SEEDS OF FICTION

By the same author

1959: The Year That Changed Our World

Blood in the Sun

Bon Papa

Una Cámara Testigo de la Historia

The Fools of April

The Ghosts of Makara

Island of Fear

Navidad con Libertad

Papa Doc: The Truth About Haiti Today (with Al Burt)

Le Prix du Sang: La Résistance du Peuple Haïtien
à la Tyrannie – François Duvalier

Somoza: The Legacy of US Involvement in Central America

Le Trophée

Trujillo: Death of the Goat

SEEDS OF FICTION

*Graham Greene's Adventures
in Haiti and Central America
1954–1983*

BERNARD DIEDERICH

LONDON AND CHICAGO

PETER OWEN PUBLISHERS
81 Ridge Road, London N8 9NP

Peter Owen books are distributed in the USA and Canada by
Independent Publishers Group/Trafalgar Square
814 North Franklin Street, Chicago, IL 60610, USA

First published in Great Britain 2012

ISBN 978-0-7206-1488-6

A catalogue record for this book is available from the British Library

Printed and bound by CPI Group (UK) Ltd, Croydon, CR0 4YY

CONTENTS

PART II

On the Way Back:
Graham Greene in Central America

ACKNOWLEDGEMENTS

Graham Greene's niece and last secretary, the late Amanda Dennys Saunders, was the first person to encourage me to write this book. She was an inspiration, and I owe dear Amanda, her husband Ron and daughter Lucy much gratitude. Yvonne Cloetta, Graham's companion, had cheered me on in spite of being a target of malicious attacks and did not live to read the book.

There are many who helped me along the road to telling the story of a man who over the years had become a father figure and to whom I turned for advice, which I treasured. I wish to thank Graham Greene's Estate, and especially Francis, for permitting me to use my correspondence with his father. As a compulsive note-taker – as was Graham – I recorded the dialogue between Graham and myself for stories, some published and others shelved, but to this day I can recall our journeys together.

There are many I must thank, beginning with our writer son Phillippe, my editor, who deserves credit for making me break with my long-held view that a journalist should not become the story and who weeded out so many distracting details that had overloaded earlier versions of this book. I also thank my son Jean-Bernard, who was privileged to know Graham – and several of the photographs he took during our last visit to Graham appear in this book – and, of course, my wife of fifty years who put up with my bringing dictators into our various homes and courageously faced several of them down.

Professor Richard Greene (no relation) wrote the book *Graham Greene: A Life in Letters* that is among the best editing of Graham's correspondence. The late Peter Glenville, although retired, was forthcoming in his interview with me. Haiti's Foreign Minister, François Benoît, allowed me to photocopy the Ministry's only remaining copy of *Graham Greene Démasqué* – a 92-page Haiti Foreign Ministry bulletin that turned to dust in the January 2010 earthquake. Tel Scott of the *Havana Post* had kept me informed of Graham's 1954 antics in Havana. Reverend Jim McSwigan, in charge of the Redemptorist Mission Home at Las Matas de Fanfan, saved us from dying of thirst on our border trip in January 1965. I would also like to thank the lawyer Sauveur Vaisse for being generous with his time in a Paris interview in 1986.

In Haiti there are so many to whom I am indebted – peasant neighbours, fellow journalists, Haitians of all ranks of society and our extended family. As a journalist I needed to break the heavy hand of Papa Doc's censors to send my stories out to the world. Among those who took great risks were RCA Cable employees, especially Josseline Bazelais Edline at West Indies Cable, the only international telephone company. My friend the late Albert Silvera, the owner of El Rancho Hotel, kept me informed of Graham movements during his 1954 and 1956 visits. The late Aubelin Jolicoeur was a great asset to my newspaper, the *Haiti Sun*; he liked to embroider his stories about Graham during his three visits to Haiti but was nevertheless a good witness. My friend Dick Eder of the *New York Times* was a superb journalist whose story on Graham in Haiti in 1963 was loved by all. Manny Freedman, Foreign Editor of the *New York Times*, wanted to know whether I had become a guerrilla when I was among the Kamoken denounced to the United Nations Security Council by Papa Doc but accepted my reasoning that a journalist must go to extremes sometimes to get the story. Mambo Lolotte was understanding and showed great kindness in arranging a red cushion and miniature rocking-chair for Graham's bottle of vodka.

I am indebted to my employers at Time-Life News Service (TLNS), who understood the importance of my close ties to General Omar Torrijos, not only because Panama was a major story but also because of Torrijos's knowledge of the crisis in Central America. They also knew that my time with Graham Greene produced stories. Editor-in-Chief Hedley Donovan, whose visit with other *Time* notables to Panama I had to arrange, produced an excellent editorial on South America that is quoted here. John Dinges's excellent book *The Underside of the Torrijos Legacy* is recommended for anyone interested in that period. My colleagues who covered the same beat, such as Karen de Young of the *Washington Post* and Alan Riding of the *New York Times*, shared the safe house in Managua during the war and were tireless reporters, and their reviews of *Getting to Know the General: The Story of an Involvement* gave a different perspective of General Omar Torrijos. I would also like to thank my late friend and colleague Gloria Emerson.

Gabriel (Gabo) García Márquez, a winner of the Nobel Prize for Literature who believed Graham Greene should also have won the prize, quietly played an important humanitarian role in Central America, unknown to the general public.

Thanks to my London publisher Peter Owen and especially to Simon Smith who welcomed me to their prestigious house.

ILLUSTRATIONS BETWEEN
PAGES 160 AND 161

The *Haiti Sun* reports Graham Greene's second visit to Haiti in 1956
Graham and Catherine Walston with artists at La Galerie Brochette,
   Haiti, 1956
Larry Allen of the Associated Press, the model for Granger in *The Quiet
   American*
Roger Coster of the Grand Hotel Oloffson, Port-au-Prince, Haiti
François 'Papa Doc' Duvalier on the day he was inaugurated as president
   in 1957
Graham talking to journalist Max Clou in the Dominican Republic, 1963
Anti-Duvalier rebels training in the Dominican Republic, 1963
A public execution of two members of the Jeune Haiti resistance
   movement, 1964
Bernard Diederich, 1965, during the civil war in the Dominican
   Republic
Members of the Kamoken, the Haitian Revolutionary Armed Forces
Fr Jean-Claude Bajeux saying Mass to Haitian exiles in the Dominican
   countryside
Kamoken leader Fred Baptiste with other Kamoken in Santo Domingo,
   Dominican Republic
Fred Baptiste at the Kamoken base at Nigua, Dominican Republic, 1965
Graham walks into Haiti, 1965
Fr Jean-Claude Bajeux at the Haitian border, 1965
Graham and Fr Jean-Claude Bajeux with Dominican soldiers at the
   Massacre River, 1965
The Hotel Brisas Massacre de Mariav de Rodriguez in the town of
   Restauración, Dominican Republic
Graham and Fr Jean-Claude Bajeux on the Bridge at Dajabón over the
   Massacre River, 1965
Graham photographs Haiti from no man's land, 1965
Bernard Diederich changes a tyre on his Volkswagen, 1965
The cover of *Graham Greene Démasqué*, Papa Doc's case against Graham
   following publication of *The Comedians*

Poster for the 1967 film adaptation of *The Comedians*

The film of *The Comedians* is finally shown in Haiti in 1986

General Omar Torrijos, the Panamanian leader, in the countryside with his people

Torrijos in Panama City

Graham and Torrijos getting to know one another on Contadora Island, Panama, in 1976

Graham and Bernard Diederich with rum punches on Contadora Island, 1976

Graham on the Panama Canal train, 1976

Graham at Cristóbal railway station, Panama, 1976

Graham fumbles with his camera, Cristóbal railway station, 1976

Graham and Bernard Diederich in the grounds of the Hotel George Wasington, Colón, Panama, 1976

Graham at the Panama Canal with Chuchu, 1978

Graham at Torrijos's house at Farallon, Panama, 1978

Graham and Chuchu searching for evidence of Sir Francis Drake at Portobelo, Panama, 1978

Graham resting in an Indian village, Panama, 1978

Graham and Chuchu flying to Torrijos's house at Farallon, 1978

Graham and Chuchu in a market in Panama City, 1980, waiting to meet Salvadoran guerrilla Salvador Cayetano Carpio to help arrange the release of the kidnapped South African ambassador Archibald Gardner Dunn

Graham is honoured by the Panamanian President Ricardo de la Espriella, 1983

Graham recieves the Order of Rubén Darío in Nicaragua, 1987

Bernard Diederich with Aubelin Jolicoeur, the model for the character of Petit Pierre in *The Comedians*, Port-au-Prince, 1986

A painting of Baby Doc in the toilet at Graham's Antibes apartment

Graham with his pen and midday martini, Antibes, 1989

Graham with Bernard Diederich the last time they met, 1989

Graham and Yvonne Cloetta in Antibes

Bernard Diederich, Yvonne Cloetta and Max Reinhardt at Graham's memorial service, Westminster Abbey, London, 1991

Yvonne Cloetta at Graham's grave, Vevey, Switzerland

Jean-Claude Bajeux lecturing on Graham's work, Port-au-Prince, 1995

Bernard Diederich giving a presentation during the Graham Greene International Festival, Berkhamsted School, UK, 2001

Greene in the World

Bernard Diederich was already a legend when I joined the staff of *Time* magazine in 1982. In those days, some writers – those seasoned, fearless foreign correspondents such as Bernie – actually travelled the globe covering the news, while the rest of us (bookish neophytes like myself) sat in little offices in Midtown Manhattan and drew on our expert colleagues' reports to produce the compressed pieces that appeared in the magazine. *Time*'s roving band of reporters were themselves the stuff of many a wild rumour, some of them former spies, others the lovers of princesses and all of them responsible for traversing the world at a time when the magazine was more or less the globe's defining news source.

Even by *Time* standards, though, Bernie stood out. He looked like Hemingway, I was told, and knew more about Haiti than any foreigner alive. He had some of Hemingway's glamour in his life, too, having run away from home to join a four-master in his teens and then started a newspaper in Haiti, before being sent to prison by 'Papa Doc' Duvalier. In my early years at the magazine Bernie was constantly sending dispatches from Nicaragua and El Salvador, both in the middle of bitter civil wars then; when Ronald Reagan invaded Grenada in 1983 Bernie, already in his fifties, was the one correspondent who somehow commandeered a boat to take him to the island where the action was taking place. I was deputed to condense and rewrite his vivid eyewitness account, as was the unbudging custom then, until our top editor saw Bernie's version and said, 'Run every word just the way he had it!'

Apart from all this, Bernie was celebrated as the trusted friend of Graham Greene, a man not known for his love of *Time* magazine (he included mischievous digs in at least three of his major novels) and a writer clearly suspicious of journalists, whose errors he loved to enumerate. Anyone reading *The Quiet American* or many other of Greene's works will note that the only characters who are always treated unsympathetically in them are journalists – a reflection, perhaps, of the fact that Greene was a rigorous and precise observer himself and, having witnessed the news everywhere from Cuba to Vietnam, had little patience for those correspondents too lazy or ill-informed to do justice to it.

In spite of all that, however, there was Bernie, invoked with warmth and respect in Greene's book on Panama. Greene often referred to him as his source and guide through the thickets of Central America and Haiti. They'd met thirty years before, I gathered, and after that Bernie had earned his way into that select, very small band of Greene companions that all the rest of us dreamed of and envied. For the many who regarded Greene as perhaps the shrewdest and most soulful chronicler of the world's conflicts in the years between 1950 and 1980, the man who was Greene's guide had something of the air of a writer's John the Baptist.

I never met Greene, though, like anyone who travels, I felt he caught the sensation of being a foreigner alone, in a treacherous turmoil, as he caught the particulars of Port-au-Prince, Hanoi, Asunción and Havana, as well as anyone I'd read. Again and again, setting foot in the Hotel Oloffson or walking through Saigon's streets after midnight, I felt Greene shadowing me almost as if I were his creation; and again and again, I read books by Paul Theroux and John Banville, by Gloria Emerson and Alan Judd, that were so haunted by Greene that I could well understand why *Time*, in its obituary of him in 1991, had written, 'No serious writer of the century has more thoroughly invaded and shaped the public imagination.'

When I began to write about Greene, I turned to only two people at first: his niece Louise Dennys and his famous travelling companion (much lauded by Louise) Bernie Diederich. One stormy night in 1995, just before the events described at the end of this book, I met Bernie near his home in Coral Gables, and he gave me a perfect illustration of why Greene had found him perfect company: he was friendly, relaxed, full of professional details and enormous fun, as he shared his adventures, with or without Greene, over many decades. Later, when I wrote a whole book about Greene, the only three writers I consulted were Paul Theroux and Michael Mewshaw, both of whom had been taken up by Greene as young protégés of a kind, and Bernie. As he described to me Greene's 'long stride', the evenings they'd spent in Panama and Antibes, how loyal and kind a friend Greene had been, I could see how the loyalty and kindness ran in both directions. Greene did not open himself up to many – and he liked to keep his own counsel, I suspect – but in Bernie he found someone whose courage he could look up to and whose practical on-the-ground, unideological wisdom he could trust.

For me Bernie Diederich is the closest I'll ever get to Graham Greene and the perfect introduction to the brand of close, undeluded, adventurous reportage that made Greene the trench-coated hero of so many. And what moves me, too – and what comes across so well in these pages – is that, unlike many others, Bernie never cashed in on his friendship with the famous author or took cheap shots at him after his death. He barely seems even to have quarrelled with a man who had a gift for picking fights even with those closest to him, although he never denies that there were moments when he was taken aback, even slightly disappointed, by his friend.

What he gives us instead is an unusually vivid, intimate, often exciting account of Greene on the road. We feel the writer's celebrated impatience in these pages, his keen-eyed curiosity, and we witness, as if we were sitting in the back of Bernie's beaten-up VW, the wild ups and downs of Greene's moods. We can hear his inimitable cadences, see the tears of laughter in his eyes as things take a tragic-comic turn, register how the great lover of paradox was now consulting his horoscope in the papers and now complaining that the papers never got anything right. Greene trusted Bernie, you can tell, not just because he was such good and informative company but because he would turn his professional eye on everywhere he knew and give an evocative and knowledgeable description of it, without agenda or presumptuous theory.

Bernie Diederich was celebrated among us at *Time* as the man who had worked at a casino, served in the war and married a legendary Haitian beauty before raising one son who became a seasoned photojournalist and another who became a writer. But it wasn't the drama of his life that made him a cherished correspondent so much as the accuracy and clarity of his reporting. I'm reminded of this every time I watch Greene here pulling out his tiny Minox camera or describing how he loves the Ritz in Piccadilly because everything goes wrong there. And for those of us who've felt Greene lead us into the most essential questions of good and bad, there's something deeply haunting about hearing him say he doesn't believe in hell as he and Bernie bump along the Haitian border (with a priest) or coming to visible life at the prospect of an ambush and sudden danger.

Yvonne Cloetta, Greene's companion for his last thirty-two years, gave us in her memoir an enduring description of the private man, confiding his fears and beliefs to a lover; the priest Leopoldo Duran has shown us Greene in his later years, tooling around Spain with his clerical friend in a spirit of fun and theological enquiry. Bernie Diederich gives us here the final and perhaps most important piece of the puzzle, an indelible portrait of the novelist at work, taking everything in, treating the dark streets as his confessional, intuitively reading those who cross his path even as they vie to become characters in the next Graham Greene novel. As Diederich points out, Greene could combine, almost in the same breath, the 'boyish exuberance' of the lifelong adventurer and the watchful, penetrating gaze of a man who was taken in by very little.

When I put down the pages you hold in your hand I felt that I had myself travelled with the man who lives on in so many of us and felt the warmth of his fond, but always unsparing, glance.

Pico Iyer
Author of *The Man Within My Head: Graham Greene, My Father and Me*
2012

INTRODUCTION BY RICHARD GREENE

This story about Graham Greene begins in the high tops of the *Pamir*. The vessel's arrangement of sails and ropes would have made perfect sense to Drake or to Nelson, but its hull and its four masts were made of steel – the ship belonged to two ages. One of its sailors was Bernard Diederich, a sixteen-year-old New Zealander who had quit school and family to sail across the Pacific in the majestic barque.

Diederich went on to serve the rest of the Second World War aboard an armed American tanker fuelling the Pacific war machine. The young sailor came ashore in more ports than I can imagine and saw for himself what Greene called 'the dangerous edge of things' – outposts of the modern age where greed and cruelty made no effort to hide themselves. Diederich was himself a mixture of old-fashioned virtues – courage, endurance and a sense of justice – all of them toughened by the demands of his life at sea. In the years that lay ahead his work would put him in the position of Conrad's Marlow – reporting on things seen in 'the heart of darkness'.

In 1949 Diederich decided to make his home in Haiti where he established his own newspaper, the *Haiti Sun*, and worked as a resident correspondent for the *New York Times* and other news agencies. In those days Haiti was free of crime and promised to become a paradise for tourists. The country had memories of freedom going back to the revolt of 1791 when Toussaint L'Ouverture led slaves to overthrow their colonial masters. Despite an American occupation from 1915 to 1934, Haiti was a democracy in the 1950s. As a newsman covering the visit of a celebrity, Diederich met Greene briefly in 1954 and then became much closer to him on a second visit in 1956 when Greene brought with him his mistress Catherine Walston, the inspiration for Sarah in *The End of the Affair*.

That was the last of the good years in Haiti. In 1957 François 'Papa Doc' Duvalier, a quiet and mannerly physician, took power and began to transform the country on psychopathic principles. He promoted a myth of terror based on elements of the Voodoo religion. Diederich tells us he became known as the *zombificateur*, the zombie-maker. His henchmen, the Tontons Macoutes, robbed, beat, tortured, abducted or killed thousands of his real and supposed opponents. The rest of the world paid little attention to events in this obscure country, and the United States was disinclined to act for fear that Duvalier might be replaced by another Castro. It was impossible for his victims to regard Papa Doc as a 'lesser evil'.

By 1963 the butchery in Haiti became widely known, largely owing to Diederich's reporting. The regime decided that he, too, was an enemy. He was arrested and locked in solitary confinement while it was decided whether to kill him. He was cut off from his Haitian wife and young son – both of them now likely targets for the Tontons Macoutes. (This can be spelt several ways. In *The Comedians* Greene writes Tontons Macoute; I prefer Macoutes for the plural.)

His printing plant, his office and all his files were destroyed. In the end he was bundled on to an aircraft and expelled from the country. His wife, moving adroitly, was able to join him in the Dominican Republic. From there, he continued his reporting on the massacres.

In the late summer of 1963 Greene decided he had better see the country again for himself. After a harrowing visit, he went on to the Dominican Republic for further briefing from Diederich, before writing his long article 'The Nightmare Republic' for the the *Sunday Telegraph* (22 September 1963). The story Diederich had been telling for six years was now given enormous attention, and while the new Johnson administration dithered world opinion shifted and Duvalier's Haiti became a pariah state.

It had been several years since Greene had written a novel – after the publication of *A Burnt-Out Case* in early 1961 Greene feared that he was near the end of his writing career. He wrote some short stories and an unsuccessful play, but Haiti now had a grip on him. In early 1965 Diederich took him on a tour of the border between Haiti and the Dominican Republic, including a memorable stop at the training camp of a tiny band of rebels in a disused lunatic asylum. For the first time in his life Greene wrote a novel with a political objective – to destabilize the Duvalier regime. Released in early 1966, and made into a major film starring Richard Burton and Elizabeth Taylor in the following year, *The Comedians* was one of his finest novels, and it created exactly the storm of publicity that Greene had hoped for. The world could not turn its eyes from the horror.

In the years that followed Diederich continued to advise Greene on political developments in Latin America. He eventually engineered Greene's visits to Panama where the novelist became a trusted friend of General Omar Torrijos, the strongman who was trying to map out a social-democratic future for his country. Greene's travels with Diederich – by then the Central American correspondent for *Time* magazine – led to close contacts with Daniel Ortega, Tomás Borge, Ernesto Cardenal and other Sandinistas in Nicaragua, as well as with Fidel Castro in Cuba.

Through all this, his guide and political adviser was Bernard Diederich, whose journalism and books made him, as Greene put it the introduction to Diederich's own book *Somoza and the Legacy of US Involvement in Central America*, an 'indispensable' historian for the region. Bernard Diederich observed the day-to-day movements of one of the century's great novelists in some of his most important 'involvements'. Himself a figure of quiet heroism, Diederich understood the broad and terrible context of Greene's work through these years, and he knew intimately the people who stood just beyond the pages of Greene's books. No writer is better placed to tell of Graham Greene's political engagements in the second half of his career – indeed, little of what follows was known to Greene's official biographer.

A work of observation and interpretation and, even more, a work of friendship, Bernard Diederich's political biography of Graham Greene is one of the most important accounts ever written about this author. It is a unique record, and we are lucky to have it.

Richard Greene
Editor, *Graham Greene: A Life in Letters*
2012

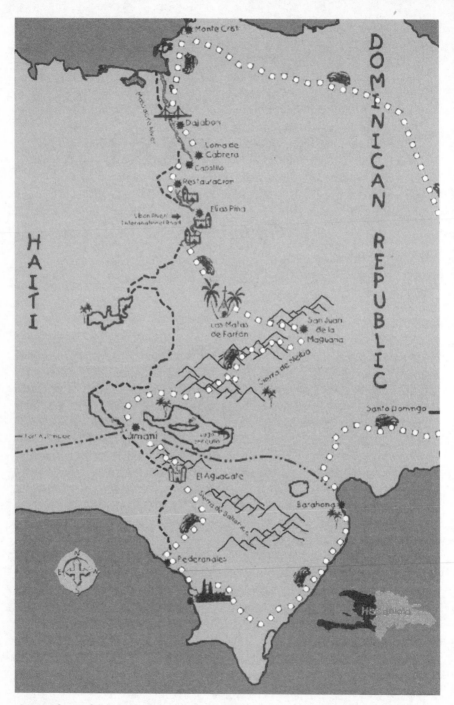

A map of part of the island of Hispaniola showing the border area between Haiti and the Dominican Republic; the route of the journey taken by Graham Greene, Bernard Diederich and Fr Jean-Claude Bajeux in 1965 is marked.

PART I

Graham Greene in Haiti

I | SEEDS OF FICTION

In Haiti they say life begins long before birth and that death is not an end but a continuation of the same long coil threading back to the beginning. The story of Haiti is certainly tragic, but unlike a work of fiction it has no end. It continues today with misery pouring down on a proud and independent people. The everyday Haitian's answer to violence, poverty, sickness and death is always the same: *bon Die sel ki kone,* only God knows. They say it with a hopeful frown and an uncertain smile. And while they speak of God – Catholicism and Christianity are prevalent in Haiti – it is Voodoo that offers the people hope; it offers them immortality. This is the magic of Voodoo. It's also the power of great fiction. It can immortalize a character, a story or a deep truth. This is why, on an overcast afternoon in January 1965, I found myself standing by the arrival gate at Santo Domingo's Las Americas airport waiting for Graham Greene.

I wanted Graham to write a book about Haiti. Like many Haitians I was at war against the dictatorship of François 'Papa Doc' Duvalier. Two years earlier I had been forced into exile with my Haitian wife, Ginette, and our infant son after living in Haiti for almost fourteen years. My first seven years in Haiti were full of the magic that some like to call the old Haiti. It was a time when the country was experiencing a cultural renaissance. There was virtually no crime. While the deforestation and over-population was noticeable, it wasn't nearly as extreme as it is today. It was a clean, charming place populated with beautiful and interesting people. There was something intimate and exotic about Haiti. It was a popular tourist destination, particularly with artists, bohemians and the Hollywood set, which is how I came to meet Graham in the first place. Marlon Brando, Anne Bancroft and Truman Capote all visited the island during this time.

En route to the South Pacific I had sailed into Port-au-Prince, quit the sea to search for my stolen camera, fallen in love with Haiti and, after a short stint working at an American-owned casino, started an English-language weekly newspaper, the *Haiti Sun*, in 1950. Soon I picked up stringing work from the US and British media. Between the late 1940s and the mid-1950s Haiti possessed more than hope and charm: it had magic.

But the last seven years had been a horrible nightmare. In 1957, after

Duvalier won the presidency, the country slowly descended into a state of fear as Papa Doc tightened his grip on power and declared himself President-for-Life. Many of my friends and colleagues were killed or disappeared. While I was busy reporting on the atrocities for the international media, I had to be careful of what I published in my own paper. I had to avoid the attention of Duvalier and his henchmen, the Tontons Macoutes. Whenever the government censors blinked I would telex or cable my stories, which were published, many times anonymously, in *Time*, *Life*, the *New York Times*, on NBC News and in the Associated Press. For seven years I walked a fine line, knowing that if Papa Doc found out I had written something critical I was certain to join the growing ranks of the 'disappeared'.

As I watched Graham's tall, lean figure make its way through customs, his blue eyes cutting across the airport with a hint of suspicion, I wondered if, indeed, he had the power to change Haiti. Could he bring down Duvalier? And, more to the point, would he write a book about Haiti?

Graham was sixty-one. His hair was thinning slightly, but he looked as robust as ever. He was dressed in tan linen trousers and a dark coat. His pale complexion stood out from the crowd of tourists and Dominican nationals arriving on the Pan American flight from Canada, where he had spent Christmas with his daughter Caroline.

We didn't need to shake hands: a smile sufficed. As he thanked me generously for meeting him, I could feel his energy. He was so eager at the prospect of our trip he was giddy with excitement.

'It's wonderful to be back in the Caribbean,' he said when he came out of customs. Then he took me by the arm. 'I hope I'm not keeping you from your work.'

'No, not at all,' I replied.

He seemed to forget I had been the one to suggest we take a trip along the Haitian–Dominican border. He stopped, and now he smiled at me again and slapped me on the back of the shoulder as we walked out of the airport. 'So when do we start?'

Hearing Graham talk this way, overflowing with enthusiasm, thrilled me. I had last seen him in August 1963. The British Ambassador in Santo Domingo had telephoned me with a message from Greene. He was coming to the Dominican Republic from Haiti and wanted to know if I could pick him up at the airport. I was taken by surprise. I hadn't seen Graham since we spent a week together in Haiti in 1956. I never imagined we would cross paths again.

The Graham Greene I'd met in 1963 looked frazzled and slightly unkempt. He arrived with little luggage and a painting by Philippe-Auguste, which he said he had purchased with his winnings from a night at a deserted casino in Port-au-Prince. He was unusually quiet and let out a deep sigh as he squeezed into the seat of my Volkswagen Beetle. It was clear he was relieved to be out of Haiti. As we drove out of the airport he rested his arm out the window and took in the smell of the summer rains and the burning charcoal from the cooking fires of the neighbourhood *colmados*.

'I thought I was doomed to stay,' he said after a long silence. His face was stark and serious. He didn't look at me; instead he stared blankly at the blue of the Caribbean as we drove along Autopista Las Américas.

'I felt something was going to happen. I was so sure of it. I thought I'd be stopped at the last minute. And just as I was about to board the plane someone pressed a letter into my hand and whispered, "Please, give this to Déjoie in Santo Domingo." I was afraid it could be a trap; perhaps a *provocateur*. I refused.' He looked at me and tightened his grip on the bag he had on his lap. I understood. The risk was too great. He was concerned about his notes. 'You think I did the right thing?'

'I'm certain of it,' I said. Louis Déjoie had lost the presidential election to Papa Doc in 1957. Like most of Duvalier's opponents he ended up in exile in the Dominican Republic where he was trying to position himself as the leader of the Haitian exile community. But the former senator had no support among the exiles. He was alone. All he could do was continually to denounce the exile groups as Communist. At one point he got us all arrested.

Graham said he had gone back to Haiti on assignment for the London *Sunday Telegraph*. He had been reading stories of the growing terror in Haiti and wanted to see it for himself. 'I had a hunch the exiles might launch an attack on Duvalier from the Dominican Republic,' he said. The promise of action had lured him back to the island.

I didn't tell Graham that I had been keeping track of his visit to Haiti. Diplomat friends returning from visiting Port-au-Prince always brought me a bundle of Haitian newspapers. Aubelin Jolicoeur's column 'Au Fil des Jours' ('As the Days Go By') in *Le Nouvelliste*, of 13 August 1963, read, 'The great writer Graham Greene is here to write an article on Haiti for the *Telegraph* of London. One of the greatest writers in the world, Graham Greene was welcomed to Haiti by the *chargé d'affaires* of Great Britain, Mr Patrick Niblock, and Aubelin Jolicoeur.' Jolicoeur had worked for my newspaper in the 1950s. Modesty was not one of his qualities. He was a fixture at the Grand Hotel Oloffson and became Greene's real-life model for the character of Petit Pierre in *The Comedians*. Graham's physical description in the novel was dead on: 'Even the time of day was humorous to him. He had the quick movements of a monkey, and he seemed to swing from wall to wall on ropes of laughter.' But it was his assessment of who Petit Pierre really was that was telling: 'He was believed by some to have connexions with the Tontons, for how otherwise had he escaped a beating-up or worse?' Years later Graham confessed to me he always suspected Jolicoeur was a spy for Duvalier. I never believed that. Like many Haitians he was a survivor. What other option did he have?

After listing Graham's published works Jolicoeur noted, 'This is Mr Greene's third visit to Haiti and he will spend ten days at the Hotel Oloffson. He has expressed a desire to meet Dr François Duvalier. We wish the author of *The Power and the Glory*, considered a great work, welcome.'

I dropped Graham off at the British Ambassador's residence. The following evening he came to our home in Rosa Duarte for dinner. I had also invited Max Clos, of *Le Figaro*, who had covered the war in Indochina at the same time as Graham and who had been on a reporting trip to Haiti.

That night Graham behaved in a way that was completely out of character. He began acting, mimicking Papa Doc's Foreign Minister. I had known him to be reserved, direct, quiet. I had never seen him this animated. He displayed a wonderful sense of mimicry.

'No interview is possible,' he said, playing the part of Haitian Foreign Minister René Chalmers. 'I regret, Monsieur Greene, the President is not receiving the foreign press at this time.' He nailed the accent perfectly. 'You know Chalmers,' he laughed. 'He's this huge frog-like man who sits behind his desk at the end of a long, narrow room and closes his eyes as he speaks.' Then he went on mimicking the minister. 'Ah, Monsieur Greene, it is not possible at this time to travel to the north. It is for your own safety, you understand. If safety considerations are to be taken into account every time a journalist covers a story, there would be no coverage whatsoever.' Coverage, we both knew, was precisely what Duvalier didn't want.

Chalmers claimed there were no longer rebels in the north and that Graham would do better to travel to Les Cayes in the south. 'As I left,' Graham explained, 'his aide told me Chalmers was very busy preparing a protest to the United Nations General Assembly because the exiled former Chief of Staff, General Leon Cantave, had led an invasion in the north with American arms.'

But even with the Foreign Minister's official blessing, Graham still had to obtain a *laissez-passer* (official pass) to travel south from Port-au-Prince. Roadblocks were everywhere. To get his *laissez-passer* he was instructed to go to the police headquarters at the new Caserne François Duvalier, opposite the National Palace. The long wait, Graham recalled, was a goldmine. It gave him a close-up look at Duvalier's repressive machine. He sat there for hours watching character after character, including a police officer who stared at him through large mirrored sunglasses. Graham was not sure of the man's name, but he could have been any of a number of Macoute officers. They had all taken to wearing dark glasses to appear tough and sinister. From his description, though, it sounded like Colonel Franck Romain, a hot-tempered officer who later became police chief and mayor of Port-au-Prince.

Graham said the stench at the station was so intense it was like sitting inside a urinal. On one of the walls, beside a large official portrait of Duvalier, were pictures of the bullet-riddled corpses of former spy chief and creator of the Tontons Macoutes Clément Barbot and his brother Harry. Both men had been killed four weeks earlier, ending a two-month war with Papa Doc. They were flushed out of a hut on the outskirts of Port-au-Prince and cornered in a sugar-cane field where they were killed by Duvalier's security forces. Afterwards a photographer was brought in to capture the bloody corpses on film.

Beyond the close-up look at the Macoutes and police, his experience at the police was fictionalized in *The Comedians* in the scene when Brown goes to get a pass to travel south. 'A pass to Aux Cayes cost so many hours of waiting, that was all, in the smell of the zoo, under the snapshots of the dead rebels, in the steam of the stove-like day.'

On his 1963 visit Graham stayed at the Grand Hotel Oloffson. But the Haiti he encountered bore little resemblance to the land that charmed him seven years earlier when he visited Catherine Walston. Roger and Laura Coster, the former managers of the Oloffson, were long gone. Sensing that politics were going to kill tourism, Roger sold his lease on the hotel in 1960 and decamped to the US Virgin Islands where he went into business with New York restaurateur Vincent Sardi. Al Seitz, an American who had come to Port-au-Prince to help run La Belle Creole department store, now ran the Oloffson. Seitz hired a Macoute for protection. It was the thing to do for many of those who could afford it. Seitz disliked newsmen; he bemoaned their stories as overblown, frightening the tourists away.

When I met Graham in 1956 he was staying at the upmarket El Rancho Hotel with Walston. I tried to convince them to move to the Oloffson, but Graham said he was a guest of Albert Silvera, the owner of El Rancho, and didn't want to hurt his feelings by moving to another hotel. But after I took them to the old gingerbread-style palace overlooking Port-au-Prince and introduced them to Coster, they needed no more encouragement. They left El Rancho and spent their last two days in Haiti at the Oloffson where Graham discovered the little barman, Caesar, who made the word's best rum punches.

When I first arrived in the country in 1949 I lived in the Oloffson, but after a month I surrendered my room to the termites, certain the place would soon turn to sawdust. The old gingerbread structure, built in 1887 as a villa for the son of Haitian President Tirésias Simon Sam, possessed incredible charm. It was a three-storey wooden structure built on to the side of the hill with two turrets at the end of the façade. The main floor of the hotel had a huge mahogany bar and a long, wide veranda which served as an elevated dining-room. Eight tall doors led into the hotel, the back wall of which was the exposed stone of the mountain. From the top floors one could see the treetops, rusty metal roofs and the bay of Port-au-Prince in the distance and until the devastating 2010 earthquake the three white domes of the National Palace.

The suite Graham and Catherine occupied became the Graham Greene Suite. Neighbouring suites were also named, hung with ornate painted nameplates of other poets and writers and famous guests who had slept there, among them the actor John Gielgud, director Peter Glenville and Anne Bancroft.

Graham introduces readers to the Hotel Trianon in *The Comedians*:

> The architecture of the hotel was neither classical in the eighteenth-century manner nor luxurious in the twentieth-century fashion. With its towers and balconies and wooden fretwork decorations it had the air at night of a Charles Addams house in a number of the *New Yorker*. You expected a witch to open the door to you or a maniac butler, with a bat dangling from the chandelier behind him. But in the sunlight, or when the lights went on among the palms, it seemed fragile and period and pretty and absurd, an illustration from a book of fairy-tales. I had grown to love the place, and I was glad in a way that it had found no purchaser.

On his trip in 1963 Graham found the rambling old hotel virtually empty. He said there were only three other guests: the Italian manager of the International Casino and an elderly American couple who had taken up extended residence at the hotel. He considered they were somewhat naïve but sincere people trying to help Haitian artists learn the silk-screen process so they could reproduce their paintings and increase their income. He thought the couple's endeavour was a noble one, if not terribly credible. Their effort ultimately came to halt because the Haitian Consul-General in New York failed to keep his promise to cut the red tape in Haiti and facilitate the import of raw material and to have the appropriate government ministry give the couple permission to work in Haiti. They were completely ignored by Duvalier's officials. This scenario at the Oloffson closely resembles the scene Graham created at the Trianon with only Brown and Mr and Mrs Smith staying at the hotel.

This time around Graham did not stay in the suite that had been named after him. Instead, he lodged at the little cottage in the grounds in front of the main hotel building known as the James Jones cottage. The author of *From Here to Eternity* had spent his honeymoon there after marrying Gloria Mosolino, a one-time stand-in for actresses Marilyn Monroe and Eva Marie Saint.

Although he was a guest at the Oloffson, in the afternoons when government offices closed and the Oloffson became too eerie Graham dropped by the Sans Souci Hotel to relax and take notes under the big caimite tree next to the pool at the back of the hotel. The manager of the Sans Souci could be trusted as he was no pro-Duvalier. The place offered peace and quiet and gave Graham a chance to discuss the political story with foreign correspondents of the daily press.

One night Graham and the Oloffson's three guests went to observe brothel life at Chez Georgina, off Carrefour Road just south of town. The place had a lovely garden set off by royal palms and an abundance of hibiscus. The only other patrons were a couple of Tontons Macoutes who stared at the group through their dark glasses. The elderly American man, an artist, began sketching the Haitian prostitutes who were dancing together. When the dance was over the girls went over and looked at what the *blan* was doing and burst into giggles. The Macoutes were not amused.

When Graham finally secured a *laissez-passer* he hired a driver and rode south from the capital. It took them eight hours to reach the town of Les Cayes, 125 miles away. Graham said there wasn't much conversation, which gave him plenty of time to think. He was sure the driver was a Macoute. He would later write, 'Fear in those weeks must have penetrated deep into my unconscious: Haiti really was the bad dream of the newspaper headlines.'

In southern Haiti it is customary to bury the dead in elaborate tombs in the family *lakou* (compound). But there are also cemeteries. As Graham passed St-Louis-du-Sud he came upon the magnificent old cemetery that rests on a hill. The weathered and strangely built tombs impressed him enough that he used them for a dramatic scene near the end of *The Comedians* when Brown and Jones are driving towards Les Cayes and their car breaks down. Brown describes the cemetery. 'It was like a city built by dwarfs, street after street of tiny houses, some nearly big enough to hold ourselves, some too small for a newborn child, all of the same grey stone, from which the plaster had longed flaked.'

Graham learned that fear permeated rural Haiti. Les Cayes had been the main bastion of support for Duvalier's opponent Senator Louis Déjoie during the 1957 election. Those who supported Déjoie paid dearly. Now, anyone who had a *laissez-passer* was treated with suspicion as a Duvalierist or a supporter of Papa Doc. The following day, when Graham returned to Port-au-Prince, the capital was filled with roadblocks. The Macoutes were constantly on the prowl.

On Sunday afternoon Jolicoeur and Al Seitz took Graham to the little Magic Ciné cinema on Rue de Centre to watch *Our Man in Havana*. When the lights went on at the end of the film Jolicoeur stood and introduced

Graham to the audience as the man who wrote the book on which it was based. The bemused Haitians gave Graham a rousing round of applause.

On another occasion Jolicoeur introduced Graham to Antoine Herard, a long-time Duvalierist and an *habitué* of the Oloffson. Herard was the owner of Radio Port-au-Prince and a well-known announcer on the station. He invited Graham to visit the regime's showplace, Duvalierville, a vaunted new town constructed on Papa Doc's orders twenty miles north of the capital. Duvalierville, a concrete monstrosity, had replaced the pretty little village of Cabaret. This trip was significant in that it helped Graham illustrate the corruption of the regime, taking up over five pages in *The Comedians* when Brown and Mr Smith drive to Duvalierville with the Minister and a Macoute.

'I've got it all right here,' Graham said and handed me the green cloth-covered book of Victorian detective stories he carried on his trip. The detective book was only a cover. Inside were blank notebook pages where he wrote in a tiny, nearly microscopic script, making it impossible for anyone other than him to read.

Graham's article on Duvalier's Haiti was published in the *Sunday Telegraph* on 29 September 1963, with the headline 'Nightmare Republic'. It was a bleak and terrifying picture of people living under a 'strange curse'. He portrayed Papa Doc as Voodoo's Baron Samedi, a spectre in top hat and tails who haunts the cemeteries smoking a cigar and wearing dark glasses.

In his article Graham classified the Duvalier regime as among the worst in history. He wrote:

> There have been many reigns of terror in the course of history. Some-times they have been prompted by a warped idealism like Robespierre's, sometimes they have been directed fanatically against a class or a race and supported by some twisted philosophy; surely never has terror had so bare and ignoble an object as here – the protection of a few tough men's pockets, the pockets . . . leaders of the Tontons Macoutes, of the police and of the Presidential Guard – and in the centre of the ring, of course, in his black evening suit, his heavy glasses, his halting walk and halting speech, the cruel and absurd Doctor.

He went on to describe the situation and his own experiences, including the searches at roadblocks in the city and how it took two days at the police station, where the 'portrait of the Doctor is flanked by snapshots of the machine-gunned bodies of Barbot and his companions, to gain a two-day permit for the south. The north, because of the raids from the Dominican Republic, was forbidden altogether.' He added, 'All trade which does not offer a rake-off is at a standstill. A whole nation can die of starvation so long as the

Doctor's non-fiscal account is safe.' He noted how the British Ambassador was expelled 'because he protested at the levies which the Tontons Macoutes were exacting illegally from all businessmen. An arbitrary figure was named and if the sum was not forthcoming the man would be beaten up in his home by the Tontons Macoutes, during the hours of darkness.'

He also mentioned his visit to Duvalierville.

> The Doctor has obviously read accounts of Brasilia and in the absurd little tourist houses with roofs like wind-wrecked butterflies one can detect Brasilia's influence. There is no beach, and the town, if it is ever finished, is supposed to house 2,000 peasants in little one-roomed houses, so that it is difficult to see why any tourist should stay there. The only building finished in Duvalierville is the cock-fighting stadium. In the meantime the peasants' homes have been destroyed and they have been driven from the area to live with relatives. Many people believe that the town, if finished, will become a Tonton garrison.
>
> As with most major constructions in Haiti, since the emperor (King) Christophe built his fantastic citadel on a mountain-top, the cement used is cruelty and injustice. Labour on the project is controlled by the Tontons Macoutes. One young labourer was taken off his job because a Tonton wanted it for another. The labourer tried to appeal to him, 'Please I am hungry. I have no work,' and the Tonton promptly shot him through the head, the cheek and the body. He now survives in Port-au-Prince, paralysed.
>
> Refugees in Santo Domingo, like the Cubans in Miami, are divided among themselves. The last presidential candidate, Louis Déjoie, plays a vain, loquacious role in the restaurants of Santo Domingo while he denounces the few men who cross the border to fight. Intervention by the Dominican forces is out of the question. Haitians remember Trujillo's slaughter of unarmed Haitian labourers at the frontier-river now called Massacre, and the Haitian pride cannot be exaggerated; it is a quality noble and absurd and comforting for the persecutors. Even a man released from the torture chamber under the palace who had been beaten almost to the point of death would not admit that he had been touched. The great-great-grandchild of slaves is never beaten. (A whip hangs on the central pillar of every Voodoo temple as a reminder of the past.)
>
> Santo Domingo is fifty minutes from Port-au-Prince by air, but the distance separating the two places must be judged not in miles but in centuries . . . neither business nor politics has any relevance in Haiti. Haiti produces painters, poets, heroes – and in that spiritual region it is natural to find a devil too.

He ended his article: 'The electric sign which winks out every night across the public garden has a certain truth. *Je suis le drapeau Haitien, un et indivisible.* (I am the Haitian flag, one and indivisible.) François Duvalier.'

One of the foreign newsmen staying at the Sans Souci Hotel was Richard Eder of the *New York Times*, who wrote an article about Graham. The piece was published on 18 August with the headline 'Graham Greene, in Haiti, talks of Double Trouble'. Although the article focused mostly on a gun-runner and thief who had been posing as Graham Greene, it also mentioned that Graham was in Haiti and thinking of writing an entertainment (the name Graham gave to his less serious fiction). Eder wrote, 'If the entertainment is written, it will begin with a hotel proprietor returning from abroad and finding his hotel has only two guests. Mr Greene is staying at the Hotel Oloffson, which has only three guests.'

I had kept a copy of the article and handed it to Graham. He looked it over and smiled. 'Yes, he is a decent fellow,' Graham said about Eder. 'I had him over at the Oloffson for drinks one night. I didn't know he was going to write this. I must say, he did a remarkable job.'

It was the only time I had seen him pleased with reporting on himself. But what excited me about the article was the possibility that he might write a novel set in Haiti. I knew enough not to intrude. I was in awe of Graham and wanted to help him as well as I could and certainly learn from him. He offered no further comment on the matter, and I didn't ask. Still, he did not deny what Eder had written in the article. It gave me hope that he might write about Haiti.

After dinner we sat on the patio. It was a hot, humid night with no breeze. Slowly the conversation began to shift back and forth from Haiti to Indochina. He and Max Clos began discussing their time covering the French war in Indochina. Talk turned to *The Quiet American,* and Graham confessed he had modelled the American newsman Granger on Larry Allen of the Associated Press. Graham and Max began telling Larry Allen stories, about how he had covered the war and even been decorated by the French. The stories were not complimentary. Graham confessed that the press conference portrayed in *The Quiet American* – in which Granger bullies the briefing officers into revealing French casualties, only to 'stare around with oafish triumph' at his colleagues – actually happened.

While the book's narrator is Fowler, a cynical old-time English political reporter who wants to remain above the fray and uninvolved, the quiet American Pyle is his opposite – youthful, naïve and out to save Vietnam from Communism. Graham said that, unlike the recognizable Granger, there was no Pyle. The best he could do, he said, was to create a composite of various Americans he had met in Saigon.

In describing his craftsmanship, Graham said he usually transposed real-life individuals into fictional characters. Sometimes he took bits and pieces of different real-life characters and moulded them into the people he needed to play the various roles he had set out for them or they for him.

I walked into the kitchen to fetch more rum and found Ginette busy preparing dessert. She was ecstatic. 'Did you hear? He never invented a character. Maybe he's searching for characters for the book on Haiti.'

'It's possible,' I said and pulled out a bottle of Barbancourt. 'You think he might write a serious book?'

'Why not?' Ginette took out an ice tray from the freezer and broke ice cubes into a small bucket. 'If he has enough characters, maybe he'll write a book about Papa Doc.'

It seemed like a real possibility. When we went back to the patio, Ginette and I began to talk of some of the people we knew in Haiti and on the Dominican border, characters we thought would entice Graham into writing a powerful novel, something that could be used as a weapon against the dictatorship. Words alone might not bring down Papa Doc, but they could bring world attention to the calamity that had befallen Haiti.

'There are scores of exiles gathering along the border,' I said. 'They're ill-prepared, but they're determined.'

'It's a real tragedy,' Graham said quietly.

'It certainly is,' I said. 'I know the guerrillas. We have been doing what we can to help them. Mainly, I have had to transport charity food to keep them from starving.'

Graham looked at me and said nothing.

I took another drink of rum.

'Do they have any guns?' he asked.

'No. They train with broomsticks and old World War I Enfield rifles. They have no logistical support.'

'At least Fidel had good logistic support effort.'

'All they have at this point is determination,' I said.

'If I came back, could you show me the border?' he asked.

'Certainly.'

I poured more rum. I could see he was turning over ideas in his head. Still, I could tell from his questions on Haiti that he was frustrated. Papa Doc's government had prevented him from travelling to the north where there had been a series of cross-border attacks by General Cantave. He had been stalled. He knew he had only scratched the surface. He needed more, but what he needed he could not get in Haiti.

2 | A QUIXOTIC INSURGENCY

The day before starting our trip to the border I picked Graham up at the British Ambassador's residence and announced my plan.

'We're going to an insane asylum.'

'Not Haiti, I hope,' Graham said.

'No. No such luck. It's where the rebels are. We're going to meet the rebels, the Kamoken.'

'At an asylum? Are you serious?'

He squeezed his tall frame into the seat of my Volkswagen, and we were off without further questions about my own sanity. As we headed west out of Santo Domingo he rolled the word 'Kamoken' over and over as a scrabble player might to try and identify it, until he finally asked me about the name.

'It's the name of an anti-malaria pill, Camoquin, they sell in Haiti.'

'Really?' Graham laughed.

'The pill gives people a yellow complexion. The first anti-Duvalier invaders were mulattos and whites,' I explained.

'Was this recent?'

'No. July '58.'

'You were still in Haiti then and covered it.'

I nodded. 'I was the only foreign reporter on the scene. Unfortunately the insurgency against Duvalier is full of fantastic plots and even more fantastic failures.'

As we drove out to Nigua I explained to Graham how in the early summer of 1958 rumours of an invasion by an exile force were circulating all over Haiti. Duvalier had been in office for only ten months and there had already been a number of bomb plots against him. Many Haitian military officers such as army captain Alix Pasquet had escaped into exile. The National Pententary prison was full of suspected anti-government agents. (Later Papa Doc made Fort Dimanche his major prison and killing field.)

Pasquet and exiled lieutenants Philippe Dominique and Henri Perpignan, who were living in exile in Miami, recruited Dade County Deputy Sheriff Dany Jones, retired Dade County Deputy Sheriff Arthur Payne and two adventurers Robert Hickey and Levant Kersten to help fight their insurgency. The Haitians agreed to pay the men $2,000 each. The eighth man in the force was Joseph D.J. Walker, captain of the 55-foot launch the *Mollie C.*

Pasquet was motivated not only by his hatred of Papa Doc but by his own ego and the delusion that he might become ruler of Haiti. He kept in touch with many of his friends and fellow officers, lining them up to support his attack on the Palace. He even sent his wristwatch to a friend to get it fixed at a repair shop in Port-au-Prince, saying he would pick it up in a couple of weeks.

Dominique had been the commander of the military riding school. He had the reputation of a playboy, romancing the younger women at the school, despite being married with children. Perpignan had spent most of his military career behind a desk and had little experience in action. He had been a member of former Haitian President Paul Magloire's 'kitchen cabinet' of unofficial confidants and managed the payroll of government spies to the tune of $12,000 a month.

The group boarded the *Mollie C* and left Key West on what they said was a lobster expedition. The cabin was crammed with arms and ammunition, and the deck was loaded with drums of fuel. They stopped in Nassau, Bahamas, where they were wined and dined by Clément Benoît, Duvalier's new Consul. Then, under a full moon, they began the 600-mile journey from the Bahamas. On the afternoon of 28 June the *Mollie C* entered La Gonave Bay and anchored in a small cove at Deluge, some forty miles north of Port-au-Prince.

The three Haitians stayed inside the boat while Jones and Payne went ashore in the dingy. They posed as typical tourists, wearing only their bathing suits and purchasing several woven straw hats. Payne used sign language to communicate with a group of local peasants, telling them they needed transport to the capital because their boat had broken down. The peasants promised to return with help, but a rural policeman was alerted to the presence of the *blans* (foreigners) and notified the nearby army post at St Marc.

At ten o'clock that night Walker brought the *Mollie C* within wading distance of the beach. As the men unloaded their weapons a three-man army patrol drove up to see what they were up to. A firefight ensued. Payne was wounded in the thigh, but the insurgents killed the three soldiers. The eight men climbed into the jeep and sped off into the night, passing through Montrouis and the army post there without being detected.

When they reached the crossroads leading to the town of Arcahaie, not far from another army post, the jeep broke down. Pasquet managed to hire a *taptap* (jitney bus). Inscribed on its front was the warning *Malgre tout Dieu seul maître* (In spite of all, God is the only master).

Dominique took the wheel. Pasquet sat next to him in the front while the others sat in the back on the jitney's two passenger benches. They bound Payne's leg in a tourniquet and sped off towards the capital, passing two more army posts without incident. They raced through the pre-dawn darkness of the capital and headed straight for the main entrance of the Casernes Dessalines (army barracks), behind the National Palace.

Pasquet barked an order to the sentry announcing they were bringing in prisoners and drew a confused salute as they sped through the gate. Dominique swung the *taptap* in a sharp U-turn and stopped in front of the administrative offices. They hopped out of the jitney and ran up the steps with Payne following behind.

They surprised the duty officer and shot him dead before he could reach for his gun. Within minutes Pasquet and his men had managed to overcome the sleeping soldiers and secure the barracks. The troops were locked inside the garrison and forced to sit in their underwear with their hands on their heads. Pasquet worked the phones, trying to recruit his friends in the military. Unfortunately none were willing to take a chance. One of his calls was to the Palace, where Papa Doc answered the phone and the two men had a quick and peculiar exchange of words, with Duvalier telling Pasquet to be a man and face him at the gate of the barracks.

Outside the Casernes Dessalines Haiti had once again woken to the sound of gunfire. The rumours circulated that a rebel force of two hundred had seized the barracks. The entire army and police apparatus appeared paralysed. Many of the army officers were literally sitting on their hands waiting to see how the scales tilted.

The early daylight hours gave some of the Duvalierists more courage. The plea came over the radio. 'Aid your president,' the announcer shouted. 'Hated Magloirists have seized the Casernes Dessalines and they have brought foreigners with them, Dominicans!'

However, few appeared to heed the call. In the downtown area a stream of tradesmen, market women and store employees went about their daily chores, setting up for the day's business, pretending to ignore the obvious. Market women with baskets loaded with vegetables on their heads walked casually past the National Palace without so much as glancing at the soldiers lying on the ground with rifles at the ready.

Duvalier himself, dressed in a soldier's khaki uniform, a combat steel helmet and two pistols at his hips, moved about the place giving orders.

Pasquet and his men held the barracks and waited for reinforcements to arrive. But Perpignan, a heavy smoker, could not control his craving. He sent out one of the prisoners, who also happened to be Mrs Duvalier's driver, to fetch a pack of Haitian-made Splendids from a street vendor. A group of Duvalierists seized and interrogated him, learning the truth: there were only eight invaders.

From there, things got progressively worse for the rebels. The reinforcements

Pasquet expected never arrived. Captain Daniel Beauvoir, a friend whom Pasquet believed would side with him and fight Duvalier, arrived with troops from Pétionville and took up firing positions in the military hospital across the streets from the barracks. The four hundred yards separating the Palace and the Casernes Dessalines turned into a free-fire zone. There was a general distribution of pistols to volunteers at the Palace side gate.

The final assault on the rebels came when the Palace guards opened up on the barracks with a .50-calibre machine-gun, making a terrible din. The rebels returned fire with a .30-calibre. Grenades exploded, and there was a loud cheer as fifty soldiers escaped from the barracks, signalling that it was all over for the invaders. The shooting stopped. The eerie silence that followed was broken when a man ran out of the barracks with a bloody cloth in his hands, yelling frantically that he had the brains of Alix Pasquet.

Pasquet's skull had been shattered. He lay face up with open eyes as if gazing into Duvalier's official portrait hanging on a wall across the room, a cynical smile on his face, his likeness pierced by a single bullet. Dominique's bullet-riddled corpse lay propped in the corner next to a door. Near him Captain Walker lay dead, shot through the right ear, a pack of Lucky Strikes balanced on his neck. Dany Jones lay half sitting, a small, clean bullet hole in the middle of his forehead.

Payne was still alive. He was wrapped up in a mattress, his complexion pale from the loss of blood from his leg wound. When the soldiers ran in he pleaded for his life and called out, 'Journalist, journalist!' But the soldiers cut him down with a burst of gunfire.

Perpignan, Hickey and Kersten managed to escape. Perpignan and Hickey ran across the street, through the grounds of the military hospital and over a back fence. Hickey was spotted by a soldier and shot through the head. Perpignan ran into the yard of a house and forced the houseboy to hide him in the chicken coop, but when the boy heard the mob outside he became frightened and ran. Perpignan shot him down with a burst from his Thompson submachine-gun, giving away his hiding place. The mob closed in. He was shot and stabbed. His clothes were torn and his naked body was dragged through the streets and into the Palace, where it left a trail of blood over the marble floors and stairs as it was hauled before Duvalier.

The mob also caught up with Kersten behind the barracks, where they hacked him to death with machetes and paraded his body through the streets.

'I can't believe it. Eight men,' Graham said when I finished telling him the story. 'They really thought they could do it.'

'It always seems to be that way,' I said.

Graham made reference of the invasion in *The Comedians* when Philipot visits Brown who is swimming in the pool. The two men speak, wondering what Jones is up to. Philipot tells Brown about the invasion. 'I told him how seven men once captured the army barracks because they had tommy-guns.'

'I'm sure that helped Papa Doc more than anyone can imagine,' said Graham.

'That's when he started his Volunteers of National Security.'

'His militia?'

I nodded. 'The National Assembly passed laws. There was a curfew, everything. It gave him the excuse to build his terror network.'

'And there were the usual repercussions, I'm sure.'

'Oh yes. And he didn't have to hide it. He positioned a new Palace military staff that was loyal only to him. He made changes in the military. A few foreigners were expelled.'

'They played right into his plans. It happens every time. It's like the Bay of Pigs. It did more for Castro than anyone else.'

'You know,' I said after a while, 'the problem with Haiti is that no one seems to care. That invasion made headlines because there were five Americans involved, but Papa Doc is committing horrible crimes every day. It just doesn't make the papers.'

'Who would believe that the Cold War would ever come to the Caribbean.' Graham was pensive, then he added, 'The US would support the devil if he was anti-Communist.'

'Fascism may flow –'

'Washington is paranoid,' Graham interrupted. 'They're obsessed with Fidel. They don't want another Cuba. Papa Doc knows how to play the anti-Communist card.'

'If they knew what's going on,' I said.

'Believe me, they know.'

'I wish Haiti would get more attention in the press. Very little truth comes out of the country, and when it does it doesn't get much play. There was Hector Riobé. I think he was in his mid-twenties. His father had been picked up by the Macoutes at a roadblock in Carrefour the day of the attempted kidnapping. They took his car, money and land. They executed him the same day but later told the family that he was still alive and needed money in prison. The family finally realized that they were lying. This became a Macoute racket to extract money from other families of the "disappeared".'

'But he was dead.'

'Yes, very dead. Riobé was an only son. He decided to fight against Duvalier, and the Macoutes turned him into an enemy. He took his Ford pick-up and welded steel plates all around it, turning it into an armoured car. He assembled a flame-thrower and attached it to the car. His plan was to take over the police station in Pétionville.'

'I heard about Riobé in Haiti,' Graham said. 'I would like to hear what you know of his fight, which would seem to be driven solely by courage. It sounds like he had no chance of success.'

'Yes, he was courageous, but it proved to be a suicidal attack,' I said and told him what I knew. Late on the night of 16 July 1963, as the celebration over the corpse of Clément Barbot was winding down, Riobé and his partisans drove the deserted streets of Port-au-Prince in his armoured vehicle. Halfway up the hill to Pétionville the vehicle overheated. The driver, Demas, jumped out and went to a house to ask for water. It turned out Riobé had welded a steel sheet in front of the radiator, blocking the truck's cooling system. But it was too late to fix. It was done.

When their makeshift tank finally reached Pétionville the overheated engine coughed and died in front of the small police post at the corner of the Pétionville market. They were only a few blocks from their target.

The policeman on duty offered to fetch some water. Another policeman walked around the strange vehicle, which resembled a Mardi Gras float. He pulled himself up to see what was in the back. Four men with 12-gauge shotguns and a .22-calibre rifle lay on the bed of the truck. The unarmed policeman ran away as the men jumped out, firing in all directions, waking up the market women sleeping beside their stalls and sending them screaming for cover.

The group abandoned the vehicle. Two of the youths figured the mission had been aborted and walked home. The other three, Damas, Riobé and Jean-Pierre Hudicourt, regrouped further up the road. They decided to make the police post in the small holiday village of Kenscoff their alternate target. They stopped a car driven by a well-known Syrian-Haitian merchant Antoine Izméry and ordered him to drive them up the mountain.

They attacked the police station, killing three policemen and two militiamen and making off with arms and munitions. The little town was in turmoil. The road was blocked, and the militia began a house-to-house search; then they began to comb the mountains. As they neared the summit of Morne Godet they were greeted by gunfire.

Near the top of the mountain there was a strategically situated cave, easily defended. Within hours government reinforcements arrived in Kenscoff and moved into battle positions, but every time a soldier or member of the militia got close to the summit and became exposed a shot from the cave sent him reeling down the mountain dead or wounded.

The authorities believed the cave was defended by a group of well-trained sharpshooters. As the number of casualties grew, the US Marine-trained Casernes Dessalines battalion was ordered to join the war with mortars and grenades. It was becoming an embarrassment to the Palace. The entire country was alive with exciting rumours of a battle that Papa Doc was actually losing.

The firefight continued for three days. Then on the afternoon of Friday 19 July the cave fell silent. The government feared it was a trick. The soldiers didn't dare approach the cave. The following day the police arrived with Hector Riobé's mother. They put her on a horse and made her ride up to the cave calling out her son's name as they followed close behind, using her as a human shield. There was no reply.

When Papa Doc's forces finally reached the cave they were astonished to find there wasn't a squad of sharpshooters but a single gunman. Hector Riobé lay dead, a bullet through his head – by his own hand.

'That's amazing,' Graham said.

'But when I reported the story it was only a short blurb. I didn't have all the facts, and since no Americans were involved it wasn't important.'

'What happened to the others?'

'All except one were captured and tortured to death.'

Graham said nothing. He looked away for a moment as we passed an open stall where a woman was selling fruit and vegetables on the side of the road.

'Life under Papa Doc,' I said quietly.

'Indeed,' he said. 'And what about this group we're going to see now, the Kamo . . .'

'Kamoken,' I said. 'Their situation's just as dire as everyone else's.'

'But you're helping them.'

I thought about this. I wanted to introduce Graham to all the characters I knew. I wanted him to know everything Duvalier was doing. He understood the problem with Haiti and the tyranny of Duvalier, but I imagined there had to be some things that would be better left untold. It was a fine line for me to navigate, and I was afraid of having breached journalistic ethics. I was as conflicted as any man fighting for a cause. I thought of Riobé and how what Papa Doc had done to his father had driven him on his suicidal mission. Events propel us into action. I did not want to be a guerrilla, but I had been forced to do something.

I explained to Graham about the Kamoken. Their official name was the Haitian Revolutionary Armed Forces (FARH), and their leader was Fred Baptiste, a former schoolteacher from Jacmel who believed Duvalier had stolen the presidential election. He was an intense, highly strung individual. In 1959 he attacked an army post at a small grass airstrip in Jacmel. Baptiste escaped, but his brother Renel was captured and spent four months in prison. In late 1962 the two brothers crossed into the Dominican Republic and joined other exiles in the struggle against Duvalier.

Baptiste had no political ideology. The Haitian Marxists thought he was a loose cannon, and the right-wing exiles led by Louis Déjoie called him a dangerous Communist.

The group had a small camp at Dajabón. When the Dominican army broke up the camp in May 1963 the exiles moved into a tiny shack on an embankment in Santo Domingo. They had no money and no support until early 1964 when Baptiste accepted the formal patronage of Father Jean-Baptiste Georges and ex-Haitian army officer and diplomat Pierre L. Rigaud.

Father Georges found an abandoned chicken farm in Villa Mella, about twelve miles south of Santo Domingo, where the rebels could stay. The troops slept in the chicken coops and learned the art of guerrilla warfare on the blackboard. There were no firearms on the farm. At night the rebels played war games with sticks. They had no radio communications, medical unit or supplies. Every morning they raised the Haitian flag and sang the anthem of the FARH.

One night I received a call from the officer assigned to the US Military Assistance Group in the Dominican Republic. 'General Wessin y Wessin is on to your Haitian friends,' he warned. Elías Wessin y Wessin had been the leader of the coup that overthrew Juan Bosch the year before. 'Be prepared. I'm sure the General's men are going to pay the camp a visit pretty soon.'

The Haitian opposition movements were fractured and constantly denouncing one another. It had been Déjoie who told Wessin y Wessin, an anti-Communist zealot, that the Kamoken were allied with Castro and Duvalier.

I made a quick visit to the US Information Office and picked up a number of pamphlets and brochures promoting President Kennedy's Alliance for Progress programme for the Americas. Then I drove out to the chicken farm and distributed the literature to the rebels. A couple of days later Wessin y Wessin's men raided the camp and arrested everyone, including a number of Haitians living in the Hotel Europa and two French soldiers of fortune.

I drove out to Villa Mella with my wife and our infant son, but as we came up to the police station along the route a policeman shouted, '*Ahi viene el hombre del carrito*' ('Here comes the man with the little car.') They arrested us and took us to the National Police Headquarters. My wife and son were left waiting in the Volkswagen for two hours in the noon heat. Finally, at my urging, an officer agreed to allow my wife to return home rather than suffer heatstroke in the police yard.

I was not held in the same cell as the Haitians. A few hours later a high-ranking officer appeared and escorted me not to the jail but to President Donald Reid Cabral's residence.

I explained the situation to the President, and he immediately sent someone to retrieve the evidence from Wessin y Wessin. Then we sat down to a drink. In a moment the telephone rang. It was the British Ambassador. Apparently he'd heard that I had been arrested.

'Diederich?' Reid Cabral said into the receiver and winked at me. 'Yes. He's been arrested. I have him right here. I'm torturing him with Johnny Walker.'

When the messenger arrived with the 'Communist' literature confiscated at the camp, Reid Cabral flipped through the pamphlets and discovered the publisher: US Information Service. The following day, on the President's orders, the Kamoken were released.

Just as the rebels were settling back on the chicken farm, Father Georges arranged to purchase rifles, munitions and explosives from an anti-Castro Cuban in Miami. One of the guerrillas, Gérard Lafontant, was assigned to take delivery of the weapons in Miami and move them to a safe house near the Miami river.

The Cuban delivered the weapons and loaned Lafontant a garbage truck to transport them to the safe house. As he drove south on I-95 the truck ran out of petrol. A Florida highway patrolman arrived at the scene, and Lafontant, who did not have a driving licence, told him he was taking the truck to Haiti. Amazingly, the patrolman didn't ask to see a licence or peer into the back of the truck. Lafontant delivered the arms, which were loaded aboard the 235-foot freighter *Johnny Express*.

The Kamoken also paid $2,000 to a member of the Jeune Haiti movement (an organization comprised mostly of young Haitian exiles, thirteen of whom later landed in southern Haiti to fight Papa Doc) in New York for the purchase of NATO-issued automatic FAL rifles. The arms arrived by ship, concealed inside the insulation of refrigerators, and the ammunition was hidden inside car batteries. The men unloaded the arms, but a few days later they were claimed by a pair of long-time Haitian exiles. At first the Kamoken refused to hand over the weapons but complied after the men threatened to blow up the house where the munitions were stored.

On the night of 27 June my wife and I attended a diplomatic party at the house of Vince Blocker, the US Embassy's CIA man in charge of keeping an eye on the Haitian exiles. I was privy to the invasion plans but said nothing. I stayed late at Blocker's house and watched the clock. I knew that if anything happened his police sources would notify him.

That night twenty-nine Kamoken were loaded into a van and taken from the chicken farm to a cocktail party at Pierre Rigaud's apartment on Avenida Independencia. The men ate hors d'œuvres and mingled until late into the night. Then they were loaded back into the van and driven to the coast near the airport, where they were ferried by a small boat to the *Johnny Express*.

As the freighter got under way the guerrillas broke out the weapons from Miami. They were stunned. The arms the Cuban had sold them were antique First World War British-made Enfield rifles.

A Dominican patrol boat fired a warning shot over the bow of the *Johnny Express*, but they managed to escape. The following day, in heavy seas, the freighter drew as close as it could to the Haitian coast near the town of Saltrou.

The landing proved difficult and costly for the guerrillas. Two men drowned, and most of the detonators for the explosives were lost. The invasion was saved when a fisherman brought his battered boat alongside the *Johnny Express* and helped the others disembark.

Immediately after landing two Kamoken deserted, but the fisherman agreed to join the group and helped carry the munitions. They were a poorly armed force of twenty-five, and their US olive fatigues confused the Haitian peasants, who thought they were members of Papa Doc's army or militia.

The following day Duvalier was informed of the presence of the rebels in the Belle Anse area. The response was terrifying and typical of Papa Doc's repression. Anyone in the area believed to be anti-Duvalier was taken from their home and killed. Sixty-seven people were executed in the town square. Because one of the Kamoken was identified as Adrien Fandal the Macoutes hunted down and killed anyone in the area with that name. They seized land from the victims, and for years the killers and the relatives of the victims had to live side by side in Belle Anse.

In Port-au-Prince Papa Doc took personal command of the armed forces. A detachment from the Dessalines battalion was sent to hunt down the Kamoken. They pummelled the mountains with mortar rounds, but the guerrillas were not there. Duvalier's small air force made daily sorties, and truckloads of militiamen were sent into the mountains. The invasion appeared to evolve into a sustained campaign. The helpless mountain peasants who were caught in the crossfire endured three weeks of terror. If they welcomed the Kamoken they would be executed by the army or Macoutes. If the Kamoken suspected them of being Macoutes they would likewise be executed.

Haiti's Foreign Minister, René Chalmers, complained to the UN Security Council, accusing the Dominican Republic of aggression. He claimed the invasion force was made up of Haitian and Dominican elements armed with automatic weapons, grenades, wireless receivers and a large store of ammunition. He said the invaders planned to dynamite bridges and gasoline tanks and accused prominent exiles of being behind the invasion.

I, too, was also denounced at the UN for providing the Kamoken with identifications. I immediately received a call from Manny Friedman, the foreign editor at the *New York Times*, asking me if I had dropped journalism and become a guerrilla.

When the Dominican government received news of the invasion, President Reid Cabral countered Duvalier's charges with his own, accusing Papa Doc of lying and declaring that no invasion force had left from Dominican territory.

The President summoned me to the Palace. He was in a good mood, pleased at how he'd rebuffed Duvalier. Then he looked at me and asked, 'Those Haitians are still in Villa Mella, right?'

I shrugged.

'Goddamn it.' Reid Cabral was furious. 'I just protested to the OAS [Organization of American States]. How the hell did they do it?'

Meanwhile the small rebellion continued. Duvalier's forces were reluctant to venture into the mountains and face a guerrilla force of unknown strength. The army and Macoutes contented themselves with occupying marketplaces and wreaking vengeance on anyone they suspected of helping the rebels. A member of the Kamoken who ventured into a market wearing combat boots was spotted and executed on the spot.

The guerrillas took over the village of Mapou. Someone accused the local shopkeeper of being a Macoute. The Kamoken ransacked the shop, distributing goods and cash to the peasants. They confiscated a bundle of mortgage notes and IOUs from the store and burned them in a formal ceremony. Then they killed the owner.

The Kamoken were forced to discourage recruits because they had no arms or food to offer them. The peasants in the mountains were dirt poor. Many couldn't even afford a machete and had to cultivate their land with their hands, scratching between the rocks to plant millet.

Water was also a problem for the guerrillas. During the sixteen days it took to cross Morne La Selle and other rocky mountains, they found little food or water to purchase. To quench their thirst and hunger some of the rebels ate chocolate-coated laxatives with disastrous results.

Baptiste was a tough leader, but he was also paranoid. He forced his men to move miles at a time and forbade them to drink from waterholes, fearing they were poisoned. Towards the end of July the Kamoken were astride the Haitian–Dominican border. Baptiste ordered the men to cross back into the Dominican Republic to find rations, but Gérard Lafontant resisted, adamant they remain in Haitian territory. Baptiste became angry at Lafontant's insubordination, which he likened to an act of mutiny. He levelled his rifle at Lafontant's head at point-blank range and pulled the trigger. Nothing happened. The gun misfired.

In the end, the sick and hungry guerrillas buried their weapons and walked across the border on to Dominican soil, where they were promptly taken prisoner by an army patrol. Two weeks later they were released back in the mountainous region along the border.

On 5 August 1964 the Kamoken returned to their old base camp in Haiti's Morne La Selle, a stone's throw from the Dominican border post at El Aguacate. The Dominican soldiers had orders from their commander to ignore the Haitian guerrillas if they re-entered the country.

The ragtag force retrieved their old firearms and began to act like disciplined fighters. Columns went out on forays against Macoutes and military targets. On 11 August they sabotaged the Pine Forest sawmill belonging to Papa Doc's sister-in-law and her husband who had the timber monopoly. Four days later another column carried out a successful night attack on the Haitian military border post at Savane Zombi. The soldiers and Macoutes fled, leaving behind their equipment and, more importantly, the post's archives. The guerrillas set fire to the post and two houses belonging to the local Macoute chieftain. That same afternoon another Kamoken column ambushed a truckload of Papa Doc's militia who were travelling slowly over the rugged mountain road that led from Thiotte to Port-au-Prince, inflicting four casualties.

Several days later a messenger arrived at my home in Santo Domingo with a request for guerrilla reinforcements, arms, food, medicines and winter wear. We supplied sweaters, which we had dyed dark green, food and medicines, but there were no heavy weapons.

I volunteered transport. Since my Volkswagen Beetle was too small I asked a friend, the owner of Santo Domingo Motors, if he'd let me borrow a car for the weekend. He said that if I 'repossessed' an automobile a Cuban exile had refused to return the car would be mine for the weekend. I took two burly Haitians with me and had no trouble repossessing the late-model American car.

At midday on 24 August, loaded down with food and clothing, three Haitian friends and I took off for the border. Hurricane Cleo was approaching the south coast of Hispaniola. The sun disappeared behind thick thunderclouds, and the sky was streaked with an eerie yellow light. We raced along the coastal road in gusting winds and heavy rain until we reached the mountain road to El Aguacate. Here the dirt road had turned to thick mud and the going became rough and slow. At times the wheels would spin and the heavy car would slide backwards on the difficult road.

When we finally drove into the military compound of El Aguacate the sentries ignored us. Fred Baptiste strode out of the mountain fog accompanied by a squad of his men. We handed over to the goods, and they gave us several rolls of film to be developed in Santo Domingo and provided to the media.

After we finished unloading, Baptiste looked at me with disappointment. 'Where are the arms?'

'There are none,' I said.

Baptiste was crestfallen. He thought Rigaud had convinced the Dominican military to release the guns General Cantave had received in an airdrop at Dajabón.

'You tell Rigaud we need arms and munitions. This is top priority. We plan to go on the offensive.'

I knew they needed arms, but all I could do was hand over a .45-calibre automatic pistol I had purchased for $400 from a fixer I knew in Santo Domingo. It was a clean weapon with the serial numbers filed off. Baptiste took the weapon and shrugged as he placed it in his belt. 'A lot of good this will do.'

We were out of time. Hurricane Cleo was beginning to turn the mountain road into a river. We made it down safely, but when we arrived in Baní the waters were too high and the car stalled. We had to abandon the vehicle and take a bus back to Santo Domingo.

Two months later a member of the Kamoken arrived at our door in Santo Domingo with a letter from Fred Baptiste. It said he was hospitalized in the Dominican army barracks in Azua with a fractured leg. The remaining members of his guerrilla force were being held in the army's *fortaleza* in Neyba. 'I must get out of the Azua *fortaleza* this week, and the fellows must be moved,' the note read. 'Alas, the inaction is killing me; I cannot stay any longer in the Azua *fortaleza*. Do your best for us. We cannot let go of the struggle . . . We are young. We will win or die.'

According to Baptiste, the Kamoken heard voices coming from across the valley on the Dominican side of the border. They decided they were Dominicans. Two hours later one of the sentries saw two dozen men dressed like Dominican soldiers approaching through the pine trees into Haitian territory deployed and preparing to attack. He fired a shot in the air to sound the alarm. The approaching force opened up with a .30-calibre machine-gun. There was no question of fighting the intruders coming from the Dominican side. The only alternative was to split up into small groups and retreat further into Haitian territory. Baptiste fell over a precipice and fractured his left leg in two places.

The weary Kamoken left their hiding places inside Haiti and straggled in twos and threes back across the Dominican border, and once again they were taken prisoner by the Dominican army. Because of his injuries, Baptiste was transported to the fort in Azua.

No one knew who had attacked the Kamoken. Speculation focused on Dominican General Elías Wessin y Wessin, who feared that the Haitian guerrillas might cause an escalation of trouble with Papa Doc. At the time the top command of the Dominican armed forces was divided. One group of high-ranking officers supported exiled President Joaquín Balaguer, while another, which had opposed the overthrow of President Bosch, was in favour of a return to constitutional rule. Only Wessin y Wessin gave full support to President Reid Cabral.

Reid Cabral had ordered reinforcement of the border but refused an army request for additional tanks in the area. He told me he was concerned that rival military groups might be trying to have Wessin y Wessin disperse his tanks around the country in order to weaken his force in Santo Domingo and bring off a coup d'état. In early March 1964 Reid Cabral set off a minor controversy in the Dominican media and military when at the urging of the OAS he suggested it might be a good thing to re-establish relations with Haiti, even at a consular level, to learn what was happening there.

There was another version of the attack on the Kamoken, in which Papa Doc's Dominican-exile recruits may have been the ones who actually assaulted the Kamoken disguised as regular Dominican soldiers and speaking Spanish.

Only twenty-four Kamoken returned from battle. The fate of the other four was never known. Still, for the Haitian peasants the Kamoken had taken on all the mystical attributes of the nocturnal airborne werewolf, the *lougarwu*. Like that fearful phantom, the Kamoken seemed to be everywhere and nowhere. The Macoutes feared the Kamoken were still in the hills.

The men were in dire need of medical attention, one for a broken arm and the others for malaria. The prison commandant provided them with a daily ration of twelve pounds of rice from his own prison allotment. The Kamoken cooked the rice at night with a little salt and an occasional plantain. They gradually sold off their clothing and boots to Dominican soldiers. Their home for seven weeks was a dark room filled with the stench of open latrines. They slept on bug-infested mattresses. They had no toothbrushes or soap, and there was no electric light. At dawn and dusk swarms of mosquitoes descended on them.

I appealed to President Reid Cabral, asking him to release Fred Baptiste for specialized medical treatment. He summoned his army Chief of Staff, who addressed a note to the commander of the Neyba garrison giving me permission to see the Haitian prisoners. As I walked out of the Presidential Palace Reid Cabral stopped me and asked me to report back to him. He wanted to know what else he could do for the Haitians.

At Neyba the prisoners paraded before me in military fashion. They resembled Second World War concentration-camp victims: emaciated and barefoot. What little clothing they had had been reduced to rags. While none of them complained about their physical state, they were desperate for news of Haiti and inquired when they might be released.

I drove Baptiste to a private clinic in Santo Domingo and checked him in under a fictitious name. Papa Doc had spies everywhere. Baptiste's leg was set and placed in a cast. I paid the $180 bill, and when he was released from the hospital he convalesced in my home office, sleeping next to the telex machine and playing with our infant son.

'So how is it they ended up in this place?' Graham said as we veered off the road and drove up a narrow dirt driveway to the grounds of the former insane asylum.

'The conditions at the garrison in Neyba were so bad I asked Reid Cabral to help us out.'

'And this is the help they got.'

'This is it.'

The asylum consisted of a series of long concrete barrack-style buildings set one after the other with a main door and barred windows. When the Kamoken first arrived, the inside of the buildings were filled with mountains of goat shit. They spent days shovelling out the manure and cleaning up.

The goats remained and roamed freely around the compound and inside the barracks. Adding a touch of the surreal to the scene, a crude barbed-wire fence separated the asylum from an empty field in which a herd of African zebras that had belonged Trujillo were pastured.

We found Baptiste in one of the buildings, which still reeked of goats. He was lying on a cot, resting his injured leg. When we entered he stood and with the aid of a stick walked with us out to the garden.

The compound did not look or feel like a guerrilla training centre. The group was using the goat manure as fertilizer to grow vegetables. They had organized a small education centre and invited the children of the Dominican soldiers guarding the property to attend, teaching them to read and write Spanish.

Graham shook his head. 'How can they succeed by determination alone?' The Kamoken were everyday Haitians, taxi drivers, former soldiers, mechanics, farmers, schoolteachers and peasants from different regions of the country. 'There are so few of them. They have no arms.'

'Yet this is the insurgency against Papa Doc,' I said.

'They're just going to end up like all the rest. Like Riobé and Pasquet.'

'They all think it's going to be different with them. Castro started his revolution with twelve men.'

Graham shielded his eyes from the sun with his hand and looked at me. 'That's different. Batista was a fool. And Castro had the support of the people.'

'I agree. But you try to tell them they can't do it.'

Graham looked away where two billy-goats were charging and butting heads against one another.

We walked back across the garden. Graham paused to observe several of the guerrillas who were completing a new bamboo aqueduct to irrigate their crops of tomatoes and beans. Baptiste pulled me aside.

'Maybe the Englishman can get guns for us,' he whispered in Creole.

'No,' I said. 'It's not his business.'

'Maybe he has connections,' Baptiste persisted.

I walked away from Baptiste and met Graham between rows of tomato plants. Later Graham gave the rebels a $30 contribution. Baptiste told him the money would go to purchase hatchlings for a chicken farm.

3 | LOVING HAITI

The following day I picked up my friend, Jean-Claude Bajeux, an exiled Haitian Catholic priest, and we went to collect Graham. The three of us left Santo Domingo in the pre-dawn darkness and began our trip across the island in my chartreuse Volkswagen Beetle. A snow-white quilt of mist hung over the fields of leafy tobacco in the rich Cibao Valley as we clattered through the Dominican countryside. Mornings are the best time of day in the Caribbean, and that morning in January 1965 was no exception. I made a comment about the air that rushed through the windows carrying the fragrance of tropical flowers, the wet earth and burning charcoal. Graham took a deep breath and said he preferred the smell of Haiti. 'It is very much like West Africa.'

The highway to the north coast had no speed limit, so we motored with the accelerator pushed to the floor, and the Beetle's 36-horsepower engine chattered away like a noisy sewing machine. The Beetle was a despised symbol during the latter years of the Trujillo dictatorship because it had become the preferred vehicle of El Jefe's dreaded secret police, the SIM (Military Intelligence Service). His *caliés* – plainclothes thugs and spies – rode three to a car with their Dominican-made San Cristóbal rifles at the ready. The noisy putt-putt of a SIM Beetle's little air-cooled engine when it came up the driveway was enough to freeze the blood of the bravest Dominican. None the less the car was economical and versatile, and it was all I could afford at the time.

Graham was cheerful. He seemed excited at our starting out. 'We'll get a good look at Papa Doc's Haiti from as close as humanly possible, and perhaps we'll provoke him a little,' he said, delighted at the prospect of action.

But as we cruised along the two-lane road, talking over the sound of the engine and the wind became laborious. Cattle and donkeys attracted to the warm asphalt of the roadway during the night were slow to give up their bed. Avoiding these slow-moving and unpredictable creatures as well as a variety of other animals became a game of Dominican roulette for Graham. He said chickens were fair game, and he displayed a mischievous, boyish delight at the contest of hitting chickens on the road. He peered out his window making cluck-clucking sounds, then snapped back in his front seat as another startled hen fluttered past our windshield, and he would credit me with another point. In the back seat Father Bajeux had managed to curl up his lanky frame and had fallen asleep.

47

We stopped for petrol in the city of Santiago. I noticed Graham had trouble with the door handle. He always seemed to have difficulty with mechanical things.

We drove on in silence, and as we passed the first crossroads out of the city I thought of my own life and the close calls I had experienced in Haiti. I feared what might lie ahead and the risk we were taking travelling a relatively unmarked and little-respected border between the two countries.

I had my own bizarre relationship with Papa Doc. The little country doctor had walked into the office of my newspaper on 5 September 1956. He sat across my desk with his hat on and stared at me through his thick glasses. He wore a thick serge suit and a bow tie and spoke in French. When I picked up a pen and a pad he raised his hand slightly and explained he was only making a courtesy call in preparation for announcing his candidacy for the presidency of the republic.

'What do the Americans think of me?' he asked. By Americans he meant the US embassy. Any candidate needed the support of the Americans ever since the 1915–34 Marine occupation. The Embassy, he appeared to think, could be an obstacle to an ambitious Haitian politician. Despite his early anthropological writings, earlier career in politics and service in the Estimé government, Duvalier's style had not brought him great public notice.

I told him that the Americans working with the Inter-American Cooperative Public Health Service (known by its French abbreviation initials SCISP) spoke well of him. I admitted that I was not privy to the Embassy's thinking.

He smiled, revealing a gold tooth. But what I didn't say, although he probably already knew it, was that the US Embassy looked kindly on the candidacy of Senator Louis Déjoie, who had actively courted them with his upper-class sophistication, charm and success in agribusiness.

Duvalier did not appear to be a strong contender for the presidency. He had trouble with newspapers misspelling his name. He wouldn't discuss his own childhood or personal life and gave no hint of his origin. Not even his close associates could furnish any details of his private life.

Watching him being driven away that day, seated alone in the back seat of a Buick, I could not help thinking that, while he had none of the charisma of populist Daniel Fignolé, none of the expertise of technocrat Clément Jumelle and none of the flamboyance of Déjoie or the other minor candidates, he had a confidence and a quiet determination about him. Still, he hardly seemed presidential material.

I covered the 1957 election and Papa Doc's rise to power. The mild-mannered country doctor, François Duvalier, became Haiti's all-powerful and feared Papa Doc. By early 1963 his gratuitous brutality had generated headlines around the world. Much of the reporting was mine. Every day I chronicled how the by now well-entrenched Papa Doc faced down the Kennedy administration in Washington and the newly elected Juan Bosch in the neighbouring Dominican Republic.

Papa Doc's bully-boys were, at the beginning, recruited by Duvalier from the city's demi-monde of thieves and other criminals. They soon became known as the Tontons Macoutes, after the Haitian folkloric bogeyman who strides over mountains snatching up misbehaving children and tucking them away in a *macoute*, a large sack he carries on his back. These street criminals had no conscience, and in their acts of brutality they were always sending Papa Doc's message: conform and collaborate – or else. The most notorious Macoutes sported Runyonesque names such as Boss Paint, Ti-Bobo, Ti-Cabiche, Boss Justin and Madame Max (one of many female Macoutes). Haiti had become the land of 'look behind'. No one began a conversation without first looking over his or her shoulder. In a land that was once uninhibitedly fun-loving, paranoia was now universal. The country had become a tropical psycho ward. Some referred surreptitiously to Papa Doc as the *zombificateur* – zombie-maker.

The quiet, seemingly moderate and pliable physician who had championed the middle class as an early proponent of the concept of *noirisme* – blacks in power – was proving to be more interested in becoming the absolute mystical master of Haiti. He had carefully tooled up his regime for the sole purpose of retaining power.

Even Duvalier's own middle class suffered. There were no sacred cows. The mulatto élite at first suffered but were quick to make the necessary accommodation to Duvalier – and he to them. Haiti's impoverished masses were offered only hyperbole. They were learning from both his rhetoric and his actions that their new Papa was not in the least permissive or forgiving. Even based on the most dispassionate analysis, the regime of François Duvalier ranks as one of the most inhuman. And covering Haiti as a newsman had become a high-risk occupation. No story equalled the naked terror of Papa Doc's Haiti in the early 1960s. It was a pervasive terror that clawed at your viscera, which haunted you day and night. Duvalier's brutality was at once predictable and capricious, meted out by savage, sick and sadistic henchmen, the Tontons Macoutes, who were given *carte blanche* – they didn't need to explain their excesses to anyone. Some of the criminals became pro-Duvalier fanatics.

Duvalier's decapitating of Haiti's Catholic Church, the university and the high schools left the country an intellectual cripple and even co-opted God. The damage wrought by Papa Doc would have long-term effects even after Duvalier was buried. Hundreds of Haiti's best and brightest – teachers, lawyers, economists, agronomists, jurists and other professionals – fled the country. It was more than just a brain drain; it was a mass exodus of the country's most talented. Semi-literate Duvalierists replaced skilled professionals in government jobs as rewards for loyalty. Many of the competent professionals who lost their jobs were even barred from joining the exodus (Duvalier personally controlled all exit visas), so they remained and vegetated, ever fearful of the knock on the door. At first Duvalier branded his enemies lizards and then, more politically profitably, communists. He outlawed youth associations and judo classes and purged the ranks of high-school and university teachers. Higher education in Haiti, as professor or student, became the domain of only loyal Duvalierists.

As for the Catholic Church, with orders to be 'rough and rapid', Papa Doc's police placed 56-year-old Monsignor François Poirier, the last in a long line of French archbishops of Port-au-Prince, on a plane to Miami with a dollar and a prayer book. The government publicly accused Poirier of financing communist students in a plot to overthrow Duvalier. The archbishop, a strident anti-communist, turned almost apoplectic when he learned of the charge. Haiti's only Haitian-born Catholic bishop soon followed Mgr Poirier into exile, as did another French bishop and the rector and priest-professors of Petit Seminaire St Martial high school. The first Haitian-born bishop was seized and deported without even time to put in his false teeth – they remained on his night table. I couldn't help thinking that Graham would be interested – as a Catholic convert and creator of the whisky priest of *The Power and the Glory* – in exploring Papa Doc's fight with the Church.

In retaliation, the Vatican in 1961 excommunicated Duvalier and all other Haitian officials involved in the expulsion of Catholic clergy. The Vatican noted that it was the first excommunication of a head of state in the western hemisphere since dictator Juan Perón of Argentina in 1955. Duvalier ignored Rome's action against him. No news of the excommunication was published in Haiti.

The once-powerful Roman Catholic Church, the army, the judiciary and the Congress had all been purged and neutralized. As Duvalier said, it was those four powers that usually overthrew a president, so he overthrew them first. Most Haitians lived in silent terror behind masks of normality, pretending to know nothing, praying for a miracle of change, playing games to survive.

Duvalier's response was to withdraw further into his surreal world whose dementia was catching like some infectious disease. Sublimely Papa Doc decreed the country would celebrate 22 April to 22 May 1963 as the 'Month of National Gratitude' – to him. It was to be a 'carnival of flowers and of joy', but it turned out to be a carnival of carnage and blood, with still more foes of the brooding dictator, real and imagined, tracked down and killed. Haiti's glistening white National Palace had known elegant black-tie banquets and formal balls for visiting heads of state. Pink flamingos had daintily stalked the lawns and gardens. The birds-in-residence now were some kind of metaphor, guinea hens and randy cocks – Papa Doc's political symbols. Haitians feared the National Palace as a house of horror.

Graham later confirmed that he was watching from afar, upset and angered to see the country he had grown to love being torn apart by someone he described as a 'madman'.

And then, on one of the bloodiest of days of the dictatorship, 26 April 1963, the dam burst.

I had just dropped my wife off at the gynaecologist in Port-au-Prince that morning and proceeded downtown *en route* to my office at the newspaper. Our first child, a son, was forty days old. As I drove near the National Palace I noticed soldiers were deployed outside the palace but their guns were pointing in different directions, suggesting they didn't know who or where their enemy was. Something had to be terribly wrong. The frantic, frightened expressions on the soldiers' faces indicated that the situation was serious. I parked my car and followed the policemen and Macoutes on foot to the Methodist New College Bird, named after an early member of the Methodist Church in Haiti. There the corpse of a Macoute was doubled over where he usually spent the day as a look-out on the veranda of an old house across from the Methodist school, which was attended by Papa Doc's son Jean-Claude and youngest daughter Simone. The two Duvalier children were safe in their school in a state of shock. Their escort and driver were both dead. I tried not to be noticed, but suddenly I faced a row of old rifles and screams telling me to get out or be shot.

Before I reached my office Macoutes were racing around the city like mad dogs on the loose, guns protruding from their battered old American-made automobiles, in search of the unknown marksmen who had tried to kidnap Papa Doc's children. Pandemonium reigned throughout Port-au-Prince. Passers-by pretended not to see Macoutes wrestle a former army officer out of his car and drag him away, leaving his automobile in the middle of the street, its engine running. Like other motorists on that street I drove around the empty car. This moment was also an opportunity to take care of personal grudges. A soldier guarding the home of the mistress of the presidential guard commander shot to death a former officer parked on the street. The city became a free-fire zone. Anyone suspected was shot on sight. Innocent people were shot because they happened to be in the wrong place at the wrong time. Some were killed because of their name – it was the same or similar to a suspect's.

That morning I rushed to the cable office to beat the censors I knew would stop all outgoing dispatches, especially mine. I filed a take to the Associated

Press and the *New York Times* on what appeared to be an unsuccessful attempt to kidnap the president's two youngest children as they were entering morning classes at the Methodist school. As I ran back to my car soldiers were arriving by truck, and I watched as they were posted before the offices of RCA. I went back to reporting first hand the bloody mayhem, knowing I would find a way to get the story out somehow as I had done many times before.

Elderly Judge Benoît and his wife had just returned from Mass in the nearby Sacré Cœur church. Macoutes and a truckload of presidential guardsmen drew up before their house and opened withering fire at point-blank range. Those in the house died instantly. The house was set on fire. It became the pyre of the judge and his wife, a visitor and servant. Their son Lieutenant François Benoît's eighteen-month-old son died in the fire or was, as some believe, taken away by an officer. For days the Benoît's ashes were scattered by the wind throughout the neighbourhood.

The Palace believed the Judge's son, Lieutenant Benoît, an army sharpshooter, was responsible for the attempt on Papa Doc's children. (It was later proved to have been an act by Papa Doc's former secret police chief Clément Barbot.) Benoît had been in political asylum in the Dominican Embassy. Soldiers violated the sovereignty of the Dominican chancellery in their search, and they were halted from entering the Dominican Ambassador's residence and massacring those seeking asylum there only by President Juan Bosch warning that it would be an act of war. We could see the Dominican Republic from our house. Generalissimo Rafael Leonidas Trujillo's 31-year iron-fisted rule had been ended by assassins' bullets on 30 May 1961, and the long-time exiled writer Juan Bosch had become the Dominican Republic's first freely elected president. But with only four months at the helm he found the military machine he had inherited from the dictatorship now slow to respond to orders. Directed by Bosch to move against Papa Doc, the Dominican military refused even to rattle their sabres. They complained that they were out of petrol – literally.

I witnessed two young friends taken away in the absence of their father. Scores of ex-army officers were seized. One, a former coastguard commander, was shot dead by a squad of Duvalierist women. Everyone and anyone was suspect, especially the military.

I arrived home late that day. Not wanting to be detained at a roadblock by berserk Macoutes, I was forced to use back roads and drive over fields and around a mountainside to our home in a hilly rural farming area of Frères outside Port-au-Prince.

It was a restless night. As the heat of the day dissipated there was no sleep, except for our baby. We knew that the terror from the Palace would not be easily sated. The bloodbath would continue. Duvalier was bound to win all his stand-offs, even with President Kennedy. He knew he could resist everything but a well-placed bullet, and he was well guarded. Two loaded silver-plated Magnum revolvers rested as paperweights on his desk, and he carried a light US Second World War carbine with him everywhere he went. A Thompson submachine-gun was propped in the corner of his bedroom toilet. Moreover, Papa Doc was a consummately cynical actor. He played many roles: the good man, bad man, evil genius and madman. He affected the Baron Samedi look, that of the Voodoo god who is guardian of the graveyard, dressed in black hat and coat. Only Baron Samedi's traditional cigar and bottle were missing – Duvalier neither smoked nor drank. (He was a diabetic dependent on insulin, but when his blood sugar got too low he would eat or drink something sugary, such as a sweet, to avoid insulin shock.) Wrapped in a red-and-black dressing-gown, the colours of his Duvalierist flag, he would shuffle aimlessly around the Palace at night like a *lougarou* – werewolf.

At daybreak I expected the Macoutes to come at any moment. Papa Doc knew that I would try to get the story out somehow. He would want to stop me. I had been repeatedly warned about reporting stories that created adverse publicity for the Duvalier government. 'After all you are a guest here,' the foreign minister had recently warned me.

At 5.30 a.m. a carload of Macoutes arrived at my doorstep. My yard-boy held his machete threateningly and looked at me, but I signalled for him to put it down. I went peacefully.

I was finally deposited in La Grande Prison in the centre of the city. It was a rambling series of tin-roofed cells encircled by a high mortar wall built by the French colonizers in the eighteenth century, covering an entire block.

I was stripped naked and placed in a cell. Every second became an hour. I knew what had happened at some of the houses of those arrested. Many times the Macoutes go back to pillage the house and 'disappear' the family. I was terrified for my family and powerless to help them.

When the sun went down and the roof cooled, the night sounds became weird, frightening omens. Occasionally there was a gunshot. Scared voices of sentries called out, trailing across the prison yard, reassuring each other at their posts along the wall. At one point I dozed, but a burst of gunfire awakened me, followed by the angry curses of an officer and mutterings from his men.

My thoughts were with my wife and little son, vulnerable to the roving bands of Macoutes. But I had some hope. My wife was from a family of fighters. General Laurent Bazalais – the mulatto Chief of Staff of liberator Jean-Jacques Dessalines' army and among the signatories of the 1804 act of independence that created the Haitian state – was one of her forebears. Our peasant neighbours were all friends and hated the Macoutes. My Catholic God remained a stranger; the Voodoo *lwa* (spirits of mystery) were more approachable.

Suddenly it was quiet – for Haiti, unearthly quiet. I strained to listen, but I heard nothing. There were no voices. From what I could tell, the prison, at least the section in which I was incarcerated, was empty. What had become of all those arrested on the street the day before? Could they all have been sent to Fort Dimanche? When a soldier brought me a plate of beans and rice the next day I asked to go to the latrine, hoping to make some human contact that could inform me as to what was going on. But instead they rolled the latrine into my cell: a 55-gallon oil drum cut in half, filled with lime and black with flies feasting on the stinking faeces.

I found a rusted Gillette razor blade resting on the crossbar of the cell. I could see it had been used to carve people's names on the walls, which were caked thick with lime from years of whitewashing. Everyone wanted to leave a trace of their existence behind. I tried to catalogue mentally all the prisoners' names etched in the wall and their dates of imprisonment, but I was too anxious to retain them. Then I decided to add my name and the date.

On the afternoon of the second day a soldier brought my clothes and told me to dress. He came back and escorted me to the prison's administration office. Captain Pierre Thomas was waiting. He was in charge of the Interior Department's Immigration Enforcement Section. We were old friends.

Several soldiers watched as Thomas sorted through my papers and pocketed my $17 in Haitian *gourdes*.

'You're leaving,' Thomas said.

'Where to?' I said. I had hardly any voice. My throat was dry, and I realized I had not had anything to drink in forty-eight hours.

'You are being expelled,' he replied.

'What about my family? I am not leaving without them.'

Thomas looked at me. His eyes were tired. I could see he was exhausted, but his eyes seemed to offer some trust.

For the benefit of our audience, some of whom would report back to the Palace, Thomas said with finality, 'They have no problem, but you do. This is the only plane. There will be no other plane for you. Let's go.'

'But I have no passport.'

'You do.'

I trusted Thomas. He was not one of them. Clearly there was a sense of urgency in his words about my leaving that made me realize I would not be of any use to my family dead. Refusing might endanger them even more. If I did get on a plane and reach the outside world, I could bring pressure on Papa Doc to allow them to leave.

Getting to the airport was another traumatic experience. A macabre out-of-season Mardi Gras band danced drunkenly in the street, blocking our way. My guard had fallen asleep in the back seat of the little car, and the muzzle of his Thompson submachine-gun had fallen against my side. I noted he still had it cocked. All I could think of was that this was Russian roulette on a grand scale. Any good bump – and there were no shortages of ruts and potholes in the streets of Bel Air – could produce a burst of machine-gun fire into my heart. I studied the dangers of awakening him, or Thomas, who was driving, having a collision, or of the soldier being startled by a bad dream. It was the last time I saw Thomas. In 1968 he was executed by Duvalier along with eighteen fellow officers.

I climbed aboard the Delta afternoon flight to Santo Domingo with four cents in my pocket, wearing a sports shirt and a pair of linen trousers, the back pocket of which had been ripped off by the butt of a Macoute's rifle. Except for a US Marine officer I was the sole passenger on the plane. At dusk, the 'Clipper' climbed out over the Cul de Sac plain and headed east across the lakes towards the Dominican Republic. There was no relief in my last look at the majestic Massif de la Selle mountain, only sadness for the country, its people and my friends – and fear for my wife and child. My beloved newspaper, the *Haiti Sun*, and printing plant were gone for ever. Of one thing I was certain: I was leaving Haiti only physically. The country had become ingrained in my soul. My wife, with the assistance of *Time*'s Editor-in-Chief Henry Luce, the British Foreign Office and the New Zealand Prime Minister, but mainly by dint of her own courage, followed me into exile with our infant son three weeks later.

Papa Doc had won this battle. It had been impossible to send out reports on the bloody violence I had witnessed. In exile I could not write a first-person account of that bloody day for fear Papa Doc would retaliate against my family and friends. I had to keep silent. No first-hand account of that day was published.

4 | A RIVER OF BLOOD

We came upon the border but had to settle for looking at Haiti from the Dominican side. For the most part, the roughly 195-mile border that separate the two countries was a desolate and ill-defined line. There was no border fence. No single highway ran its length; only a series of feeder roads or narrow paths linked the few towns that populated both countries. Rivers served as the demarcation line in the valleys. In the mountainous sections the border could be delineated by the fact that the Haitian side had been eroded by tree-cutting for charcoal to the point where the land was virtually bald, while the Dominican side was still green with trees and vegetation. The border had an aura of evil, the uneasy feeling of a place not to wander about. The demarcation line, such as it was, had been soaked in the blood of ancient enemies.

The natives of Hispaniola, as Christopher Columbus baptized the island in December 1492 on his first voyage of discovery, suffered dearly under Spanish rule. In 1650 French settlers took over the western third of the island; it became known as La Partie Française until officially named Saint-Domingue with the Treaty of Ryswick in 1697. The Spanish side first introduced African slaves to the island in the early sixteenth century to toil in their gold mines after the Indian population had literally been worked to death. Much later, as the French settlers evolved into traders, Saint-Domingue became an important market for the thriving commerce in African slaves.

Following thirteen years of warfare, in 1804 an ex-slave, Jean-Jacques Dessalines, led his armies to victory against the French and declared the new nation of ex-slaves Haiti (the Indian word for 'mountainous lands'). The black Caribbean nation entered a hostile white world. It was the second free country in the hemisphere after the United States. Fearful of foreign invasions, the victorious Haitian leaders led their armies across the border in conquest to occupy much of the Spanish part of Hispaniola. In 1821, seventeen years after independence, Haitian President Jean-Pierre Boyer occupied the entire island, and the eastern two-thirds became known as 'Spanish Haiti'. The border disappeared for twenty-three years until 27 February 1844, after Boyer was overthrown and, taking advantage of the political chaos in Port-au-Prince, a group of Dominican patriots led by Juan Pablo Duarte seized Santo Domingo and brought about the capitulation of its Haitian garrison. The Dominican Republic came into existence, and the border reappeared.

We reflected sombrely on the fact that no strip of land in the Caribbean had seen so much killing. Graham displayed a keen interest in the border history and lore. The Haitianization of the border area dated as far back as the early 1930s. Haitian currency and the Creole language dominated the region. Dominicans were fearful of crossing the border because they believed that powerful old Papa Legba, the Voodoo deity and interlocutor between man and his gods, guarded the roads leading into Haiti. They associated the Haitians with black magic. Yet Haitians crossed over into the Dominican side, looking for work in the sugar-cane fields and as market traders and to flee political oppression. The Dominicans feared a 'black tide' was engulfing their country.

We arrived in Monte Cristi on the north coast. From there we headed west to the frontier at Dajabón, but before entering the town we branched off again, heading north towards the coast to inspect an area where exiled Haitian General Leon Cantave's ragtag army had been trained. Cows grazed peacefully in the pastures. We passed *saco mangles*, men who made a living collecting the bark of the mangrove tree which was used for dyeing animal skins. At Pepillo Salcedo a smart-looking Dominican navy corvette was berthed at the Granada Banana company dock. A small empty Haitian military post was within shouting distance on the other side of the river mouth.

I parked the Beetle on the side of the road, and we walked through the wild vegetation in the Punta Presidente bird sanctuary. As we struggled through the undergrowth on the bank of the river we startled a flock of flamingos that rose and flew like a pink cloud. Then we heard an engine start, and two men in a motorboat ploughed off into the open sea, the throttle wide open.

'They are up to no good. I bet they're Cuban *gusanos*,' Graham said, using Castro's word, worms, for Cuban exiles.

We got back in the Beetle and headed south to Dajabón. The old customs gate looked more like the entrance to a fort than the entrance to the Dominican border town on the banks of the Rio Dajabón, more commonly known as the Massacre River. The river originally got its nickname in the seventeenth century when Spanish troops ambushed buccaneers on the river bank while they were hunting cattle on Spanish territory. The Spanish slaughtered the men.

The water under the Dajabón bridge was green and sluggish. Dominican soldiers were amused by our visit and our interest in the border. They allowed us to proceed to the middle of the bridge, but one of the solders warned me. '*Con cuidado.* Carefully,' he said, as I stepped over the yellow line in the middle of the bridge to take a picture of Graham taking a picture of the Haitian side of the river.

The soldier set his rifle down and pointed to the Haitian side. '*Alli están los Haitianos*. The Haitians are there.' He nodded meaningfully at the foliage that cloaked the river bank. It all looked pristine and deserted. Graham focused his little Minox camera and snapped the view of Haiti. It was the only time during all the years I knew him that his camera worked on the first try.

Graham had a mischievous look in his eye, as if he wanted to provoke the Haitian soldiers into showing themselves or perhaps even shooting at us. The Dominican guards were cautious. 'Haitian soldiers and Macoutes have you in their gunsights,' one of the Dominican soldier warned. 'They are watching your every move.' As if to show proof of what he meant, he pointed to the pockmarks left by bullets that had struck the Dominican customs house when Haitian troops had opened fire with a .50-calibre machine-gun on General Leon Cantave's retreating army of Haitian exile recruits and cane-cutters. It had been a real war scene along this section of the Massacre River in September 1963. Cantave's forces fled in total disorder, throwing away their weapons in terror, after trying unsuccessfully to capture the army barracks in the border town of Ouanaminthe, which could not be seen from the bridge. Since that incident the border had been closed. There was no traffic or contact between the border guards on each side of the river.

Graham was fascinated by one story that had emerged after the battle for Ouanaminthe. One of Cantave's toughest fighters, Captain Blucher Philogenes, was killed in the encounter. According to a radio message intercepted by the Dominicans, Duvalier had ordered that Philogenes's head be flown back to Port-au-Prince in a pail of ice. The story of the special plane dispatched by the Palace to fetch the head soon spread on both sides of the border.

'What did Papa Doc want with the head?' Graham asked.

Bajeux and I offered answers, but who knew really knew the mind of a butcher? I assumed he wanted to savour contemplating it, but Bajeux suggested he needed to verify that the officer was dead before paying a bounty to a member of his garrison who claimed to have killed him. There was also the possibility of a simple scare tactic, suggesting an act of black magic, which Graham believed to be the best possible answer. 'Shakespeare,' he said. 'Hamlet talking to Yorick's skull.'

Despite its bucolic atmosphere, Dajabón was far from silent. Dominican *meringues* blared full-blast from radios in shops and homes along its dusty streets and from a scratchy loudspeaker system attached to the roof of a neighbouring bar.

We sat in the shade in one of the *colmados*. We had to raise our voices to be heard above the music. Graham brought up the so-called 'Parsley Massacre' of October 1937 when the Dominican military had macheted and bludgeoned Haitians to death by the thousands, many on the banks of this river (and it is popularly believed that this is the origin of the name Massacre River). Only when the soldiers' arms grew tired were they permitted to use their old Krag rifles and shoot those trying to escape across the river. Black corpses choked the water and along the ravines, according to survivors I interviewed for a feature on the massacre. El Jefe's men conducted a literacy pronunciation quiz, and failure to win the quiz was instant death. 'Say *perejil* ('parsley'),' every black person was asked, and if that person did not pass the test with the correct pronunciation, *perehil*, they were dead. Some twenty thousand Haitians were slaughtered throughout the Dominican Republic on dictator Trujillo's orders.

The fact that the news of this horror had taken so long to reach the outside world troubled Graham. It illustrated how tightly, in those days, a Latin American *caudillo* could control communications in his country. Quentin Reynolds of *Collier's* magazine, alerted by six lines in a United Press wire service dispatch, flew down and discovered the terrible truth that Trujillo had attempted to hide. Albert C. Hicks in his book *Blood in the Streets: The Life and Rule of Trujillo* tells of the killing by a Dominican army captain of his family's elderly Haitian servant who had been with them for decades. The officer's wife, who witnessed the murder, 'for a considerable period after that day had to live locked in a room in a sanatorium, a raving maniac. She couldn't understand that her husband was simply acting on orders from *El Generalissimo*.'

Before resuming the journey I cleaned off the mass of splattered insects on the car's windshield. Then I poured drops of water on the dirt road, on each of the cardinal points of the compass. Graham liked the idea that we had appealed to Papa Legba to 'open the gate' for us – '*Papa Legba ouvri barye pou nou*' – and for a safe trip. Graham saw the invocation as the equivalent of Catholics beginning their prayers with the sign of the cross. Papa Legba is invoked at the beginning of ceremonies when a person wishes to communicate with his gods. This powerful Voodoo *lwa* is keeper of the keys, guardian of the highways, crossroads and man's destiny. 'And this,' Graham asked, pointing to the St Christopher medal attached to the dashboard. 'Is this Papa Legba's Catholic equivalent? We are not taking any chances, are we?'

With the sun directly overhead the car felt like the inside of an oven. 'I shouldn't have had that beer,' I grumbled.

'But you did.' Graham disagreed with my view that one should not drink in the Tropics until the sun went down over the yardarm. 'I think it's ridiculous,' he said. 'One should not be limited by any such code. A drink is good any time, and it is especially good for the digestion at noon – in the Tropics or anywhere.'

The road meandered from the lush green riverside over dry, brown rolling hills where goats nibbled at stubbles of burnt grass. In the distant blue haze appeared the mountains where Maroons, escaped slaves from the large plantations that then occupied Haiti's bountiful Plaine du Nord, had established their campsites. These Maroons, or Cimarons as the Spanish called them, led the early slave revolts against the French colonialists and played an important role in Haiti's independence war.

'How good it is you have no radio,' Graham said. 'We are quite cut off. Excellent!' We could, he said, survive at least a couple of days without news or music.

It worried me, though. There could be a coup d'état or civil war could break out, and we wouldn't know it.

Graham was surprisingly at ease as I drove along the rutted narrow dirt track, which required most of my concentration. I tried not to think of what could or might happen. Graham had an insatiable appetite for facts but also liked to hear all the fiction (rumours) from Haiti. We passed through Capotillo, at the small pueblo near which on 16 August 1963 Cantave's troops had made a swift incursion into Haiti and seized the picturesque little coffee town of Mont-Organisé. That attack had been a special embarrassment to Dominican President Bosch, who had been near by commemorating the Dominican Republic's independence from Haiti. The exile force quickly retreated to the Dominican side when reinforcements began arriving from Cap Haïtien to retake Mont-Organisé. These attacks were launched without the knowledge of President Bosch.

Near the Dominican town of Restauración a sawmill that once had belonged to Generalissimo Trujillo was in disrepair and appeared abandoned. The mules used for dragging pine trees to the mill grazed on a neighbouring hill. El Jefe had sold the mill to Antonio de la Maza, who established a coffee plantation near Restauración. His pinewood home here had once been the centre of the area's social activity. Years later, de la Maza led the team that assassinated Trujillo. He was later shot to death near Santo Domingo's Independence Square by the SIM (Military Intelligence Service) one night while I was having dinner near by with a group of colleagues.

As we came into Restauración Graham pointed to a little sign. 'Look, they even have a Massacre Hotel.' It was a modest wooden building with a tin roof displaying the sign: *Hotel Brisas Massacre de Mariav de Rodriguez.*

'Before all the trails run cold you might think of writing a book about the massacre,' Graham suggested.

'An American, Alfred Hicks, already wrote it,' I said.

'I haven't heard of it.'

'It came out in 1946. *Blood in the Streets.* But it's been out of print. I've never been able to find a copy.'

'When I get back to London I'll see if I can find you one,' Graham promised.

Dust rose up like a blanket from the road and our little car sucked it inside like a vacuum cleaner. We had the swirling dirt in our eyes, and it ground like sand on our teeth.

We reached Villa Anacaona, a gritty village that carried the name of the

Taino-Arawak Indian poetess-queen of the region of Xaragua, today the southern part of Haiti. 'Anacaona' in her people's language meant 'golden flower'. She had married Caonabo, the *cacique* (chief) of this central region through which we were passing. Christopher Columbus had ordered his soldiers to take Caonabo prisoner, and *en route* to Spain the ship sank and all aboard were drowned. In a treacherous act Governor Nicolas Ovando had his men seize Anacaona and hang her in Santo Domingo.

The last time I had been on the border was on 14 July 1963, when Duvalier's collaborator-turned-enemy, Clément Barbot, had been caught and killed outside Port-au-Prince. There had been a rumour of yet another uprising against Papa Doc, and the border was the closest I could get to Haiti.

We knew that Papa Doc's terror was only as far away as the other side of the road; his long shadow loomed all along this sad frontier. Again and again we found our thoughts and conversation returning to the enigma of the regime's violence. What lay behind its grotesque terror? Many people had been murdered, and for what? So that one power-driven psychopath could totally control the destiny of five million impoverished people? Graham knew about such things in other countries, but he saw Haiti under Duvalier as a true nightmare with Papa Doc exuding a unique evil.

'Why are we stopping?' he asked when I pulled over.

We had reached the centre of the island of Hispaniola and the so-called International Road, which was a 54-mile stretch of mostly gravel and grass that passed for a road and wound back and forth through Haitian territory alongside the Libon River.

'If something is going to happen it will be along this stretch,' I said. 'We should be alert.'

Graham stared out the window. 'I have never felt such pervasive fear in a country as in Haiti,' he confessed. His words were always measured, like those slow miles of the rough border track, even though he had to raise his voice above the rhythmic rattling of the little Volkswagen engine.

We continued. And a few minutes later Graham sounded the alarm. 'There in the hill.' He pointed. 'Tontons Macoutes.'

Bajeux, who had been sleeping in the back, was now wide awake. The hill was on the Haitian side. But Graham's sighting was not confirmed.

'We are a good target,' he said, still scanning the low brown hills.

We were the only target, I thought.

Both countries were supposed to have maintained this section of the road, which crisscrossed the boundary, but it was obvious that neither had bothered to do so for years. Papa Doc couldn't care less about a road he didn't wish to share in the first place. To discourage incursions by the Kamoken, in June 1963 he had ordered a swath three to five miles wide cut along this central section of the Haitian side of the frontier. He called it a *cordon sanitaire* and warned that he regarded it as a war zone and anyone caught trespassing would be shot on sight. Graham called it a Voodoo Curtain. Peasants and their livestock were herded by Tontons Macoutes out of the no man's land. For days the whack of machetes felling trees and slashing undergrowth was heard along certain sectors of the border. A huge cloud of smoke from the burning homes of peasants, their corn crops, grass and underbrush hung over the region for days.

'There they are!' Graham pointed ahead. 'The Macoutes!'

But his sighting proved to be a group of poor Haitian children who scrambled down the hill and on to the road in tattered clothes begging for *cinq cob* – five cents. These emaciated children were defying Papa Doc in search of food.

'Ask them where they come from,' Graham said. But it was too late. They'd scampered off into the hills, their little fists holding tightly to the Dominican coins we gave them.

'Where can they possibly spend the money?' Graham asked, contemplating a border that appeared so empty.

'They will find a vendor of bread or candy somewhere,' Bajeux explained. 'Haiti is one big marketplace, with everyone trying to sell something. It's the only way to survive.'

We came around a small bend in the road, and once again Graham moved forward in his seat. 'There. I think I've spotted some movement over there.' He pointed to a clump of bushes near a deserted military post on the Haitian side ahead.

We detected no Macoutes or troops, but a guinea hen, that mascot of the Duvalier regime, darted across the road in front of us and disappeared into the Dominican Republic.

'That hen is a defecting Tonton Macoute,' I joked.

'What a windfall the three of us would be to the Tontons!' Graham said. He had started to call the Tontons Macoutes Tontons. 'Imagine what Papa Doc would do if he knew we were here?'

I knew what I would do. I had been thinking about it constantly: drive into Dominican territory as fast as the little car could take us. Indeed we were constantly on the look-out for three of Duvalier's most notorious border henchmen – Zacharie Delva, an apprentice *houngan* (Voodoo priest), and Ludovic (Dodo) Nassard, smuggler and augur, who had divided up the central and northern sectors of the border; and legislative deputy André Simon, scourge of the southern region. This trio, with licences to kill, were very much alive, and one of my concerns was an unscheduled meeting with one of them.

As we neared the next village, Loma de Cabrera, we could see five tall medieval-looking watchtowers resembling an East German border rather than one on a Caribbean island. They were evenly spaced along the entire length of the Dominican side of the international road.

Loma de Cabrera had been Trujillo's effort to build his side of the border into a buffer zone. It had proven a notable failure. Paroled convicts had been transported to the small town from urban prisons on condition that they live and work there. But that effort, as well as another involving settling Hungarian refugees to help colonize the border, did not prosper. El Jefe had wanted these settlements to act as a human fence blocking what he perceived as 'the black tide of Haitians'. However, few settlers wanted to live out their lives in such a lonely outpost, and eventually they fled. Trujillo, who had a Haitian ancestor, both feared and hated his black neighbours.

After we passed the town we came upon a rare road sign at the end of the International Highway near the town of Pedro Santana. The plain metal sign said 'Haiti' with an arrow pointing to the east. We got out of the car, stretched our legs and took photos of ourselves with the sign as if heading into Haiti.

'Perhaps we should take a walk,' Graham suggested, indicating a narrow path that led off in the direction of Haiti's Central Plateau.

I suggested it might prove foolhardy. We moved on.

This was an area once home to the Haitian Caco guerrillas who rose up against the US Marine occupation and fought a tough guerrilla war under the leadership of Charlemagne Péralte, who vowed to drive the Americans into the sea. There was intense combat in 1919, but Péralte was finally killed by two Marines disguised as blacks who slipped into his camp with the aid of a traitor. One Marine received the Congressional Medal of Honor for killing Péralte. The Marines displayed the guerrilla leader's body in Cap Haïtien to prove to the more superstitious that he was indeed dead. The near-naked body of Péralte, spread-eagled on a door, was a shocking exhibit that for Catholic Haiti recalled the crucifixion of Jesus Christ. More than three thousand Haitians died in this guerrilla insurgency.

Graham was fascinated by this little-known guerrilla war. He said he had heard the Marines had committed atrocities. He wanted to know how Duvalier, posing as a nationalist, could get away with inviting the Marines back to Haiti to train his army. Father Bajeux and I explained that Duvalier was incredibly cunning and believed that the end justified any means. By inviting the United States Marines to return and train his army he brought the United States into his corner, and this helped him consolidate his power. While the Marines helped rearm his troops, their old arms went to the Tontons Macoutes. During the 1960 student strike against Duvalier I had been arrested by one of the most powerful gang leaders, threatened with death and the loss of my manhood until I was finally taken to the Palace where I was later released. The Macoutes were armed with old military Thompson submachine-guns.

The Artibonite River wriggles its way across both sides of the border. At one point, in pre-Duvalier times, it served as a common water fountain, public bath and laundry for both Haitians and Dominicans near Pedro Santana. Haitians coming out of the parched hills did their washing alongside their Dominican neighbours. Now the once-thriving commerce between these border people – it wasn't really contraband, more like a free-market system – had come to a standstill. Dominicans no longer dared buy Haitian *clairin* (raw rum), while Haitians couldn't acquire basic necessities. There were only a few Dominican women washing and drying their clothes on their side of the river. I was relieved when we completed our reconnaissance of this section of the border without mishap.

The Dominican town of Banica, through which we now passed, had also been the scene of many killings of Haitians during the 1937 massacre; and these killings were not just on the border but took place inland all the way east to San Pedro de Macoris. We churned into Elías Piña, across from the Haitian town of Belladere. It was here that I had first stepped on Dominican soil when, in 1951, I covered a rare meeting between the chiefs of state of the two countries – in this case Dominican dictator Trujillo and Haitian strongman Paul Magloire, during which they signed a peace pact with the usual insincere phrases. Each side was suspicious of the other, but the harmonious façade was symbolized by a public embrace by the two chiefs. However, when Trujillo embraced Magloire the Dominican tyrant's coat-tail inched up to expose a finely embroidered gun holster; Magloire's face was frozen by the camera in an expression of startled discovery. One of his hands had landed on the butt of Trujillo's pistol! After I published the photograph of this famous embrace in my newspaper, I had a visit from the Dominican Ambassador to Haiti. Pointing to the photo, he called my attention to the cane that President Magloire was holding in one hand. 'You think he needs this to walk with? This is in fact a gun,' he declared angrily.

Graham loved this example of Latinesque mutual trust. 'Very Mexican,' he laughed. He told how on his first trip to Mexico in 1938 he had learned about the famous *abrazo* or embrace. 'It is supposed to be an embrace of friendship,' Graham said, 'but its practical purpose is to pin the other fellow's arms down and keep him from drawing his gun.'

Not far from the bridge over the Massacre River Graham thought we should eat. We found our lunch under a handwritten sign: '*Rico – Pintada y arroz.*' The day's special, guinea hen and rice, was a rewarding discovery. Under the open-sided thatched-roof little restaurant Graham was ecstatic, savouring the wild bird, all the more when he reminded us that it was Papa Doc's emblem and on the badge of the Tontons Macoutes. A large black pig rooted in a pile of garbage at the side of the adjacent gravel street, and chickens pecked near our table. We drank a silent toast of Cerveza Presidente to the countless massacre victims slaughtered in 1937 only a few yards away.

5 | THE POETRY OF FAITH

We were tired and dirty, caked with dust. I suggested we stop at the American Mission House at Las Matas de Fanfan. I had stopped off there before. 'I assure you the priests will give us a good stiff drink,' I said.

Graham perked up. 'Let's not lose any time then.'

Bishop Thomas F. Reilly, who headed the Roman Catholic Congregation of the Most Holy Redeemer in nearby San Juan de la Maguana, was a hero to Dominicans. Graham wanted to learn all about the tough Bostonian who had been a US Army chaplain during the Second World War in the Pacific. Reilly had also been an outspoken critic of Trujillo during the dark latter days of El Jefe's reign – in 1960 Reilly and the country's other bishops had read an unusually candid pastoral letter in their churches condemning the widespread arrests and imprisonment of Trujillo's critics. El Jefe responded by sending a mob to wreck the bishop's residence in San Juan de la Maguana, and then accused him of leading a terrorist conspiracy. The bishop and most of his priests and nuns were forced to flee to the capital, where they took refuge in his order's convent. Reilly was then placed under house arrest. Trujillo was assassinated a month later, and Reilly was detained by the dreaded SIM. However, he was saved by the timely intervention of Joaquín Balaguer, a long-time Dominican bureaucrat who was by then acting President.

I had interviewed Bishop Reilly on a number of occasions. He was a reliable news source.

'What order did you say these priests are?' Graham asked.

'Redemptorists,' I said.

'Redemptorists!' His tone changed as he repeated the name and explained that the order had been established in Italy in 1732 and was known for its strict theological principle that the beginning of wisdom was fear.

Father Bajeux, who had been quiet through our entire trip, became animated. He was impressed with Graham's knowledge of the Church and agreed with him.

Graham looked at me. 'If you don't mind, I'd rather you didn't introduce me.'

'What's the matter?'

'You see, I don't believe in Hell,' he said. 'I really don't wish to be drawn into a discussion on my beliefs.'

Bajeux and I were stunned.

'If there is one congregation that is big on Hell it is these people,' Graham said, sounding apprehensive about meeting the priests.

'I understand,' I said. As far as I knew, all Catholics had to believe in Hell. I was brought up as an Irish Catholic, in a tradition that threatens one, at a very early age, with burning in eternal fires in the hereafter for even questioning one's faith. I was shocked by Graham's pronouncement. Nevertheless I had reached what I felt was a truce with my celestial judge and believed that the day of payment for sins took place on earth. There was a tradition of blind faith in my family with which I found it difficult to identify. Still, I felt, a convert like Graham was often a better Catholic than Father Bajeux and I, who had been born into the Church and basically accepted its teaching as part of our spiritual inheritance. Graham the convert, we were learning, was continually questioning his adopted faith, a theme in many of his books.

Graham must have known what Father Bajeux and I were thinking. 'I do believe in Purgatory, though. It makes more sense than Hell.'

I waited for him to express his opinions on Heaven, but he said no more. But I learned something about Graham that day. In most cases he preferred to remain anonymous, and in future travels I seldom introduced him by name. Besides, it was customary for leftist and guerrilla groups in the Caribbean and Central America not to introduce people by their real or full names. To ask names could be considered impolite or could raise suspicions.

Explaining that we would probably have to introduce Graham because these alert American missionaries would expect us to, Bajeux and I decided that he should be addressed as Mr White, the title Haitians applied to all foreigners, *blan*.

'But am I Monsieur Blanc or Mr White?' Graham asked, noting that he had spent much of his professional life selecting names for his characters, and it had often been a tricky business. After a brief discussion, we agreed that Mr White was a common enough name and would do the job.

We put the issue of our souls and Heaven and Hell aside, and focused on a more earthly issue. Clearing our throats of dust was the highest priority. We didn't have any water, and had spent most of the day in the hot car as we drove the dusty roads. In the back seat Father Bajeux had made a strange rasping sound, clearing his dust-coated throat, possibly to ask Graham a question about his Catholic belief, but he had evidently thought better of it and remained silent.

I had felt Graham might welcome the company of the young, activist Haitian cleric – which the famed Catholic author indeed did. Father Bajeux would, among other things, be able to answer any ecclesiastical questions that Graham might have concerning Papa Doc's success in controlling Haiti's once-powerful Roman Catholic Church. Enlisting Father Bajeux for the trip had not been difficult. It was an escape from his latest exile in a small parish in a Dominican sugar town where he was suffering deep depression. Tall, with the gaunt, malnourished look of most Haitian exiles, our pastor-companion was a Greene literary fan well acquainted with the author's whisky priest in *The Power and the Glory*, and he knew all about Graham's conversion to Catholicism. Bajeux was no whisky priest but an intellectual, a writer and somewhat of an existentialist, a perfect Greene character, although I knew it was impossible to predetermine such things.

Bajeux believed that the Church had a responsibility not only to alleviate the economic conditions of the poor but also to play a part in liberating them from political and social oppression as well. As a young man he had gone to France, where he studied theology and philosophy for nine years and was ordained to the priesthood. His Holy Ghost Order first sent him to Africa for five years to teach. In the Cameroons he edited the Church-sponsored newspaper *L'Effort Camerounais*, dedicated to the Cameroons' drive for independence. He also collaborated on several books dealing with the national clergies in the Third World that were published by the Church. Still later Bajeux was involved in the exciting activities that accompanied preparations for Vatican Council II. He had met Pope John XXIII in Rome while assisting in the consecration of the young Archbishop of Yaoundé, Jean Zoa. After returning with Zoa to the Cameroons as his secretary, Bajeux accompanied the Archbishop on some of his official trips.

In 1960, as Bajeux was preparing to accompany Archbishop Zoa to the Vatican Council – where Zoa would distinguish himself as secretary-general of the African Episcopate – fate intervened. Bajeux was packing his bag when he was directed to return to his native Haiti by his superior in the Holy Ghost Order. Back in Haiti, Bajeux became Professor of Philosophy at the Holy Ghost Order's St Martial College, one of the two major high schools in Port-au-Prince and a hotbed of anti-Duvalierism.

In the Haiti of the early 1960s Bajeux found a country virtually paralysed and in the vice of dictatorship. With other young Haitian priests he embarked on the important work of creating a Creole liturgy. He edited the Catholic cultural magazine *Rond-Point* and directed Port-au-Prince's Catholic youth centre, Bibliothèque des Jeunes. He also helped launch another religious magazine entitled *Church on the March*.

It was a dangerous and difficult time. Young Haitian priests and their students had become the core of anti-Duvalier resistance. In many ways Papa Doc had helped them by decapitating the old conservative hierarchy of the Haitian Church. No more dour-looking Frenchmen from Brittany would be added to the photo gallery of former archbishops, dating from 1860, covering the walls of the waiting-room of the Port-au-Prince archbishopric. However, Duvalier became even more disturbed by the threat from the young Haitian priests and would eventually send them into exile.

During the crisis of the summer of 1963 Bajeux had spent twenty-one days under house arrest after he tried to establish a residence for the chaplains of the Catholic Youth Movement in a large house in the capital. He was finally expelled from Haiti in February 1964, going first to New York. The following April he decided that a priest was needed in the Dominican Republic to administer to Haitians who were crossing the border in greater numbers, fleeing the Duvalier dictatorship. In Santo Domingo, with a group of prominent Dominicans, he established a 'Friendship of Peoples Foundation', whose announced mission was to give what spiritual and material aid was possible to Haitians living in the Dominican Republic. In a white flowing soutane, Bajeux was a familiar figure swishing into Dominican police or army headquarters to get a Haitian released from detention or celebrating Mass for poor civilian exiles or guerrillas. He was a one-man human rights mission who wrote reports, complaints and protests and dispatched them to the Dominican authorities.

Unfortunately, Bajeux had not been as communicative a passenger as I had hoped, but he would provide us with a perfect alibi for travelling along the border. Our cover was that we were checking Dominican border jails for missing Haitians. But Bajeux, I felt, was searching spiritually for his own family. Papa Doc had 'disappeared' them only three months earlier. In October 1964 I had had the unfortunate task of informing Father Bajeux that his family had been seized at their home in Port-au-Prince by Duvalier's police. Bajeux was truly alone, struggling with his God. Sometimes, while speeding through the Dominican countryside, I thought I could hear his prayers, begging God to protect his family. It was the worst Duvalier could inflict on an exiled opponent – reprisals against the exile's helpless relatives. An opponent could suffer deprivations and estrangement in a foreign land and still bear up, but to be made responsible for the 'disappearance' of one's family was the cruellest punishment of all. It was Duvalier's ultimate retribution: kill the families of exiles – men, women and babies. Papa Doc believed this horrifying strategy would make his exiled enemies weigh the high cost of their actions against him.

The anguished priest, then aged thirty-three, was to live for years with this personal Calvary – not knowing whether his loved ones were dead or alive, visualizing the horrors they might be suffering because he was an activist priest. During our border trip he could only guess what had happened, but years later he finally pieced together the sickening story.

Duvalierists had heard Father Bajeux's name cited on a newscast on 10 July

1964 on the Santo Domingo radio monitored in Haiti. The newscast reported that the exiled priest had opened an office to help poor Haitians in the Dominican Republic, especially those toiling as cane-cutters. The Papal Nuncio accredited to the Dominican government had attended the opening ceremony, as had the Archbishop of Santo Domingo. Eleven days preceding the broadcast, on 29 June, Fred Baptiste's guerrillas had staged a landing on the west coast of Haiti, coming from the Dominican Republic. There was at least one Duvalier spy in the Baptiste camp in Santo Domingo. Papa Doc had the names of all those involved with the guerrillas, according to evidence he was able to present to the Organization of American States and the UN Security Council. Bajeux had been a chaplain to the guerrillas and said Mass at their initial training camp near Villa Mella. I also had been listed and accused of issuing identification cards to the Kamoken. In fact I was interested in knowing each and every exile, where they came from and as much of their lives as possible for an eventual news feature. I had photographed each of the Kamoken and prepared a card with their background – in fact I was trying to weed out Papa Doc spies. I failed.

On the night of 11 July the Bajeux family was preparing for bed. The mother was nervous, with a premonition of trouble even though she had been reassured by the French Ambassador and the Papal Nuncio that she had nothing to fear. Albert, her eldest son, was comforting her, as was Maxim, her youngest daughter. Another daughter, Anne-Marie, a pretty woman who was engaged to be married, had come to spend the night with her mother and comfort her and a third daughter, Micheline. The three sisters were all in their nightdresses getting ready for bed. Suddenly it happened. The quiet Bois Verna Street filled with cars loaded with big-name Tontons Macoutes and police officers. Neighbours watched terror-stricken from behind shutters. The Macoutes and police burst into the Bajeux house. Neighbours saw the family being dragged in their night clothes into vehicles and driven away. No one bothered to switch off the lights. The front door of the house remained open. The neighbours dared not enter the house to close the door and turn the lights off. It remained a strangely silent illuminated house for days, a reminder of Duvalierist terror. The Bajeux family's yard boy, who was also seized but later temporarily released, told neighbours that everyone had been beaten at the police headquarters before the family were disappeared. The yard boy was later seized again and also disappeared. All were later reported executed at Fort Dimanche.

Bajeux had asked me not to tell Graham about what had happened to his family. I agreed that we didn't want to become the story and divert Graham from concentrating on Papa Doc.

The American Mission House at Las Matas de Fanfan came into view, and we all sighed deeply in anticipation of something cold and fresh to drink. As we walked up to the building the door swung wide open. Reverend Jim McSwigan, a tall Irishman from Pittsburgh with a shock of blond hair, stood there with a wide smile on his face. 'Welcome, welcome,' he said, thrusting out his hand, as if he'd been waiting all day for our arrival.

We shook hands, and he said it was good to see me again on the border. Then he reached past me and took Graham's hand and pumped it excitedly. 'Graham! What a pleasure this is. Come in. Please come in.'

We were stunned. None of us dared look at each other. As Father McSwigan escorted us upstairs to the mission's common room I asked him, 'Do you have any whisky?'

'No. With the taxes and all, it is far too expensive now. But I can make a good rum Manhattan!'

And so he did, quickly mixing a batch and handing one to each of us. When Father McSwigan went out to order our dinner – the priests had just finished their evening meal when we arrived – Graham, Father Bajeux and I burst into laughter.

'It is their intelligence service,' Graham said when he regained his composure, his eyes filled with tears of laughter. 'They have people everywhere. They knew we were coming. Missionaries are well informed. They have their network.'

Father Bajeux walked over to examine the mission's well-stocked common-room library. He found a copy of Graham's most recent work, *A Burnt-Out Case*, a Book-of-the-Month-Club selection published by Viking in 1961. 'Mr Greene, you gave yourself away,' Bajeux said and waved a copy of a book featuring Graham's photograph on the back flap. The image was a relatively recent likeness, and Graham had not changed much. 'You allowed them to publish your picture in one of your books. They know you well in this house.'

It was the first time I had seen Bajeux smile in three months. The library also contained copies of two other Graham Greene tomes, *The Quiet American* and *The Power and the Glory*. Graham confessed that until lately he had not permitted his picture to appear on the jacket of his books, in order not to be recognized.

Bajeux picked up a copy of *The Power and the Glory*. 'It is my favourite,' he said.

When Father McSwigan returned to announce that the cook had agreed to prepare us a spaghetti dinner we regained our decorum and took our seats like innocent schoolboys. Graham drained his second drink and complimented the Father on his rum Manhattans.

'Call me Gredo,' he said. 'That's how I'm known around here, Padre Geraldo.' We never learned if it had been the photograph on the flap of *A Burnt-Out Case* that had given Graham's identity away. Nor did we ask, because it didn't really matter. Graham was treated like a visiting bishop. He was quickly made to feel a member of the mission family. 'I'll admit,' Padre Gredo said. 'We make Graham required reading in the seminar.' He was a good and generous host – especially with his rum – and he didn't spoil the visit with talk of Hell or redemption.

Father Bajeux explained that we were on the border looking for missing Haitians and wanted to know whether there was any news locally of Haiti or border crossings.

Padre Gredo said he'd heard the horror stories from Haiti but that this sector of the border had been relatively quiet during the past several weeks.

'How is the road along the border to Jimaní?' I asked.

'What road?' Padre Gredo shook his head. 'Is there a road?' I supposed the Redemptionist was not trying to be funny. 'It is more like a track than a road. My guess is it's hardly ever in use. When there is trouble with Duvalier the army might make a trip, or timber thieves may move out some wood, but hardly anyone goes from here to Jimaní along the border. It is much easier to go inland and cut across on a good road.'

There was no room for the three of us at the mission house, and Padre Gredo suggested we drive the short distance inland to San Juan de la Maguana, the country's fourth-largest town, assuring us that the hotel had plenty of space. We thanked him and his fellow priests for their hospitality and promised to return for early-morning Mass and breakfast.

The relaxing visit to the mission house, the rum Manhattans and the generous helpings of spaghetti allowed the subject of religion again to arise, as we sped the twenty miles into the Dominican interior in search of an inn. Graham had thoroughly enjoyed the Irish-American missionary priest.

'So what was your religion before you converted to Catholicism?' I asked.

'None,' Graham said, adding that his family had been Anglican but that he had been an atheist before being baptized a Catholic. After his conversion, he said, 'I took as my patron saint St Thomas Didymus, the doubter.'

I said something about how in Haiti Catholicism and Voodoo have become intertwined.

'They are not so entirely different,' Graham said. 'They both accept the existence of God.'

A lot of old Breton priests who had served in Haiti would have been shocked at that. While Judaeo-Christianity is distinguished by its concept of a single deity and a plethora of saints and guardian angels, Voodoo-worshippers must keep their peace with a plethora of *lwas*.

We entered the Hotel Maguana, which had been built by El Benefactor, Generalissimo Trujillo, father of tourism and virtually everything else. We were told that Trujillo had had a reserved suite here, as in most of the

Dominican Republic's hotels. A large black Dominican man was registering as we were handed our registration cards.

'What is this?' Graham asked the desk clerk, pointing to a line that demanded to know the guest's colour. Trujillo was sensitive to race and colour and had decreed his country officially 'white'. To help confirm this, hotel guests were required to list the colour of their skin in addition to their nationality. The registration cards with the requisite line for this data were still in use nearly four years after the dictator's demise. The black Dominican registering before us had put down his colour as '*indio oscuro*', meaning a dark-hued Indian. It was difficult even then for a black Dominican to admit to being black. The Dominicans were proving Trujillo right. There were no blacks in the Dominican Republic. The hotel industry could confirm that, because no blacks ever registered.

Graham was indignant. The registration card requirement was blatantly racist. He complained to the desk clerk and, fuelled with Padre Gredo's Manhattans, he decided to provide a literal description of his colour and wrote 'Pink' on his registration card. He showed Bajeux and me his card with a touch of triumph. 'That settles that. I am pink.'

The desk clerk, himself a swarthy 'Indian hue', looked slightly confused. If someone had made such an impertinent statement prior to Trujillo's assassination he or she would in all probability have been overheard by an informer, and the police would have joined us in the lobby for a quick arrest. Even then, being politically 'pink' or 'red' was still extremely dangerous in the Dominican Republic. After all, President Juan Bosch had been overthrown only two years earlier by the military who accused him of having been soft on communists.

Ideologically, Graham said he felt more comfortable being pink than white. Black, he reminded us, could be even more beautiful. Father Bajeux, although he was a very light-skinned mulatto, listed his colour on the registration card as '*morado*' (purple). I wondered if he harboured the ambition of one day wearing the purple colours of a cardinal.

I inscribed my own colour as black, deciding it would probably be the first time in the Dominican Republic that anyone had registered under that pigmentation.

After we checked in we strolled around town until we found a quiet bar. We sat outside at a table by the street, sharing a bottle of straight rum. Graham showed no signs of being tired and was in no hurry to retire for the night. He was also in an uncharacteristically talkative mood and told us how he had loathed the tedious Bible-reading at the Sunday services of his former Anglican faith.

'I had a grandfather who was an Anglican clergyman and ended up in a mental institution,' he said. 'I converted to Catholicism in 1926 because a priest who offered me instruction finally won me over. But I read a lot of theology, too.'

As for Father Bajeux, his faith was taken for granted by Graham and me. Nor did our Haitian priest-companion offer any startling revelations. His mind was miles away. His struggle with God was very personal.

When we returned to the hotel the desk clerk handed Graham his registration card. For a moment I thought our little prank of writing different colours on the card had got us in trouble. But the clerk pointed to the back of the card and said, 'You had visitors.'

Graham turned the card over. There was a handwritten verse on the back, which ended with, 'What a rainbow of colour in Room Sixteen.' It was signed by an American nun of the Dominican Order who was working in the local hospital. She had heard of Graham's presence in town – those Catholics did have their grapevine after all – and had paid a visit to our hotel, hoping to meet Graham, of whom she was an avid fan. She invited us to breakfast, but we had already made arrangements to drive back to the mission house for Mass and breakfast with Father McSwigan (who later told me he had been the one who advised the sisters of Graham's arrival in town).

For a while Graham's adopted religion remained on our minds as he discussed his favourite Pope, John XXIII, for whom he had a 'lot of affection'. None the less, he was not optimistic about reforming the Church. The age-old alliance between the army, Church and oligarchy in Latin America would not be broken by wishful thinking, he predicted. Yet he agreed with the view of Father Bajeux and myself that the leading advocates of change in the Church were in Latin America. Papa Doc's persecution of the conservative Church hierarchy in the name of Haitianizing it was a masquerade, because he could no more stand a Haitian priest than a French priest, unless the cleric agreed to be a Macoute-priest. It was all about control.

The following morning there was no struggle to rise before dawn; Graham was an organized traveller and lost no time in bathing and dressing. On the way to Mass he confessed that he didn't like being called a Catholic writer and declared that he was adamant about this matter. 'I just happen to be a writer who is a Catholic.'

It was evidently a sensitive subject for him. Travelling with him in Central America years later I heard Graham explain time and again his status as a writer who happened to be a Catholic. At the mission chapel we heard two Masses. Father McSwigan said his regular 6.30 a.m. Mass while at a side altar dedicated to Our Lady of Altagracia, patron saint of the Dominican Republic, Father Bajeux said Mass in Latin. Graham acknowledged that he had enjoyed the ritual and that he especially preferred Latin. Not comfortable with the Mass being said in the vernacular, he stressed that the Second Vatican Council had not outlawed Latin. The Tridentine Mass was always in Latin.

It was still early, and the mission cook had not yet arrived. We were in a hurry to resume our trip, so instead of the typical Dominican breakfast of boiled and mashed green plantains with eggs (*mangu*) the Mission Superior went to the stove and cooked up an all-American breakfast of bacon and eggs.

'For years,' Father McSwigan said, 'one of the most important events in my life will be that I can say I prepared breakfast for Graham Greene!'

He served us a cup of strong coffee. 'How do you like it?' He wasn't referring to the breakfast but the fact that in the church the altar had been turned around so the priest now faced the congregation during Mass.

'It looks like the priest is having a good meal up there,' Graham replied, because it was now possible to see the priest symbolically consecrate and consume the body and blood of Christ. Father McSwigan laughed heartily and was still laughing when he said goodbye.

6 | A MATTER OF POLICY

We putt-putted back towards the border feeling physically and spiritually refreshed. As we bounced along, searching for the road, we could see in the distance behind the rounded hills the darkened region of navy-blue mountains that awaited us. This was to be our longest and most harrowing day on the border.

It was slow going as we crept up the mountains. It appeared as if no one had navigated this stretch of road in a long time in any kind of vehicle. As we progressed, we had to pause more and more as our path was strewn with fallen trees and boulders. Graham had written about priests and their weaknesses, helplessness and human fragility, but here he had to join forces with a priest to remove obstacles from our common path.

When he was brushing off the dirt from his road work, I asked him whether he would prefer to drive.

'No, no, I am quite content not to,' he replied.

This section of the border needed no international markers. The Haitian side was an ecological disaster. It was all rock. Haitian peasants in the mountain regions are lucky to grow a few strands of corn on the steepest peaks where some soil may remain, but, largely because of deforestation, when the rains come tons of remaining topsoil cascade down the mountains into the sea. A brown ring encircles Haiti's shores, the unsightly stain of eroded earth that is too thick to filter easily into the turquoise Caribbean. Haiti was literally bleeding to death.

As we approached the misty summit we came to a forest called Angel Felix, where we encountered a group of woodcutters. I slowed the car and headed towards them, but they quickly disappeared into the dense tree line. The mountain forest, which looked as if it still had virgin timber, was in stark contrast to the eroded Haitian landscape next door.

'I can see some trees at the bottom,' Graham said and stuck his neck dangerously out of the window. 'If we fall we will not fall into Haiti.'

'Why?' At that moment I was not particularly concerned about where we would land on our fatal plunge.

'Because the Haitian side no longer has any trees.' He laughed as if I'd flunked his riddle. He was enjoying every minute of our plight. Adversity seemed to animate him.

We made a pit stop (each chose a tree to pee against) in the forest's cathedral-like interior, beneath the tall pine trees, taking in the incense-like scent of a smoking charcoal pit, a choir of songbirds and the shrill buzz of cicadas.

Further on, the scenery was breathtaking. The mountains were steep and the clouds covered the mountains below us. But this was no carnival ride. I felt responsible for Graham's and Bajeux's safety, and as we climbed the precarious road the possibility of our toppling over the side grew. Graham had been a good travelling companion. He had a youthful curiosity and exuberance, but he could be obstinate. Every time I asked him and Bajeux to get out of the car so I could manoeuvre it alone over the seemingly impossible landslide that might confront us, he refused. I tried explaining that the car needed less weight, but Graham ignored me, refusing to get out – although Bajeux had – saying it reminded him of his mule trip to San Cristóbal de las Casas where he had faced many such deep ravines.

We must have had all the prayers of the American Redemptionist mission with us because every time that it appeared the path would end and we would have to backtrack we found a way to move on. Graham was the determined one. Nevertheless, we were now in trouble. We reached a place where a landslide had buried the road completely. There was no other way around the mountain. Our trip was only halfway through. Still, Graham insisted we continue. He was not about to turn back. And slowly, inch by inch, with Graham sitting stolidly next to me, I edged the Beetle forward in first gear. If the tyres slipped we would topple over the edge and drop into a deep ravine.

Later, after we'd passed the landslide, we joked that if we'd gone over the edge the death notice in *Time* magazine's 'Milestones' section would be: 'Died: English author Graham Greene, 61, in an auto accident on the remote Dominican–Haitian border.' The British newspapers by contrast, in line with their tradition, would run a lengthy obituary. The Fleet Street dailies would be a lot more prolix and a lot less kind, questioning what Graham was doing in such an isolated setting and blaming the death of the famous author on Papa Doc Duvalier.

We had a good laugh over it, and I explained to Graham that Trujillo's favourite method of ridding himself of someone was to arrange for them to have an 'accident' by diving into a cliff or ravine in their car. We thanked God the Generalisimo had been assassinated in 1961. We had no such worries about Papa Doc. Although he had a propensity for revenge, he never bothered to cover up his crimes.

As we came around the side of another mountain the view was spectacular. Far below in the smoky, bluish haze was a huge valley and Lake Enriquillo, simmering in the scorching heat of this sunken region's eternal summer. At 160 feet deep and with a surface some seventy feet below sea level, the lake occupies the lowest inland topographical point in the Caribbean and its water is three times as salty as ocean water. Indian carvings on large rocks surrounding Enriquillo are the only visible reminder of the indigenous communities that once lived beside the lake. It was still home to pink flamingos, and, years earlier, it had not been uncommon to see a caiman sunning itself along the 33-mile shoreline. Beyond the lake was another range of mountains that we would have to cross. This had been the theatre of war for Fred Baptiste's guerrillas prior to their internment in the old lunatic asylum near Santo Domingo.

As our trip grew more difficult Graham became more affable. He showed no sign of exhaustion. He was excited at the prospect of the unexpected. The ordeal actually seemed to energize him, a reflection perhaps on his stubborn resilience. The only thing that seemed to bother him was the vultures. He admitted to being spooked by vultures since his days in Africa. He said the repulsive birds were signs of death and evil. But the large birds we had sighted gliding overhead and which had drawn Graham's worried attention were actually red-tailed hawks – *Buteo Jamaicensis* – which had been christened *Mal Fini* ('Badly Finished') by Haiti's French colonizers because of the species' habit of leaving its prey, mostly chickens, in a sorry state. An old Haitian saying holds that if a *Mal Fini* spits in your eye you lose your sight.

Suddenly, as we came around the bend on the way down the mountain, a young dark-skinned Haitian – or Dominican – appeared on the side of the road. He was miles from nowhere. As we slowed to a stop he approached us and got into the back seat of the car next to Bajeux without a word. We were apprehensive, but the youth didn't appear threatening. Bajeux and I attempted to question him in Creole and Spanish, but he remained silent. We drove on, came out of the mountain and continued across the plain to the town of Jimaní at the mouth of a valley that opens up into Haiti. Then, just before we reached the town, our hitchhiker tapped me lightly on the shoulder to stop. When I did, he got out and simply walked away, disappearing into the dust.

'Perhaps he was deaf and dumb,' Graham suggested as we watched him go.

Bajeux and I didn't believe so, yet we couldn't explain the youth's strange behaviour. The incident remained one of those ineffable Caribbean mysteries. In Haiti the mysterious stranger would have been considered a zombie. Nevertheless I suggested to my two sharp-eyed companions that they relax their 'Macoute watch', as Graham called our constant paranoia.

Jimaní, the main Dominican border town through which Dominican forces were expected to storm into Haiti during the 1963 crisis when the two countries nearly went to war, was fast asleep. It was siesta time. We were hungry and thirsty. The government hotel was closed for repairs, and the old woman who ran the local eating house was asleep. Her young maid was terror-stricken when we suggested she wake her up, so we went into a *colmado* and purchased three tins of miniature sausages, several stale bread rolls, a box of toothpicks and room-temperature soft drinks.

'There must be a brothel where we at least can get a cold drink,' Graham said, unhappy about our lunch arrangement.

'Dominican brothels close down for siesta,' I said. I was not about to go racing around the stifling hot, awful little border town in the middle of the day in search of a whorehouse.

Graham glanced at me. I could tell he was sceptical, but he said nothing.

My main concern was getting over our final mountain range before nightfall. The prospect of this last section of the border made me nervous. Anything could happen. We sat under a thorny *bayonde* tree that offered a few speckles of shade and opened the first can of sausages. A horrible smell rose up and invaded the still air. Bajeux plucked out one of the little morsels with a toothpick and offered it to Graham. He reacted to the taste with revulsion. None the less our hunger drove us on; we held our breath and devoured the *saucissons* until the little cans were empty.

'And to think,' said Graham, still grimacing and chewing on a piece of bread to rid himself of the pungent taste of the sausages, 'in a few days I'll be dining at the Tour d'Argent in Paris.'

His comment angered me, but I said nothing. It took Graham out of our world. His thoughts were of eating at the pricey Parisian restaurant while our concern was providing survival food for the Kamoken and other Haitian refugees. For the past three months I had been transporting sacks of grain, flour and tins of oil from the Catholic Relief and CARE to keep them alive. I was reminded that Graham didn't belong to these surroundings after all.

We washed our meal down with the warm drinks and returned to the car under the scorching sun.

'We could be at the Oloffson in an hour if the border guards let us cross,' I said trying to make light of lunch. 'I'm ready for one of Caesar's rum punches.'

'It would be your last,' Bajeux said.

'Indeed,' Graham muttered.

The joke went down like a deflated balloon.

Past the salt flats, just across the border from the town and glued to the foot of a mountain, was the Haitian military post of Malpasse. In the late 1950s I had begun to cover the Dominican Republic from Haiti. During those last years of Trujillo's thirty-year reign I was one of the few travellers returning to Haiti to cross the border at Jimaní. It was only a fast hour's ride to Port-au-Prince, road and politics permitting. Once, when I was returning from the Dominican Republic, I slept in the little Malpasse jail after the Haitian army chief ordered the sergeant in charge not to allow me and my car to re-enter Haiti. I was returning to Haiti in my Volkswagen. At Malpasse a new sergeant took my passport, and, expecting a short wait, I kept the engine running – that is, until this bright sergeant showed me my passport and told me it was no good as my visa to travel back and forth to the Dominican Republic did not have the police stamp. (All such visas were difficult to get and a friendly pastor working in the passport division who read my newspaper had issued it, but I knew I would not get a police stamp.) No one had noticed. The sergeant did. The officer in charge was an old friend, but he could do nothing but wait until evening to contact headquarters. The reply came back: Don't let the *blan* pass. I chose my bed in the empty prison and kept the door open even after the officer tried to close it to make sure I didn't take off to Port-au-Prince. In the dark I noticed the door closing slowly and pushed it back open and sent the officer tumbling down the embankment in his underwear.

In the morning I raced back to Santo Domingo full of mosquito bites and the memory of a nightmare about Trujillo's 1937 massacre of poor Haitians along the border. I caught the noon plane to Port-au-Prince and breezed through immigration. In the days that followed I had my car driven to the Dominican side and asked my the sergeant friend to drive me across the border. I invited him to toast my Beetle with several cold Presidente beers.

The saline flats are a no man's land between the two countries. It's the devil's oven. In December 1958 Duvalier signed a 'peace pact' with Trujillo – having kept him waiting for more than an hour in the steaming heat. While photographing El Benefactor as he sat in the 38-degree heat in a three-piece business suit waiting for Papa Doc, I noted rivulets of perspiration eroding his pancake makeup. The droplets trickled down his flabby jowls. When Papa Doc eventually arrived, he and El Jefe exchanged saccharine smiles. It was the first and last time the two tyrants of the island met. Each promised to refuse safe haven to the other's enemies. Trujillo vowed in particular to protect Duvalier if the bearded rebel leader in Cuba's Sierra Maestra across the Windward Passage from Haiti should come to power. A month later the bearded one, Fidel Castro, was in Havana and the Cuban dictator, General Fulgencio Batista, was in exile in Ciudad Trujillo.

With the Dominican sausages growling in our digestive tracts, we began the climb up the last mountain range. As we came to round the first leg of the road the back of our little Volkswagen sank into the gravel. I raced the engine, but the Beetle refused to budge. A huge thorn had punctured a tyre through to the inner tube. It was a miracle we'd managed to get this far without car trouble. We replaced the flat tyre with the spare, but since it would have been foolhardy to try to climb the mountain range without another tyre we backtracked to a construction camp where, with the help of workmen, we patched the punctured tyre and tube.

As we toiled up into the cool Sierra de Bahoruco, it became familiar ground for Bajeux and me. He pointed out a steep hillside where the thatched hut that Fred Baptiste's Kamoken had used as a shelter and rendezvous for incursions into Haiti stood. It remained there, abandoned like some arcane symbol of defeat. From there the road branched off to El Aguacate, but we decided not to tempt fate further and avoided the Dominican army post there despite Graham's wish to see it. Bajeux and I knew members of the garrison might recognize us and be hostile.

At the summit we were greeted by fog and an afternoon drizzle. Graham surveyed the rugged landscape as Bajeux sat transfixed, gazing at the Haitian side of the frontier. This section of our narrow route was paved with large shiny rocks. It was more like a washboard than a road and was slippery in the rain. We met a group of scowling soldiers manning a small Dominican army post. Bajeux stepped out of the car and got to work. He asked the suspicious troops whether they had any Haitian 'guests'. They didn't answer, but when Bajeux identified himself as a priest – he was dressed as we were – the soldiers allowed him to enter the post. The single cell at the post was empty.

It was a jolting, sliding, bumpy ride down to Pedernales. Closer to the lowlands giant trucks, their tyres taller than our car, rumbled along their own red-dirt roadway parallel to the one we were travelling on. They were transporting bauxite, the red earth and raw material for aluminium, from the mines to the Alcoa docks at Cabo Rojo for export to the United States. Our rough little road eventually led into the wide well-graded bauxite-transporting road.

We arrived in Pedernales at dusk. At our request, Dominican army officers gave us a gratifyingly comprehensive tour of the city's prison facilities. We spoke with several jailed Haitians, but the charges against them were non-political; none was one of the missing Kamoken.

The few hotels in Pedernales didn't look inviting, so I suggested that we go to Cabo Rojo, to the big Alcoa bauxite complex where I knew the manager, an American named Pat Hughson, who had often extended an invitation to visit when I met him socially in Santo Domingo. Graham and Bajeux thought it was a splendid idea: the prospect of a drink, dinner, a shower and a good bed at Cabo Rojo appealed to them. Hughson, I explained, had once been either a pilot or an aviation mechanic who had been brought down from the United States by Trujillo to work with the Dominican air force. He married a Dominican and was now employed by Alcoa. He had seemed a friendly, hospitable and affable enough fellow.

It was dark when we arrived. The Beetle's lights lit up the sturdy high chain-link fence, and we followed it until we came upon a padlocked gate. The enclosure looked forbidding. It was situated in the remote extreme south-west corner of the Dominican Republic; we had travelled from ocean to ocean. A man in uniform stepped out of the guardhouse with a flashlight and asked us to state our business. He made no move to open the gate. I identified myself as a good *amigo* of the boss. I needed to talk with him.

He took my name and told us to wait, then he disappeared inside the guardhouse. We could hear his muffled voice as he made a call. There was a long silence. We waited. Graham looked at me, his eyebrows arched quizzically.

'Do you see a water tap?' Father Bajeux said. We were all terribly thirsty. I felt uncomfortable. I called to the guard. He told me again to wait. Finally he came back to the gate, beckoned to me, unlocked it and opened it just enough for me to slide through. He pointed to the guardhouse phone, the receiver resting on the side of the table.

I took the phone. 'Hello?'

'Yes?' It was Patrick Hughson, and there was nothing friendly in his voice. I thought perhaps we had interrupted his dinner.

'Hello, Pat. Could you put us up for the night? There are three of us.'

'This isn't a hotel. You can find a hotel in town,' he said.

So much for the jovial Hughson I'd met on the Santo Domingo cocktail circuit. Still, I explained that we'd been out in the boondocks all day travelling from San Juan de la Maguana, adding, 'I thought you had said to drop in and visit if . . .' If I hadn't been with Graham and Bajeux, both of whom deserved a good night's sleep, I would have told Hughson to go to hell and gone for any of the decrepit lodging places in Pedernales – even the prison.

Finally Hughson relented. 'Put the guard on,' he said. I handed the phone to the guard, who received his orders. He unlocked the gate again, and we drove into the compound. But once more we were told to wait. The additional delay was infuriating. Finally an unarmed guard on a motorcycle wearing a shiny silver hard hat arrived. We were issued visitors' badges and ordered to follow the bike.

A mountain of red earth loomed next to the adjacent Caribbean Sea. A long low-slung bauxite cargo ship was berthed at the dock. 'This is right out of *Dr No*!' exclaimed Graham. 'Dr who?' Bajeux and I chorused. Neither of us was familiar at the time with the James Bond thriller set in Jamaica at a bauxite port much like this.

'And this is obviously Dr No himself,' Graham laughed when we drove up to the main house where Hughson, a large heavy-set man with a rotund girth, awaited us on his spacious open veranda.

I apologized to Hughson for not calling in advance, explaining that we hadn't known we would make it over the mountains, but he did not appear to be in a forgiving mood. He gave us a cool reception, making us feel like intruders, suspicious at our sudden night-time arrival. I could see that Graham was equally dubious of Hughson and his inhospitable manner. I introduced my two companions, mumbling their names, but Hughson was not interested in who they were.

'You missed dinner,' Hughson said, sounding almost pleased.

'We've been travelling all day from San Juan de la Maguana. It's been a long tough trip,' I explained, but he was not impressed.

He sent orders to prepare cold sandwiches for us. Later Coca-Colas arrived. Graham was mortified. 'You wouldn't have a whisky?' he asked. Graham was never shy when it came to asking for a drink. Hughson must have seen the plea in Graham's pale blue eyes. Three whiskies arrived, a single drink each. Graham drained his with such obvious relish that any reasonable host would have quickly ordered a refill – but not Hughson.

When the dry ham-and-cheese sandwiches arrived, without condiments, we wolfed them down. As we ate Hughson sat back, seeming to find us a little disgusting. There was a little small talk. With no whisky refill in the offing, we thanked him and said goodnight.

Again we were taken under escort and were deposited at the junior executives' billet where we would spend the night.

'What a bloody awful fellow!' Graham exploded. 'The man has no humanity. Dreadful chap.'

But even Graham's latent anti-Americanism, which Pat Hughson had caused to flare up like a fever, was soon lost in the sheer comic relief of the moment. Graham and I had to share a room. Despite our long day on the road neither of us was ready for sleep. Like two English schoolboys we sat up talking and laughing as long as our dry vocal chords would permit about this strange encounter and Graham's imaginary comparison with *Dr No*. Graham thought up all kinds of sinister plots that could be going on around us at Cabo Rojo. He told me about his stay at Ian Fleming's Goldeneye residence on Jamaica's north coast. He hadn't liked the housekeeper, Vivian, whom he accused of putting the 'evil eye' on him. I realized much later the depth of Graham's superstitious nature. Fleming, he said, had offered to loan him Goldeneye rent-free if he would do the foreword to an omnibus of his James Bond books. 'I told him I'd rather pay the rent than write the foreword.'

We discussed the day's events, and I apologized about the Dominican sausages.

'No, no. Not at all. It happens sometimes. You had the best of intentions,' he said. 'It was quite fun.'

I told him I had obviously misjudged Hughson and apologized for the Alcoa man's inhospitality. 'We should have stayed in town,' I said.

'No, no, on the contrary, this is interesting,' Graham insisted as he laid out his toilet gear. He carefully folded his clothes over a chair. 'Shame about the whisky, but I would enjoy a pipe about now.'

I thought he meant tobacco, but then he added, 'Opium gives you a good sleep. I often had a pipe in Indochina during the war. I set myself a limit far, far below that of the habitual pipe smoker.'

I looked around the room. 'If Dr No has our room bugged he'll hand us over to the police in the morning.'

Graham laughed. 'I am sure the awful fellow would.'

We lay in bed, and Graham recounted that while completing *A Burnt-Out Case* in Tahiti in 1959 he was walking along a street in Papeete when he got the feeling that someone was watching him. 'I turned,' he said, 'and there in the doorway of a little shop was an elderly Chinese man staring at me. We looked at each other, then he invited me in, and I followed him to the back of the shop. He asked me whether I had been in Indochina. I told him I had, and he offered me a pipe. He had his own little South Pacific fumerie. When I was back in London some time later I received a lumpy letter postmarked Papeete. It was a plug of opium sent courtesy of the French and Her Majesty's Royal Mail from the old Chinaman in Tahiti.'

I came to understand that, despite my reaction to his remark under the *bayonde* tree, he didn't really aspire to luxury living *per se*, but he did enjoy good food and wine, crisp vodka martinis and smooth Scotch whisky. And he confessed to Bajeux and me that what he missed most about living abroad were bangers and mash washed down with good ale. I admitted that I would die for a pork pie at my favourite Fleet Street pub. We were all human, I reflected, and maybe Graham had a date planned at the famous Parisian restaurant.

He was not completely opposed to nightmares; he admitted to being in favour of dreaming. It seemed that at an early age he had put his night-time subconscious to work for him. Whereas I was often plagued with dreams involving journalistic anxiety – such as losing my portable typewriter or my copy or missing the big story – Graham described his dreams as being much more creative, producing results that aided him in his writing. He talked about Freud's interpretation of dreams, that a dream is an opening to the unconscious through which one can examine a disguised version one's anxieties and problems. 'Your brain works continually,' Graham believed, adding, 'Dreams also give you rest.'

Next morning we were escorted out of the American company's compound. We returned our badges at the gate and didn't wait for breakfast. We never saw Hughson again. Outside our bedrooms before departing (Bajeux was lodged in the adjacent room) we found a Coca-Cola machine to slake our thirst. Graham was still laughing. I didn't know it then, but he had found his ugly American.

After departing the Alcoa plant the three of us made good time over the saline flats. Even dodging the squat, thorny *bayonde* trees was fun. When we reached the coastal road close to the cliff, during a short pit stop, we stood watching the sea angrily pounding a beach piled high with flotsam and jetsam. Among the timber on that wild and desolate coast were uprooted trees, their trunks worn white by the surf and sun, yet too big to be buried entirely by the sand. The scene must have stirred some memory of Joseph Conrad's writing about the sea, because Graham began talking of Conrad and how he often reread his favourite Conrad books. It was a pleasant change of subject. I feared we had over-marinated Papa Doc. Graham said that it is important for a writer to experience at first hand what he is writing about and that he thoroughly enjoyed the legwork for his novels. I noticed his blue eyes had become bloodshot, but when I made a comment about it he shrugged it off, saying, 'It is all that dust.'

We now left the border behind. The main trip was over. Waving fields of sugar-cane welcomed us to Barahona. The town's hotel was open, and we chose to sit on the terrace at the water's edge. I knew what to order. The fare at La Tour d'Argent or any other overrated Parisian restaurant could never match it: deliciously grilled, freshly caught lobster and ice-cold Cerveza Presidente.

Graham agreed that the succulent lobster more than made up for all our lost meals and was worth the wait. Our conversation returned to our border odyssey. I recalled the warning by an old Haitian named Moy who had survived the 1937 massacre and for years tended gardens at Frères outside Port-au-Prince. Fortified with *clairin*, he cautioned that the frontier was an 'evil place, abandoned by the *lwas*' and where you 'never hear drums'. 'He was right,' Graham remarked. 'We didn't hear any drums.'

We felt relaxed for the first time in three days. Graham leaned back on his chair, and we reminisced about when we first met in 1956. I had really met him for the first time in 1954, but it was a fleeting moment he did not remember.

That first time Graham had been invited to Haiti while staying in Jamaica by Peter Brook, the stage director who was turning Truman Capote's short story, 'House of Flowers', set in a Port-au-Prince bordello, into a Broadway musical. Graham explored Haiti in his own way with Mrs Brook, enjoying its culture and people. The circumstances then were recorded in my weekly newspaper: 'Celebrated English writer Graham Greene arrived Saturday [21 August 1954] at [Port-au-Prince] Bowen Field airport. Author of such works as *Epitaph of a Spy* [*sic*, and incorrectly included, as *Epitaph for a Spy* is actually by Eric Ambler], *The Heart of the Matter, The End of the Affair,* Mr Greene has won many honors in the literary field including the Nobel Prize for Literature. On hand to welcome him was Mr André Supplice of the Tourist Office, who escorted Mr Greene to the El Rancho Hotel where he will spend three weeks.' The item appeared on the front page of the *Haiti Sun* on 29 August. Brook and his wife played host to Haitian newsmen at an El Rancho lunch during which, to allay officials' fear that a musical set in a brothel would be terrible publicity for the country, he declared, 'It will be the best publicity Haiti ever received. It will be produced in the great theatrical capitals of the world: London, New York, Paris and so on.'

At the time I had just returned from Ireland, visiting relatives with my mother, to find my staff had not bothered to seek out the famous author and write him up as 'Personality of the Week'. At least they had honoured him with the coveted Nobel Prize for Literature, whereas the Swedish Nobel Committee had not. Rather than interview the famous American playwright Capote and the British-born artistic stage director Brook, they had translated a story from President Magloire's daily, *Le National*.

Even Mark Twain would have objected to our journalism – because of technical problems the *Haiti Sun* broadcast Graham's arrival after he had departed on Monday 27 August. As to my meeting with Graham, it turned out disastrously brief.

It was the afternoon before his departure that a waiter at El Rancho pointed to a man alone with his long legs wrapped around a tall stool at the hotel's huge mahogany outdoor circular bar. Graham was clad in tropical tan trousers and open-neck shirt, and his glass was empty. I had time to feel his shield of intimidating aloofness, and it threw me off guard. When he stood up, I noted he was about my own height, six feet two inches. As he stretched his legs I had the feeling he was prepared to make a run for it.

'Good afternoon,' I said.

'Hello,' he said.

And then he was gone, swallowed up by Brook's and Capote's group, who arrived in haste. I noticed his distinctive manner of speech as he greeted his friends and bounded out of El Rancho, leaving me with the impression that he was a starchy Englishman.

My friend Albert Silvera said he liked Graham and described him as 'an English gentleman'. The famous writer and Mr Brook's wife, Natasha, he commented, had a wonderful time together and had driven to Cap Haïtien and climbed up to see the Citadel (King Henry Christophe's famous mountain fortress). Using his own hand signals, Silvera indicated that Graham and Natasha were just good friends and that there had been no monkey business. Silvera was a womanizer, so he would know. After Mrs Brook left Haiti Graham continued playing tourist. That routine included visits to the hilltop village of Kenscoff, a Voodoo ceremony in a dingy sector of the capital and a reef in the middle of the bay off Port-au-Prince where marine life could be observed from a glass-bottomed boat.

Silvera joined me at the bar, which had evidently been Graham's command post. The handsome hotelier was the son of one of Haiti's wealthiest Sephardic Jews. Debonair and Paris educated, Albert delighted in playing host to famous people. In conspiratorial tones he quickly unburdened himself of his worries about the *House of Flowers* musical. We were alone. The barman was busy preparing for the cocktail hour. Haitian officials, he said, were very uneasy about the Broadway version of the 'House of Flowers' story – written by Truman Capote following a 1947 visit to Haiti – as it was set in the red-light district along the bay, south of Port-au-Prince. 'Will it be good for us?' the image-sensitive Silvera asked me. While supporting the musical as a 'great boost for Haitian tourism', he wondered whether the musical might attract 'the wrong kind of people'. 'We cannot afford to have our image tarnished so early,' he warned with finely honed distinction.

The story is about a brothel madam (played in the Broadway version by Pearl Bailey) who takes in a ravishing beauty from the Dominican Republic, the picture of innocence and who has no idea of her new profession. Madame Pearl is determined to trick her out of her innocence and put her to work. On the point of losing her innocence, the beauty meets a young man at a *gaguerre* (cockfight) and falls in love. It's wedding bells, and they dance from the *House of Flowers* to the wonderful music of Haitian carnival.

It was easy to sympathize with Silvera. Many brothels were spread along the Carrefour road south of the city in old gingerbread houses, once the property of the rich before they moved up to the coolness of hillside living. The exteriors of the bordellos were covered with flowers, bright red and white bougainvillaeas. At night hundreds of colourful Christmas lights competed with neon signs, such as for the Paradise Bar. Some of the houses were staffed by Dominicans while others featured Haitian hostesses.

Capote had become a familiar sight in Port-au-Prince, dressed in his Bermuda shorts and straw hat. (Haitians at the time were unaccustomed to knee-length attire and found the ensemble strange and funny.) And it was Capote and Brook who made the news the summer of 1954.

Haiti was at last reaping its share of the Caribbean tourist harvest. Dollars were rolling in. The country's father figure was President 'Papa' Paul E. Magloire, an army general and a much more genial strongman than many of his predecessors. Moreover, he was basking in the floodlights of history, having himself appeared on the cover of *Time* magazine as 'Bon Papa'. That year Haiti was observing its 150th anniversary as the hemisphere's second independent nation (after the United States) in what was the world's most successful slave revolt. President and Mamie Eisenhower had given President and Mrs Yola Magloire a full-dress official welcome to Washington, and they had slept in the White House, the first black Haitian President to be so honoured. (Playing on Broadway at the Alvin Theatre during Magloire's January 1955 official visit to the city was the big hit, *The House of Flowers*. The State Department cancelled the President's plan to see it, fearing it was too bordelloish. Magloire, his friends said, would have loved it.)

Back in those days Port-au-Prince was alive and vibrant. The population was less than 250,000. At night the seaside Harry S. Truman Boulevard was a lively scene, with the wealthy cruising back and forth to see and be seen. Automobiles were so few that their owners were easily identified. The centrepiece was the Bar Italia, offering fine espresso Haitian coffee and ice cream. Near by, chic young girls of the élite families enjoyed a moment's freedom from their parents' watchful eyes, cavorting around the ornate statues amid the sounds and flashing light show of a large musical fountain. Across the street was the statue of Christopher Columbus, on his knees, holding a cross, depicting how he discovered the island in 1492; here romantic couples made love in their cars. Haiti truly had a wonderfully magical and mysterious atmosphere, and visitors loved the 'Pearl of the Antilles'.

The hurricane season had officially ended. There was a Brazilian circus in town with a ballet as well as a big elephant. Mrs Wilhelm Oloffson, who had founded the Grand Hotel Oloffson, had died that week at the age of seventy-nine. Students were permitted to demonstrate against Cuban President Batista's bloody violation of the Haitian embassy in Havana in which Cuban police killed ten of their countrymen who had taken refuge there. Six of the dead Cubans had been granted asylum in the Haitian embassy and were awaiting safe conduct out of the country. The other four had only hours earlier entered the embassy seeking political asylum. (Also killed was Cuba's national police chief, who had led the charge into the embassy.) At home Haitians were being encouraged to register to vote in what many hoped might be the country's first attempt at universal suffrage.

However, the island republic's golden era proved to be losing its glitter. General (Bon Papa) Magloire wanted to extend his rule past the constitutional deadline, but the general's 'iron pants', his own metaphor for toughness, had rusted badly, and he no longer frightened his enemies. The old Haiti they had shared was soon to disappear for ever.

The day after Graham had departed Aubelin Jolicoeur burst into my office, gushing over the great stories I had missed. Jolicoeur never sat down. He had to gesticulate his story with his whole body. At the El Rancho he said, Truman Capote had asked him, 'Jolicoeur, have you met the celebrated author of *The Power and the Glory*? Greene left the bar,' Jolicoeur asserted, 'and crossed on to the El Rancho dance floor to come to meet me! He must have walked ten metres to greet me!' Jolicoeur's description of their meeting was uncharacteristic of both men. I had observed my friend Aubelin many times, gurgling with joy, declaring 'Oh-la-la' and flitting forward to greet a tourist like a *oiseau-mouche*, the tiny hummingbird with gyro-like wings that allow it to hover over a hibiscus flower, sip pollen and then dart on to the next flower at remarkable speed. Graham, by contrast, would (I then believed) appear reluctant to respond to the gesture and would detest the interruption, cringing at the public attention. As the capital's society reporter, he had managed to crash Haiti's tough caste and colour barriers by dint of his deft pen, writing the most exaggerated and outlandish prose conceivable in even his republic of hyperbole.

The following day when I arrived at the Bowen Field airport to pick up my copies of the Dominican and Puerto Rican newspapers from the Delta fight, I was startled to see Graham again. He had left Haiti the day before; now he stood on the tarmac arguing with the American manager of Delta Airlines. I was about to approach him but had second thoughts, and I joined a small group at the transit bar and gift shop facing the tarmac and listened to the argument. Embarrassed, I denied knowing him.

The Delta man kept insisting that Graham had to stay, that he had obtained a Haitian visa for him. He would have to wait until midweek for a flight to Jamaica, where he needed no visa as it was British territory. He could not proceed because he didn't have a visa for Cuba, the plane's next stop, or to New Orleans. We all heard Graham snap, 'What?' Then he made it definite. 'I'm going on this plane!' The Delta manager, a white American Southerner, was beside himself. 'But you're not going on my plane.' I could see that Graham was being pushed too far. He appeared ready to explode.

The plane's pilot joined them. Like a boxing referee, he raised a hand to separate them. With a dignified gesture the pilot invited Graham to board his plane. We heard the pilot tell the Delta man, 'Thank you, I'm taking this gentleman on my plane.'

We watched as they took off for Havana. The Delta manager, crestfallen, kept repeating to himself, 'I was just trying to help him.' The spectators at the bar were sympathetic.

My weekly had a story. Graham was back on our front page (at the bottom, because it was a good news week). While later he loved to make light of his Puerto Rico 'lark', it had not seemed to be fun at the time. It had provided a glimpse of a man who didn't take kindly to being pushed around.

At a diplomatic cocktail party the next night I learned further details of Graham's adventure. US *chargé d'affaires* Milton Barral told me that he had met Graham at a dinner party on the Friday night before his departure. Greene, he said, had decided to return to England the quickest way. Perversely, it became the longest route. The quickest way was via San Juan, Puerto Rico, and on to New York, and then across the Atlantic. However, Graham knew it would take days for the US Embassy to receive permission from Washington to issue him even a transit visa. Barral thought Graham might be able to swing it without a visa as he was only in transit to London. The worst scenario Barral envisaged – not quite accurately, as it turned out – was that Graham could be detained briefly between plane connections in Puerto Rico or New York. The embassy official said Graham had told him that on two recent occasions he had received special permission from the US Attorney-General to visit New York City, but each waiver had involved a lot of red tape and had taken three weeks. Detesting red tape and not prepared to wait in Port-au-Prince, he decided to take the risk of travelling as an in-transit passenger without a US visa.

We used the basic Reuters report, which Graham had himself scripted.

> In 1925 at Oxford University, at age 19, as a prank to escape boredom, Greene and a friend had become probationer members of the Communist Party of Great Britain. They had teamed up to play a trick on the party. They paid two shillings [24 cents at the time] – actually four sixpenny stamps – as membership dues for the first month. Their original idea was to wangle a free trip to Moscow or at least Paris. When the scheme failed, they allowed their memberships to lapse, by which time the party hierarchy had seen through them.

Graham's escapade certainly didn't interfere with his later becoming a wartime member of the Secret Intelligence Service. (Graham informed me that he had got on the US blacklist by mentioning his collegiate prank 'stupidly to an American fellow in Belgium who put it in a report'). I published the story in the *Haiti Sun* the following Sunday, where we decided Graham's writing deserved to win the Nobel Prize for Literature, and we even noted he had won it in 1951 – or should have done.

When Graham won the verbal sparring match at the airport, which we had witnessed, I anticipated that he might have further trouble in Havana and envisaged him becoming a permanent fixture, flying back and forth around the Caribbean. However, this time Graham took the initiative. When he got to Havana he managed to leave the airport without going through the immigration formalities. (Strongman Batista, a one-time army sergeant, was still very much the boss in Cuba in 1954. Fidel Castro, his brother Raúl and other survivors of the abortive 26 July attack on the Moncada army barracks in Santiago de Cuba the year before were behind bars on the Isle of Pines. They would later be released and exiled to Mexico.) Graham had booked into the lovely old Hotel Inglaterra on Havana's Parque Central and was about to enjoy a siesta when the phone rang. He had alerted Reuters, and now it was the British news agency alerting him. They had taken up 'his' story. This was a rare occasion on which I knew he had played his own publicist.

The *Daily Telegraph*'s correspondent, New Zealand expatriate Ted Scott, and a friend, sent me an update from Havana. Scott, an ex-British spy, had found Graham and told him, 'You know the police are searching for you. I've been inquiring about you at the airport, and they say you have come in without going through immigration, and they are looking for you.'

The British ambassador to Cuba sent Graham a message that he wouldn't invite him to a meal because it might offend the Americans.

I realized years later that Graham had a habit of always registering at British embassies abroad, and he enjoyed being invited to them for dinner or even staying in the Ambassador's residence. Rested up, he flew on to London, managing to escape any exit problems at the Cuban capital's Rancho Boyeros International Airport.

There was some good in Graham's lark: he had ridiculed the McCarran-Walters Act of 1952, which barred entry into the United States to anyone who might have had connections with the communists.

Two years later, in November 1956, I met a different Graham Greene. He was sitting with a woman bent over a Scrabble board near the pool at El Rancho. It was late morning, and the hotel was almost deserted. I approached, not wishing to disturb their game. I was holding a copy of the *Haiti Sun* that announced their arrival. His interest was in the lady who was beating him at Scrabble. I watched him as he reached down to consult a dictionary at his feet. I thought that was cheating. He gave off a series of 'Oh yes, oh yes' when he spotted me standing in the sun. His companion was cool and collected – and winning. She had a pleasant smile, and Graham invited me to sit with them. It was fun to see him wrestling with the spelling of a word. Graham Greene a poor speller? Catherine, as he introduced his handsome and lively female friend, was indeed the winner. Graham had to buy the rum punches.

Perhaps it had been Catherine who brought him to life and made him a much more open and entertaining person. He already sounded like an expert on Haiti. He explained it was a quiet time at the El Rancho as the other guests were on city and mountains tours, and he ticked off the sights: the Iron Market, mahogany factories and the marketplace at Kenscoff in the cool mountains; he confessed that he had become another victim of Haiti's strange charm.

They were on a six-week Caribbean holiday, and he had decided to show Haiti to 'Cafryn', as he called his friend. I told them I would be only too pleased to show them around, whenever they wanted. I did not wish to intrude on their holiday. I did not take out my notebook and pen. I was in awe of the writer, and I decided against an interview, posing any questions or asking

Catherine about herself. I had almost forgotten I was a reporter. But I did ask him if I could take a photograph. He confessed to hating having his picture taken and didn't wish to be recognized by the tourists. I promised I would publish the photograph only after they departed. Catherine said, 'Fair enough,' and instructed him, laughing, to 'stand up like a man and be shot'. She herself did not wish to be in the photograph and told me to stop calling Graham 'Mr Greene'. He also preferred Graham. Snapping his picture was painlessly quick. In one frame I captured a youngish Graham Greene posing by the pool in a dark shirt and with his hands in the pockets of his linen trousers. The image appeared on the front page of the *Haiti Sun* on 2 December. The caption noted that three of author Greene's greatest discoveries on this trip were: first, the ten-cent taxi, a communal automobile called *la ligne,* that dropped passengers anywhere within the city limits for that price; second, the *taptap,* a colourfully painted small pick-up truck with a specially designed passenger section, sporting brazen sayings and biblical messages to and from God that were designed to assure the rider that God cared, even if the fare was seven cents; and, third, another means of transport, the *camionette,* an unadorned estate car, also seven cents a ride, that plied the hill between the capital and Pétionville. The average tourist didn't use these forms of transport. However, they appealed to Graham's thrifty side, and, besides, he was not a typical tourist.

After their Scrabble game they invited me to lunch. I made suggestions, such as attending a show at the Centre d'Art. When we met again Graham asked whether we could visit a 'house of flowers'. I agreed. Catherine also agreed. I had no idea who she was, only that she was outgoing and fun-loving with a saucy sense of humour with which she often baited him and brought him out from his shell. They seemed like old friends, and he was obviously very fond of her. Graham stipulated that we choose brothels staffed by Haitians girls not Dominicans. It was quite acceptable for visits to take the form of sitting, imbibing, dancing and watching the dancing. We sat and drank Barbancourt rum and soda at the large café-brothel opposite a private Thorland country club on the Carrefour road. The café portion was open-air and structurally not unlike a Voodoo *peristyle* (religious centre); it was painted the colour of the wicked red eyes of *Erzulie Ge-Rouge,* the religion's love goddess who had a bad case of jealousy. The jukebox was blaring a rendition of Perez Prado's 'Mambo Number Five'. The clientele were obviously not the wealthy, who patronized the Dominican houses; in fact there were few customers.

The girls were dressed in tight clothes and bright colours. Some of them danced with each other. One customer was hunched over a plate of *griot* and fried plantains. The scent of the pork mixed with cheap cologne. Graham drew our attention to one Haitian Aphrodite and commented on her grace and beauty. 'What an exquisite long neck! Look at that profile . . . She could be an African princess!'

Catherine, noting that he was quite taken with the girl's natural beauty, feigned jealousy, as if Graham had found his choice for the evening. 'Well,' she announced loudly enough to command attention, 'I think I'll leave you boys to your wiles. Can I get a *taptap* back to the hotel?' Graham smiled, 'Fine', as if to admit he was smitten. It was worth a chuckle to observe their games. But for a moment I thought she was serious, and I was about to call it quits for the evening.

We moved on to another bar, which was much the same. Catherine, smiling, turned to me during a lull of the loud *meringue* playing on the jukebox and said she thought writers were particularly interested in brothels. She nodded her head gaily towards Graham. 'Of course as observers . . . they are attracted by the world's oldest profession. It allows them to see,' she went on coyly, 'and sometimes feel humanity in the raw.' She broke into laughter as Graham looked at her quizzically; she added, 'You know it's the male oppressor's workplace!'

It was when he spoke of his personal aversion to the crowds of tourists that I suggested that they would be more at home at the Grand Hotel Oloffson. After introducing Graham and Catherine to Roger Coster and his wife Laura, they needed no more encouragement and agreed to spend the last two days of their stay there. 'We sell a soul, not a bed,' Coster had told them, rattling off his sales pitch. During their nineteen-year occupation of Haiti (1915–34) the US Marines had turned the hotel into a hospital and built a ten-room maternity wing for expectant Marine wives. Coster claimed that lots of babies had been born at the Oloffson during the Marine occupation, but more had been conceived there since the Marines left.

Both Graham and Catherine displayed keen interest in the primitive Haitian art movement. At the time most expatriate Americans living in Haiti attended the *vernissages* of new artists at the Centre d'Art in Port-au-Prince run by an American, Dewitt Peters. (The 1954 painting by Rigaud Benoît, of a flood sweeping all before it as a priest and his flock kneel helplessly watching the *lavalas*, as Haitians called the flash floods, remained with Graham for the rest of his life. Along with other Haitian primitive paintings – such as the one by Phillippe-Auguste that he'd bought in 1963 with his winnings from a night in the nearly deserted Casino in Papa Doc's haunted Port-au-Prince – he kept it hanging in his last apartment in Switzerland. He loved them. They reminded him of an exciting time in his life, according to Yvonne, with whom he last lived.)

One afternoon I drove Graham and Catherine out to La Galerie Brochette, an exhibition centre for a new colony of young Haitian artists situated in the village of Carrefour. They included the painters Gérard Dorcely and Luckner Lazard, whose work was not actually primitive but modernist. Catherine became enthusiastic and wanted to know whether the artists had ever exhibited abroad (most at that point had not) and whether they would consider exhibiting their works in London. *Mais oui, madame!* The artists were then struggling for recognition, and their responses to her were understandably enthusiastic. The group photograph I took shows a tanned and smiling couple, Graham and Catherine, with the artists at La Galerie Brochette. Another artist, Max Pinchinat, a member of the Galerie, later returned to work in Paris, and it was he, as things turned out, who played the Voodoo priest in the movie version of *The Comedians*. After long being repressed, Voodoo was now out of the closet. Each hotel had its night for a special folkloric show, and at the International Casino dancer Pierre Blain and his troupe performed an extravaganza entitled *Invocation to Dambala*. Many of the folk dancers were actually *ounsis* (women dressed all in white who assist in the ceremonies) or other practitioners of Voodoo, and their floor-show rituals followed closely the rituals in the temples. Drums were heard nightly not only in the open-air Théâtre de Verdure, in the tourist hotels or the International Casino; they lulled one to sleep in most districts of the capital. After years of official persecution of Voodoo, it was the late Dumarsais Estimé, President between 1946 and 1950, who had allowed Haiti's folk religion to blossom once more, even though it was technically illegal.

Graham's anti-tourist bias and his thrift drove him away from pricey tourist guides and chauffeurs and into the crowded backs of the *taptap* buses. He and Catherine squeezed in with the chickens and produce and wares of the *marchands* (market women). Catherine was resourceful in avoiding the throngs of vacationers in other ways. Both had about them a spirit of mischievous glee that summer.

Years later, in search of the perfect rum punch in Panama or Central America, Graham often spoke with fondness of the diminutive Oloffson bartender Caesar's superb rum punches, which he served with an ear-to-ear smile just visible above the hotel's huge mahogany bar. The Oloffson's long, wide veranda served as an elevated dining-room.

One afternoon, as a soft reddish glow illuminated the veranda while the sun dipped into La Gonave Bay, Graham began to ruminate about his family's having had a Caribbean connection. As he had never mentioned his family before, I credited Caesar's punch with exerting special powers, as if the hotel's playful bartender had planted some Voodoo powder in the drink. I was intrigued by Graham's surprising airing of his ancestral linen.

'According to Greene family lore,' he said, 'the Greenes have roots in the

Caribbean.' As he told the story of his family link to this tropical sea I felt it might explain why he was so at ease with Caribbean people. A branch of the Greenes, he continued, had had sugar plantations on the island of St Kitts in the last century; Great Uncle Charles had died there at age of nineteen of yellow fever. (It could have been cholera.) But he had accomplished what most men don't do in an entire lifetime. He had fathered, said Graham after a brief pause, 'thirteen children'. The siring, he went on, savouring his rum punch, took place after the emancipation of the slaves on St Kitts. (Graham gave no details of the mothers of the thirteen children, leaving that to the imagination.) Two years before Charlie died of the fever, Graham's grandfather, William Greene, then only fourteen years old, sailed across the Atlantic to help his brother Charles run the plantations. Grandfather William went back to England after Charlie's death but later returned to St Kitts, where he, too, died and was buried on the island near his brother. Graham clearly relished telling the story of his forebear's sexual exploits. (He had at one time mentioned the fact that he was a distant cousin of Robert Louis Stevenson, whom he obviously admired, but it was Uncle Charlie he respected.) He told the latter story matter-of-factly but with a certain amount of irreverent humour. Catherine had heard the tale before and was talking with an artist at another table down the long veranda. She looked towards us and smiled as Graham delivered his punchline about the thirteen offspring.

During Graham and Catherine's last evening in Haiti, the Centre d'Art's founder and director, Dewitt Peters, held a farewell cocktail party for them. The next morning I drove them from the Oloffson to the airport. They took the Delta flight, this time non-stop to Havana.

Graham had two paintings that the Haitian artists had given him and four bottles of five-star Rhum Barbancourt, my gift to them both. (He would try unsuccessfully to reproduce Caesar's rum punch in England with the recipe the little Oloffson barman had confided to him.) I remarked that Haiti was a quiet place, ideal for him to write, and suggested he return. He showed interest in the idea but worried about how to finance a much longer stay. He made no promises but asked about renting a house and the cost of living. As he drained his last rum punch at the Bowen Field airport bar, gripping his battered leather briefcase in one hand and his paintings in the other, I knew he would be back.

However, instead of returning to Haiti in the late 1950s Graham went to Cuba, which had a rebellion of its own. Fidel Castro had been released from jail, gone into exile in Mexico, and on 2 December 1956 had returned at the head of an invasion force of eighty-two men. Their arrival was anticipated by the regime, and they were almost wiped out by Batista's army. With a dozen survivors Fidel reached the rugged Sierra Maestra, the brooding mountain chain in eastern Cuba visible on a clear day from north-west Haiti. From there he launched his guerrilla war. It turned out that the book manuscript Graham had been carrying in his battered briefcase during his 1956 visit to Haiti was one spoofing the British Secret Service. He ultimately adapted it to Cuba. *Our Man in Havana* was published in 1958, a few months before Castro came to power, and made into a film in 1959 starring Alec Guinness, Noël Coward and Ernie Kovacs. The Cuban revolutionaries were not amused. It was not comedy hour in Havana – nor was it in Haiti.

7 | BLOOD IN THE STREETS

Following our border trip Graham flew back to England. Bajeux went back to his exile in the Dominican sugar-mill town and to questioning his God. I went back to my reporting assignments. I wrote a story about the journey and then decided against sending it to *Time* as I had not consulted Graham. I didn't wish to hex his book project. We all went our separate ways, but a nightmare – Papa Doc's Haiti – tragically remained with us. I was certain Graham would write a book and it would be the end of our friendship, as he would move on to other places and other books.

I wrote to Graham reporting that the day following his departure my Beetle suffered a flat tyre and I had discovered that the spare was also flat. How lucky we had been, I noted; the gods had truly been good to us. We might still be in the mountains if we had punctured another tyre.

Graham greeted the news with characteristic concern. 'I always suspected that that tyre was no good,' he wrote. 'I tried to point out a hole in it to our friend the priest, but he didn't seem to think it mattered!' Then he added, 'How much I enjoyed our time together and how grateful I am to you for giving up two days to the trip.' To me that was a good sign that the trip hadn't been boring; it had actually lasted three days. There was no news from Graham himself or of any book in progress. He did write to tell me he had sent me a copy of his new play, *Carving a Statue*. 'I hope you won't find it as boring as the critics did.'

Closer to home it was a busy time for my family and hard times for the Dominican people. There were endless strikes and anti-government demonstrations as well as rumblings of coups d'état. Our second son, Phillippe, had been born. The exiled Haitian priest, Father Jean-Baptiste Georges, had taken time out from planning his next invasion of Haiti, this time from Miami, to baptize our new infant. Father Bajeux attended the church ceremony as Phillippe's godfather before departing for New York. I read Graham's most recent book, *A Burnt-Out Case*, and couldn't help feeling that Querry, the central character in the novel, which is set in a leper colony in Africa, was Graham – or at least his *alter ego*. I felt this despite the fact that there are a lot of seeming disclaimers in the book, as for example when Querry tells Maria, the wife of the disgustingly pious Rycker, the palm-oil factory

manager, 'No, you mustn't draw parallels. They always say a novelist chooses
from his general experience of life, not from special facts.' And again when
Querry insists, 'You mustn't accuse a storyteller of introducing real characters.'
I also found a warning to those who would seek to influence writers in what
they write. Querry tells Maria, 'You are like so many critics. You want me to
write your own sort of story.'

We wanted Graham to write our sort of story on Haiti. But *A Burnt-Out
Case,* which I thought was one of his best works, reassured me that if and when
he did take up Haiti he would treat the country and the people right. After
reading the passage in *A Burnt-Out Case,* 'He looked around the church, at
the altar, the tabernacle, the brass candles, and the European saints, pale like
albinos in the dark continent,' I knew Voodoo would be portrayed with the
understanding it deserved. Graham obviously understood Africa (the book
had been conceived during his fourth sojourn there) and the creative
imagination and spontaneity of the Africans. *A Burnt-Out Case* also illustrated
Graham's eternal struggle with faith, belief and disbelief. The book evokes no
outright laughter, but Graham dabbles with a certain dark humour, and I
wondered whether he would carry this over to his next work. Although the
backdrop he chose was the worst disease then known to mankind, leprosy,
Graham managed to lighten the tension of the tragedy with subtle sarcasm.
Querry says, 'A writer doesn't write for his readers, does he? Yet he has to take
elementary precautions all the same to make them comfortable.'

There also appeared during this time a slim volume Graham called *In
Search of a Character*, first published in 1961, containing two of his African
journals. 'Neither of these journals,' he wrote in the foreword, 'was kept for
publication, but they may have some interest as an indication of the kind of
raw material a novelist accumulates.' In it he hinted that *A Burnt-Out Case*
might be his last novel. 'As one grows older,' he wrote, 'the writing of a novel
does not become more easy, and it seemed to me when I wrote the last words
[of *A Burnt-Out Case*] that I had reached an age when another full-length
novel was probably beyond my powers.' I did not believe it. He was not the
type of person to stop putting pen to paper. Writing was his life.

Graham proved that he kept promises, no matter how inconvenient and
time-consuming. He wrote to me in April 1965:

> I have failed utterly to find a copy of *Blood in the Streets* in England,
> but a bookseller unearthed one copy in the United States and after
> reading it I am posting it to you. You will find that the account of the
> [1937] massacre is very brief and I should have thought deserved a
> whole book in itself if you ever had the time and opportunity to write
> it. How are things with you and your family? I hope all goes well. Since

Feb. 13 I have been having one attack after another of the flu and have only just got rid of the beast (touch wood!). I'm hoping to go out to Indochina again during the summer if I can procure my visa to Hanoi.

It was ironic that he should write that he had found *Blood in the Streets*. Only four days later, and long before the letter reached me, the Dominican capital erupted in violence. Eventually the blood of more than two thousand Dominicans, and a dozen Americans, was to be shed in the streets.

The revolt caught me *en route* home from New York City where I had gone to sign a publisher's contract for a book about Haiti's François Duvalier entitled *Papa Doc*. The idea for the Haiti book was that of a colleague, Al Burt, then the *Miami Herald's* Latin American editor. I had been hesitant about writing such a book, fearing it might bring reprisals against my wife's relatives in Haiti. While I was pondering the idea, a representative of McGraw-Hill happened to be in Santo Domingo and made an offer on the spot. 'You can always blame your co-author,' he suggested when he saw I was hesitant. I sent word to Haiti about the project; my wife's family did not scare easily. They made no objection. They would take their chances. Their family history since Haiti's war of independence had been one of taking chances. They came from a long line of distinguished fighters, not least General Laurent Bazelais.

While I was in New York I warned my foreign news editors that a coup against the Dominican triumvirate, headed by Donald Reid Cabral, was imminent because Cabral had made it clear that neither ousted Liberal President Juan Bosch nor former Trujillo aide and ex-President Joaquín Balaguer would be allowed to return from exile and participate in forthcoming elections. The military was divided. One section favoured a return to constitutionality by permitting President Bosch to complete his term of office, while the other was loyal to Balaguer. Lieutenant Hector Lachapelle, who had been cashiered by General Elías Wessin y Wessin for opposing the military coup that ousted Bosch, was now running a petrol station in Santo Domingo and had warned me to be watchful, saying that 'things' were about to happen. They did, and Lachapelle was soon back in army uniform as commander of an area of the capital seized by the Constitutionalists, as the rebels called themselves.

I had hardly proffered my warning to my editors when Ginette called me from Santo Domingo to advise me to hurry home. The coup was about to happen. The food shops were swamped by customers fighting to stock up on provisions. Events exploded while I was on my way back. I reached San Juan, Puerto Rico, just as the coup unfolded. Commercial air traffic to and from the Dominican Republic was suspended. I interviewed ex-President Bosch, who was in exile in Puerto Rico, and filed as best I could on the situation in the Dominican Republic, with my wife now playing the role of reporter, monitoring the radio and passing along vital information by telephone. But with Ginette and our two infant sons caught in the turmoil in the capital, I became desperate. I managed to hitch a ride on a US Marine landing ship, the USS *Wood County*, a modern LST (landing ship tank) heading to the Dominican Republic to evacuate American citizens. It was the night of 28 April 1965, exactly two years to the day since I had been booted out of Haiti.

Other newsmen and I joined the US Marines enjoying the evening movie aboard ship. Just as the actor William Holden disappeared from the screen for the love scene, the ship's public address system boomed, 'Now hear this, now hear this. Darken ship.'

The Marines on board buckled up for war. They began breaking out live ammunition. I couldn't believe what was happening. This was 1965, not the early part of the twentieth century when the US, exercising its doctrine of 'manifest destiny', sent Marines ashore in Haiti, the Dominican Republic and Nicaragua.

'It can't be!' I exclaimed to the ship's captain. 'It's not that serious.'

'Tell that to President Johnson.' He laughed.

Maybe matters were worse than my wife's reports. Once again I became deeply concerned about their safety.

There was little sleep aboard ship that night as the Marines prepared to land, but we newsmen couldn't file our stories about the imminent invasion because the ship's commander told us he could not authorize the use of the ship's communications facilities.

It was a clear and beautiful Caribbean night as we sailed, blacked out, listening to President Johnson over the Voice of America explaining in his Texas drawl that he had ordered Marines ashore in the Dominican Republic to 'protect American lives'. Johnson's doctrine of 'no more Cubas' was being put into practice. More than twenty-seven thousand US servicemen would be involved and would remain until the crisis was over in September 1966.

The day after we landed Dick Duncan of *Time*, Louis Uchitelle of the Associated Press and I ventured into the rebel-held 'Constitutionalist zone' in downtown Santo Domingo, just off Plaza de la Independencia, and came upon an old bakery, busy and alive with the sound of Haitian Creole. The Kamoken were working away, not baking bread but repairing an ancient machine-gun. With their knowledge of firearms, the Haitians had been quickly integrated into the Dominican Republic's new Constitutionalist army, now at war with both the Dominican status quo forces and the American troops. At the outbreak of hostilities, Fred Baptiste, his brother Renel and most of the other Kamoken fled the lunatic asylum at Nigua and joined the Dominican Constitutionalist side. It was the first time in anyone's memory that Haitians and Dominicans had joined to fight a common enemy on Dominican soil. On entering the bakery we found the Haitians in high spirits. They announced that their side was winning the battle and that the landing of the US troops had been a terrible mistake. As soon as the war was won, they added, they could resume their war against Papa Doc; meanwhile they were perfecting their urban-guerrilla tactics.

A few days later I was in the Constitutionalist sector at the cable office when the gunfire had died down, sending a story. Suddenly I heard a commotion in the street and ran to the door. Fred Baptiste, a bazooka over his shoulder, was moving his troops down Calle el Conde on his way to blow the door off the historic Forteleza (Fortress) Ozama. The US-trained Cascos Blancos (White Helmets), Santo Domingo's tough, loyalist riot police, were still holding out there. It was Fred's and his men's finest hour. The fortress capitulated. Fred was getting a reputation as a tough disciplinarian – far too tough for Colonel Francisco Caamano Deno, who had been made leader of the Constitutionalist forces. One day Caamano told me he had received reports that the Haitians were executing some of their own men for unknown reasons. He was angry and concerned, declaring that all he needed was for word to leak out that people were being executed in his zone.

I confronted Fred about this, but he denied that anyone had been executed. 'Let me tell you what happened,' he said. 'Puma [Jean-Claude Romain] died playing Russian roulette.'

The other Kamoken backed up Fred's story. With a revolver loaded with a single bullet, they said, Puma shot himself in the head and died instantly. I thought of Graham's stories about how he had played Russian roulette as a bored youth.

The American forces laid siege to the Constitutionalist-occupied area of Santo Domingo, while junta forces continued their fight against rebels in the northern part of the city. There were fierce firefights. My little Volkswagen with 'Prensa' (Press) taped on its windows became a familiar sight throughout the city. Reporting the war meant covering all three sides: the daily US Army briefings in the Embassy Room of the Hotel El Embajador; the Constitutionalists at the Copello Building on Calle el Conde (after passing through US Marine and Army checkpoints and driving rapidly across streets receiving fire from the Palace, where loyalist troops were holed up); then on to the fairgrounds, where the new right-wing Government of National Reconstruction had its headquarters. There was a good deal of dangerous travel every day, but my hardy Beetle sustained only minor war damage. In fact, I credited my manoeuvrable and speedy little 'Bug' with getting me out of the line of fire a number of times. My colleague Al Burt of the *Miami Herald* was not so fortunate. While travelling in a taxi with a photographer he became a target for skittish US

Marines at a roadblock. The Marines believed they had received incoming fire and opened a withering barrage on the taxi. Both newsmen and the taxi driver were badly wounded.

The US intervention finally ended, and President Johnson gave his approval for the seasoned conservative Dominican politician, Joaquín Balaguer, to take power. The Dominican Republic would no longer compete for headlines with Vietnam.

Graham had certainly been right – grim things had happened in the wake of his departure.

8 | THE COMEDIANS

In a letter dated 20 December 1965 Graham finally broke the news. He preceded it by alluding to the Dominican upheaval. 'I was afraid that something might have happened to one of you during the revolution – a revolution which alas I could not attend!' Then, sounding slightly sheepish, at the end of the letter he announced, 'I've got a novel about Haiti coming out at the end of January, of which I am sending you a copy in the hope that it may arrive. I'm sure you will find a great many errors there, but perhaps you will be amused by the last chapter, which reflects our visit to the bauxite works. Forgive the errors for the sake of the intention.'

In the midst of the Dominican civil war, in spite of the erratic postal service, *The Comedians* arrived at our home. It was a thrilling moment, mixed with apprehension. This book, I hoped, would affect Haiti's future or at least Papa Doc's tyranny. The pen could indeed be mightier than the sword. I felt that much depended on the little parcel I held in my hand that afternoon. I examined its careful wrapping and waited a moment before tearing open the package and showing it to my wife. The book's cover was several shades of green. The brief blurb on the inside jacket flap said it was Greene's first novel in five years and noted that 'Like one of its predecessors, *The Quiet American*, it is a story about the committed and uncommitted.' Graham opened the book in the form of a letter, both as a salute to his old publisher, A.S. Frere, and as a way of establishing its geographical location. 'Poor Haiti itself and the character of Doctor Duvalier's rule are not invented,' he wrote, 'the latter not even blackened for dramatic effect. Impossible to deepen that night.' The UK edition had been published by the Bodley Head of London. In his tiny script Graham had written: 'For Bernard – hoping you will not find this too much of a travesty – with love, from Graham. Christmas 1965.'

Unconsciously I lifted the book to feel its weight, as if it were a precious metal. Then I sat down, forgot about deadlines and news reports and devoured *The Comedians*. I didn't sleep that night. Graham had given us a novel in which fiction was reality. There had been no need to worry. He had protected everyone concerned. There was not one breach of confidence. I was reassured he was honourable and compassionate. He had given the poor people of Haiti something Papa Doc had deprived them of: a voice. The horrors of the Papa

Doc dictatorship and its gratuitous brutality were there. Graham had managed to capture, in this imaginary love story, the 1963–4 climate of Duvalier's terror and its surrealism. Only those who had lived through that terror could appreciate the accuracy with which he painted it. The dark comedy left me depressed, and for several nights after rereading the book I suffered painful flashbacks of my last years in Haiti.

The comedians of the book's title are not the Haitians but the *blans* (whites), a term synonymous in Haiti with foreigners – whom Graham introduces sailing to Haiti aboard the *Medea*, a Dutch ship named after the jealous sorceress of legend. Their names are as vacuous as their moral philosophies – Brown, Jones and Smith. However, Jesuit-educated Brown is well read, citing Wordsworth and Baudelaire, and he reads Henry James's 'The Great Good Place' at the Trianon – Port-au-Prince's gingerbread landmark, clearly patterned after the venerable Grand Hotel Oloffson – during a long Sunday afternoon.

But comedy in *The Comedians* is of the bitter kind, about dark human emotions. There are no belly laughs, just a deep sadness at watching a country sink into a living hell because of the cruel and capricious contempt for human life of its despotic leader and his sadistic Tontons Macoutes. Papa Doc does not make a personal appearance in the book, but his presence permeates the air like some awesome, terrifying vulture. Graham achieves this by portraying Duvalier as the Voodoo god Baron Samedi, guardian of the dead. As such, he casts a demonic shadow that darkens all.

Graham uses a first-person narrative. Brown, the book's anti-hero and main protagonist, was left by his worldly mother to be raised by Jesuits. He even contemplated becoming a priest at one stage but lost his faith and became a cynical, jaded, middle-aged beachcomber-type. He refers to God 'as an authoritative practical joker'. Determinedly uncommitted, Brown wants to remain uninvolved in any social or political cause (which was so true of many foreigners and effete Haitians living under the dictatorship). But Brown's cynicism does not prevent him from knowing what is going on around him. He returns to Haiti unable to sell his hotel, which his well-travelled mother has ended up with in Port-au-Prince.

Aboard the *Medea* there is also 'Major' Jones, who is sailing under false pretences. He is a con man in the British genre, at times a charming cad but a pathetic figure none the less. He boasts of having battled the Japanese in Burma during the Second World War when in fact – as he confesses to Brown in a Haitian cemetery towards the end of the book – he was an actor performing far behind the front lines (which reminds me of Noël Coward). In Haiti Jones has high hopes of striking it rich by making a lucrative arms deal with corrupt government bureaucrats. Unfortunately, as the winds blow, so do the officials; Jones's letter of introduction is to an official whose current address is the national prison.

The only committed members of the group of seafarers travelling to Port-au-Prince are Mr and Mrs Smith, a noble-minded but naïve and elderly American couple who have not the slightest idea of what Haiti is like under Papa Doc's dictatorship. As evangelical vegetarians (he was the presidential candidate on the US Vegetarian Party ticket) the Smiths absurdly seek to set up a vegetarian centre in Haiti that they hope will 'one day remove acidity and passion from the Haitian character'. Still, they are likeable, and Graham shows that there are good Americans as well as quiet ones.

From the moment the *blans* descend the gangplank in Port-au-Prince, they move deep into the terrifying darkness of Papa Doc's regime and his eerie hell on earth. (Graham told me more than once after his 1963 visit that he had never elsewhere confronted the type and extent of evil that pervaded Papa Doc's Haiti. The place, Graham said, reeked of malevolence – a malevolent dictator, a malevolent secret police and a malevolent system.) Upon disembarking Brown is given an effusive greeting by the ubiquitous Petit Pierre, the most recognizable character in the book after the all-pervasive Papa Doc. Because Petit Pierre seems to have escaped being beaten up or worse, he is suspected of having connections with the Tontons Macoutes. But Brown questions whether it is true because 'there were occasionally passages in his gossip-column that showed an odd satirical courage – perhaps he depended on the police not to read between the lines'. It is also true that in a dictatorship any survivors are suspect. In his portrait of Petit Pierre Graham adds that he was 'always gay. It was as though he had tossed a coin to decide between the only two possible attitudes in Port-au-Prince, the rational and the irrational, misery or gaiety; Papa Doc's head had fallen earthwards and he had plumped for the gaiety of despair.'

Brown heads off in the country's customary nightly black-out to the eerily majestic Hotel Trianon only to find a corpse in the hotel's pool, which has no water. The body is that of Doctor Philipot, Papa Doc's Secretary of State for Social Welfare, who has chosen suicide at Brown's mother's hotel, slashing both his wrists and his throat, rather than face death at the hands of the regime's terror specialists, the Tontons Macoutes. Although Brown is unmoved by this distasteful discovery, the incident eventually draws him into Haiti's drama and even affects his sex life. While making love to Martha, the wife of a South American ambassador, Brown sees in his mind's eye Doctor Philipot's corpse again and is rendered impotent.

On a visit with the Smiths to see the Cabinet minister who has replaced the unfortunate Dr Philipot, Brown observes, 'Above his head hung the portrait of Papa Doc – the portrait of Baron Samedi. Clothed in the heavy black tail-suit of graveyards, he peered out at us through the thick lenses of his spectacles with myopic and expressionless eyes. He was rumoured sometimes to watch personally the slow death of a Tonton victim. The eyes would not change. Presumably his interest in the death was medical.'

The dictatorship is exemplified by Captain Concasseur, who took pleasure 'in breaking limbs' and 'missed nothing through those dark glasses'. It was he who mutilated and emasculated Joseph, Brown's servant at the hotel. Typical of the regime's entrepreneurial insanity is the construction of an ice-skating rink in the mountains at Kenscoff, overlooking Port-au-Prince. (This was actually a short-lived project undertaken by a businessman connected to the Duvalier regime during that time.)

Except for the unworldly Smiths, who are oblivious to their murderous surroundings, the cynical, uncommitted foreigners see themselves only as players in a cosmic bad joke. Life to Brown is a form of dark comedy with the actors and actresses – comedians all – directed by the Almighty. Brown's world therefore lacks any profound purpose. Even so, the comedians' superficial environment is so totally dwarfed by the frightening enormity of Papa Doc's Kafkaesque darkness enveloping them that they appear laughably trivial and insignificant. 'We are only the sub-plot affording a little light relief,' Brown tells Martha, commenting on Dr Philipot's suicide. 'We belong to the world of comedy and not to tragedy,' he tells her on another occasion. He has no moral moorings and is not even able to sustain his romance with Martha. Their affair is growing cold, and besides being married she is the daughter of an executed Nazi war criminal. She mentions her harsh father, the German, to Brown who says, 'Cruelty's like a searchlight. It sweeps from one spot to another. We only escape it for a time.' And elsewhere he observes, 'Haiti was not an exception in a sane world: it was a small slice of everyday taken at random. Baron Samedi walked in all our graveyards.' Later when he calls on the British *chargé d'affaires* to help the imprisoned 'Major' Jones, whose deal is dead, Brown says he 'felt a little like the player king rebuked by Hamlet for exaggerating his part'. He is unaffected even by the death of his mother, Maggie Brown, a brave, worldly woman – Madame la Comtesse de Lascot-Villiers. She leaves him the hotel, and he treats Marcel, her Haitian lover, as just another member of the cast of the theatre of farce. Before she dies, the Comtesse says to Marcel, 'I know I'm an old woman and as you say a bit of an actress. But please go on pretending. As long as we pretend we escape.' But Marcel cannot escape. He is no comedian; he cares. Filled with grief, he, too, commits suicide in the hotel. Suicide, Brown worries, is bad for business. On the other hand, there is no business.

It is the book's Haitian characters who try to inject some transcendental life into the comedians like Brown, who is the equivalent of a Haitian zombie in that his moral and spiritual decay has been caused by a loss of faith – in God – that makes him resemble the walking dead.

The towering figure of commitment is the Haitian physician Dr Magiot.

The antithesis of Papa Doc, Magiot is a Marxist but one attuned to the more gentle, bourgeois Victorian age in which Marx himself lived – a time when Marxism had a human face. Like the Hotel Trianon, Magiot is almost a relic from a bygone era. He helps bring about Brown's slow regeneration. Brown first encounters Magiot crouched over the body of the ex-Social Welfare Minister 'in the shadow cast by my torch like a sorcerer exorcising death', and gradually succumbs to his influence as a sort of father confessor.

Graham, through a letter of introduction from the French Roman Catholic philosopher Jacques Maritain, met the Haitian physician Dr Camille Lherisson, a big man with an even bigger ego who had been Minister of Health in the Magloire government for a brief time. He was Graham's opposite. Graham shunned the public spotlight, while Lherisson bathed in it. The high-profile physician had been one of the first Haitian doctors to be sent abroad by the Rockefeller Foundation. Under Rockefeller auspices he received a scholarship and undertook his postgraduate work in biology at McGill University, Montreal. (The Rockefeller Foundation had granted scholarships to a number of Haitian doctors to specialize in various medical fields abroad. Dr François 'Papa Doc' Duvalier studied public health at the University of Michigan for a semester on a Rockefeller scholarship. There he learned a great deal about racial discrimination in the United States, if not about democratic values. Indeed, because of colour prejudice in the United States, most Haitians granted foreign scholarships had earlier been sent to Canada.)

Engaging and physically impressive, 'Bibi', as Lherisson was known to his friends, was attending physician to some of Haiti's oldest families. He was a devoted doctor who had saved lives but who had become increasingly egocentric with age. He had finely chiselled features and could be described either as a dark mulatto or a light-coloured *griffe* (one of the many shades of colour between mulatto and black). Apart from a wandering eye, philosophy was another of his passions. He spoke English well and made a deep impression on Graham, who had difficulties with any language but his own. Lherisson's moment of fame, at least locally, had come during the last six days of September 1944 when, as president of La Société Haïtienne d'Etudes Scientifiques (the Haitian Society of Scientific Studies) he organized an international conference on philosophy. It was an extraordinary event for Haiti, made more so by the fact that it was held while the Second World War still raged. In retrospect it might appear that Haiti had priorities other than a five-day discussion on Kant and the anti-intellectual mysticism of Luther, 'Object of Sensible Intuition According to Kant' and 'Object of Physics-Mathematics' by Eugene Babin. Lherisson himself spoke on the philosophy of mathematics. The star of the event was the Catholic philosopher Jacques Maritain, whom Lherisson introduced as *'notre cher et grand ami'* (our beloved good friend). It was Jacques

Maritain who Graham said had helped him publish his first book in France, *The Man Within*, and who had suggested he meet Dr Lherisson.

As things turned out, Lherisson became the model for Dr Magiot in *The Comedians*. This choice of a model was a shock to me. There were numerous Haitians who could have been the model for Dr Magiot. It was not until August 1980 that Graham told me who the inspiration was. He told me this as he and I waited for Panamanian strongman General Omar Torrijos's personal jet to take us to Managua, Nicaragua. Graham lamented the demise of the late Hotel Oloffson bartender Caesar and his famous rum punches. His musing took him back many years. 'Did you know Dr Camille Lherisson?' he asked. 'I had him in mind when I created the character of Dr Magiot in *The Comedians*.' Of all the heroic figures I believed were possible models for Dr Magiot, Lherrison had never crossed my mind. Up to that moment Graham's powers of observation and judgement had seemed extraordinary to me; now I was not so sure. I was shattered. All I could say in getting over my astonishment was that Graham had got Dr Lherrison's colour wrong.

'He was black,' Graham said, his lips puckered up, seeming to hold back his words, as he usually did whenever he spoke with force and conviction.

Lherrison was a right-wing mulatto. He was an elitist doctor. He couldn't be the black Marxist Magiot. 'It is a good thing Lherrison's dead,' I said. 'This conversion of colour and ideology would have killed him.'

'But he was black,' Graham insisted, looking at me as if I was the one who was colour-blind. When I didn't say anything more, he insisted. 'He was very dark, black!'

Unknown to even his mulatto friends, Lherrison had entered Graham's narrative as a *noir*. They would consider it the ultimate irony, given the colour caste system in Haiti, for a man as pompous as Lherisson to be turned by an author who despised pomposity into a 'tall elderly negro with a Roman face blackened by the soot of cities and with hair dusted by stone'.

Graham could see that I was upset about his choice of a model for Dr Magiot, so later he sent me a copy of an article he had written four years earlier for the *Sunday Telegraph* magazine in which he had identified Lherrison not by name but by colour in the following effusive terms:

A man I liked above all who was the model for Doctor Magiot in *The Comedians*, a novel I never dreamed then that I would come to write. He was a doctor and a philosopher – but not a Communist. For a time he had been Minister of Health, but found his hands too tied, so he resigned (something which would have been very dangerous to do under Duvalier). Every other year he visited Europe to attend philosophical congresses. He was a very big man and very black, of great dignity and with old-world courtesy. He was to die in exile, more fortunately than Doctor Magiot. Who can tell?

The Comedians leaves no doubt that Graham is firmly on the side of the oppressed. US foreign policy is astutely criticized by Dr Magiot, who predicts that Papa Doc will keep his 'window open towards the east until the Americans give arms to him again'. Magiot notes that the fear of another Cuba, a second communist state at its back door, is reason enough for the United States to forgive Papa Doc his sins. 'There will be no Cuba and no Bay of Pigs here,' says Dr Magiot.

Police Captain Concasseur says, 'We are the true bastion against Communists. No Castro can succeed here. We have a loyal peasantry.'

While the *blan* comedians are self-centred and only half-alive, the Haitians they meet at least exhibit purpose. A young poet, Henri Philipot, nephew of the dead minister, decides along with Dr Magiot to take up arms against Papa Doc. Together they have commitment enough to spare, and they try to breathe some spiritual life into the comedians. But overcoming Brown's cynicism about life is not easy. The Smiths' vegetarian scheme also withers. They, too, get caught up in the violence and corruption of Papa Doc's Haiti, but at least they care about something. As they sail off to neighbouring Santo Domingo, Brown concludes that they are not comedians after all.

Pineda, the cuckolded Latin American ambassador, likewise mirrors the book's title: 'Come on, cheer up, let us all be comedians together. Take one of my cigars. Help yourself at the bar. My Scotch is good. Perhaps even Papa Doc is a comedian.'

Henri Philipot, the would-be guerrilla, replies to the Ambassador, 'He [Papa Doc] is real. Horror is always real.'

The Ambassador rejoins, 'We mustn't complain too much of being comedians – it's an honourable profession. If only we could be good ones the world might gain at least a sense of style. We have failed – that's all. We are bad comedians, we aren't bad men.'

In his way Graham pays just tribute to the role of Haiti's folk religion, Voodoo. 'Certainly I am not against Voodoo,' Dr Magiot tells Mrs Smith. 'How lonely my people would be with Papa Doc as the only power in the land.' Voodoo, Magiot says, 'is the right therapy for Haitians'.

And it is Voodoo (Graham, who attended a Voodoo ceremony in 1954 gets it right) that the young poet Philipot turns for help when all else fails him. 'The gods of Dahomey may be what we need,' he concludes.

Of Philipot, Brown notes, 'Governments had failed him, I had failed him, Jones had failed him – he had no Bren gun; he was here, listening to the drums, waiting, for strength, for courage, for a decision.' Voodoo did not fail him. Brown attends the Voodoo ceremony above Kenscoff, high in the mountains, and the description of the service is remarkably well done for an author who had attended only one Voodoo ceremony in his life – and that more than seven years earlier.

In a letter to Catherine dated 30 August 1954, from El Rancho Hotel, Graham scribbled down his impressions of the Voodoo ceremony he had attended the night before, which had 'lasted until 3 in the morning'. The letter, reproduced in *Graham Greene: A Life in Letters* edited by Richard Greene, is headed with a request to Catherine: 'Will you keep this letter in case I need it to refresh my mind?' In fact, the rite Graham described in his letter was typical of the ceremonies that catered to the tourist trade.

The importance that Haitians attach to sanctifying the dead came through in *The Comedians*. Haitians worship their ancestors. (A body-snatching by Duvalier's police recounted in *The Comedians* is based on an event following Duvalier's 1957 election when a kidnapping took place during the funeral procession of ex-candidate Clément Jumelle.)

'Major' Jones, the charming cheat and boastful liar who is pursued by Captain Concasseur, tries to escape dressed as a Haitian woman and takes asylum with Ambassador Pineda. Jones is finally conned by a jealous Brown, who believes he is having an affair with Martha. This is a chance to put his phoney wartime experiences to use. Undergoing a spiritual transformation and shedding his comedian's mantle, Jones dies a hero's death with poet Philipot's guerrilla band. As the guerrillas withdraw from Haiti across the border into the Dominican Republic – our 1965 trip along the Dominican–Haitian border served Graham well in this last chapter of the book – Philipot, carrying the corpse of the torture victim Joseph, reports that Jones has vowed to keep Papa Doc's pursuing soldiers at bay until the others have had time to reach the border road. Philipot and his guerrillas are interned in an abandoned lunatic asylum near Santo Domingo, not unlike the Haitian guerrilla camp that Graham and I visited in 1965. Brown, himself now not so remote, concedes that he would like to erect a stone where Jones died. 'I shall get the British Ambassador, perhaps a member of the Royal Family.'

Father Bajeux, our melancholy travelling companion during the three-day border trip, enters Graham's novel as the Haitian refugee-priest who says Mass at the Franciscan church in Santo Domingo. Father Bajeux and I had told Graham about the Mass said by Bajeux on 27 April 1964 in memory of those killed during the bloody repression in Haiti the year before. After Mass the Kamoken had posed for their photograph together outside the church. Towards the end of *The Comedians* Philipot leads his dishevelled troops from the lunatic asylum to attend another Mass, this one for Joseph, limping no more from Concasseur's blows, and for Jones, 'whose beliefs were not known' but who 'was included out of courtesy'. Besides the guerrilla survivors there are Brown,

Martha and her family. In the sermon the priest, a liberationist, condemns the indifference of the Browns of the world as evil. Graham's description fits Bajeux: 'a young man of Philipot's age with the light skin of a métis'.

Thus Graham was continually questioning faith, ideology and human behaviour. Shortly after *The Comedians* was published the Roman Catholic Church fell into a state of ferment, especially in Latin America, and 1968 was the year of the Second Vatican Council. The age-old image of the implacable, intolerant and inflexible Catholic Church was being buffeted by the winds of social change. The bishops of Latin America had met in Medellín, Colombia, and promised to sever the Church's centuries-long alliance with the region's military and entrenched élites. Graham was well aware of these events and was devoted to Pope John XXIII, the most popular pontiff in the century.

Graham had written in his foreword:

> A word about the characters of *The Comedians*. I am unlikely to bring an action for libel against myself with any success, yet I want to make it clear that the narrator of this tale, though his name is Brown, is not Greene. Many readers assume – I know it from experience – that an 'I' is always the author. So in my time I have been considered the murderer of a friend, the jealous lover of a civil servant's wife, and an obsessive player at roulette. I don't wish to add to my chameleon-nature characteristics belonging to the cuckolder of a South American diplomat, a possibly illegitimate birth and an education by the Jesuits. Ah, it may be said, Brown is a Catholic and so, we know, is Greene . . . It is often forgotten that, even in the case of a novel laid in England, the story, when it contains more than ten characters, would lack verisimilitude if at least one of them were not a Catholic. Ignorance of this fact of social statistics sometimes gives the English novel a provincial air.
>
> 'I' is not the only imaginary character: none of the others, from such minor players as the British chargé to the principals, has ever existed. A physical trait taken here, a habit of speech, an anecdote – they are boiled up in the kitchen of the unconscious and emerge unrecognizable even to the cook in most cases.
>
> Poor Haiti itself and the character of Doctor Duvalier's rule are not invented . . . The Tontons Macoute are full of men more evil than Concasseur; the interrupted funeral is drawn from fact; many a Joseph limps the streets of Port-au-Prince after his spell of torture, and, though I have never met the young Philipot, I have met guerrillas as courageous and as ill-trained in that former lunatic asylum near Santo Domingo. Only in Santo Domingo have things changed since I began this book – for the worse.

The few Haitians privileged to read the book were eager to identify the players. I myself was increasingly persuaded that Brown, the principal character and narrator, was a composite, blending together slight resemblances to several real-life individuals, including the Hotel Oloffson's American operator at the time of Graham's 1963 visit. This Caribbean entrepreneur appeared blithely uncommitted as far as Papa Doc's dictatorship was concerned and seemed to care only about the effects of media reports on the country's tourism and specifically his clientele. And, in spite of Graham's sweeping disclaimer, other characters in the book brought to mind certain actual people and settings. 'Major' Jones is reminiscent of many wheeler-dealers who were attracted to Haiti by the dictatorship's need for guns. Mr and Mrs Smith, the elderly vegetarians, evoked a similarly idealistic but naïve American couple who were the only other guests besides Graham and the Italian casino operator at the Hotel Oloffson in August 1963.

Henri Philipot closely resembled Fred Baptiste, the commander of the little guerrilla band that invaded Haiti from the Dominican Republic as poorly armed as any guerrilla group ever was. Years later Graham confirmed to me that Fred Baptiste and Hector Riobe, another young Haitian who fought the regime, had inspired the young idealist Philipot. Graham also revealed that the individual he had in mind when he created Captain Concasseur was the intimidating officer who stared at Graham during his long hours in 1963 waiting in the Caserne François Duvalier, the Port-au-Prince police headquarters, for a permit to travel to the south of Haiti.

Graham used the graveyard he found on his 1963 trip to south Haiti as the stage for the dramatic scene in *The Comedians* when the two main characters, Jones and Brown, 'come alive'.

'You expected a witch to open the door to you or a maniacal butler, with a bat dangling from the chandelier,' Graham wrote, describing the Grand Hotel Oloffson as the Trianon.

Our border trip along the Dominican–Haitian frontier was not wasted as source material. The last chapter of *The Comedians* draws heavily upon it. Graham's description of the border was remarkably accurate: 'I was glad enough when we came in sight at dusk, from our grey eroded mountain range where nothing grew, of the deep Dominican forest. You could see all the twists of the frontier by the contrast between our bare rocks and their vegetation. It was the same mountain range, but the trees never crossed into the poor dry land of Haiti.' The vaunted international border road he described as 'a grand name for a track little better than the Great Southern Highway to Aux Cayes'. And he later observes, the road 'was more suitable for mules and cows'.

The mean manager of the Alcoa bauxite operation at Cabo Rojo, Pat Hughson, bore more than a slight resemblance to the book's Mr Schuyler

Wilson, 'a large fat man with an anonymous face shaved as smooth as marble'. Brown's arrival at a mining site in the Dominican Republic after having fled Haiti recalls our arrival seeking a drink and a bed; he describes the scene faithfully if not a little colourfully.

In his introduction to the US edition of *The Comedians,* published in 1966, Graham also noted, 'The best I could do in January 1965 was to make a trip down the Dominican and Haitian border – the scene of my last chapter – in the company of two exiles from Haiti. At least, without Doctor Duvalier's leave, we were able to pass along the edge of the country we loved and to exchange hopes of a happier future.'

Few Haitians living abroad read *The Comedians* for its literary value. They were interested in its political content. It was the opposite for the reviewers. Literary critics and pundits were more interested in *The Comedians* in terms of its literary merit. Much to his mirth, they forever dissected his books in microscopic detail – perhaps because of Graham's eclectic intellectualism – and because this was his first book in five years it received even closer scrutiny. '*The Comedians,*' Graham himself later wrote, 'is the only one of my books which I began with the intention of expressing a point of view and in order to fight – to fight the horror of Papa Doc's dictatorship.' He dragged the enigmatic Dr François Duvalier from the shadows into the floodlights of the world stage.

There were few Haitian exiles around to share my copy of *The Comedians* since, by the time it appeared, most had been forced to flee Santo Domingo because right-wing death squads had them in their gun sights. It was not until the following year that I caught up with Father Bajeux and was able to discuss the book with him. Bajeux was by then working with the Rev. Ivan Illich, who headed a liberal think tank called CIDOC (the Centro Intercultural de Documentación) in Cuernavaca, Mexico. Father Bajeux had just published an all-encompassing document entitled *Un Cri pour Haiti* (*A Cry for Haiti*) in which he analysed the political and economic situation under Duvalierism and called for drastic change. He was still struggling with his personal God.

The Comedians enjoyed wide press coverage. Photographs that I had taken of Graham on the bridge over the Massacre River at Dajabón, using his little Minox camera, were published in both *Time* and *Life* magazines. (By then I was a full-time correspondent for both sister publications.)

When I finally closed my copy of the book and handed it to my wife I thought this would be the end of our story and the end of Graham's Haiti period. As he did following his Indochina, South America and Mexico periods, he would now move on to another place and another book. It was a little sad. Graham's aim in Haiti was nearly perfect. His pen had proved to be a powerful sword against Duvalier. Although it did not decapitate Papa Doc – who managed to retain power for the rest of his life – the book was equivalent to winning a major battle against his evil tyranny.

While Graham and I were later rarely at odds on any topic, we always disagreed about Jolicoeur. He was convinced that Jolicoeur was a government informer, a spy. To me, Aubelin, like so many Haitians, was simply a brash survivor. I had known him since the early days following his arrival from Jacmel and in 1952 had made him 'Personality of the Week' in my newspaper. As a social columnist, one of the first of that journalistic genre in Haiti, he wrote a column for my newspaper. If anything, he was simply over-zealous and adjective-driven.

Graham, I learned later and unbeknownst to him, was under tight Tonton Macoute and police surveillance night and day throughout his 1963 stay. He was not aware that the street people, hangers-on and drivers around him were either Macoutes or police agents with orders to monitor his every move.

Back in Haiti, iron censorship enforced by harsh penalties, possible imprisonment or even death kept *The Comedians* from entering the country. Haitians knew only too well that to be caught with any document or book that was unfavourable to Duvalier was suicidal. Customs inspectors were trained to weed out any literature that could be deemed to impugn Papa Doc. They examined books and even private papers carried by passengers arriving in Haiti. One man was especially assigned at the Port-au-Prince airport to censor foreign newspapers and magazines; scissors unabashedly in hand, he would clip out on the spot any mention of Haiti. Years later, after the Duvalier dynasty collapsed, the censor identified himself to me upon my return via the Port-au-Prince airport, declaring with shameless guile, 'I used to enjoy your stories' (referring to those bylined from elsewhere). It was one of the more bizarre compliments of my journalistic career.

Gradually, however, Haitians learned through their *telejiol* (grapevine), and from other sources, about a book called *The Comedians* written by a famous English writer. They immediately presumed that they were the comedians, and it is not unusual to hear a Haitian say, even today, 'Graham Greene was right. We are *comediens* – actors!' This point of view was not without some logic. For all their earthiness, they exhibited many of the shoulder-shrugging characteristics of the uncommitted, but their masks were often more in keeping with the escapism of carnival, as they endeavoured to shut out reality and survive. Petit Pierre was not alone in his desire simply to stay alive.

The survivors of Papa Doc's death chamber reasoned that they might be safe so long as they did not provoke the beast. As an old Creole saying goes, '*Tout bête genin mode*' (All cornered beasts bite). Graham had provoked the beast; now we waited for Papa Doc to bite.

9 | PAPA DOC REACTS TO THE COMEDIANS

One can see that Graham Greene and his accomplices managed to get
off cheap, because on a simple order from President Duvalier he [Greene]
could have been shot down like a wretch in any corner of the universe.
– *Le Nouveau Monde*, Papa Doc's newspaper

In January 1966 the poet Gérard Daumec, one of Duvalier's top publicists and
literary advisers, returned from London with a copy of the British edition of *The
Comedians*. Papa Doc was not always receptive to bad news, so Daumec later
explained to me that he had handed the book to Duvalier saying, 'We need not
be concerned about this book, it is a *salopré* (a piece of shit). Duvalier, Daumec
recounted, chuckled when he saw the book's title. For several days it reposed on
Papa Doc's desk, next to his Bible and loaded Magnum revolver. It was the only
known copy of *The Comedians* in Haiti. Years later his son Jean-Claude Duvalier
described his father to me, saying, 'Papi was a good actor, a comedian.'

Papa Doc's English was limited and not sufficient to comprehend the novel
fully. He didn't bring up the subject of the book publicly until one day when
he allowed himself to be interviewed on camera by a European television crew
visiting Haiti. During the interview Duvalier dismissed *The Comedians* as
having 'no literary merit whatsoever'. Daumec recalled long afterwards that he
thought that would be the end of it. But it was only the beginning.

Later Duvalier asked Daumec about 'Mister Gween', as Papa Doc pronounced
Graham's name in his nasal whine. Daumec explained that 'Mister Gween' was
a Catholic writer of considerable repute. Papa Doc, Daumec said, became visibly
upset. *The Comedians* was particularly disconcerting to Duvalier because 1966
was the year he had decided to change his image. He had officially pronounced
the end of what he termed the initial 'explosive' phase of his 'revolution' and
had begun to patch up his relations with the Vatican. In his paranoid mind Papa
Doc was convinced that *The Comedians* was part of a wider conspiracy to
sabotage his negotiations with Rome.

Duvalier showed his copy of *The Comedians* to Paul Blanchet, his xeno-
phobic Minister of Information. Blanchet, it was said, understood that Duvalier
was instructing him to 'take care' of Graham and his book. So in his 'newspaper'

Panorama, the circulation of which was limited mostly to government offices, Blanchet published the only review of the book that was permitted in Haiti at the time. His broadside, in fractured French, was headlined, 'Graham Greene: *La machine à faire peur*' ('The machine that frightens'). 'As for Greene,' the review intoned, 'he invents and makes machines to frighten us with. This is a compulsion: he must build up sinister and morbid situations.' Graham's message in *The Comedians*, in *Panorama's* interpretation, 'is a monstrous one and reveals only the Greene-type sensibility, that of the unsatisfied, or a Catholic living in hopelessness; it means a failure of Greene in so far as the difficulty of being a Christian could not be conquered'. The review made no mention of Duvalier or Haiti.

Travel writers were invited to Haiti specifically to dispel the 'lies' spread by *The Comedians*. Duvalier pulled out all the stops to publicize a visit by Emperor Haile Selassie of Ethiopia as well as the opening of the Dr François Duvalier International Jet Airport, constructed at a location known infelicitously as Maïs Gâté (Rotten Corn). Emperor Selassie was on a visit to the Caribbean, and Haiti was one of his stops. Decked out in top hat and tails, Duvalier greeted the Ethiopian ruler at the new airport, which together with the architectural monstrosity known as Duvalierville was one of his pet projects.

When Aubelin Jolicoeur first learned about the book and its characters he was delighted to find himself in a novel by such an illustrious writer as Graham Greene. But when he weighed the potential consequences of his enthusiasm, he became uncharacteristically aloof on the subject. He knew the dangers of attracting the wrong publicity in Papa Doc's Haiti. He was careful for a time not to mention or write a word about *The Comedians*. It did not take long, however, before, true to form, he was bending over feminine hands and introducing himself as Petit Pierre. He confided to his friends, 'If Greene had described me as he knew me, I would have looked like an angel among devils – and that would have made me vulnerable to the Tontons Macoutes. I was grateful to Greene.' However, years later he complained to me, 'Greene is haunted by spies, and he made me into a spy, which I was not. The government saw me as against the regime because I had appeared in a book that was anti-Duvalier. I suffered both ways. People were afraid of me, both sides were afraid of me. The truth is they couldn't touch me because I had no greed for money or power. I don't care for either . . . I live in harmony with myself.' Sitting in his art gallery in Port-au-Prince among unframed, unsold paintings of primitive artists during a 1991 interview, and by then sixty-seven years old, Jolicoeur had lost little of his *joie de vivre*. 'How could I worry? I don't drink or smoke. I indulge only in sex. Oh, la, la!' he said his high-pitched laugh, making the paintings on the wall dance. 'More champagne?' In 2005 Jolicoeur passed away. He was buried in the Jacmel cemetery in which he claimed he had been born. He died a poor man.

In a letter to me dated 20 December 1965 Graham announced, 'I am leaving England on January 1 to take up residence abroad and my address will be 130 Boulevard Malesherbes, Paris 17. Do look me up if you are ever in Paris at the same time as me.' Just as *The Comedians* appeared in the bookshops, he was busy writing the screenplay for the movie version of his novel. In another letter to me, written from his new base in Paris and dated 5 January 1966, he could hardly conceal his excitement. The film rights had been sold, he reported, even before the book was finished. Hollywood's Metro-Goldwyn-Mayer had bought the rights and intended to make it a big-budget film with a stellar cast; the studio hoped to begin filming within days. In his letter Graham added:

> It was a very happy surprise when I came back here from Canada after Christmas to find your long letter. Even more pleasant was the fact that you liked *The Comedians*. I was very much afraid that you might find that I had got everything wrong owing to my short acquaintance with the country, and it gives me enormous pleasure that you praised it. I had heard in Havana that they were broadcasting extracts from the book so Papa Doc must be quite irritated by it.

He was also pleased, he said, that the film's director would be Peter Glenville, a Brit who had directed Graham's play, *The Living Room*. Glenville had abandoned his law studies at Oxford to pursue a career in the theatre. He became a celebrated stage director in London and eventually moved to Hollywood.

In Port-au-Prince, the poet–sycophant Gérard Daumec broke the news to Papa Doc: *The Comedians* was going to be made into a movie. A dangerous silence ensued, Daumec recalled to me. When Papa Doc finally lifted his head from his desk he uttered one word. 'Conspiracy!'

To Duvalier, this was another phase in a plot to sabotage his self-styled 'revolution'. His terror apparatus continued to operate but on a slightly more sophisticated level, as he was making an effort to entice tourists back to Haiti. In fact, a government communiqué had recently instructed Haitians to go out in the evenings and enjoy themselves. The government wanted to make the capital's night life more attractive, and the official communiqué directed 'state employees and Duvalierists in general . . . to frequent bars, restaurants, and the International Casino'. During the height of repression the regime had turned the city after sundown into a morgue. Now the Duvalier faithful were under orders to bring it back to life. It was not an easy transition. Only the highest-ranking bureaucrats and gun-toting Macoutes ventured out at night to paint the town red.

Meanwhile Papa Doc had triumphed over Rome. His excommunication was revoked, and he returned to a state of grace in the Catholic Church. The

Holy See had agreed to Duvalier's choice for the post of Archbishop of Port-au-Prince, Monsignor François Wolf Ligonde. He was Haitian-born and considered a Duvalierist.

To Papa Doc the film version of *The Comedians* was a distraction of the worst kind. Feeding his paranoia, Duvalier's palace ghostwriter, Gérard de Catalogne, who was also in charge of reviving Haitian tourism, suggested that the impact of the film version of *The Comedians* could be disastrous for tourism. The film, according to Daumec, was suddenly seen by Papa Doc as a threatening monster. Foreign Minister René Chalmers and Gérard de Catalogne were called to the Palace for what amounted to a council of war. Daumec sat next to Papa Doc. Various options and plans were presented and studied. Duvalier was more than ever convinced that the film was part of a larger CIA conspiracy and that Graham was working for the CIA.

According to Daumec's account, Chalmers was instructed to deprive the producers of the movie of a location in which to film it. He was to inform each and every country where the film could potentially be shot, including the United States and the Caribbean and African nations, that allowing it to be made on their territory would be interpreted as a hostile act against Haiti and its President-for-Life and that it would lead to grave consequences. In retrospect, Papa Doc's attempt to extend the long arm of his censorship around the globe must go down as one of the more bizarre episodes in diplomatic history.

The Comedians (the book) was still being reviewed in the United States when Peter Glenville began his search for the film location. It would have to be a place that resembled Haiti yet offered all of the necessary amenities to shoot a major motion picture. 'I must have done the world looking for a location,' Glenville recalled. He said he had visited Salvador de Bahia in Brazil, Martinique and Guadeloupe in the French Caribbean and several other islands in search of a Haiti lookalike. 'French Guinea wasn't bad, but it had its limitations, and I finally settled on Dahomey in Africa,' Glenville explained in a 1993 interview with me at his summer home in San Miguel de Allende, Mexico.

Dahomey, now known as Benin, was chosen for a number of reasons, he added. Dahomeyans spoke French in addition to their native Fon language; and there were daily flights to Paris, which meant the film rushes could be sent back to the editing studio there every day. Not least important for an all-star cast working on location in West Africa, 'We could receive food flown out daily from Paris.' The President of Dahomey, General Christophe Soglo, was hospitable and wise enough to understand that the film would bring business and an influx of money to his country of 2,300,000 people at a time when its economy was at a standstill. Revenues from Dahomey's principal exports of palm-tree products and castor oil were not enough to cover the government's $29 million annual budget. Moreover, the government had guesthouses available, which it was only too happy to rent. The country's largest city, Cotonou, is close to the sea on the Gulf of Guinea, which was important for the film. The government had also built an impressive four-lane sodium-lit boulevard along Cotonou's seafront. 'And I had six stars to worry about, so I chose Dahomey,' Glenville concluded.

In another important step in preparing for the movie Glenville decided it was worth the risk to visit Haiti. Posing as a tourist, he flew to Port-au-Prince in October 1966 to see the country for himself and savour the character of the Grand Hotel Oloffson. Glenville was accompanied by a French architect (Glenville identified him to me as an interior decorator) whose job would be to design the movie-set replica of the Oloffson, which would be reproduced in the film as the Hotel Trianon.

Glenville had barely been shown into his room at the Oloffson – the 'John Gielgud Suite' – when, as if on cue, Aubelin Jolicoeur appeared and introduced himself, adding that he was the famous Petit Pierre of the Graham Greene novel *The Comedians*. Years later Jolicoeur charged that Glenville 'lied to me, saying he was here to make a film on the life of Toussaint L'Ouverture, our great revolutionary hero'.

Glenville got more than a taste of the fear and anxiety that permeated Duvalier's police state. His most memorable experience occurred while he and his architect colleague were waiting at the Port-au-Prince airport preparing to depart. 'It was a horrendous experience,' Glenville recalled. A Haitian friend had informed him that an edition of a New York publication containing an article about *The Comedians* being made into a movie had just arrived, and a Duvalierist airport censor was dispatching the article to the Palace. The article mentioned that Glenville was going to direct the movie.

'There we were waiting at the airport when an announcement said our plane was delayed. I really thought they were going to nail us at the last moment,' Glenville recounted. 'The American ambassador had warned us that there was very little foreign embassies could do for their nationals in Haiti when they were imprisoned.' Glenville and his architect worried about the innumerable photographs they had taken for reference to recreate Haiti in Africa. Had Papa Doc by now got word of their mission? Finally their flight was called, but neither allowed himself a sigh of relief until Haiti was far behind.

When Papa Doc read the news that Dahomey would be the location for the filming of *The Comedians,* he was, as described by Daumec, apoplectic. Dahomey of all countries! Duvalier saw this as a treasonable act. The people of this West African nation have a special kinship with Haitians. Dahomey was the ancestral home of many Haitians whose forebears had been taken away and sold as slaves. Besides being their original home, the country had spiritual significance for

Haitians, who still practised the Dahomey Voodoo rites. Duvalier ordered Foreign Minister Chalmers to make a strenuous protest to Cotonou. President Soglo, no shrinking violet himself – he had been instrumental in ousting three of his predecessors since the country's independence – shrugged off Duvalier's efforts to quash the filming.

The cast of *The Comedians* began descending on the small African nation and setting up house. Their behind-the-scenes experiences during the filming were a saga in themselves. Cotonou was not exactly a replica of Port-au-Prince. Although it is near the sea, it lacks the backdrop of mountains. Still, there were plenty of similarities. Dahomey was also a tropical black country that had been colonized by the French. Following independence in 1960 it also suffered a series of coups d'état.

The film luminaries arriving in Cotonou included Elizabeth Taylor, her husband and co-star Richard Burton and actors Alec Guinness, Peter Ustinov, James Earl Jones (who played Dr Magiot) and Raymond St Jacques, whose character was the sadistic police officer Concasseur. Roscoe Lee Browne, who was an uncanny Jolicoeur lookalike, was on hand as Petit Pierre. Max Pinchinat, a Haitian painter who lived in Paris, was persuaded to act as the fictional *houngan* (Voodoo priest). (During the filming Pinchinat insisted on biting the head off a live chicken and not a fake one, despite worries about protests from the Society for the Prevention of Cruelty to Animals.)

'In the papers yesterday there is news that Richard Burton and Elizabeth Taylor . . . have received anonymous threats of what will happen to them if they play in the film which is starting in a few days in Dahomey,' Graham reported in a letter to me. 'I hope to go there for ten days in February to see how things are getting on.'

When Graham arrived in Dahomey, he recalled, he got a 'terrible shock'. While driving from the airport to the capital, he was marvelling at certain similarities to Port-au-Prince when suddenly an iron sign loomed ahead along the roadway, with a look of permanence, that announced: 'Welcome to Haiti.' Although the sign was only a prop for the movie, for an anxious moment Graham thought he had landed at the new Dr François Duvalier International Jet Airport in Port-au-Prince instead of Cotonou.

Because of various misfortunes that plagued the set, many members of the film crew began to suspect that Duvalier had laid a Voodoo curse on them. In his autobiography, *Blessings in Disguise*, Alec Guinness relates:

> There was an ugly rumour that Papa Doc, who bitterly resented Greene's account of his country and its politics, had sent a Voodoo priest to Dahomey to disrupt the film. Apparently Voodoo spells cannot travel over water and have to be operated close at hand. All great nonsense, I

am sure, but, whether the rumour was true or not, on the first day of filming one of the unit stumbled on the beach, possibly from a heart attack, and drowned in a foot of water before anyone could assist him. Several people complained of difficulty in breathing, suffering from acute headaches and deep depression; one or two had to be sent home.

There were also real-world concerns. In his book *Rich: The Life of Richard Burton* Melvyn Bragg recounts that because the book of *The Comedians* had upset many people the threat of kidnapping hung over the Burtons through their connection with the film. The family were receiving a number of kidnapping alarms a week, and their children all had individually assigned guards accompanying them when away from their home in Gstaad or school.

By September 1966 the Dominican Republic's civil war and US intervention had ended. Following the truce and elections, the long-time Trujillo bureaucrat, Joaquín Balaguer, a seasoned, crafty politician, was back in power, and Washington was appeased. The Haitian exiles in the Dominican Republic, including their leader Fred Baptiste and his brother Renel, scattered as if to the wind. They were no longer welcome, partly because they had fought on the side of the Constitutionalists. In retaliation they had become targets of La Banda, right-wing death squads. Balaguer also re-established diplomatic relations with Papa Doc. The Dominican Republic was no longer hospitable territory for anti-Duvalier exiles. *Time* magazine transferred me to its Mexico City bureau, so again my family, and I also started a new life in a new land.

In a letter from Paris, dated 4 May 1968, Graham wrote, 'I feel a little sad about having shot my bolt as far as Haiti is concerned, and wish I could find another arrow in my quiver.' Despite intensive research into Graham's background, the team at Duvalier's Foreign Ministry had learned relatively little about the real-life Mr Greene. Yet even Graham admired the amount of work that went into producing what would become Papa Doc's official exposé of Graham's 'flawed character'.

In Haiti, as in any nation where politics are personal and partisan, character assassinations of writers were as old as the publishing business. Nevertheless an attack in the form of a slick government-printed booklet, as was produced on Duvalier's orders against Graham, was unprecedented even in Haiti. This was no ordinary government protest. It was an official highly orchestrated effort to discredit an internationally renowned author. Styled as an official Haitian Foreign Ministry bulletin, the 92-page document was devoted entirely to denouncing Graham Greene and the dark conspiratorial forces that allegedly motivated him. It was a classic example of the paranoid's complaint – 'It's all a plot against me' – while cheering the achievements of Dr Duvalier and his 'revolution'. The main text consisted of ten essays. The authors, who were duly credited, were all staff members of the Foreign Ministry, with several drawn from the protocol section. Father Bajeux has referred to them as Papa Doc's 'intellectual Macoutes'. The broadside's purple prose was interspersed with gripping photographs reflecting Papa Doc's paranoid narcissism – the President-for-Life himself, the Dr François Duvalier International Airport, the Dr François Duvalier Police Headquarters, the Dr François Duvalier Tax Office. There were pictures of the still-uncompleted Duvalierville, which Graham had described in *The Comedians* as a 'wilderness of cement'.

A memorandum dispatched by Foreign Minister René Chalmers to all Haitian chiefs of diplomatic missions abroad, and to all foreign diplomatic missions in Haiti, left no doubt as to the seriousness of purpose of the government bulletin. Dated 15 January 1968, the book-length memorandum announced that it was being distributed to 'call attention to the film *The Comedians* staged by the Metro Goldwin [*sic*] Mayer, the theme of which is inspired by Graham Greene's novel of the same name'. The document, printed in French and English, warned:

> The frankly hostile character of this film in which the Republic of Haiti, its government and its Chief are criticized, the acrimonious tone of each sequence in which the most unlikely facts are supposedly true to life, the very price paid for staging of the film permit one to infer that Graham Greene's novel and the film drawn from it are part of a vast plan tending to prepare international public opinion for an action that might be carried out on a larger scale against the Republic of Haiti, the last episode of which could be an invasion of our territory with all its detrimental incidences [*sic*].
>
> Therefore, this Chancellery is inclined to believe that the shooting of this film and its showing in different countries constitute an act of indirect aggression against the Republic of Haiti. This is why it would appreciate it if the Chiefs of the Diplomatic Missions of Haiti accredited in foreign countries would lodge protests in the name of the Haitian Government, with the Chancelleries of the countries to which they are accredited, against the showing of this film that is considered an act of indirect aggression against the Republic of Haiti, and conse-quently likely to weaken the traditional bonds of friendship existing between those countries and Haiti.

Lucien Montas, who headed the cultural department of the Foreign Ministry (while doubling as a journalist for the local daily *Nouvelliste*), was instructed by Chalmers to write the foreword. He called Graham 'the prey to a thousand complexes and obsessions' and went on to declare that Graham's 'nightmarish images in his frenzied imagination, together with a pessimistic vision of the world', were a 'reflection of an unbalanced and proudly perverted self'.

The essays were entitled, in order: 'Graham Greene's Biographical Panorama'; 'Graham Greene's Swindle'; 'Could Graham Greene Be an Advocate of the Theory of Existence of Superior Races?'; 'Does Graham Greene Know the History of Haiti?'; 'Achievements of the Haitian Government'; 'Graham Greene, or the Scaring Machine'; '*The Comedians*: A Commissioned Work'; 'Graham Greene's Contemner of [*sic*, evidently meaning 'Contempt for'] the Negro Race'; 'The Political Philosophy of the Government of His Excellency Dr François Duvalier'; 'Aren't Graham Greene's Novel, *The Comedians* and Peter Greenville's [*sic*] Film an Episode of the International Plot Against the Haitian Government?'

Yves Massillon, a protocol officer at the Haitian Foreign Ministry, wrote two of the essays. In the first, entitled 'Graham Greene's Biographical Panorama', Massillon alleged that Graham, after a 'morbid adolescence', became a 'young Communist stool pigeon'. After a wasted youth, Massillon further alleged, Graham launched

> an all-out drive for money in 1938. At long last, the war! The war and the opportunity to get rich! He is a secret agent in Africa under cover of a writer. But this pseudo-writer, spotted in Indo-China and Havana after the war, is shadowed wherever he is. Yet, he goes on with his activity of novelist–secret agent and writes a commissioned novel, *The Comedians*, about the Republic of Haiti where he stayed less than fifteen days.

Warming to his subject, Massillon declaimed:

> Will Graham Greene ever stop his many repudiations, 'stool-pigeoning' and spying activities; his malignant attacks, lies, and belated apologies? Will he ever stop contributing his talent to purposes unworthy of a true writer? That is the question. Considering the man's career, we can't expect anything good from him. A [religious] conversion may have some value only in respect to its motivations, significance, and results. Graham Greene's didn't bring about any amelioration which could have made him study the problems of the Haitian people with more open-mindedness with a view to finding the root causes of a revolution which – like all revolutions – had its excesses, these excesses which we think are nothing as compared with what goes on elsewhere. But Graham Greene did not understand at all the Haitian revolutionary reality, this reality that would have ended up in plain anarchy had it not been for an eminently intelligent control by the Chief of the nation, Physician,

Ethnologist and Sociologist, Dr François Duvalier. Greene is fretful because of the reserved attitude of a friendly Big Power [presumably an allusion to the United States] which has more than once stumbled against the complexity of our problems. Such reticence should have taught Greene a lesson. When one does not understand, either he asks for information or he shuts up.

Another contributor concluded his disquisition, 'Graham Greene's Swindle', by decrying what he termed Graham's physical description of Haiti:

The rusty colors of our crops deprived of water, the barrenness of our hillsides ravaged by erosion, misery, disease, illiteracy, and even the infirmity of our poor are more in keeping with the pessimistic vision of a Graham Greene or a Mr Brown in his novel than an unbiased consideration of under-development which is not specific to Haiti.

A fourth jeremiad branded Graham a 'tormented racist' on the 'payroll' of leading racists of the day. Another contributor proclaimed, 'Graham Greene thought he was going to destroy Haiti's prestige; he may now bite his lips, gnaw his thumbs; sooner or later, he will have to rid his sickly mind of the despicable comedians of his own kind.' Still another diatribe asserted without elaboration, 'Former torturer Graham Greene is annoyed no end upon finding that Haiti is the chosen land for social justice in this world of hatred and violence.'

Massillon, in his second blast at Graham, expanded on the theme that he was a secret agent at work to defame hapless Haiti. Massillon charged that Graham's putative connection with the British Secret Service had just been brought to light in Moscow by Harold 'Kim' Philby who, while himself a British Secret Service officer, was also a Soviet agent. Indeed, Massillon pointed out that in the Latin American edition of *Time*, in the issue of 29 December 1967, on page 20 under the heading 'Espionage' one can read the following: 'Between the caviar and cognac, Philby managed to sandwich in a few new fascinating revelations about his past activities. He had worked, he claimed, with such unheralded British spies as novelist Graham Greene . . . and the late Ian Fleming.' Crowed Massillon: 'Thus it is that the present is better understood through a study of the past; however, one must have a thorough knowledge of the past to understand why the novel *The Comedians* was written. Why millions were spent in the making of the film and why none other than Graham Greene was called upon for the work.'

The principle thrust of the Haitian Foreign Ministry broadside was that both the book and the film were part of some vast amorphous plot against

Haiti. The expelled British Ambassador G.T. Corley-Smith was brought into the purported conspiracy, accused by Massillon of 'insolent dealings'. Another essayist accused Graham of fostering 'psychological preparation for a frantic counter-revolution'.

In a hyperbolic wrap-up, Clément Vincent of Duvalier's protocol staff declared:

> Once more the countries using Graham Greene and Peter Greenville [*sic*] as a cover-up have committed the crime of indirect aggression against the Black Republic which is only guilty of pride and dignity. Obviously Graham Greene and Peter Greenville are only puppets in a tragic-comic show put up by some well-known countries against Haiti which still faces some of the most strenuous hardships in its existence as a free and independent nation, after having fought unaided against the slavery system for three centuries and a half, broken its fetters, proclaimed its independence in the face of an astonished world 164 years ago, and paid with the blood of its people for the place it occupies among civilized nations.
>
> We will not be caught off guard. Our knowledge of the fighting tactics of our opponents supports our beliefs that Graham Greene's novel *The Comedians* as well as Peter Greenville's movie inspired by the said novel constitute a prelude to some action that may be carried out on a large scale against our country. This unprecedented performance in the art of disparagement can be nothing else than the first step toward a bolder plan against Haiti.

If Duvalier thought his publishing offensive would intimidate Graham, he was sadly in error. Graham, although usually reserved and modest, revelled openly in the verbal assault coming from a tyrant such as Papa Doc. The whole charade appealed to Graham's contrarian sense of humour, so he mischievously promoted the attack on his character. As an ingenious practical joker, Graham exploited Papa Doc's canards to startle others. With Graham himself acting as a publicist for Duvalier's bizarre broadside – spreading word among friends and interviewers about the 'remarkable document' – it quickly became a collector's item.

The first I heard of Duvalier's literary assault was in a letter from Graham, dated 20 February 1969, which I received in Mexico City. He could hardly conceal his excitement and mirth. 'Have you seen his book about me in French and English called *Graham Greene Démasqué (Finally Unmasked)*? If you haven't seen it get somebody to ask for it from the embassy in Mexico City. It's a treasure.' In a letter to me two months later, Graham again recommended that I get a copy of the booklet before it disappeared. Still clearly elated, he wrote, 'Papa Doc honoured me.'

Despite my efforts, I could never find a copy in Mexico. The Haitian embassy there said it didn't have any. It was only years later, after the Duvalier dynasty collapsed in 1986, that I finally managed to locate one in the archives of the Foreign Ministry in Port-au-Prince. (The Foreign Ministry collapsed into rubble along with its archives in the January 2010 earthquake.)

In an op-ed article in the *Sunday Telegraph* on Sunday 3 December 1976, entitled 'Black Humour in Haiti', Graham commented:

> If I had known the way the President regarded me, my fears would have seemed more rational. *The Comedians*, I am glad to say, touched him on the raw. He even attacked it personally in an interview he gave in *Le Matin*, a paper in Port-au-Prince – the only review I have ever received from a Chief of State. *'Le livre n'est pas bien écrit. Comme l'œuvre d'un écrivain et d'un journaliste, le livre n'a aucune valeur.'* ['The book is not well written. As the work of a writer and journalist it possesses no value whatsoever.']
>
> Was it possible I disturbed his dreams as he had disturbed mine? For five long years after my visit, his Ministry of Foreign Affairs published an elaborate and elegant brochure, illustrated, on glossy paper, dealing with my case. A lot of research had gone into its preparation, with many quotations drawn from the introductions I had written for a French edition of my books. Printed in French and English and entitled *Graham Greene Démasqué (Finally Exposed)*, it included a rather biased sketch of my career. This expensive work was distributed to the Press through the Haitian Embassies in Europe, but distribution ceased abruptly when the President found the result was not the one he desired.

Graham even quoted from the booklet in which he said he was called 'A liar, a cretin, a stool pigeon . . . unbalanced, sadistic, perverted . . . a perfect ignoramus', accused of 'lying to his heart's content' and of being 'the shame of proud and noble England . . . a spy . . . a drug addict. . . a torturer'. 'The last epithet has always a little puzzled me,' Graham concluded. 'I am proud to have had Haitian friends who fought courageously in the mountains against Doctor Duvalier, but a writer is not so powerless as he usually feels, and a pen, as well as a silver bullet, can draw blood.'

On 9 October 1968 I had received a brown envelope addressed in Graham's small script. In it was a transcript of a British television programme, *Twenty-Four Hours,* which had a hilarious field day with the 'official counter-blast from Duvalier against Greene's last novel, *The Comedians*'. The commentator ends by noting, 'All in all it's the kind of accolade he [Greene] may well prize even more highly than his Companionship of Honour, his Honorary Doctorate and the other bits and pieces he's collected since he began writing forty years ago. By the way,' the commentator added in a final dig at Papa Doc's literary *chef d'œuvre*, 'there's one misspelling the Haitians missed. On page 33 of their glossy book they call President Harry Truman President Hairy Truman.'

Naturally Graham was not about to retreat or apologize for *The Comedians*. For him the Haitian government's published 'bulletin' and its essays proved only that he had bloodied Papa Doc with the pen, if not the sword, and he was even optimistic – overly optimistic, it turned out – about Papa Doc's political demise. Graham ended a letter to me dated 6 January 1970 with the words, 'Let's hope that before the end of the year we can all meet again in Port-au-Prince!' It didn't happen – but not because he was anything like his uninvolved character, Brown. Papa Doc hung on to power until his death from natural causes in 1971.

Alan Whicker of Yorkshire Television interviewed Papa Doc in 1968 while riding in the presidential limousine. He asked Duvalier what he thought of Graham Greene's *The Comedians*. Duvalier is seen touching his right temple with his index finger while responding, 'He is crazy, he is a poor man mentally . . . he didn't say the truth about Haiti, because maybe they say he was out of money, he got money from people in Haiti or from political exiles.'

The MGM Distribution and Production Company, along with its owner–partner Maximilian/Trianon, released the film version of *The Comedians* in late 1967. The producer and director was Peter Glenville, with a screenplay by Graham. It was the first film made of a Graham Greene book in seven years, since the 1960 release of *Our Man in Havana*. Whether *The Comedians* was a good or bad film from a critic's perspective, its star cast ensured that millions would see this feature production around the world. It would establish Papa Doc and his Tontons Macoutes once and for all as men of evil.

When I finally had an opportunity to see the film, while on assignment in San Diego, I found it extremely painful to watch. The reason Graham had written the script, the last he would write, he later told me, was to make sure that his arrow hit its mark, portraying the terror of the Duvalier years. To achieve maximum effect he had dropped the early part of the book, in which *The Comedians* are introduced sailing aboard the *Medea* to Haiti. He had also changed the ending. At the end of the movie, Martha (Elizabeth Taylor) looks down from the Miami-bound plane and laments, 'Poor Haiti.' And the film makes it resoundingly clear that Papa Doc's dictatorship and his Tontons Macoutes are responsible for turning this once beautiful country into 'poor Haiti'.

The film opens with young voices singing praise to 'Duvalier, President-for-Life, creator of the New Haiti, supreme leader of the nation, idol of the masses and spiritual leader of the nation'. While Papa Doc himself is portrayed only fleetingly, walking inside the Palace followed by two nurses, signs and references to him abound. Duvalier's image and his red-and-black flag are plastered everywhere – on a billboard, even in a brothel. The atmosphere of terror is established near the beginning of the film as the camera pans along a row of photographs of grotesque corpses, all marked with a large red 'X' indicating that the victims have been eliminated. Captain Concasseur is seen tracing another red-pencilled 'X' across the photo of yet another victim. The Macoutes are real enough in their dark glasses and fedoras. Overlooking the nightmarish panorama, exuding its own haunting Charles Addams-like decadence, the replica of the Grand Hotel Oloffson was almost perfect.

Dr Magiot (who in the book is shot) has his throat cut by the Tontons Macoutes, collapsing dead on top of a patient on whom he is operating. The scene sent a communal shudder through the audience in which I was seated. There were reports of Haitian women, exiled in New York, fainting while viewing the film and being carried out of the cinema and others screaming and yelling when they saw the captured guerrillas Drouin and Numa being executed. The film was far too realistic for many expatriate Haitians, especially those who had lost relatives in the real world of Papa Doc's Haiti.

Time magazine gave *The Comedians* a column-and-a-half movie review on 3 November 1967 entitled, 'Hell in Haiti'. Noting that the film ran for two hours and forty minutes, the *Time* critic commented:

> *The Comedians* has everything but economy. The director, Peter Glenville, has tarried with a story that might have been twice as good at half the length. Unlike the novel, in which Greene's obsessive concern with mankind's spiritual underworld is subdued, his scenario seems as overtly moralistic as a passion play . . . [However,] French Photographer Henri Decae's location shots offer a remarkable re-creation of a land where images of Voodoo gods and the Virgin Mary are worshipped at the same rituals. The cast of supporting villains and victims – led by Peter Ustinov – is uniformly excellent. As a fading beauty with a German accent, [Elizabeth] Taylor is reasonably effective, but [Richard] Burton, playing an exhausted anti-hero in the same style as his memorable *The Spy Who Came In From The Cold*, seems to have stepped from the pages of the novel. Ironically, the film's most stirring moments are not its overheated love scenes but the brief encounter between Burton and Guinness. In one, Guinness, a short day's journey from death, recounts his wasted life of lies in a graveyard retreat. Priest-like, Burton answers the tortured confessions with a symbolic absolution. At such moments

of transcendent drama – and there are enough to make it worthwhile
– *The Comedians* is easily forgiven its other sins.

Similarly typical of the mixed reviews was John Russell Taylor's assessment
in *The Times* on 18 January 1968: 'It is just loaded with production values.
Unfortunately, loaded is the operative word. Under there somewhere is perhaps
quite an interesting little film trying to get out, but if so, it is smothered at
birth.'

Graham, of course, had his own after-the-fact critique. He told Gene D.
Phillips in a 1969 interview published in the *Catholic World*:

> My biggest problem when adapting one of my novels for the screen is
> that the kind of book I write, from the single point of view of one
> character, cannot be done the same way on the screen. You cannot look
> through the eyes of one character in a film. The novel (*The Comedians*)
> was told from Brown's point of view. Brown remains the character who
> is on the screen more than any of the others. His comments on others
> are often there. But we still do not see others completely from his point
> of view as we do in the novel.

As noted, Graham had changed the film's ending from that of the book.
'Brown is a beachcomber-type character. He has been washed up on the beach
of Haiti,' Graham explained in the *Catholic World* interview.

> He is a person who could not be better than he is, although he would
> like to be. At the end of the novel, which is black comedy, he becomes
> an undertaker: he is just being washed up on another shore. In the film
> the ending is different but the point is the same. Brown is forced to join
> the guerrillas in the hills because he cannot return to Port-au-Prince.
> He does not want to go and he has no experience in guerrilla warfare,
> but he makes the best of the situation.

Discussing the film in a letter to me, Graham said he had hoped to have
the film shot in black and white, feeling that colour gave it a phoney look.
However, as a long-time film critic himself who was quite familiar with the
industry, he acknowledged that the major film studios of the time wouldn't
support a black-and-white film. One of the reasons, he said, was television sales;
colour television had arrived on the scene only a few years earlier. He thought
black and white would have made it a better film, more of *cinéma vérité*.

The most common criticism of the book and the film among Haitian
intellectuals who were able to read the novel and view the film overseas was

that the love story took up too much time, which is against the tradition of Haitian fiction, where politics reigns supreme. Moreover, many non-Duvalierist Haitians resented the scenes in the movie in which Brown addresses a band of anti-Duvalier insurgents.

Brown has finally been persuaded by the young Philipot to join the guerrillas in the hills after Captain Concasseur kills Major Jones and is in turn killed by the guerrillas. Forced at last to make a commitment, Brown says, 'I'm cornered', and the young artist–guerrilla says, 'My men are waiting . . . For some reason they believe that white men are the only true experts in killing.'

With Philipot and barman Joseph, Brown climbs the mountain and joins the assembled insurgents, who stand in ranks armed with a motley assortment of weapons including gardening tools and even a tin insecticide sprayer. Of the latter weapon Brown asks Philipot, 'What is this supposed to be?'

'The closest we could come to liquid fire,' Philipot responds. 'It's full of petrol. Don't discourage them.'

Then, standing before the ragtag band of rebels, Brown launches into his speech – in English (which none of them understands): 'Tomorrow we attack the Tontons Macoutes. We are crazy fools. You don't know how to fight. I don't know how to fight. We are going to get the Tontons, we, with a handful of shotguns, machetes and a garden spray, a hotel keeper, a painter, a barman and you. You stupid bastards, the rabble of the cockpits and the slums, my ragged regiment!'

Some Haitians felt Brown's oration was unjust and humiliating. They saw it as a manifestation of the white foreigners' superiority complex. They saw it as an insult to the Kamoken. But Brown's soliloquy was closer to the truth than many Haitians would admit: a none-too-exaggerated caricature of the anti-Duvalier insurgents – brave, untrained, mostly unarmed and, as Brown himself exemplified, badly led.

The Comedians was not a particularly successful film in terms of mass audience appeal, despite it being a Graham Greene adaptation with a star cast. In his book *Blessings in Disguise* Alec Guinness wrote that he was impressed by Richard Burton's 'generosity as an actor', noting, 'He gave himself and his talent in the most unselfish way I have ever encountered in a great star.'

Papa Doc's guile was not to be underestimated. A few weeks after the film was released, Guinness recounts, he and his wife received an invitation from Haiti 'to spend Christmas in Haiti' as Papa Doc's guest, so that 'we could see for ourselves what the country was *really* like. I had a notion that if we were rash enough to accept we might end up as zombies, turning spits in the kitchen of some Haitian palace; so we declined, with flowery politeness.'

Nevertheless there was one footnote that doubtless gave Papa Doc a moment of glee. Four weeks after the movie opened in cinemas around the world, on Christmas Day 1967, President Soglo of Dahomey was booted out of office by his subordinates. As Soglo flew off to Paris to join the three other ex-presidents of Dahomey living in exile, several mundane explanations were cited for his overthrow, among them Soglo's tough austerity programme which had included reducing the salaries of civil servants and even turning off their air-conditioning. However, there were those who suspected a darker cause – the long arm of Papa Doc and his powers of Voodoo, in retaliation for the filming of *The Comedians* in Dahomey. Jokingly, even Graham said he felt that Voodoo should receive some credit for Soglo's downfall.

The reports that Duvalier received from his agents abroad painted the film as shocking – but not for the reasons that shocked most viewers. Doc didn't see himself as others did. To him there was nothing wrong with his use of violence and bloodshed to retain absolute power. He saw nothing wrong with his role as judge and jury. Both Duvalier and God, in that order, should decide who would live or die. Like most dictators, Papa Doc suffered from pathological narcissism; having lost touch with reality, he firmly believed that he was the embodiment of right and that his ends justified the means. What outraged him was that *The Comedians*, in both its book and film versions, did not join his claque.

By now Duvalier was killing his own loyal officers, many of whom had killed for him. After a full decade in power, Papa Doc worked long hours, sometimes past midnight, micro-managing the details of his tropical tyranny. Diabetic and with a weakened heart, he looked much older than his sixty years. Within the Palace's private quarters he was at war with his own family, upon whom he had lavished all that money could buy. His eldest daughter, Marie-Denise, had defied him and married an army officer whom Doc accused of plotting his assassination.

Confronting the outside world, Papa Doc and his demons were angry. 'Mr Grem Gween is attacking me in a movie too!' Doc raged to his aide Gérard Daumec, who in turn parroted to a visiting newsman, 'Everyone in Haiti knows that the CIA paid Graham Greene to publish this book attacking Haiti, and now they've made a movie of it.'

As outrageous as it may sound to anyone who appreciates literary integrity, the view that any book or magazine article not favourable to the regime must have been paid for by the regime's enemies was common in Haiti (as in much of Latin America). It wasn't a question of whether the writer or reporter was stating facts about the country. Money, it was assumed by Duvalierists (as well as by many Haitians on the political sidelines), was the only motivating factor that would induce a writer or reporter to risk incurring Papa Doc's wrath. Even such a well-known and successful author as Graham had to have an ulterior motive for writing such a book and making such a movie. Of course, in Haiti under Papa Doc there was no such thing as literary freedom; Duvalier had executed four of Haiti's best-known authors.

Papa Doc became particularly mesmerized by the audience-shocking scene described to him in which Dr Magiot meets his gory end. In the scene Papa Doc's Tontons Macoutes arrive to confront Dr Magiot in his hospital's operating theatre. He sees them coming, but he doesn't run and calmly continues his operation. While two Macoutes stand guard with guns drawn, a third takes a surgical knife from the table and, seizing Dr Magiot from behind, proceeds to cut his throat. The audience is treated to a lifelike throat-slitting with blood spurting from Magiot's jugular vein. The Marxist physician collapses on top of his patient and dies with his surgical cap still on his head. 'It has never happened. It is a dirty, dirty lie,' Papa Doc protested to Daumec.

'This barbaric act, above all, made Dr Duvalier mad,' Daumec explained. Interestingly – and in a bizarre reflection of Papa Doc's twisted mentality – he found the ghastly scene an affront to *his* Hippocratic oath.

Graham had no idea just how deeply his arrow had struck its mark with the film version of *The Comedians*. It would be years before the ensuing reaction in Haiti's hermetically sealed National Palace could be pieced together. When I eventually informed Graham of the pain he had caused the regime, he reacted with almost youthful glee and quipped sarcastically, 'I'm so glad I could be of help.'

So far as is known, Papa Doc never actually saw the film version of *The Comedians*. The ban on the film in Haiti was total, with not even a sneak preview reported at the Palace. Papa Doc, it was said, relied completely on the reviews of the film provided by his agents abroad, and he read with alarm the glowing reports in the exile press about the movie. Thus the battle over the celluloid version of Graham's dark novel was joined within days of MGM releasing the film. Duvalier spent hundreds of thousands of dollars (of depleted public funds) waging war against a movie. It would average out to an extraordinary amount of money – according to one source $5,000 for each of the 150 minutes of the lengthy film. For Papa Doc, however, this was a crusade. Graham Greene became Haiti's Public Enemy Number One. Duvalier ordered his diplomats abroad to attack the film as baseless fiction, a grossly distorted portrayal of Haiti under his stewardship. Ironically, with his protests Papa Doc became the film's chief publicist.

On 1 November 1967 the Haitian embassy in Washington, DC, issued a lengthy statement blasting *The Comedians* – possibly the first time in diplomatic history that a national embassy had ever officially protested against a movie. The diatribe, printed and distributed on Duvalier's black-and-red official letterhead, declared:

The embassy of Haiti strongly protests to Metro-Goldwyn-Mayer against the film *The Comedians*, which constitutes an inflammatory libel against Haiti and has been publicly released to mislead the American people. No effect has been spared to slander the people, the government and the entire Haitian Nation. It is not less than a character assassination of an entire nation. From the first to last the film presents an utterly distorted picture of Haiti, its people and its government.

Filmed in Dahomey, *The Comedians* shows Haiti with a wrecked port, dirty customs, shabby taxis, dilapidated hotels and houses, broken up streets and roads, a nation of cripples, beggars, voodoo worshippers and killers.

This is not only indirect aggression against a government representative of the masses and the peasantry in their fight for religious and economic freedom from an oligarchy allied to exploiting foreigners, but this is also an economic assault and propaganda aimed at disgusting and scaring the American tourists at the beginning of the season. Our Department of Tourism, our national associations of hotels and resort owners, taxi drivers, our Chamber of Commerce are now investigating and estimating the damages . . . Haiti is one of the most beautiful, peaceful and safe countries in the Caribbean.

Also, it is a pity that even the diplomatic representation of a great South American Nation has been ridiculed in many scenes of adultery, one of which is truly bestial and shocking.

The Embassy of Haiti has also sent a note to the State Department protesting the release of the film on the territory of the USA, based on existing Treaties and Charters and remembering that Haiti and its Government according to the same Charters, Treaties and Laws have never allowed any aggression, or assault, to take place on its territory against the prestige and dignity of the noble American people, its government and its president.

Papa Doc's attempt to suppress the film in the United States drew the attention of the *Miami Herald,* which on 25 November 1967 devoted an editorial to what the South Florida newspaper called the 'comedy of Haiti's protest':

Papa Doc is raving through the mouth of his ambassador in Washington. He has been irked by a film version of Catholic author Graham Greene's *The Comedians*. The picture stars three British subjects, Elizabeth Taylor, Richard Burton and Alec Guinness.

The comic side of *The Comedians* is the fact that the bloody Haitian dictator's official agent in Washington seems to think he is at home when he protests exhibition of the picture.

Perhaps he believes that President Johnson will join Queen Elizabeth in an agreement to suppress the producers and actors and deny their right to work. Freedom of expression is sadly exotic in the Haitian Republic . . . The picture was filmed in Dahomey because Duvalier prohibited shooting in his country . . . *The Comedians* doubtlessly symbolizes the oppression, fear, anxiety and the insupportable conditions to which Haitians have been subjected by the former physician who betrayed his mandate and renounced and violated all the principles of his humanitarian profession.

In Mexico, Papa Doc's Ambassador, Rudy Baboun, the first Lebanese-born Haitian to be appointed to such a diplomatic post, also protested at the showing of the film. His protests were ignored by the Mexican government and only kindled further interest in the movie. In Haiti's next-door neighbour the Dominican Republic, however, President Joaquín Balaguer was quick to oblige Papa Doc. He immediately issued a decree banning the film. Then, when the Dominican government – after the fact – organized an official private showing to see what they had banned, they discovered that someone had stolen their only existing copy of the film. The movie remained banned, sight unseen. In Spain Generalísimo Francisco Franco made the expected gesture to his fellow Haitian dictator and forbade projection of the film on Spanish territory. Meanwhile Haiti's Foreign Minister René Chalmers complained to the UN General Assembly that Graham was paid with 'gold from mercenaries'.

The censorship battle over *The Comedians* made good news copy, and Graham enjoyed every minute of it. On 4 May 1968 he wrote to me:

> There has been a battle in France, too, and I rather think Papa Doc has succeeded finally in having the film suppressed. On the whole with a few bright exceptions the film had a very bad press. Film reviewers now seem only to enjoy avant-garde films which of necessity deal with very simple stories with two or three characters so as to give the director plenty of room for imaginative film cutting. When you have a rather solid story there's nothing to be done about it but make a rather solid script. I am glad anyway that it has had a certain effect.

He again mentioned meeting Fred Baptiste in the south of France and an 'ex-major in Duvalier's army who only defected of recent years. He was an intellectual and I couldn't help suspecting him of being an informant for Papa Doc. I wish you had been around so that I could have spoken to you about the affair.' Graham explained that Papa Doc – having failed to evoke tears of sympathy in the United States with his campaign against *The Comedians* – had turned to Haiti's former colonial master, France.

A Parisian lawyer named Sauveur Vaisse recounted in an interview with me in 1991 how one day near the end of 1967 he received a telephone call in Paris from a former student named Samuel Pissar, who at the time was with a Los Angeles law firm that specialized in the movie business. 'I have a very special case,' Pissar said. 'I am not sure whether you will accept it.' His client was Dr François Duvalier, the President-for-Life of Haiti. Duvalier, Pissar explained, was seeking legal action against MGM to halt the showing of *Les Comédiens* in France. The movie, its original English-language dialogue dubbed into French, was scheduled to open in France soon afterwards. For all he knew, Vaisse recalled, Haiti 'could have been on the moon'. He did have some recollection that, like his native Algeria, Haiti had once been a French colony. 'Curiosity got the best me,' he admitted, and he told Pissar, 'Sure, why not.'

So began a lawyer–client relationship between Duvalier *père* and attorney Vaisse that eventually would continue with Papa Doc's son and successor in power, Jean-Claude 'Baby Doc' Duvalier, for more than a quarter of a century. But if Vaisse had any misgivings about taking on Papa Doc as a client to do battle with a giant Hollywood movie studio, the Paris attorney admitted that he became fascinated with Haiti – as happens with so many foreigners. At the time of our interview Vaisse was Jean-Claude Duvalier's attorney. Baby Doc was by then was living in exile in the south of France, following his overthrow in 1986, and Vaisse agreed to an interview to discuss the case of *The Comedians*, whose plaintiff had now been dead for almost ten years.

The law firm Vaisse, Lardin et Associés occupied well-appointed offices at 51 Avenue Montaigne in Paris whose accoutrements reflected a conspicuous interest in Haiti: a Haitian painting hung in the foyer leading to Vaisse's office and was visible from the waiting room. On his desk were copies of Haitian newspapers including *Le Petit Samedi Soir*, printed by an exiled Duvalierist in Coral Gables, Florida.

The Papa Doc film case lasted nearly three years, Vaisse told me. 'At the end of the first year, when we had begun to get some good results, François Duvalier asked us to [visit] Haiti. That was my first visit to Haiti. It was November 1968.' In Port-au-Prince, Vaisse and another French attorney met Papa Doc.

'He was in very good shape,' Vaisse said. 'We had two working sessions with him at the National Palace. He explained to us his doctrine. He spoke quietly in a very low voice. He had a very good sense of humour. This was one of the things which impressed me – his very good sense of humour.

'Duvalier generally tried to show us how he was upset by the book *The Comedians*. He said Graham had written this book because he had "personal problems" with the Haitian government. But Duvalier,' Vaisse added, 'did not explain what he meant by personal problems. There were so many people to whom we were introduced. We were honoured guests. Even the French Ambassador was a little frustrated because we were being treated better than himself.' After spending less than a week in Haiti, lodged at the El Rancho Hotel, Vaisse 'left more convinced than ever before that both the book and the film were a travesty'.

Vaisse explained that the grounds alleged for the lawsuit in France were that the film insulted the chief of state of a friendly nation recognized by France, adding that 'We argued Haitian history and what François Duvalier was trying to do – it was a classic tragedy. If you did the same with De Gaulle, publicly, that had been done to Duvalier, you would have obtained similar results. There had been plots against De Gaulle and people were arrested and shot.'

The first success achieved by Papa Doc's lawyers was to obtain a court order prohibiting the film from being shown in France while the case was being tried. The case lasted from 1968 until March 1970. Haitians, at least those who read *Le Nouveau Monde*, which had become Duvalier's newspaper, did not learn about the court case of *François Duvalier* v. *The Comedians* until Friday 13 March 1970. On that day the paper reported, for the first time, that the case was being argued before the 17th Court of Appeals in Paris. *Le Nouveau Monde* claimed that Metro-Goldwyn-Mayer had denied all responsibility for the production of *Les Comédiens,* alleging that it had been produced by Maximilian/Trianon. The article went on to recount the arguments presented by the Duvalier government's lawyers and their demand that damages be paid to Haiti's President-for-Life amounting to 10 million francs (then $2 million). To justify this amount it was alleged that a plethora of wrongs had been done: 'To Duvalier, admired as a man of letters and ethnologist. To Duvalier, as a learned doctor. To Duvalier, as an eminent statesman to whom the great personages of this world . . . have paid visits. To Duvalier, the president of Haiti, incarnation of the Haitian state . . .'

The presiding judge, a woman who later became a French Supreme Court justice, ruled partly in Papa Doc's favour. All scenes considered injurious to François Duvalier were to be cut from the film before it could be shown in France. So mutilated would the film have been that it would have been impossible to exhibit.

Even twenty-one years later Vaisse was ecstatic in recalling that portion of the judge's verdict. He was less enthusiastic about the rest of it. The court ordered that Duvalier be paid damages amounting to 'one franc' – clearly a note of ridicule. Graham relished the irony of the one-franc victory and sent me a small clipping, a paragraph from *The Times* of 23 March 1970, under the headline: 'One Franc Damages'.

Paris, March 22, 1970 – A French court has ruled that the film of Graham Greene's novel *The Comedians* was a libel against President Duvalier of Haiti, and parts of the film were ordered to be cut. President Duvalier, who asked for ten million francs (two million dollars) damages from the French distributors, was awarded symbolic damages of one franc.

Back in Haiti, 'Great National Victory on the Soil of France. President-for-Life Dr François Duvalier wins his lawsuit against Metro-Goldwyn-Mayer,' blared the headline across the front page of *Le Nouveau Monde*. The newspaper waxed ecstatic over what it cast as Duvalier's triumph over *The Comedians*.

A cable from Papa Doc's newly resurrected son-in-law in Paris, Max Dominique, whose death sentence for plotting against Duvalier had only recently been commuted, was published in full:

> suppression of all offending parts Stop Recognition of wrong experienced by President Duvalier Stop Symbolic franc [granted] as damages and reparation of moral wrong to great personage Stop Report follows. Congratulations and affections from Dédé [Doc's daughter Marie Denise]. Respects Ambassador Max Dominique.

An unsigned editorial in *Le Nouveau Monde* – which would have been dictated in the Palace or on orders from the Palace – contained, in addition to the usual lavish praise of Duvalier, a not-so-veiled threat against Graham. Neither he nor I realized at the time the extent to which Duvalier seemed prepared to go to exact revenge. *Le Nouveau Monde's* editorial declared:

> It is a political and moral victory from which we must draw the high meaning . . . There was no doubt that Haiti should have obtained damages against an organized defamatory action . . . by the American Secret Services, who have been able to find in the mercenary Graham Greene the agent who could be useful to feed their slanderous propaganda . . . Publication of the novel, *The Comedians*, followed briefly by a movie of the same name, had for its goal to intoxicate international public opinion against our Republic and its president and prepare a favourable ground for an invasion that was condemned to failure.
>
> If one remembers that the regional president of Metro-Goldwyn-Mayer, for having produced a movie against Lebanon, was assassinated in the streets of Beirut as reprisal, one can see that Graham Greene and his accomplices managed to get off cheap, because on a simple order from President Duvalier he (Greene) could have been shot down like a wretch in any corner of the universe.

As was said by a man greater than we in a memorable circumstance: 'For that we need only a stout-hearted man, and we have thousands of them.'

At the time Graham and I did not know of this apparent veiled warning. It was only after Graham's death, when I was looking over some old Haitian newspapers, that I discovered the editorial. Graham had good reason to fear Papa Doc.

No matter the cost to the Haitian treasury, in the end François Duvalier had undeniably won a symbolic victory. It was perhaps Papa Doc's best year, a year before his death; he had prevailed against both *The Comedians* and the Kamoken, whose leaders were slowly rotting to death behind bars in Fort Dimanche.

Graham wrote to me on 2 July 1971: 'I thought of you naturally a great deal at the time of Papa Doc's death, and I am very sorry indeed to hear that things are as bad as ever.' There was no gloating on Graham's part over the passing of his old adversary. For all of Duvalier's attempts at retaliation for *The Comedians*, Graham just hoped that the tyrant's passing would finally bring change in Haiti. It was too much to hope for.

As the thirteenth year of his rule ended in 1970, Papa Doc had become more suspicious than ever of those around him. As his health deteriorated, his paranoia increased. By now the enigmatic but ruthless king of Haiti's political jungle was a tired and sick old man. Three French doctors were rushed to his bedside from Paris by his daughter Marie-Denise and son-in-law Max Dominique after Papa Doc suffered a mild heart attack on 12 November 1970, due to the deterioration of his vascular system. The French specialists found a wizened little figure wasting away in bed. Everyone was afraid to touch him. One of the French physicians recalled to a Haitian friend how he had sat Duvalier on his lap in order for technicians to X-ray his chest. Duvalier, said the French doctor, had pleaded, 'Give me six months. That's all I ask.' But the physician said, 'The *machine* [body] was a wreck. Diabetes has taken its toll.'

Duvalier had steadfastly refused to go abroad for specialized treatment that might have prolonged his life. None the less he got his six months, sufficient time to secure his successor in power and with it a Duvalier dynasty. Most high-ranking Duvalierists, and even some ambitious Macoutes, lusted after Papa Doc's throne. They refused to believe he intended to pass them by and instead name his nineteen-year-old son, Jean-Claude, to succeed him as President-for-Life. In a speech on 2 January 1971 Papa Doc gave a clear hint of his intentions when he declared that it was time for the youth to take the helm in Haiti. Then, with characteristic modesty, he took the opportunity to liken Jean-Claude to the Roman Emperor, Augustus, who 'took the fate of Rome into his hands when he was nineteen years old, and his reign is still known as the century of Augustus'. (Gérard de Catalogne, who had become a close aide to Papa Doc, claimed he researched and wrote the succession speeches for him.)

Jean-Claude's friends claimed he would have been happier racing cars than ruling Haiti. Nevertheless, whether he liked it or not, the youth had no choice but to obey his father. Papa Doc, a close aide later confided, took great pleasure in naming his son to assume power and cheating those around him who believed they should have been the chosen one. They could only watch in dismay as Papa Doc's mantle was handed to a uninterested young motorcycle enthusiast who, when he was told the anointment was official, left the room, went out on a balcony and cried. Jean-Claude had no illusions about his inheritance, which meant he would have to watch his back and regard his friends as possible traitors.

Following the announcement of his successor, and with his opposition imprisoned, disappeared or intimidated into silence, the only adversary Papa Doc had to face at the age of sixty-four was death itself. The old dictator held on to life until 21 April 1971. The death certificate read: 'Dead of a myocardial infarction'.

The body of François Duvalier was placed (it was later removed) in a relatively simple blue-tiled mausoleum in the Port-au-Prince cemetery. A military guard was posted on round-the-clock duty at the tomb for the next fourteen years. In February 1986, after Jean-Claude Duvalier fled the country, crowds who hated Papa Doc broke open the tomb. It was empty. The whereabouts of Papa Doc's body remain a mystery to this day.

Haitians who had become afraid to leave their homes thanked God for an easing of repression. Many applauded the transition, but along with some Duvalierists they also believed that Baby Doc (as Jean-Claude was quickly nicknamed by the foreign media) would not last long as Haiti's new President. They were wrong. In spite of his flaccid leadership qualities, Baby Doc remained in power even longer than his father.

A number of factors contributed to the seeming paradox of Jean-Claude's political longevity. For instance, when the United States realized that Papa Doc was truly near death they began helping to facilitate a peaceful transition. Neither the United States nor Papa Doc's political heirs wished to see the embittered exiles return to exact revenge. It was arranged, through back-channel negotiations and the pro-regime US Ambassador Clinton Knox, that Jean-Claude Duvalier would receive US support. Repression was given a new face.

So change came – but only up to a point. In spite of the general easing of repression, political prisoners remained locked in filthy, crowded cells. The new government grandly announced an amnesty for all exiles, 'except Communists and troublemakers'. The announcement effectively barred all exiles from returning.

Jean-Claude Bajeux, who had by then left the priesthood and was teaching at the University of Puerto Rico, decided to put the amnesty to the test. He requested permission to return home to give his mother, two brothers and three sisters (who had been arrested and disappeared in 1964) a Christian burial. His request was ignored.

An exile by the name of Tony St Aude, who had returned from New York, was promptly arrested and sent to Fort Dimanche. The outcry over his arrest was so intense, however, that the regime had no choice but to release him and ship him back to the United States. On his return to New York St Aude reported that among those with whom he had shared a cell at 'Fort Death' was Renel Baptiste. His brother, Fred Baptiste, was said to be in another cell. After hearing this news in December 1971 I informed Graham that both Fred and Renel were still alive but languishing in the putrid cells of Fort Dimanche. I told Graham I would try to confirm the news and make certain the Baptiste brothers were still alive.

Another exile who tested Baby Doc's regime was my wife, Ginette. She had not been home in almost a decade. In August 1972 she flew home from Mexico City to visit her parents. During her second week back, while she was enjoying the Haitian countryside at Frères with our three children, the police arrived and told her she had to go with them. They refused to answer any of her questions or allow any family member to accompany her. The children were left with her parents, and she was taken to the Casernes Dessalines where she spent three hours waiting until an officer, who introduced himself as the aide to Haitian Army General Breton Claude, said she would have to return the next day because the general was busy. She had to find her own ride home.

The following day she complied, and General Claude, who then headed the Duvalier regime's political police, appeared. He told her that the government of Jean-Claude Duvalier liked to keep in touch with returning compatriots, especially those who lived in Mexico, which he said was a centre of international communism. Then he began to question her. During the interrogation her attention was drawn to mugshot photos pasted on the wall of General Claude's office. The general noted her interest and explained, 'Subversives, madame.'

A man in a sharkskin suit, later identified as the regime's strongman Luckner Cambronne, joined the interrogation. 'It soon became obvious that they were not interested in me but my husband,' Ginette recalled.

'Is it true your husband is writing a new book?' Cambronne asked, taking over the questioning from General Claude. Where General Claude had spoken in a patronizing manner, Cambronne was overbearing, and while he made an effort to control his anger he quickly began to parrot the new government so-called change of image – an image, he said, that was hardly a year old. 'Any adverse publicity, especially in the form of another book, would not be helpful.'

'He writes his books. I have my own work,' Ginette said.

Cambronne became visibly irritated and began to dispute Ginette's suggestion that she had been arrested. 'But surely you read his book on Papa Doc. He had the right to criticize the chief of state, but he was mean towards the Haitian people,' he said.

Ginette then realized Cambronne hadn't read *Papa Doc* and volunteered that at the moment I was working on a book about the 1961 assassination of Trujillo.

Cambronne left as angry as he had been when he entered the interrogation session. Then Breton Claude asked her whether she would ever come back to live in Haiti. 'You heard what the man [Cambronne] said, General. My husband can never return,' she replied.

The General smiled. 'But men change, madame.'

She was finally allowed to leave. In recalling the exchange after departing Haiti, Ginette was of the opinion that Breton Claude had meant that Cambronne could be changed. And indeed, a month later Luckner Cambronne, the first power behind the throne of Jean-Claude Duvalier, found the Palace gates closed to him. He sought refuge in a Latin American embassy and eventually went into exile in Miami, where he became a permanent resident and died in 2006. When he left, his home in Haiti was looted by partisans of the regime.

In a letter dated 12 October 1972, written from his apartment in Antibes – which by coincidence bore the name, Le Residence des Fleurs (The House of Flowers) – Graham wrote:

> Your letter written on my 68th birthday came to me as quite a shock. Thank goodness, Ginette and the children came back safely from Haiti. What a brave girl she is to have attempted the visit. Your story of her being taken under guard to see Cambronne and Claude was terrifying. In Haiti on that last visit was to me quite a traumatic experience and I still at intervals dream of the place. My dreams even keep up to date – so that the last one I had Baby Doc was in charge and not Papa Doc.

He continued, 'I suppose there's still no news of our friends who may be in Fort Dimanche?' There was no news. Graham was deeply affected by the imprisonment of Fred and Renel Baptiste and insisted that he was still ready with 'my signature for any protest or appeal'. We waited.

Around that time I had complained to Graham about how many of the stories I wrote for *Time* magazine were being killed. In a March 1973 letter he addressed the issue:

> The kind of material they seem to like best from France are trivialities like the tailor who makes Picasso's clothes in return for paintings. Personally I find it a more readable paper now than in the old days – they have at any

rate abolished that awful *Time's* style which meant that every character had to have three adjectives in front of his name. I now read it perhaps two dozen times a year when before I only read it in airplanes. I would have liked to have read your story of Colonel Francisco Caamano Deno. [He had been the leader of the 1965 Constitutionalist rebellion in the Dominican Republic who returned from exile in Cuba to launch a guerrilla movement, only to be killed in the hills of his homeland. My story for *Time* had been 'outspaced'.] I knew very little about him and I don't think I even remarked his death. *The Times* is almost as bad as *Time* about Latin America, perhaps worse, and somehow I can never bring myself to read *Le Monde* regularly.

Conditions in Haiti under Baby Doc were less dire – if only comparably so – than under his father. Then suddenly, in late 1975, I received belated information that Fred and Renel Baptiste were still alive in Fort Dimanche. Fred was said to be delusional, and both he and Renel were suffering from advanced tuberculosis. Help was urgently needed. At the time the Duvalier regime was seeking more US aid, so I imagined public pressure from the outside might be effective in getting help to the Baptiste brothers. I alerted Graham. I received his reply dated 13 February 1976.

It's rather horrifying to think that Fred Baptiste and his brother are still alive. Amnesty International have suddenly become very interested in Haiti and I don't think you will mind if I give them your address. They want to revive interest. I am giving a talk to the American Press Corps in March in London and propose to bring up Haiti then. Any up-to-date information you can give me about conditions there would be welcome.

The British journalist Greg Chamberlain, then working in Paris for the Agence-France Presse (AFP) English-language news service, had become interested in Haiti and did part-time reporting on Haiti for the *Guardian* and other British publications. He arranged to interview Graham after his rare appearance at the foreign press luncheon in London in March 1976. They met in a small hotel room not far from Covent Garden and near the offices of Graham's publisher, Bodley Head. The interview appeared in the *Guardian*.

Graham was quoted as saying, 'To kill them [the Baptiste brothers] tomorrow would be a mercy, a release. They have suffered so much.'

During the luncheon, Chamberlain reported, Graham had thrown 'into the ring his prestige as the origin of most of the world's image of the Duvalier dictatorship and offered the late Papa Doc's son and heir, President Jean-Claude

Duvalier, a deal to free his friends Fred and Renel Baptiste, and perhaps hundreds of other political prisoners'.

'I want to go back to Haiti to see if it's true that things have improved as the regime claims,' Graham said in the interview. 'But I will only be convinced and only go back if they bring my two prisoner friends as free men to meet me at the airport.' Chamberlain went on to add:

> Greene made his last public statement on Haiti in 1970 when he exposed, in a letter to *The Times* which enraged Papa Doc and more discreetly the State Department, a massacre of about 80 opponents of the regime in the northern town of Cap Haïtien. The colonel who was named then as the leader of the operation was appointed five months ago as head of the Haitian Tourist Office in New York.
>
> 'A blanket of silence seems to have descended on the world press about the Duvaliers,' he says. 'One reads about the place only in the glossies now, and in such fulsome tones that they seem to have been put up to it. Only a few months ago the Duvalier family inaugurated a three-million-dollar mausoleum built for Papa Doc. That's a large chunk of the national budget. Yet a few days later, they announce that hundreds of thousands of peasants were dying of starvation in northern Haiti.
>
> 'The British press exposed the scandal of low wages paid by British firms in South Africa, but no one in the United States seems to have made much noise about the virtual slave labour conditions in the new American offshore factories and industries in Haiti. Everyone seems to have forgotten about the hundreds of political prisoners still unaccounted for. Attempts by groups like Amnesty International to obtain lists of prisoners have always met with silence. Prisoners' releases are sometimes announced, but they are often of people long dead or who never existed.'

When Port-au-Prince learned of Graham's challenge of a visit by him in return for freedom for the Baptistes, Paul Blanchet, the late Papa Doc's long-time aide and Information Minister, responded with an anti-Greene editorial in his newspaper, *Panorama:* 'The Incorrigible Graham Greene'. The broadside called Graham 'facetious' and 'as extravagant as the novels he dreamed up'. The Port-au-Prince newspaper purported to be

> convulsed with laughter at this latest joke of Greene. What a waste of talent. As a good Catholic he could have used it in a wiser crusade. But gallows humour isn't enough for him. Nor nightmares. Nor the inspiration

he affects of someone just back from hell. A mortal sin torments him. But the 'rabid Catholic' neglects to do penance for having written *The Comedians*. He is a sinner who loves good but does evil.

Panorama declared that Graham had 'defied and denigrated Haiti, which he feels nostalgic about'. Echoing the government line, *Le Matin*, the Port-au-Prince daily, said Graham would be 'mad with rage' at the economic progress it claimed the Baby Doc regime was promoting in Haiti. However, Chamberlain noted in a reaction story published in the 25 May 1976 issue of the *Guardian*, 'The exigencies of political discretion in Duvalierist Haiti . . . prevented the paper from telling the reader what the author [Greene] had demanded.'

Graham wrote to me on the same day, 'I am glad to see that I am not forgotten in Port-au-Prince . . . My interview with the American Press got through to them . . . and there's a little attack on me in the local paper.'

In September 1965 when the Dominican civil war ended, Fred and his Haitian combatants had to flee the country. We managed to aid Fred and Renel Baptiste with clothes and money. Together with Gérard Lafontant, they departed for Belgium and eventually moved to Paris where the Baptiste brothers joined Lieutenant Sean Pean, a former Haitian military academy instructor, who was top of his academy class of 1956. In Europe, Fred Baptiste began seeking funds for what he termed 'his' revolution. Along with Lieutenant Pean he visited Graham in Antibes during the filming of the film version of *The Comedians*. Graham introduced them to the cast, and Fred pleaded for funds from them. Peter Glenville told them he had already contributed generously to Father Georges for the Haitian revolution.

In his letters to me from Paris, Fred Baptiste spoke of his frustration but also of his determination to continue his fight. In early 1969 Fred and Renel were arrested upon their return to Santo Domingo. They were in possession of false passports. Fred was later released, but some of his old Kamoken still living in the Dominican Republic had been rounded up and jailed. It was suspected that President Balaguer's well-organized secret service had let Baptiste go for the express purpose of learning more about his intentions.

Then, on 24 February 1970, an article in the *Washington Star* datelined from Port-au-Prince by Jeremiah O'Leary reported that the Baptiste brothers had returned to Haiti.

The two leaders of the anti-Duvalierist group had been in custody until recently . . . Evidently Balaguer, who had troubles of his own with a presidential election coming up in May, was anxious to convey to Duvalier that the Dominicans were not responsible for helping the rebels cross the frontier. The Communist band is led by Fred and Renel

Baptiste, who are brothers and who took an active part in the Dominican civil war of 1965 on the side of the leftist rebels.

Fred Baptiste went into hiding when he was released on bail and
Dominican authorities subsequently learned that he was gathering men
and arms. Last week, Santo Domingo intelligence officials say, the brothers
plus seven other armed men made their way into Haiti in the vicinity of
Jimaní in the south. Evidently hoping to round up the Baptiste band
quickly, Duvalier has not announced to his people that they are in the
country. The Dominicans similarly have not made public disclosure
about the incursion. The Baptistes are tough and well trained. In the
past their small group has accepted financial assistance from Fidel Castro
and Moscow.

Precisely how the Baptiste brothers ended up in Papa Doc's hands remains
a mystery, but it was believed that they were arrested and handed over by President
Balaguer to the Haitian authorities.

Papa Doc had decided their fate in 1970: the Baptiste brothers should rot
to death in Fort Dimanche. They did. Fred died on 16 June 1974. He was
forty-one. His corpse was reportedly dragged from his cell and dumped near
the sea to rot and be eaten by dogs. Renel, who was thirty-five, died on 19 July
1976. Both were said to have contracted tuberculosis, and Fred had become
insane.

Curiously, O'Leary had described the Baptistes as Communists. In 1964
they had been given a clean bill of health by the CIA as non-Communists. It
was only later revealed that Fred Baptiste, in his quest to find funds for his
revolution, had become a quasi-Maoist and had travelled to China during the
Cultural Revolution. There are various versions of whether in fact Red China
supplied Fred Baptiste with funds and, if they did, whether they were stolen. It
is true that at the time of his death Fred was left with only a Maoist cap, which
he had worn proudly in Paris.

Graham wrote their epitaph in the *Daily Telegraph* magazine on 12 March
1976. 'I am proud to have had Haitian friends who fought courageously in the
mountains against Doctor Duvalier . . . They were patriots, simple men, not
from the élite. Unlike many exiles, they were brave enough to go back and fight
the Duvaliers on their home ground.'

I had just completed my work on a *Time* cover story on the Panama
Canal and the treaty negotiations when *Time* assigned me to cover the last
leg of a twelve-day mission to the long-neglected Caribbean by President
Carter's UN Ambassador Andrew Young. In Venezuela I joined Young and
his entourage. While most of the journey was dedicated to spreading Jimmy
Carter's gospel of goodwill, Haiti was to be the exception. Ambassador

Young had an important human rights message for Baby Doc that the US envoy intended to be loud and clear.

When I had first heard of Young's trip I asked Georges Salomon, Haiti's Ambassador to the United States, to ask Jean-Claude Duvalier whether he had any objection to my visiting Haiti with Young, even though I was still officially *persona non grata*. Salomon reported back that Jean-Claude had no objections. However, when I arrived in Santo Domingo with Ambassador Young's delegation to spend the night prior to flying on to Haiti, an official from the local US embassy placed my bags to one side, explaining that I was not going to Haiti. When Young heard what the embassy official said, he became angry. 'You are going with us,' Young assured me. The US embassy in Santo Domingo was instructed to notify the US ambassador in Port-au-Prince to advise the Palace. I was coming back to Haiti.

US embassy officials in Haiti were visibly irritated by my presence and complained to their colleagues in Santo Domingo, and later to me personally, about the many trips they had to make to the National Palace to gain entry for a newsman who was – in diplomatic protocol terms – officially unwelcome. Nevertheless they had a stubborn human-rights advocate on their back. Young was determined to see that I returned to Haiti for the first time in fourteen years. In retaliation, the Palace was placed off-limits to all the media, and Young's entire news entourage was, according to a furious State Department official, prevented from covering the meeting between Duvalier and Young at the Palace.

My problems aside, it turned out Ambassador Young's 24-hour visit to Haiti saved the lives of at least 104 political prisoners. A general amnesty and the release of many political opponents followed the US envoy's quiet lecture to Baby Doc Duvalier. Young was respected in Haiti because he had marched with Martin Luther King Jr, and a speech Young made from the steps of the old plantation-style US ambassador's residence, overlooking Port-au-Prince, was remarkably plain-spoken.

Young recalled the United State's own tortuous civil-rights history, and while professing that he had no intention of telling Haiti how to run its internal affairs he made clear that Haiti's human-rights record would in large part set the tone of relations between the two countries, particularly the amount of US aid. He cautioned the Baby Doc regime to take some sailing lessons from Washington. 'When people understand the way the winds are blowing, they trim their sails accordingly,' Young said, emphasizing that the prevailing wind blowing out of Washington was in support of human rights.

Jean-Claude Duvalier must have felt that wind because later at the Palace, when Young handed Duvalier a list of Haitian political prisoners prepared by Amnesty International, Baby Doc promised the prisoners would be freed, at least in cases that did not involve serious crimes of violence. That was a major caveat since presumably any political prisoner could be so accused. Still, Duvalier added that his regime, which had long exercised unlimited powers of arrest, was preparing to announce *habeas corpus* guarantees – previously unheard-of in Duvalier-era Haiti. Haitians were impressed with Young's visit. Eleven of the 104 political prisoners released were expelled from the country as so-called 'terrorists', too dangerous, Baby Doc's government said, to be left on domestic soil. One of the released prisoners said of his fellow inmates, 'Those who lived were the ones who nurtured the flame of hope. Those who died were the ones who gave up. A man who decided he couldn't live didn't.'

I was excited at the prospect of obtaining first-hand news about the fate of the Baptiste brothers. It was just possible, I hoped, that if they were still alive Ambassador Young could obtain their release. Unfortunately, I was wrong.

The question that was to haunt both Graham and me was whether we could have done more to save the Baptiste bothers. Had we pressured the regime earlier, might they have been released? If Fred had been released to the local insane asylum, only a few miles from the prison, at least he would not have rotted away like forgotten garbage in Fort Dimanche.

According to prison survivors, both of the Baptiste brothers were carried out, like other victims, wrapped in the traditional Fort Dimanche shroud, the lice-infested straw mats that had been their beds for all those years. The fellow inmates pressed into service to handle the corpses were careful not to remove them head first, as Haitian superstition says that if a dead person is removed the wrong way (head first) from a room, the other occupants are sure to follow the corpse to the grave.

Jean-Claude Duvalier permitted me back again in 1980 and granted a three-hour interview. He had just wed the divorcee Michèle Bennett, and the story I reported appeared in *Time*'s Hemisphere edition. From then on I visited Haiti regularly, observing the forces of change evolve. In early December 1985 I predicted that the political end was near for Jean-Claude.

My photographer son Jean-Bernard and I attended the January Independence Day church service at the cathedral in Port-au-Prince. Although we were both arrested, the events proved us right. The service was to be the last public ceremony for the young couple and the last full-dress parade of the Duvalier dynasty's hated thugs, the Tontons Macoutes. The popular revolt succeeded, and on 7 February 1986 Duvalier fled.

Far from improving the disastrous situation, the succession of self-serving and authoritarian neo-Duvalierist 'interim' governments further undermined ideals and provoked even greater misery and hardship. In the aftermath,

Haitians faced greater duress. Corruption, thievery and state terrorism had become institutionalized under the Duvaliers as had the drug trade. Greed had become a creed. An entire generation of Haitians sought to imitate their role models, the super-ministers who practised grand larceny on a grand scale.

Yet even as Duvalierist thugs both within and without the army, commanded by General Henry Namphy, roamed the streets, wreaking their savagery at will – evidenced by the massacre of thirty-four voters on a bloody November election day in 1987 – the Haitian people persevered in their non-violent struggle. From the depths of their anti-Duvalierist, anti-politician feelings they chose a different destiny. In overwhelming numbers they turned out to elect Jean-Bertrand Aristide, an ambitious 37-year-old Roman Catholic priest, to the presidency. Aristide had waged a campaign based on his public opposition to Duvalierism, and his platform had been simple and what the people who mistrusted politicians wanted most: justice and transparency. His was a movement of hope, and the little priest-turned-prophet won the most democratic election in Haiti's history.

But the Haitian people's hope for change brought only more of the same. With the former priest, the people's hope was once again tragically dashed, as he, too, proved to be just another politician whose use of violence as an instrument of power harked back to Papadocracy.

Graham continued to be prophetic in writing about Haiti. In one of his last letters to me, on 20 November 1990, he predicted that if Father Aristide won the presidential election 'he wouldn't survive long'. Aristide lasted only seven months in office before he was overthrown and the Haitian military assumed power once again. That bloody coup of September 1991 and the repression that followed the ousting of Father Aristide from office triggered an unprecedented flood of boat people trying to escape Haiti. More than forty thousand were intercepted at sea by the United States Coast Guard; unknown numbers of others drowned. Thousands were imprisoned at the US naval base at Guantanamo, Cuba.

During a 1992 hearing in Washington, DC, US Supreme Court Justice Harry A. Blackmun, obviously displeased with the policy of then President George Bush of summarily returning Haitian boat people without determining their refugee status, asked a US Justice Department lawyer, 'Have you ever been to Haiti?'

She answered, 'No, your honour. I'm sorry. I have not.'

Justice Blackmun asked, 'Are you familiar with a book called *The Comedians* by Graham Greene?'

'No, your honour. I'm not.'
Blackmun then told the attorney, 'I recommend you read it.'

In a sense Graham Greene's influence over the fate of Haiti will endure. The reason why is perhaps best explained in a passage at the end of *The Comedians*, reflecting the eternal struggle between good and evil, darkness and light and the plight of humankind – caught in the middle – in trying to cope and choose. The young exile priest – Bajeux – preaches a short sermon based on an exhortation by St Thomas the Apostle, 'Let us go up to Jerusalem and die with him'.

> The Church is in the world, it is part of the suffering in the world, and though Christ condemned the disciple who struck off the ear of the high priest's servant, our hearts go out in sympathy to all who are moved to violence by the suffering of others. The Church condemns violence, but it condemns indifference more harshly. Violence can be the expression of love, indifference never. One is an imperfection of charity, the other the perfection of egoism. In the days of fear, doubt and confusion, the simplicity and loyalty of one apostle advocated a political solution. He was wrong, but I would rather be wrong with St Thomas than right with the cold and the craven.

PART II

On the Way Back:
Graham Greene in Central America

11 | A DICTATOR WITH
A DIFFERENCE

In December 1971, on my return from covering the third anniversary of a military coup in Panama, I wrote enthusiastically to Graham about a different breed of Latin American dictator, Brigadier General Omar Torrijos Herrera. This heretic populist Panamanian strongman, then forty-one years old, was struggling with Washington, demanding a new treaty for the Panama Canal. If peaceful negotiations failed, he hinted that violence was in the offing. For foreign correspondents the story had the stereotypical ingredients: an underdog 'banana republic' challenging Uncle Sam and a charismatic *caudillo*. But, more substantively, Torrijos's challenge was a major policy issue for Washington that would not only affect the fifty thousand Americans living in the Panama Canal Zone but touched a nostalgic and proud nerve in the American people. The strategic Panama Canal had been the young United States' greatest engineering feat. It likewise symbolized American hegemony in the hemisphere. The spirit of Teddy Roosevelt was still alive in the United States, particularly among 'Zonians' on the isthmus. On the other hand, Panama's 1.3 million citizens, along with most Latin Americans, if not all, were sympathetic to Torrijos's cause. Instinctively, I knew that Graham and the General would get along.

During possibly the largest rally ever in Panama City, held on 11 October 1971 to mark the third anniversary of Torrijos's revolution, I had noticed how ill at ease he was when speaking in public. Yet the enthusiasm of the thousands that crowded into Plaza Cinco de Mayo was not the ritual cheering of a rent-a-crowd; he didn't have to buy their emotions. Their love affair with the charismatic general was genuine. Torrijos had given them a new sense of national pride.

Absent was the clutch of politicos whose ambitions and perquisites he had upset. Most of the *rabiblancos* – white tails (wealthy members of the upper class whose nickname comes from a white-tailed songbird) – didn't like his populist rhetoric. He was the butt of their jokes at the élite Union Club. Torrijos was a graduate of the Salvadoran Military Academy. He was a country boy without a university degree. Still, he was a shrewd, wily negotiator with a folksy intuition. He had an unusual ability to coin one-liners that provided slogans for his political battles, and he spoke in parables steeped in rural logic. That day, in 1971, in a neat white dress uniform, Torrijos was obviously uncomfortable in his role. But once he launched into his speech his emotions took over and his voice rang strong with conviction. He had provided the slogan for the banners, '*Nunca de rodillas*' ('Never on our knees'), and he wanted the US administration of President Richard Nixon to take notice. The crowd roared ecstatically.

There were tense moments when it appeared his words might trigger an assault on the American Zone on the other side of the fence behind the crowd. 'What people can bear the humiliation of seeing a foreign flag planted in the very heart of its nation?' Torrijos demanded. The people's patience, he warned, had limits; their anger could be directed at the Zone, and 'we' were prepared to die. However, unlike the riots of 1964 when the Panama National Guard was nowhere to be seen, Torrijos had taken the precaution of stationing guardsmen with orders to halt any movement towards the Zone. The only thing to die that day was my story. Without a riot there was no interest from *Time*'s editors in New York.

The American Zonians, the canal workers and their families, were shaken by the giant rally, which had also set off alarm bells in Washington. Concerned Zonians wrote to their congressmen, and back in the United States an emotional anti-Panama Canal Treaty campaign began to gather steam. For the Americans working and living in the Canal Zone – an insular enclave and quaint relic of the days of US gunboat diplomacy – the barbarians were at the gates. The canal and the Zone must be saved.

On the Panama side of the fence, General Torrijos had promised that gaining sovereignty over the Panama Canal and the Canal Zone was no longer a Panamanian pipe dream. It was a matter of sovereignty, pride and dignity.

The helicopter was buffeted by the storm, swinging back and forth like a pendulum. The green jungle canopy suddenly appeared perilously close to the chopper's window. We were in the full embrace of a heavy tropical rainstorm. Visibility was near zero. Some of my journalist colleagues suggested General Omar Torrijos, who was bounce-dancing in his seat in front of me, was crazy – a real nut. That Monday morning in early October 1972 I was wondering whether they might be right. We were swinging about in the thunderstorm's blind fury, almost grazing the jungle roof. The very nature of the General's authoritarian profession would normally have made security the highest priority. Not for this fellow. The chopper had no escort. The pilots didn't fiddle with the radio to report our position to the Comandancia, headquarters of the National Guard in Panama City. They didn't know where they were anyway. The Comandancia, I later learned, usually had no idea of their commander's whereabouts.

With nature in command, the General appeared in high spirits. A woman from one of his embassies abroad occupied the seat beside me. Occasionally the wild gyrations of the chopper brought us together; the ride had its pleasant moments. Besides a pistol the General carried a water bottle on his hip which some suggested was filled with vodka. Unlike his *caudillo* counterparts who fussed over their dress, often bedecking their chests with medals (usually bestowed for diplomatic victories), the General's only distinctive accessory was his bush hat, which he wore at a cocky angle.

Tapping him lightly on the shoulder and giving him the 'What's up, Doc?' gesture with the outstretched palms of my hands, I wanted to know what was making Torrijos dance in his seat. He smiled and shared his earphones with me. I received a blast of Panamanian music. He unveiled his secret: a cassette player with his favourite Panamanian and Colombian *boleros*. As he savoured my surprise I shouted over the engine's roar, *'General, estamos perdidos?'* ('General, are we lost?') He shook his head and laughed as the pilot locked on to a swollen stream and began bucking down towards the Atlantic coast. Not to worry, the General assured me, still grinning. 'If we crash I'll get you out of the jungle. I graduated from the *gringo* jungle warfare school.' I strained to hear his heavy country-accented Spanish.

I had visited the Jungle Operations Center near Fort Sherman in the Canal Zone, which was part of the multifaceted military curriculum at the US Army School of the Americas. They had created a replica of a Vietnamese village and called it Gatun Dinh for training purposes (after the Canal's Gatun locks). The trainees' lunch featured barbecued snake. The Bolivian Army Rangers who tracked down and killed guerrilla icon Che Guevara had been trained at the School of the Americas. Leftists throughout Latin America called the School of the Americas many things, from 'The Coup d'État Factory' to 'Gorilla University' to the 'School for Dictators', implying that the institution taught Latin officers to usurp civilian power. 'I am not comfortable with such a school in my parlour. Who would be?' Torrijos asked me this question between jolts of the helicopter.

A squad of the General's Red Berets – special forces – had picked me up at dawn from my little hotel in downtown Panama City, and when the General arrived on the helicopter pad behind the house on Calle 50 we flew off into stormy weather. What kind of strongman was Omar? Based on my observations, he didn't crave the usual trappings of power. He was essentially a shy sentimentalist who detested public and social functions, preferring the company of a small group of friends who did not always share the same ideology. He detested the protocol that went with his job and left most of such chores to his friend, engineer Demetrio B. 'Jimmy' Lakas, a huge US-educated man of Greek descent who had been involved with Omar in the 1968 coup that brought him to power and who remained a loyal friend.

It was obvious that Torrijos was trying to avoid the image of a *caudillo* dictator. Three of his closest international associates were from the short list of the region's democratic leaders. There was much of Fidel Castro's style of now-you-see-him, now-you-don't in Torrijos's personal performance. Like any head of state in those latitudes, he had a practical interest in disorienting aspiring assassins. His ministers and colonels had trouble firming up appointments. They came to understand that the fellow himself was a creature of the spur of the moment. In a little country like Panama, with a helicopter and plane, he could be anywhere in the nation in an hour or so at most, on a whim, at any time. That was his spontaneous unprogrammed style.

Our helicopter had emerged from the rainstorm, and the pilots were ordered to set down the Vietnam-vintage 'Huey' in a soggy Atlantic coastal village. The chopper's rotor backwash had shredded several thatched roofs. Out bounced the General in his olive-green fatigues. Wading through floodwater that covered his jungle boots, he adjusted his familiar bush hat and called out, 'What village is this?'

'Santa Isabel, *mi Colonel*,' replied a village elder, not realizing the visitor's true rank. The General was in his element. He was happiest in the boondocks with his own rural people. This was the last day of a gruelling two weeks of travel to sixty-four *pueblos*, from the isolated Darien jungle bordering Colombia to Atlantic Coast fishing villages, mostly by helicopter and mostly at tree-top level. At each stop the people would gather and Torrijos would make a speech extolling his new 'revolutionary democracy', which he explained as a new kind of participatory government designed to bring the marginal classes into the process of economic development.

Lighting up his fourth cigar of the day, he told me, 'This is the first experience of this kind in Latin America. I want to bring up those who are down. This revolution is being made without blood or *paredon* (the wall) executing people. Our main task is to change the people's mentality.' He strode through the adjacent village. Passing a cemetery overgrown with tropical weeds he exclaimed, 'Look at that!' Minutes later he was chastising the villagers, lecturing them, 'If you can't take care of your dead, how the hell can you expect to take care of the living?' When the villagers for their part complained that the government hadn't kept up deliveries of cement to complete their new school, he took note.

He strode through village after village without bodyguards or an official entourage, like some tropical Pied Piper of Hamlin, with scores of shouting and laughing children running at his heels. At Portobelo, amid the ancient Spanish fortifications, he swore in the newly elected town councillors, telling them, 'You must work with the people. We must make our revolution Panama-style. Things from the outside don't grow here. I brought some eggs from the

Dominican Republic that were supposed to give me great fighting cocks. They didn't hatch. It's the same with fruit from Europe – it doesn't grow here. In the same manner we must grow our own revolution.'

He added, 'No one is being persecuted in Panama, nor will anyone be persecuted in the future. I want no one in jail because of their ideas.' Those statements, however, could be challenged. Under General Torrijos, Panama's political parties had been banned and the press effectively muzzled or co-opted. For all his charisma, he was a strongman none the less. Now, with his rule secure, he could afford to speak magnanimously. Leaving one village, visibly upset, he told the people he would not return until they stopped arguing among themselves.

The General stopped for lunch in a little jungle village. We sat down to an exotic meal. Watching as I navigated my plate heaped with yucca, *gallo pinto* (rice and beans) and an unknown meat, he identified the last-mentioned delicacy for me. 'It is *tigre*,' he explained. After the meal the villagers, armed with their customary ancient shotguns, asked their celebrated visitor to do what he could to bring down the high cost of shotgun cartridges. He said he would, and several raised their old shotguns to cheer him. Was it right to encourage hunting jungle animals?

'What about conservation, General?' I asked.

'Living comes first,' he replied. 'These people have lived in the jungle as long as the animals.'

Back in Panama City that evening, in the modest but over-furnished house of his long-time friend, businessman Rory Gonzalez, the place he said was his favourite residence in the capital, Omar Torrijos came to the point. He didn't like being interviewed. In fact, he hated it. But talk he did, encouraged by liberal slugs of Johnny Walker Black Label, his favourite whisky. The conversation in Spanish was wide-ranging. He talked about his early assignment as National Guard commander in Colón. During Panama's January 1964 riots he had been ordered back to take charge of the Caribbean seaport. Three US soldiers had been killed there and fifteen American soldiers and three civilians wounded, while on the country's Pacific Coast nine US military personnel and three civilians were wounded and a total of 126 Americans were hospitalized. (The total death toll on the Panamanian side during the riots was twenty-four dead and more than a hundred injured.)

The act that had set off the riots was the flying of the US flag at the Canal Zone's Balboa high school. For both Panamanians and Americans this was a matter of sovereignty, and the riots left deep scars on both sides of the fence. Had Torrijos been asked whether he was a Communist? 'Yes.' It was often the first question posed by an American. 'When they ask me if I'm a Communist, I say much less than Jefferson, less than Lincoln and just an inch less than

Kennedy.' He recounted how he was wounded in 1959. 'The guerrillas had won in Cuba, and all of the youth in Latin America, it seemed, wanted to duplicate Castro; at least his victory inspired them. Just sixty miles from Santiago, in the Panamanian province of Veraguas, my hometown, forty young men went into the hills as guerrillas. I went up there with forty National Guardsmen. After five days we had our first encounter. There were two killed on our side and four on their side. I was wounded, not seriously. I had a bullet in my arm, and I cannot move the index finger, and I recently took the lead from a bullet out of my leg.'

As for Panama's relations with Uncle Sam, Torrijos said he didn't want any more shooting, but he frankly didn't know how his country's struggle for a new treaty would end. What he hated most in the 1903 treaty that gave the United States control over the waterway and 550 square miles of Canal Zone was the phrase 'in perpetuity'. The Canal Zone was a 'knife cutting through the heart of Panama, dividing the country in two', he said, adding, 'What people would tolerate a foreign flag planted in their own heartland? The American people would not tolerate a foreign colonial enclave across the river from Washington, DC.'

Torrijos believed he was thrown into his leadership job by fate. On 10 October 1968 he had been among a group of officers who ousted the master Panamanian populist President Arnulfo Arias from power. This was hardly an unexpected event. Arnulfo, or 'Fufo' as he was nicknamed, had been overthrown on three previous occasions. His latest presidency lasted only eleven days after he broke a promise not to meddle with the National Guard. As executive officer of the Guard, Torrijos had been among the officers Arias had unwisely decided to move out of the country by sending them to diplomatic posts abroad. The Guard officers had failed to get their commander, General Bolívar Vallarino, to take over the country and dispatch 'Fufo' once again into his near-perennial exile. It fell to Torrijos to lead the coup in Panama City. He mobilized much of the Guard's 3,500-man force, took over the radio stations and closed down the airport, quickly completing a bloodless overthrow.

Unlike his fellow countrymen, Torrijos was not a gambler or fan of horse-racing, Panama's major sport. Yet he had been persuaded to visit Mexico City by Panamanian businessman Fernando Eleta, who had two horses running in the December 1969 Clasico del Caribe in the Mexican capital. Taking advantage of Torrijos's absence, two Panamanian National Guard officers declared a pre-Christmas coup and advised Torrijos to stay in Mexico – he had been overthrown. Torrijos simply smiled. He managed to get word to his wife Racquel and instruct her to go with their two sons to the American Zone, to the house of an American friend who Torrijos believed was working for the Defense Intelligence Agency (DIA). Then he arranged a flight from Mexico

City that dropped him off in the northern Panama town of David, near the Costa Rican border. There he was greeted by the local commander, Manuel Antonio Noriega (a major at the time). Torrijos's return caught the imagination of Panamanians. With loyal troops joining in as he travelled down the isthmus, General Torrijos's motorcade took on the appearance of a carnival parade. Thousands lined the Pan-American Highway to cheer him on. The gates of the American-controlled Canal Zone remained wide open, and the 'Bridge of the Americas' over the canal (also known by the Americans as the Thatcher Ferry Bridge) leading into Panama City was lined with cheering Panamanians. The leaders of the counter-coup, who had no popular support, were arrested and jailed. They eventually escaped from prison, into the Zone, and went into exile.

It was only after he returned, Torrijos said, that he learned that his American friend, who was indeed an agent of the DIA, had been in touch with the plotters before the coup. This revelation brought a change in his attitude towards the US military, along with a deep suspicion that the United States could not be trusted. It ended a friendship with Washington. He ordered his officers to keep their distance from the US military and personally broke off his informal contacts with American military officers, delegating such contacts to Major Noriega, who became his intelligence chief. This suspiciousness remained with Torrijos for the rest of his life.

The conversation during our Scotch-fuelled interview session in Panama City unexpectedly turned to writers. Torrijos praised 'Gabo' (Gabriel García Márquez), the noted Latin American author from neighbouring Colombia. I was surprised. Dictators aren't usually known for reading books. Torrijos, born to school-teacher parents, the seventh of twelve children (three of his sisters also became teachers), said he read at night and recommended García Márquez to anyone who wants to 'understand us'.

The literary turn of the conversation gave me the opportunity to introduce Graham Greene. Torrijos seemed not to recognize the name, so I went on to describe the writer whom some in Latin America now referred to as the *Viejo Ingles* ('Old Englishman'), telling him of Graham's politics and sympathy for Haiti and Latin America. In military terms, I explained how his novel on Papa Doc Duvalier had been more powerful than a fully equipped exile army.

The conversation switched to Haiti. Torrijos was well acquainted with the Duvalier dynasty. Papa Doc had been dead for less than a year and Torrijos had already considered aiding the Haitian exiles who were trying to overthrow his son Jean-Claude. He said he had agreed to meet the exiled Haitian army lieutenant François Benoît. They had discussed a plan that included assistance from Costa Rica and Venezuela, but the Haitian exiles, in Torrijos's words, had been too disunited.

When Omar said he would like to meet this Englishman I cited as an endorsement Graham's literary friends, naming the poet Victoria Ocampo of Argentina as well as the novelist Jorge Luis Borges. The fact that Graham had only recently visited President Allende in Chile, a visit arranged by the poet Pablo Neruda, who was Chile's envoy in Paris, clinched the deal.

It had been a long day, and as we parted Torrijos said, 'Now I want to meet your friend the Englishman.' But it would take four years before the meeting would take place.

The following day I was forced to move into the bathroom of my room in Panama City's Hotel Executivo, and I sat on the toilet with my Olivetti portable typewriter in my lap. I had picked up a serious case of diarrhoea either from eating too much *tigre* with the General in the jungle or drinking too much of his Black Label Scotch.

As I looked over my notes I wondered about the scepticism I had shared with my collegues about the 'nutty' Panamanian dictator. For all his Latino strongman characteristics, the General seemed sincerely dedicated to the dignity and development of his small country – created, shamefully in the eyes of many historians, as an offshoot of US imperialism. (Panama, once a province of Colombia, had gained independence in 1903 with the heavy-handed support of the United States, which then proceeded to build the canal under a 'treaty' with the new nation.)

Searching for the right words to best describe the good-natured, part-romantic, part-pragmatic and only slightly Machiavellian strongman was not easy. Moreover, on my return to Mexico City a few days later that October I learned that my Panama story had been 'outspaced' from *Time* magazine by more immediate news during the week. US presidential elections were coming down to the wire. Henry Kissinger was engaged in secret peace talks with the North Vietnamese, and Chile's President Allende was being destabilized by his right-wing opponents. The bloody coup ending the Allende government was less than a year away, but I knew Panama, too, would soon be a major world story.

In Mexico I found a letter from Graham, dated 12 October 1972, in which he once again politely declined my offer to use our house in Mexico during my wife Ginette's and my absence on holiday in my homeland of New Zealand with the children.

> I feel too old now to attempt Mexico on my own, and I shall probably have to stay with my daughter for Christmas in Switzerland. Anyway I'd rather be with you in Mexico and with Ginette than on my own.
> This summer, which I dread more than winter, was the first in four years when I had not escaped to South America, and it felt strange

Haiti's English-language newspaper, the *Haiti Sun* (2 December 1956), owned by Bernard Diederich, reports Graham Greene's second visit to the country (far right-hand column)

Graham with Catherine Walston during their 1956 visit to Haiti. The couple visited the village of Carrefour where some of Haiti's top artists had set up La Galerie Brochette; both were captivated by the work on show.

The American newspaperman Larry Allen of the Associated Press who was the model for the character of Granger in Graham's novel *The Quiet American*

Roger Coster, proprietor of the Grand Hotel Oloffson, Port-au-Prince, Haiti, in welcoming mode; Graham stayed here in 1956, then again in 1963, by which time Coster (and most of the guests) had left.

François 'Papa Doc' Duvalier on his election day, 22 September 1957; he was inaugurated as president for a six-year term a month later.

Graham talking to French newsman Max Clou at the house of former Dominican dictator Rafael Trujillo near San Cristóbal, Dominican Republic, following his 1963 trip to Papa Doc's terrifying Haiti

The first group of Haitian anti-Duvalier rebels training with antiquated weapons in the Dominican Republic in May 1963 for an incursion into Haiti that never happened

Above, left and right: A public execution ordered by Papa Doc in 1964 of two members of the Jeune Haiti resistance movement; Graham worked this into *The Comedians*.

Bernard Diederich (with camera) talking to combatants on the Constitutional side in Santo Domingo, Dominican Republic, during the civil war of 1965

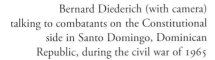

The Haitian Revolutionary Armed Forces, known as the Kamoken, in Haiti's pine forest

Fr Jean-Claude Bajeux, a Haitian priest of the Holy Ghost Order, celebrating Mass for Haitian exiles in the Dominican countryside

Kamoken leader Fred Baptiste (centre with hat) and his guerrillas sheltered in a small 'chalet' in Santo Domingo

In the centre of Hispaniola, divided between the Spanish-speaking Dominican Republic and Creole-speaking Haiti, were a few miles of highway called the International Road. Here, during the border trip in 1965, Graham tempted fate and insisted on taking a walk into Haiti where he was then considered an enemy of Papa Doc's regime.

Above: Fr Jean-Claude Bajeux at the border; not long before, his family had been seized by Papa Doc and 'disappeared'.

Left: Fred Baptiste in 1965, around the time Bernard Diederich took Graham to meet the Kamoken at their base in an old asylum for the insane at Nigua, Dominican Republic

Graham and Fr Jean-Claude Bajeux during the 1965 trip in the company of Dominican soldiers at the Rio Dajabón, which forms part of the border between Haiti and the Dominican Republic; it is commonly known as the Massacre River as it has been the scene of a number of atrocities, most recently in 1937 when Dominican soldiers killed some 20,000 Haitians, many on the banks of the river.

The Hotel Brisas Massacre de Mariav de Rodriguez, named after the events of 1937, in the border town of Restauración

Graham and Fr Jean-Claude Bajeux (left) on the bridge over the Massacre River at Dajabón, from which Graham photographed Haiti from the relative safety of no man's land (below).

Bernard Diederich changing a tyre on his Volkswagen after returning to Santo Domingo following the border trip

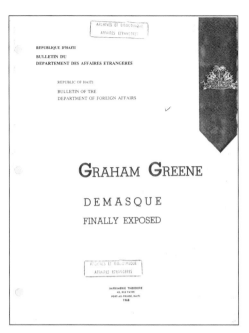

RÉPUBLIQUE D'HAITI

BULLETIN DU
DEPARTEMENT DES AFFAIRES ETRANGÈRES

REPUBLIC OF HAITI

BULLETIN OF THE
DEPARTMENT OF FOREIGN AFFAIRS

GRAHAM GREENE

DEMASQUE

FINALLY EXPOSED

IMPRIMERIE THEODORE
42, RUE PAVEE
PORT-AU-PRINCE, HAITI
1968

Graham Greene Démasqué, Papa Doc's case against Graham following publication of *The Comedians*; the 92-page pamphlet included such denunciations of its subject as 'a liar, a cretin, a stool pigeon'.

The poster advertising the film adaptation of the 1967 film of *The Comedians* (left); the film was finally shown in Haiti in 1986 (above), nineteen years after its original release.

Left and below: General Omar Torrijos, the Panamanian leader, in his element among his people in the countryside

Above: Torrijos looking less than comfortable while undertaking his duties in Panama City

Above: Graham and Torrijos getting to know one another on Contadora Island, Panama, 1976, the day they met

Graham and Bernard Diederich
(with rum punches) with Torrijos's
friend Rory Gonzales on
Contadora Island, Panama, the day
Graham met the General in 1976

Graham in 1976 on the Panama
Canal train linking Balboa with
Cristóbal (above) and (right) at
Cristóbal station in the then
American-run Canal Zone

Graham fumbles with his camera on arrival at Cristóbal railway station; he was never at home with mechanical items.

Graham and Bernard Diederich in the gardens of the George Washington Hotel, Colón, Panama, 1976

Graham at the Panama Canal, 1978, with (above) José de Jesús Martínez, known as Chuchu, a Panamanian poet and professor of mathematics who was one of the men closest to Torrijos

Graham with Torrijos on one of several visits he made in 1978 to Torrijos's house at Farallon on the Pacific coast; they enjoyed one another's company.

Graham and Chuchu rest against the sea wall at Portobelo, Panama, where Sir Francis Drake's body had been buried at sea; in 1978 Graham, Bernard Diederich and Chuchu had set out to try to locate the coffin. Torrijos provided a helicopter for the trip.

Graham as co-pilot in Chuchu's Cessna flying to Farallon to visit Torrijos in 1978

Above: Having given up the 'search for Drake', the party set off in search of Nombre de Dios, the Spanish town at the end of the Camino Real. They came across an Indian village where Graham rested.

On his last fleeting trip to Havana in 1983, Graham and Gabriel García Márquez drank whisky while they waited for Fidel Castro. They had previously met in Panama, and both were friends of Torrijos.

Left: Graham in a market in Panama City with Chuchu, 1980; Graham and Bernard Diederich were waiting to meet the legendary Salvadoran guerrilla Salvador Cayetano Carpio to arrange for the release of the kidnapped South African ambassador Archibald Gardner Dunn.

Graham was decorated with the order of Vasco Nuñez de Balboa by Panamanian President Ricardo de la Espriella (second from right) in 1983; Torrijos's two sons also attended (Martín Torrijos, far left, won the presidency in 2004).

Bernard Diederich with Aubelin Jolicoeur – on whom the character Petit Pierre of *The Comedians* was based – in 1986 after a popular uprising finally forced Jean-Claude 'Baby Doc' Duvalier to flee to France

Graham is honoured for his literary work by the Sandinistas in Nicaragua, 1987; they awarded him the Order of Rubén Darío, named after Nicaragua's most famous poet.

This painting of Baby Doc was in the lavatory at Graham's Antibes apartment.

Graham with his pen and midday martini at his writing desk in Antibes, 1989

Bernard Diederich with Graham in his flat in Antibes, 1989; this was the last time the two men met before Graham's death in 1991.

Graham and Yvonne Cloetta, his partner, having lunch at Chez Félix au Port in Antibes

Bernard Diederich, Yvonne Cloetta and Graham's publisher Max Reinhardt at the memorial service for Graham at Westminster Cathedral, London, 6 June 1991

Jean-Claude Bajeux lecturing on 'La Métaphysique du Mal Chez Graham Greene' in Haiti in 1995; having left the priesthood he subsequently served as Minister of Culture in the post-Duvalier government.

Yvonne Cloetta at Graham's grave at Corseaux Cemetery, Vevey, Switzerland; Graham died there on 3 April 1991.

In September 2001 Bernard Diederich was invited to give a presentation at Graham Greene's alma mater, Berkhamsted School, as part of the annual Graham Greene International Festival. The title of the talk was 'Graham Greene: Among Demons and Dictators'.

being in Europe. However, my novel is finished (called *The Honorary Consul*) and it should be coming out in September next year. Of course you shall have one of the first copies. I wish you could both look in here on your way back from New Zealand.

He later told me that, of all his works, *The Honorary Consul* was the book he liked best. 'An author has the right to like and dislike his own books,' he asserted in his characteristically droll way.

Still, I wanted him to visit Panama. It loomed as his next destination. Logistical problems had to be overcome because just visiting Panama would not be enough; he had to meet General Omar Torrijos. Fortunately for my plan, towards the end of each of Graham's letters his plaintive cry for escape to a new setting was getting louder.

In Mexico City I scoured bookshops for Spanish-language copies of Graham's titles and shipped them to Torrijos. I have no idea if he read them all, but I do believe from a later conversation that he had read *The Quiet American*. A month later I was filing another story on Panama. In March 1973, as he had promised, Torrijos succeeded in persuading the UN to hold an unprecedented Security Council meeting in Panama. It was no secret that his motive was to bring pressure on Washington. In the first of two stories on this development which I reported, headlined 'Omar versus the Canal Zone', Torrijos in his twenty-minute speech to the session assailed the United States, declaring, 'It is difficult to comprehend how a country that has characterized itself as non-colonial insists on maintaining a colony in the heart of our country. Never will we add another star to the flag of the United States.'

In response, John Scali, US Ambassador to the UN and a former television newsman, said Torrijos was 'knocking on an open door' and that the 'world knows the United States is ready to modernize our treaty arrangement with Panama to the mutual advantage of both countries'. Panama then introduced a resolution calling for the United States to draft without delay a new treaty that would guarantee Panama sovereignty over all its territory. The resolution won the support of thirteen of the fifteen delegates, with Britain abstaining. However, Scali, not at all happy, had to raise his right hand and cast the third US veto in the UN's 27-year history. Panama's Foreign Minister, Antonio (Tony) Tack, was jubilant. 'The US vetoed the resolution, but the world vetoed the US,' he said.

In a long three-page letter dated during the time the UN meeting in Panama was under way – 16 March 1973 – Graham, who could normally say a great deal in a small missive, lamented again being immobilized in Europe.

Unfortunately my sole excuse for visiting South America has gone now that I've finished my three-year-old novel (*The Honorary Consul*). I wish we could have another trip together like our Dominican one before you shake the dust off your feet. Have you any useful contacts, preferably English-speaking, in Panama as I really would rather like to visit that country perhaps in the summer or would it be a terrible climate then? I have managed to take Cuba in August without suffering too much . . .

Our letters – mine being the one commending Torrijos to Graham – had crossed! I quickly responded, telling him about Panama and the General. A meeting was all set if Graham wanted to go to Panama. I had arranged things with the General's friend, Rory Gonzales, to ensure that Graham would be welcomed and well taken care of.

Had he packed his bags, Graham would have met the General years earlier than he did. But he was hesitant. It took another three years for his Panama adventure to materialize. In his 25 April 1973 reply, he wrote:

Many thanks for your long and useful letter about Panama. I shall certainly write you if I decide to go and contact the man Rory Gonzales . . . I haven't yet made up my mind as *Playboy* wants me to go to South Africa which I have always wanted to visit, but the problem there is that my chief friend is the Afrikaans novelist Etienne Leroux and I don't want to get him into trouble. If I go to Panama I will try and stop off and see you. I am delighted to hear you have given up the idea of New Zealand.

I had mentioned in my letters how our children wanted to move to New Zealand because they were in love with the farms and horses. Graham opposed the move. He was certain I would die of boredom. Boredom, he warned, must be avoided at all cost. It was life's real enemy.

I had found Graham's novel *Travels with My Aunt* (1969), a copy of which he dispatched to me, to be thoroughly enjoyable entertainment – light and merry and for Graham a change of pace. He said he had had 'a lot of fun' creating the indomitable Aunt Augusta and her black lover Wordsworth, then having them traipse around the world. When the book was published in the United States, Graham's publisher – Graham often told this story – wanted to change the title, believing it was not saleable. Graham cabled back, 'Easier to change publisher than to change title.' He changed publishers.

The Honorary Consul was another matter. Little did either of us realize in 1973 that in five years we would be caught up in a kidnapping drama that could rival his fictional account in that book. In *The Honorary Consul* the British consul is kidnapped by Paraguayan guerrillas by mistake. They had been after the American ambassador. The setting is a river town on the Parana River, on the border between Paraguay and Argentina. I considered *The Honorary Consul* a much better book than many critics did at the time and wondered whether its setting, like that of *The Comedians*, had not affected their judgement. There is an old saying in journalism that Americans will do anything for Latin America except read about it. Yet for those of us covering the region the kidnapping was only too close to reality. The human drama Graham constructed was not unlike so many that were unfolding around us during the terrorist-ridden 1970s.

Often the General would give me a signal of recognition at public sessions where his boredom was apparent as he toyed with an unlit cigar. When we met, he would ask, 'What news from your *amigo inglès?*' It had become almost a game between us. When I replied that there was no news regarding Graham's visit to Panama, Torrijos would laugh, saying his public relations man, Fabian Velarde, whom he had instructed to take care of the details of inviting Graham, was as slow as a 'Panamanian sloth'.

Meanwhile the United States, notwithstanding its veto of the UN Security Council resolution, was moving ahead on its own with the negotiation of a revised Panama Canal Treaty. Chief US negotiator Ambassador Ellsworth Bunker, at seventy-nine America's most venerable troubleshooting diplomat, had become a regular commuter between Washington and Panama's Contadora Island where the talks were being held. A set of eight principles, which would lay the groundwork for a new partnership, was agreed by the two countries, and on 7 February 1974 Secretary of State Henry Kissinger flew to Panama with Bunker and a group of US congressmen. Torrijos was at the airport to greet them and rode with Kissinger into Panama City. The US diplomatic team was applauded by Panamanian legislators, who were particularly elated over principle no. 4, which read, 'The Panamanian territory in which the canal is situated shall be returned to the jurisdiction of the Republic of Panama.'

The following year was an especially busy news year in Panama. *Time*'s editors allowed me a four-column story in the 28 July issue headlined, 'Collision Course on the Canal'. In the piece Torrijos was referred to as a 'dictatorial but populist strongman'. At a press conference in Minneapolis Secretary of State Kissinger had worried aloud that the Panama Canal Zone, the quasi-US colony harbouring the strategic waterway that links the Atlantic and Pacific oceans, could become the focus of a 'kind of nationalistic guerrilla-type operation that we have not seen before in the hemisphere'.

As the year drew to a close the Time Inc. Editor-in-Chief Hedley Donovan and Board Chairman Andrew Heiskell decided to visit Panama at the end of a six-country fact-finding tour of Latin America, accompanied by their wives. When I requested an interview with Torrijos for my bosses, Omar agreed and named the venue: the island of Contadora. Ambassador Bunker was in Washington. The Time Inc. VIPs would be lodged at Bunker's Contadora bungalow. In his *Time* essay following his return to New York, under the headline 'South America: Notes on a New Continent', Donovan wrote:

> The most interesting thing to watch in South America's near future, apart from the obvious potential for economic growth, is the groping for political forms somewhere between all-out democracy and rigid authoritarianism. Peru and Brazil think they are exploring this ground and priests and professors talk about it in Chile. It comes near the heart of the problem that a dictator, General Torrijos of Panama, should say, 'I feel ashamed when I notice that somebody sitting next to me starts trembling. I feel guilty that there are people who are still afraid.'

Donovan devoted much of his essay to Panama, noting:

> The subject of the Panama Canal unites South Americans. The Zone is seen as an odious relic of the imperialist age. All the governments support the Panamanians' demand for a new treaty granting them unmistakable sovereignty over the Zone, with details of canal operations and US military presence to be negotiated. General Omar Torrijos Herrera, Panama's strongman, is willing to wait until after the [1976] US elections for the new treaty (he has heard of the 'Teddy Roosevelt lobby'). But something must give in 1977. He speaks of restraining 'the students' (at the University of Panama) as another general might speak of withholding his paratroopers.

Meanwhile Panama finally began to loom as a destination for Graham. His letters reflected an almost desperate yearning to travel. 'I wish we could meet somewhere else – say in Panama. I want very much to go to Panama one day and it would be fun to do it with you.' He went to Greece instead. Then on 25 May 1976 he replied to a letter from me in which I asked him again whether he wanted to go to Panama, a repetitive question by now:

> I certainly am still interested in visiting Panama and the pleasure would be greater if I had your company. Unfortunately the time when I am most free is the summer when I have to get away from Antibes because of the crowds. Summer, I imagine, is not very agreeable in Panama. For example the most likely times this year, as I promised to go to Spain for ten days around July 12, would be say the last week of July and the first week of August. This is the period of greatest heat in

Panama, but I could stand it if you could. I would much appreciate an invitation from General Torrijos and I could probably cover my expenses with an article in the *Daily Telegraph* Magazine. I would probably come by KLM, and would plan to stay around two weeks. I don't think the General would find my article unsympathetic! Oh, I have just seen in rereading your letter that July is bad for you. Would August be better?

Then on 15 July he wrote:

I am just off to Spain tomorrow the 16. I got your letter of July 1 but there has come no word from Mr V [Torrijos's PR man Fabian Velarde]. Perhaps the General has changed his mind or Mr V is too lazy . . .

I tried about fifty times to get you at the telephone number in Paris [where I was visiting at the time] but there was never any reply except once when I got the wrong number! It would be lovely to see you in Panama, but I don't feel like pressing the General for the invitation. Let it come or let it not come.

On 26 August he wrote:

I have just got your letter of August 13 as I have been travelling around. It's sad that we weren't able to have a meeting in London or elsewhere for I was in England for some days. I am afraid any invitation from the general would come too late for this year now. I have too many things that I have to finish. Perhaps a good plan would be to wait until next summer when [US presidential candidates] Carter or Ford's attitude to Panama will become clearer.

In a letter dated 15 September he told me:

I have at last had a telegram from Mr V and I have replied that the earliest I can go is December. There is a KLM flight from Amsterdam which I propose to take, arriving in Panama on 4 of December. I wanted to avoid passing by way of New York. Is there any chance of your being able to come up for a few days anyway and see me? I suppose in due course Mr Velarde will be booking me in a hotel etc. Have you any idea whether the government plans to pay my passage or only for my stay in the country? If all goes well I would plan to stay the best part of three weeks. It would be lovely to see you. I doubt if the CIA will enjoy having me around! They didn't like it in Chile.

Then on 18 October he wrote:

> I was relieved to get your letter as I had no reply from Mr Velarde to either my telegram or my letter. Anyway today I booked my seat and am due to arrive by KLM soon after 9 a.m. on the morning of December 4. How very good it will be to see you, if only for a few days. I plan to stay about three weeks if the General will continue to pay for me! I would be grateful if you would continue to send me snippets on Panama. The visit should be well timed as negotiations presumably will have begun again with either Carter or Ford. (P.S. Can you suggest anywhere for urgent letters and telegrams, if possible not in the American Zone?)

13 | RENDEZVOUS ON
A PEARL ISLAND

Despite his years, Graham was rearing to go, prepared to explore new territory, size up new faces and match wits and tangle with whatever Byzantine politics the 'crossroads of the world' – Panama – had to offer. At seventy-two he dropped in on one of the most important foreign-policy issues for Washington of the time – not as just an observer but as a man who believed deeply in the rights of small nations. At issue was the new Panama Canal Treaty, a topic charged with powerful emotions and nationalistic nostalgia on both the US and Panamanian sides. It was an explosive mixture. His experience would produce a book, *Getting to Know the General,* which Graham described as the story of an involvement. 'I was surprised and a little mystified,' he wrote in the book, 'to receive a telegram . . . telling me that I had been invited by General Omar Torrijos Herrera to visit Panama as his guest.' Graham and I had an agreement. As a foreign correspondent I did not wish to become part of the story. However, Torrijos's invitation to Graham was no mystery and certainly no surprise. It had been four years in the making.

On 4 December 1976 my flight to Panama City from Mexico City was terribly late. I worried about Graham. If things went wrong I would feel responsible. I hoped someone would be at Panama City's Tocumen airport to meet him. Omar's evanescent public relations man Velarde did not answer my frantic telephone calls from the Mexico City airport. I had visions of Graham stranded, alone at the airport, waiting. Velarde was notorious for operating on Latin time, which assumes delayed arrivals for every event.

When I finally reached the El Panama Hotel after a three-hour flight Graham had already checked in. He had been met by Velarde after all. He brushed aside my apologies and said he was relieved that I had arrived safe and sound. He had aged well. He was still as lean as an athlete, with plenty of bounce in his step. It had been nearly twelve years since we had last seen each other, after I bade him goodbye in Santo Domingo. His letters in the interim had made it seem like yesterday. He was a wonderful pen pal, never failing to answer correspondence. Like travel, he said, letter-writing was a form of therapy.

As we chatted I realized something else. He had mellowed; he was much more talkative, open and humorous than he had been in the 1950s and 1960s. But he was still shy with strangers, and he could still be finicky. His driver spoke no English, and Graham, who spoke virtually no Spanish, didn't think he could get along with him. Nor was Graham too happy with Mr Velarde. (Graham's opinion of Velarde was shared by many foreign correspondents who covered Panama.)

Travel seemed to energize him, and he dismissed the idea of jet lag. He was anxious about the chances for a new Canal agreement. The Panamanians were on tenterhooks because the newly elected US President Jimmy Carter had said during his campaign that he would never give up US control of the Canal Zone. None the less, signals out of Washington suggested that the 'never' had only been campaign rhetoric.

Meanwhile Torrijos had just returned from a non-aligned nations' conference in Sri Lanka to find troubling headlines at home. Students had rioted over an increase in the price of milk and rice. A Zonian policeman – a tall, skinny American named William Drummond, one of the more vocal opponents of a new treaty – had filed a civil suit in the Zone's US district court to block Canal negotiations. Three days later a series of bombs exploded in the Zone. The first partially demolished Drummond's car. Some Americans pointed the finger at the Panamanian National Guard, saying it was an effort to intimidate Drummond, while Omar's inner circle suspected it was all part of a *gringo* plot to destabilize his government. Washington believed that the National Guard had had a hand in the bombings in an attempt to speed up negotiations. Omar, angry at the suggestion that his Guardia was involved, ordered his spy chief, Colonel Manuel Noriega, to go to Washington and talk to the CIA chief, George H.W. Bush, to assure him it wasn't so. 'It seems like a good time to visit,' Graham chuckled. 'I'm looking forward to meeting the General. He must have his hands full.'

Next morning Graham was up early and already in the hotel lobby when I came down to meet him. We had been instructed to wait for a driver. Appointments, I warned Graham, had a habit of changing in Panama at the last moment, and the General was notorious for altering his itinerary without warning. We would be playing it by ear. Smelling adventure, Graham was in high spirits – cheerful at breakfast and cheerful while waiting for the driver. We sank into the comfortable chairs on the El Panama's open veranda, enjoying the delicious tropical morning and watching the cars come and go.

After a while a man approached. 'Greene?' he asked.

'Yes,' we both said at the same time.

The man motioned to us, and we followed him to a Jeep Cherokee. He said nothing more and we got in the vehicle and started off. I played tour guide, pointing out places of interest to Graham as we drove through the city. 'This is the old Panama City,' I explained, waving towards some ruins. 'It was set on fire and destroyed by the Welsh pirate Henry Morgan. He sacked Panama

City in the seventeenth century. Afterwards the city was moved to where it is today.'

Suddenly I realized that something was amiss. 'Wait a minute,' I interrupted the driver. 'I thought the General said we were going to Contadora.' We were driving in the wrong direction.

The driver made a sharp U-turn and sped back to the hotel. The driver had picked up the wrong Greene. He left us with a flurry of embarrassed apologies and went in search of the other Greene.

Graham and I laughed. We could imagine the headlines: 'Author Graham Greene and Journalist Abducted from Panama Hotel Lobby.' Normally I was careful to take only *bona fide* taxis at Latin American airports because kidnapping was becoming a growth industry with leftist guerrillas seeking funds for their respective war chests. Graham found the whole strange episode hilarious. Gazing after the driver as he disappeared into the hotel, he said, 'I wonder if I should follow him and meet the other Greene. You know there is another Graham Greene, an impersonator, and I have been unable to catch up with him.'

We sat back on the hotel's veranda. Graham rubbed his hands and intertwined his long thin fingers. 'The day is starting out well.'

Later, when we obtained a Panama Canal Company telephone directory, we found half a dozen Greenes listed in the Panama Canal Zone. Graham commented that they could be the West Indian branch of his family.

Another driver arrived, dressed in the uniform of Panama's Guardia Nacional. He was short with a lined, leathery Mayan face. His hair was closely cropped, military-style, and tinged with grey, and he wore a sergeant's stripes.

'Sergeant José Jesús Martínez,' he said in excellent English. 'At your service.' He turned out to be the correct driver. He drove us the relatively short distance to the house of Torrijos's friend Rory Gonzalez on Calle Cincuenta. He ushered us to the door, saluted and departed.

It was as if we had entered a wax museum. The two figures in the over-furnished sitting room sat motionless. They appeared to have struggled out of bed and collapsed into the easy chairs. One of the figures, Rory Gonzalez, broke the silence. 'Good morning.' He spoke in perfect English. The other was wearing a bathrobe with a towel hanging from his shoulders. He was dishevelled and clearly suffering the devil's hangover. This was General Torrijos.

There were no introductions. We sat, and I leaned my head towards the General to let Graham know this was Torrijos, the Maximum Leader of the Revolution. Graham was making his own deductions. After a while the General got to his feet, nodded towards us and left the room. We were served coffee, and about fifteen minutes later Omar returned. He had showered and was wearing sports clothes. With a wave, he gave the order for us all to head for the small Paitilla airport.

Waiting in the small terminal for a propeller plane of Panama's internal Perlas airline to be readied, Torrijos puffed on a cigar, obviously lost in thought, or still struggling with his hangover. He had said barely a word to Graham and me. Instead, we chatted with Rory.

A small boy suddenly ran up and wrapped his arms around the General. Taken by surprise, Omar pretended to be angry. 'You don't know me!'

The lad laughed and pointed a finger at him. 'You are Omar Torrijos.'

Such was Torrijos's relationship with his people. The General asked the boy where he was going, and when he said 'To Contadora' Omar invited the child and his family to accompany us in the plane. The boy cheered, and his parents thanked the General and accepted the ride.

When we arrived on Contadora the businessman Gabriel Lewis Galindo, who was developing the island, welcomed us. We sat under a young coconut tree outside the Galleon seafood restaurant and drank rum punches. I could tell Omar and Graham were sizing each other up. The General spoke no English, so the job of translator fell to me.

The General told Graham of his aversion to intellectuals. Graham declared he was not an intellectual, putting emphasis on the word 'not', and adding, 'I do not aspire to being an intellectual.' I figured they were both on safe ground. They had discovered a mutual dislike.

Suddenly, Torrijos stopped talking in mid-sentence. We followed his stare to a lithesome Latin beauty with the figure of a model who had stepped out of the restaurant, removed her sandals and was wriggling her toes in the sand. She gave out a little squeal of pleasure at the contact with the hot sand. Then she slowly climbed the hill, her hips swaying invitingly, towards Gabriel Lewis's bungalow. We all sat transfixed. Then, as if hypnotized, the General rose to his feet and without a word or a glance marched up the hill after her.

Graham looked at me and chuckled.

'She is a Colombian singer,' Roy explained. 'He listened to her sing last night in Panama City. She's hot stuff.'

We ordered another round of rum punches and drank to the General's health.

We heard the drone of the little plane returning to the island from a trip to the mainland. A short while later Jorge Carrasco showed up. Carrasco, a heavy-set and well-known presenter of television evening news, was also Omar's official translator. His obesity was a topic of jest among his Panamanian viewers, but he knew how to keep his mouth shut off-camera. He had had the task of translating for the Panamanian negotiators of the Canal Treaty.

Graham didn't like Carrasco's arrival. The four of us – Graham, Omar, Rory and I – had been getting on fine. None the less we made small talk with Carrasco. About half an hour later the General returned; beads of sweat glistened on his forehead. He picked up the conversation where he had left off. I could see that Graham was impressed. He later told me it was like his meeting with the Mexican rebel, General Saturnino Cedillo, at his ranch in San Luis Potosí nearly forty years earlier, which Graham recounted in *The Lawless Roads*. There was the same unhurriedness about both generals.

Torrijos himself led Graham on a tour of Contadora. The conversation turned to the newly elected US President Carter. 'What kind of man is this man, the farmer from Georgia?' the General wanted to know.

'We will have to wait and see,' Graham replied cautiously. 'He does appear to be much more sympathetic than his predecessor.'

When the waiter at the Galleon came to check on us, I declined another round of rum punches.

'Absolute rubbish!' Graham snapped.

'The sun is too high,' I said, and explained how the strong rum punches in the tropics can glaze the eyes and cloud the brain of even a dedicated drinker.

Graham disagreed, and the General agreed with Graham.

I must concede that even after several rounds Graham remained fresh and alert. He never required a siesta, even after our lobster lunch accompanied by a bottle of wine. In many respects he defied all the usual medical advice and expressed horror at the idea of engaging in any special physical exercise. He was healthy, and his loping gait kept comfortably apace with Omar's long strides.

Walking us to the plane, Torrijos was obviously gratified. He and Graham had hit it off, and the small isthmus country's economic woes and the seemingly never-ending Canal negotiations had been momentarily forgotten.

Graham was excited. Back in Panama City he said he liked the General and believed his political compass was pointed in the right direction. I had taken a number of black-and-white photographs, one of which was eventually to become the cover of his book *Getting to Know the General*. I telexed a brief news item to *Time* the following day, and air-expressed the pictures to the magazine in New York. The item appeared in the 20 December 1976 issue in the 'People' section:

> It was like a scene out of a Graham Greene novel: a Central-American strongman and an Oxford-educated Briton sat beneath a coconut tree on a tropical beach philosophizing. The strongman, Panamanian Dictator Omar Torrijos, noted that both their fathers had been teachers, and that he had left his family at 17. The Briton, author Greene himself, mused between sips of rum punch: 'You should thank God you did escape from home, because if you hadn't you might be an intellectual today.' Greene quickly added: 'I am not, because to be an intellectual is rather academic. A creative writer seems to me to *be* emotionally involved, and that is not being an intellectual. They are people who regard from

a distance and don't involve themselves. When an intellectual like Kissinger gets involved in events, it's a disaster.' 'Intellectuals,' added Omar, 'are like fine glass, crystal glass, which can be cracked by a sound. Panama is rock and earth!'

Before setting out to show Graham Panama City I suggested Mass at the Church of Christ the Redeemer, built in the *barrio* of San Miguelito by a group of progressive Chicago priests. Their *misa tipica* (folklore Mass) with guitars and bongo drums was one of the first to be celebrated in the hemisphere. When I finished quoting the pastor, Father Mahon, as saying that 'the old Roman Catholic service had lost its spiritual appeal and reflected the monastic mentality of the Renaissance', Graham's expression told me I had forgotten his preference for the Tridentine rite said in Latin. So we skipped Mass and instead visited Panama's ancient Cathedral of San José in the old section of the city. While on the topic of religion, the subject of the priest in *The Honorary Consul* came up. Graham said, 'My priest is not, as some have suggested, modelled after Father Camilo Torres.' (Camilo Torres was a Colombian priest who died fighting as a guerrilla in 1966.) 'As a revolutionary Camilo is on par with Che Guevara, and they are much more romantic than my priest, for whom I invented a little personal theology.'

Graham was like a schoolboy on a journey of discovery. The days were far too short for him. I couldn't believe a man who had travelled as much as he had could still be so enthusiastic about new surroundings. His curiosity and enthusiasm were unabated by Panama's heavy humidity and heat. He seemed to want to see everything, including Colón, the city on the Atlantic side of the isthmus.

I said it was a good idea and suggested we travel by train. The train ride across Panama's Canal Zone from ocean to ocean would be via the world's oldest transcontinental railway which had opened in 1855, fourteen years before the last spike was driven on the first rail line to span the continental United States. British author David Howarth in his book *Panama* had noted that before the Atlantic–Pacific isthmus rail link came about, gold-seekers in the California gold rush were paying $100 each to cross by canoe and mule. The railway, constructed by a group led by New York financier William Henry Aspinwall, a grand-uncle of Franklin D. Roosevelt, charged them $25. It became a highly profitable enterprise. Thousands were said to have died in its construction, mostly from yellow fever.

Graham and I paid $1.50 each for the ninety-minute trip from Balboa on the Pacific side to Cristóbal on the Atlantic (and literally across the street from Colón), which covered not quite forty-eight miles. Although it broke no speed records, the train ran on time.

We settled down in a first-class car where we were the only passengers except for two Panamanian boys using the aisle as a playground while their parents travelled in the second-class section. The yellow-and-blue diesel-powered train clattered along with open windows and a view of the Panama Canal on one side and tangled rainforests on the other.

We had a date to meet the General's aide, Sergeant 'Chuchu' Martínez , at the George Washington Hotel in Colón and were to return by automobile with him on the Trans-Isthmian Highway.

Graham did not share my enthusiasm for the old railway. As we were clickety-clacking through a section of jungle I could sense that he wanted to tell me something important. 'There is this writer, a professor of English literature named Norman Sherry,' Graham said rather sheepishly, 'who wants to write a book on my work.'

I could see that accepting the biographer's offer had not been an easy decision for him.

'I liked what he did on Conrad . . . and I was wondering if you wouldn't mind talking to him. He also wants to retrace my steps in Mexico, do *The Lawless Roads*, *The Power and the Glory* . . .' Graham left the sentence hang without an ending and seemed to be deep in thought. Then he added, 'You can tell him anything you wish, but don't mention my personal life.'* By personal, he said, he meant private. Graham was very protective of his family and friends.

The boys playing in the aisle had left our car momentarily and rejoined their parents in the second-class section. The American conductor (the railroad was operated by the US Canal Zone administration) came by and punched

---

*It was after attending Graham's memorial service at Westminster Cathedral on 6 June 1991 that I understood what he had meant in cautioning me about his 'personal life' on that train in Panama. The *Sunday Times* published a photograph of the 'Catherine' who had accompanied Graham on their visit to Haiti in 1956, identifying her as Catherine Walston. 'At precisely the same hour as the Westminster memorial service, Lord Walston, a socialist millionaire whose life had been closely bound up with Greene's, was being buried. Only with his death has the long-kept secret emerged of Greene's love for Catherine Walston (Lord Walston's beautiful American wife),' stated the report by Geordie Greig. 'Even though Lady Walston died in 1978, aged 62, Greene always insisted that matters of the heart should remain private.' It was said that their affair, begun in 1949, had ended in 1960. Yet it was hardly the secret the *Sunday Times* suggested. The literary world knew about it, and Evelyn Waugh's letters mention Catherine. Waugh appeared to have approved of the liaison and wrote admiringly of both Catherine and Graham.

our tickets. Then we were alone and I could see that the subject of a possible biographer bothered Graham. I admitted I had not read Sherry's book or books on Conrad.

Graham explained that he had selected Sherry's book on Conrad as the British Book of the Year in 1971. Sherry had been pleased, and his correspondence with Graham had led to a request to undertake a critical biography of Graham and his work, similar to the book he had done on Conrad. Among the considerations that had persuaded him, Graham said, was the fact that Sherry was neither a Catholic nor a friend. It was an odd conversation, and I felt as if Graham were reassuring himself that he had made the right decision. He commented that some of his friends had suffered from their biographers, and he mentioned Evelyn Waugh as a victim.

I knew little of Graham's personal life. I had only seen him with one woman, Catherine, who had accompanied him to Haiti in 1956. I remembered her as a very pleasant person, but he had never mentioned her again. In fact, except for Yvonne, his lady friend back in the south of France whom he did talk about, he had rarely discussed his relationships with women. He had mentioned his wife Vivien, from whom he had been separated since the end of the Second World War, telling me on one occasion that she was living in Oxford and had written a book on doll's houses. He spoke of her in the most respectful manner. He talked about Francis, his only son, and his daughter Caroline. But he was very private about his family. His life seemed to be carefully compartmentalized and organized, much as he described his dreams. As foreign correspondents often do, he would talk at times about visiting brothels – he mentioned Havana and Hanoi – but he gave the distinct impression that he went there more as an observer than a participant.

'He [Sherry] may soon look you up in Mexico. He may need help in travelling over my old trail,' Graham said.

'It will not be a problem,' I said. 'I'll certainly talk to him.'

I gazed out at the jungle rolling by and wondered whether it may have been my puzzled look or inner embarrassment over the term 'personal life' that had set him talking about his past romances. Then, even more out of character, he began discussing a Swedish actress with whom he said he had been romantically involved after his 1956 trip to Haiti. He referred to her as Anita.

We were crossing the Continental Divide. The boys had returned to play in our train car, and I interrupted Graham's romantic ruminations by snapping his picture. He didn't protest.

Later, when we arrived at Cristóbal, Graham paused to take a photograph of a Zonian policemen in his wide-brimmed hat which he believed dated from the US Civil War. 'Awful thing. It won't work,' he complained and fussed with his camera.

We crossed the street from the US town of Cristóbal to Colón, Panama's second city. We admired Colón's dilapidated French architecture of two-storey balconied houses, and Graham mentioned how they reminded him of Haiti and Hanoi. We headed for a camera shop, but the Panamanian attendant at the shop had no idea how to fix Graham's camera. (The camera was eventually stolen in Panama, but Graham was not at all upset.) We asked for directions to the George Washington Hotel from the camera shop attendant. It was only eight blocks and it wasn't yet lunchtime, so we decided to walk. The street was empty except for a Guardia Nacional police van.

As we passed the van two Guardia policemen barred our way. 'Where are you going?'

I was about to reply, 'What the hell business is it of yours?' but Omar was their commander and I didn't want to make trouble. 'To the Hotel Washington,' I answered.

'Get in, please,' the policeman ordered, and waved to the back of the van. We got in and sat looking at each other, perturbed. I thought: What a great photograph: Graham Greene in a paddy wagon! The two policemen took places on each side of us and tapped the hood of the van to signal the driver. We drove off down Front Street.

'Are we headed for jail?' Graham asked.

'This is a very bad street, lots of *ladrones*, plenty of thieves,' one of the Guardia policemen said in English. 'They have sharp knives and they like cameras like yours.' Then he made a gesture with his finger running across his throat. We could have had our throats slit.

Graham looked at me. 'Why didn't they tell us at the camera shop that it was dangerous when we asked directions to the hotel?'

'Maybe the shop buys the stolen cameras,' the policeman replied. He was very serious-looking and added that only recently they had terminated the career of two thieves. He didn't elaborate on how the early retirement had occurred. We thanked the stony-faced policemen for the ride and clambered down from the van at the entrance of the Hotel Washington, with curious staff and guests staring at our inglorious arrival.

We went to the bar and sat. Over our first planter's punch, which Graham pronounced 'excellent', we discussed Colón. The city had become a sad, seedy and neglected place.

Graham said he had read a French novel many years earlier set in Colón. It described the rip-roaring Colón of the Second World War. It was the fleshpot that provided countless servicemen with their last tryst before heading out to the Pacific. None the less Graham found the elegant old George Washington Hotel, built in 1913, delightful. At one time it ranked with the Raffles of Singapore and other celebrated hotels around the world. Will Rogers slept there, and the exiled Argentine dictator Juan Perón met and wooed his future wife María Estela Martínez Cartas (better known as Isabel) there.

Later in the afternoon Sergeant José Jesús Martínez, General Torrijos's aide and our driver that first day, arrived. He insisted we call him Chuchu (the Latin American nickname for Jesus). Chuchu proved himself a formidable conversationalist and a chatterbox. He talked virtually non-stop over lunch in the old hotel's high-ceilinged dining-room and throughout our fifty-mile drive back to Panama City. Graham and I listened to Chuchu expounding on his Marxist ideology and life as Omar's aide. That evening over a nightcap, after Martínez had left us, Graham wondered aloud, 'How sincere a Marxist is Chuchu? He certainly talks well.'

I had heard that Chuchu, politically, was Omar's left-hand man, but I had no clue as to how influential he might be. Torrijos had both capitalists and Marxists in his camp and personally embraced neither extreme. In fact he prided himself on being a pragmatist and knowing how to balance both groups. He had the ability to take advice from both sides, reflect on it and then make a final decision. He was the first to admit it was not always the right decision, but his intuition was rather good. He trusted Chuchu. That was apparent. But Graham and I agreed that Chuchu, for a man of so many eclectic interests and loyalties, must find it hard to be a dogmatic Marxist.

The next day we were invited to a town meeting over which Omar was presiding in a hall across the street from the Comandancia, the National Guard headquarters, in El Chorrillo, a damp, decrepit *barrio* in downtown Panama City. The sagging wooden tenements always seemed to have drying laundry hanging out their windows: flags of poverty. We stood among the crowd and watched. Omar sat among several of his top Guardia officers. He twisted his unlit cigar, listening to the complaints and suggestions of the poor people of El Chorrillo. Speakers were introduced by a bongo drum-roll.

Graham was enthralled. He commented how the black Panamanian drummers sounded Haitian. He asked me to identify each member of the high command, who they were and their alliances. He gave Chief of Staff Colonel Flores low marks because he sat chewing gum. Omar later told us Flores was one of his most trustworthy officers. The General didn't say whom among his military staff he didn't trust. Later, the television commentator Jorge Carrasco caught up with us, and Graham went back into his shell. He wasn't happy about the intrusion. He distrusted the newsman-translator.

Graham played his own game, quietly assessing who were the good guys whom he believed the General could trust and the potential bad guys who could be secret backers of El Hombre, ex-President Arnulfo Arias. After having heard stories of Arias's early days in Europe and his infatuation with Mussolini and Hitler, Graham had concluded that the former president had an evil streak.

Later he asked me to take him to the British Embassy. I was at a loss. In all my travels I had never bothered to check in with the British or US embassy to sign their respective visitors' books. However, if he wasn't staying at the British Embassy in whatever foreign land he was visiting Graham was a stickler for registering with the Embassy to make his presence known. When we got to Her Majesty's Embassy in Panama City it was closed. We later returned when it was open, and he duly signed their book. 'Let's see if the old fart [the British ambassador] invites us to tea,' Graham chuckled.

No invitation came.

The next evening we listened to the other side of the Canal issue. Virtually across the fence from El Chorrillo, the baseball diamond in the Canal Zone was lit up as if for a night game, but instead it was for a Zonian rally. Politically at bat was the policeman Drummond himself. He addressed the crowd of barely a hundred American Zonians about the legal actions he had taken to block the Canal Treaty. Graham thought it was interesting how the Americans called Secretary of State Kissinger and President Ford by their first names and accused 'Henry' and 'Gerry' of being 'traitors'. We both felt a little sorry for the Zonians; they were bound to lose the game. They believed in American hegemony over the Canal and honestly felt they were the only ones who could run it properly. Graham recorded in his book *Getting to Know the General*, 'The protesters looked lost and lonely in the vast stadium and the hot and humid night, and one felt a little sorry for them. God and Country would almost certainly let them down just as surely as Gerry and Henry had done.'

I regretted having to leave Graham in Panama, but before departing I mentioned to Rory Gonzales that Graham needed a better driver, that he couldn't communicate with the first one assigned to him. Rory reported to the General and the General assigned his aide to be both driver and guide to Graham. As we parted, Graham said he wasn't sure he would remain for the entire planned three weeks. 'Must get back to Yvonne,' he said. It was obvious that Yvonne was very special to him. Indeed, upon his arrival I had attributed his new tropical wardrobe to her. He was wearing slightly more stylish tropical clothes and shoes than in his earlier days. *Time* had noted in a 1951 cover story on Graham that 'he dresses like a careless Oxford undergraduate'. Yvonne told me years later that when she met Graham in the early 1960s he owned just three suits, each of them grey pinstriped. Clearly he was not fashion-conscious. I left Panama to cover general elections in Jamaica and then join my family on a prearranged holiday.

14 | GETTING TO KNOW CHUCHU

PR man Fabian Velarde had sought to market Graham in the usual press agent's fashion. I did my best to explain that Graham was not in Panama as a publicity stunt to publicize Panama or Omar or to fight for the Canal Treaty. 'Graham,' I said, 'is a writer who decides what he writes when he likes.'

When Velarde said he wanted a professional American photographer to follow Graham around and take pictures of him, I spoke up indignantly. 'On no condition,' I declared.

'But the General likes this photographer,' Velarde said.

'Graham doesn't,' I replied. He hated having his picture taken.

When I told Graham about the exchange he said, 'Quite right. I don't want to end up in *Playboy* magazine between some big tits without my knowledge.'

And when Torrijos heard of the episode he said, 'Leave Graham alone.'

The order was that Sergeant 'Chuchu' Martínez would take charge of Graham after my departure. Omar assigned Chuchu as Graham's driver, guide, translator and professor of local lore and history. Appointing Chuchu to this task was a sign that the General had accepted Graham into his close circle of friends. Few generals share their aides, and Chuchu had at times made himself indispensable to Torrijos. While Chuchu often romanticized his version of things, the origin of his relationship with Torrijos was indeed intriguing. Omar explained to us that Chuchu had joined the National Guard to fight him but instead had become a loyal aide. He said he had met Chuchu at the Guardia boot camp at Río Hato. The officer at the camp in charge of basic training for an anti-guerrilla force told Torrijos, 'General, we have a professor of mathematics here who wants to become a soldier.' Torrijos was understandably baffled by such an anomaly.

'What the hell are you doing here?' the General asked Chuchu, who had been a faculty member at the University of Panama.

'General, I came to the conclusion that I couldn't beat you on the outside, so I've decided to try from the inside,' Chuchu said.

'The son-of-a-bitch was only half joking,' Torrijos said. When the laughter died down Omar's instructions to the officer were: 'OK, let's see if the old bastard [Chuchu was forty-five] can survive the training.'

As a professor of philosophy (his initial discipline) at the university Chuchu had joined the protests, often violent, against the 1968 military coup that ousted Populist President Arnulfo Arias. Chuchu's involvement cost him his university job. Eventually he obtained a two-year scholarship to study mathematics at the Sorbonne in Paris. Afterwards he was permitted to return to the University of Panama to teach mathematics but spent much of his spare time with an experimental cinema group. He then joined Torrijos's Guardia Nacional. Chuchu's campus student friends ribbed him about changing his profession from academic to *militar*, and anti-Torrijos students believed he had sold out to the enemy. Later, Chuchu accepted the General's offer to join his security detail after they had lunch together. Torrijos had won over the enemy, and Chuchu had switched sides.

Chuchu became more than a security aide; he also became Omar's staff intellectual, interpreter and troubleshooter. He was promoted to sergeant – he said he didn't want an officer's rank. One of his many troubleshooting tasks, assigned to him personally by Torrijos, was that of assisting Latin American leftists on the run from Chile, Argentina, Nicaragua and El Salvador. Omar, who didn't own a chequebook or even know how to write a cheque – his wife ran their family finances – gave Chuchu a figurative blank cheque to aid the refugees. From all indications Chuchu was scrupulously honest in dealing with the funds. He himself lived modestly and appeared to have no particular interest in money. His underground railroad moved rebels escaping from Argentina's military and Chile's General Pinochet in and out of Panama. By the time Graham arrived, Chuchu's 'Pigeon House', the name he gave his combination rebel guest quarters and safe house, was the nesting place mostly of Sandinistas fighting President Anastasio (nicknamed Tacho II) Somoza of Nicaragua.

Chuchu admitted that he did not always see eye to eye politically with Torrijos and that he did his best to influence the General. However, he would not allow his ideology to encroach on his loyalty to the General. It was not long before Chuchu was extending his loyalty to Graham. They discovered that they were fellow playwrights. Chuchu told us he had published two plays the year before, one entitled *El Caso Dios* (*The God Case*) and the other, which won the Ricardo Miró prize of 1975, entitled *La Guerra del Banano* (*The Banana Wars*). In 1952 he had won the National Theatre prize in Madrid for his play, *La Perrera*. Chuchu explained that his *Banana Wars* play was about United Brands, known as the Chiriqui Land company in Panama. The villains were the big banana producers who had exerted such a powerful influence in Central America's 'banana republics'. The heroes were leftist workers.

One day Chuchu proudly showed us around Panama University and introduced us to its Experimental Cinema group. The students excitedly asked

Graham whether they could interview him on camera, for television. Knowing his aversion to being interviewed on television I was surprised to hear him say, 'All right.' (As far as I know, the only other time he went on television was much later, in 1983, on a regional French station when he appeared to attack a story on Nicaragua that he found offensive in *Time*. He told me where to obtain a video of the show if I wanted it.)

Graham and Chuchu were soon a couple of fellow conspirators. It was a merry ideological mix. Omar's other aides, to whom Graham had taken a dislike, were soon pushed into the background as far he was concerned. Meanwhile the eclectic multilingual Chuchu was perfecting his Italian as he was courting a young Italian woman who resided in Panama and whom he was soon to marry.

Graham was smitten by Panama. On his return to France on 30 December 1976 he wrote to me:

> I am writing after my return from one of the most charming countries I have visited! I was very grateful for your support those first days and as you can imagine we had a running struggle with Mr Velarde. He told Chuchu to report at every Guardia Nacional on the routes we took so that he could know where I was, but Chuchu completely disobeyed instructions. In any case the General on, I think, our second meeting had told us to do the opposite of anything Mr Velarde required. The downfall of Mr Velarde occurred just before I left when the General was having one of his Saturday binges, which began at 5 o'clock and ended at 10.00 and Mr Velarde may have begun earlier. Anyway, Velarde was quite incapable and when he left me at my hotel he just managed to get out that he hoped that I would have a cup of tea with him and the General next day, which seemed something of an improbability. Chuchu was a tower of strength though, unlike what you thought, he always carried a revolver in his pocket! In fact his car had been blown up by a bomb a little before my arrival and so we travelled always in one of the General's cars. I saw a great deal of the General and liked him more all the time. He soon came to realize that I was not an intellectual!
>
> I got involved even in his private life as well as Chuchu's, although it was a complete holiday and, apart from Mr Velarde and that fat translator, I liked everybody. My only dislikes seemed to have been shared with the General. I even got an idea for a novel when I was in the country with Chuchu and, if it does seem to take root, I shall go back to Panama in July.
>
> I was very touched by the little note [you] left under my door and I

was sorry to be out when you telephoned. With the help of Chuchu I tried to telephone [you in] Mexico several times but without success. I do hope you have had a nice holiday with your family in New Zealand, and perhaps we can meet again next summer. Everybody appreciated your piece in *Time* magazine, which occurred at psychologically the right moment, because of Mr [Ellsworth] Bunker's arrival with the negotiators.

The article was one of many I reported from Panama on the potentially explosive issue of conceding sovereignty over the Canal to Panama.

Graham and I corresponded a great deal during 1977. He had asked me to keep him abreast of developments in Panama as he was writing an article about Panama. The General and Chuchu were of no help since they were not letter-writers. Although covering the Canal Treaty negotiations was taking up much of my time – I was virtually commuting back and forth between my bureau base in Mexico City and Panama – I kept Graham as informed as possible.

Graham was a fast worker. On 18 January 1977 he announced in another missive:

> I have done a rather lengthy 4,000-word article on Panama and *Playboy* is showing interest in America as well as the *New York Review of Books*. *Playboy* of course would probably need illustrations. My camera shutter went wrong just before leaving with Chuchu for the country so I had to depend on him for photographs. Unfortunately the two he took of me and the General at the General's house in the country are very dark and I am not sure that they are useable. Could I have permission to show anyone who publishes the article that very good photograph which you didn't use in *Time*? Naturally, of course, a fee would have to be negotiated and credit given you, but is this impossible because of your connection with *Time*? I really believe a novel is emerging into my sub-conscious as the result of Panama with Chuchu as the main character.

On 5 February I received a handwritten letter in Graham's tiny script which I had great difficulty in reading. Omar's press agent Fabian Velarde had by now suffered a heart attack and died, and I had facetiously reassured Graham that it had had nothing to do with him. 'You have relieved my guilt about Velarde,' he wrote back. 'I told the General I called him fishface and he became a standing joke between us.' Graham announced that the *New York Review of Books* had published his article on Panama and that the *Sunday Telegraph* magazine in London would 'follow suit in early March . . . I chose one of the two photos you gave me. I hope you'll find the article reasonably truthful and

I'd be glad to hear what the General's reaction has been.' He ended with 'I envy your going back to Panama. I feel quite homesick for the place.'

A week later in another letter he wrote:

> I do hope by this time you have seen my story – I asked a copy to be sent to you. I think the *New York Review* is a good place for it to appear and better, except financially, than *Playboy*. I hear from John Ansty of the *Sunday Telegraph* magazine that *Playboy* might be interested in the article for its Spanish edition. He has the syndication rights apart from the United States and France. Tell Chuchu I have just had his letter and a copy of his play – an excellent little one-act play, by the way. I hope he will have received the *New York Review* by this time.

The anxiety that Graham displayed in his letters, one seeming to follow the other, over how his Panama article would be seen by the General and Chuchu was striking. It was as if Graham were a cub reporter waiting for a response to his first story:

> I feel a little nervous in case the General feels that I was a bit too personal. I did leave out a very interesting story of his wife and his father-in-law and Dian [*sic*] which Chuchu can tell you. I was very touched by the fact that the General confided it to me. The telephone directory [which I had sent him] is a fascinating bedside book for me and the plans [maps] of Panama City and the Zone are invaluable. I am doing my best to finish off the novel which was begun eight years ago [*The Human Factor*] and in which I have no confidence, but am determined to get to the end of it if only in order to try this Spring to begin the Panama novel. One of the things which fascinated me about Panama was the communications. The General obviously can't rely on telephone or codes and therefore, like in the 18th century, he uses couriers. Chuchu is sometimes used as a courier. Once when he was spending the day at the General's house in the country a letter arrived from Venezuela by jet plane at his little airport there. I am always delighted when the 20th century goes back through the multiplication of technology to the 17th or 18th century.
>
> If this arrives before you go to Panama do tell Chuchu that the Swedish paper *Aftonbladet* are publishing the article in their magazine as soon as it has appeared in England. Chuchu was rather against me writing an article because he felt it would damage a possible novel. I can quite see his point of view and it is a very sensitive one, but I felt I had to get a little bit down on paper first. I wonder anxiously how

you will take my article. P.S. I am sending a few of your photos to *Aftonbladet* assuming that your permission extends that far. Of course I have told them to credit you.

P.P.S. A brief examination of the [Zonian] telephone book makes me curious. Why are the only Diplomatic and Consular representatives those of Denmark, Finland (strangely), Norway and Sweden? I am fascinated under Churches to find a Baha'i faith. Presumably they have got a branch in the Zone as well as the extraordinary building they have in the Republic. Have you ever visited that? It too seemed to be run by Americans. I must say I like a telephone book which includes instructions for 'attack without warning'. 'Your first warning of an attack might be the flash of a nuclear explosion.' One is advised to get quickly underneath a motor car! Surely the advice before the last war for ordinary bombs was less innocent than that.

Elisabeth Dennys, Graham's sister, who took care of his correspondence, included a letter of her own in the envelope. 'Graham dictated this letter over the Dictaphone,' she wrote, 'and I am not very happy that I have got the word in line 12 correctly. It sounded like "Dian" but I may not have spelt it right! I did not want to hold up the letter until I could ask him, knowing that you may be off to Panama quite soon.' The name was actually that of Moshe Dayan, former Israeli defence minister and hero of the 1967 Arab–Israeli War. Graham later revealed to me that the 'interesting story' was that Dayan had helped to bring Torrijos's wife and her estranged Jewish father, then living in New York, together after twenty-five years.

I was finally able to assure Graham that his *New York Review* article, entitled 'The Country with Five Frontiers', which I had taken with me to Panama, was a hit not only with Chuchu and the General but among Panamanians who read Chuchu's published Spanish translation. The article was impressively accurate and generous, the General said. And I had watched Chuchu waxing ecstatic after reading the piece. Graham need not have been concerned. Indeed his essay on Panama was remarkably free of mistakes, as was the picture he drew of the General and his struggle *vis-à-vis* the United States:

> Panama is not an insignificant banana republic with politicians and presidents for sale, nor is General Torrijos in any way a typical military dictator. Panama is dangerous and so is Torrijos, a man fighting to exercise prudence as Fidel Castro advised him, but a man bored with prudence – you can see it in the lines of weariness around the eyes, the sudden wicked smile which greets a phrase that pleases him. 'You can choose your enemies, but you can't choose your friends.'

General Torrijos in seven years has given Panama a national pride. It would be a tragedy for Latin America if he fell a victim to the impatience of the left or the chicanery of the right. A guerrilla war is less to be feared than the sudden limited violence which kills one man and solves nothing . . . As Chuchu said, as he regretfully laid the revolver, which he always carried in his pocket on our travels, down on his bedside table, 'A revolver is no defence.'

Later that year I wrote to Graham and informed him I was setting out on a reporting trip to the Southern Cone of South America. *Time* had offered me the Buenos Aires bureau (and I could move it to Rio de Janeiro if I wished). Graham wrote that he was

envious . . . What a trip you are having! I only spent an unhappy ten days in Rio once with a Pen Congress and decided never to go to another. I and Alan Pryce-Jones bathed alone on the Copacabana beach with nobody in sight and only a flag which we realized after a little meant that bathing was dangerous! I have always wanted to see Manaus, but your account of the tourists puts me off. I see that Air France runs a direct flight there now. Brasilia I hated but I suppose it's changed a lot since those days in the sixties. Paraguay I loved, but I don't think [then dictator Alfredo] Stroessner was pleased with my presence there.

I've finished my novel [*The Human Factor*] which I don't like but which has met with the approval of others who are perhaps better judges. I am now free to contemplate the Panama book and a lot depends on whether I decide to go ahead with that. If I do decide then I must go back. The French refused to publish my article although it's been published twice in America, in England, in Sweden, in Brazil, and in Spain and I think Holland. In the meantime I have been conquering a month's cough and am only beginning to return to life.

In a letter on 13 June 1977 Graham announced:

I'm off to Anacapri [Capri] on the 16th and I expect to come back to Antibes around July 5. Then it's likely that I shall be off to Spain for a trip with my nice Father Duran [a Spanish priest friend] for about ten days beginning on the 12th July. August therefore would be free for Panama, but I am doubtful. It partly depends on how I get on in Anacapri with the novel if I begin it. I'm not certain that I want to go back yet. It was such a vivid and amusing trip that I am afraid of a kind of anti-climax with my return. All the more so perhaps if everything is quiet again and a treaty to please everyone signed. I might even then be a slight embarrassment to the General as belonging to the earlier period. Anyway if you do go back to Panama I'd very much like to hear your reaction to the situation there. Curiously enough I dreamt of the General last night and your letter arrived this morning. It's the only time I have ever dreamt of him.

In a letter the following day he thanked me for my letter in which I told him I had decided to remain in Mexico City as I felt there was more news at this end of the hemisphere than in the Southern Cone. He agreed. He again gave me his travel plans and said he was still undecided about Panama.

I am in two minds about returning to Panama. At least returning to Panama in the immediate future. If there is trouble I would like to go back, but I am wondering whether the novel won't go ahead in its preliminary stages better because of the vivid memories of my first visit. As for *The Quiet American* I can always go back later to check up. This is if the novel gets off at all and that depends on how I see it when I am in Capri. Anyway I don't want to foist myself on the General again unless invited. If negotiations with America are going on in a satisfactory way I think the General might well feel that my presence was an embarrassment. If things go badly then he might like a return visit, but I think I should leave it to him rather than force myself there again. Chuchu of course would always welcome me I am sure, but I wouldn't want to go back if it was an embarrassment to the negotiations. Perhaps you can find out a bit about that if you are going back in June.

What a time the General must have had with 20 women. I can't tell you how much I appreciate your keeping me in the picture.

The women Graham referred to were members of an *ad hoc* Mexico City newswomen's association denominated 'Twenty Women and One Man' – the one man being their chosen interviewee, or victim as they liked to say. The organization was made up principally of female Mexican journalists. In the summer of 1977 they had flown to Panama for a scheduled hour-long interview with the General. He figuratively swept them off their feet. They descended on his house and the interview ended up lasting three days. While several of the ladies were concerned about their journalistic reputations – they had been flown around the country and lodged in Torrijos's seaside home at Farallon – the more focused reporters among them came away with scoops, revealing that a breakthrough in the Canal negotiations was imminent (which it was). Moreover Torrijos's comments to the ladies accusing Guatemala of preparing to seize its small neighbour Belize the moment the latter gained independence from Great Britain triggered a break in diplomatic relations between Panama and Guatemala.

Finally in a letter of 9 July Graham announced that he had received a telegram from the General inviting him back to Panama.

> As a matter of fact I didn't particularly want to go this summer. I started the novel in Capri and wrote 6,000 words but I am doubtful whether it will work. However I always believe in going with Providence [he was always interested in what might happen next, so I see that he was wagering that his adventures might be given him by God] and so I accepted the invitation. Perhaps the General anticipates a crisis this summer as I can't believe Congress will approve any agreement that old [Ambassador] Bunker makes. Are you going to be around those parts? I plan to go somewhere around August 20.
>
> P.S. I wonder if it was your visit which made the General send me the telegram. Do you believe that Congress will ever pass the new treaty?

I had chided Chuchu, telling him of Graham's wish for a return invitation and the General was happily surprised when he heard that Graham would like to return.

| ## GREENE GOES
TO WASHINGTON

Graham returned to Panama on 21 August 1977 and was soon involved in a caper close to his prankish heart that gave him a ringside seat at the historic signing of the Canal treaties. If he had entertained any doubt about the favourable impact of his article on his new friends in Panama, their warm welcome reassured him. He was now considered a *compadre* of the General.

As Graham was arriving from Europe on his second trip to the isthmus I was departing Panama City after reporting for *Time*'s cover story on Panama and the treaties. My departure was necessitated by an opportunity I couldn't afford to miss: I finally had a chance, if only briefly, to return to Haiti. Meanwhile Graham's visit to Panama turned into high drama – exceeded only by high irony. It included nothing less than a trip by Graham Greene – who had once been barred from entering US territory in Puerto Rico – to Washington, DC, as a member of the Panamanian delegation equipped with an official Panamanian passport.

Torrijos's delegation also included the Colombian writer Gabriel García Márquez who recalled:

> Some journalists speculated at that time that the invitation had been one of Torrijos's manoeuvres to jazz up his delegation with the names of two famous writers who had nothing to do with the occasion. In fact, both of us had worked on the treaty's negotiations much more than the press suspected, but that wasn't why General Torrijos invited us to accompany him to Washington. The real reason was that he couldn't resist playing a friendly joke on his friend President Jimmy Carter. Both Graham Greene and I (like so many other writers and artists) had been denied entry to the United States for many years for reasons that not even the presidents have ever been able to explain, and General Torrijos had decided to solve the problem for us. He raised the matter with many of the high-ranking officials who visited him at that time, and finally he took it up with President Carter, who was surprised that the problem existed and promised to solve it as soon as possible. However, his term ran out before he could give us his reply.

When Torrijos was deciding on who should form part of the delegation going to Washington, it occurred to him to smuggle Graham Greene and me into the United States, and the idea quickly became an obsession. Shortly before that, he had suggested that Greene disguise himself as a colonel of the National Guard and go to Washington on a special mission to President Carter as a joke. But Graham Greene, who is more serious than may appear from some of his books, didn't want to lend his glorious body to some shenanigans that, doubtless, would have been one of the most entertaining episodes in his memoirs. Nevertheless, when General Torrijos suggested that we attend the treaty signing ceremony, under our own names but with official Panamanian passports and as members of the delegation from that country, both of us accepted with childish glee.

That is how we arrived at Andrews Air Force base together, both of us in jeans and denim shirts, in a delegation of Caribbeans [*sic*] dressed in black and bewildered by the 21-gun salute and the martial notes of the US national anthem, which seemed to be all part of the joke. Aware of the literary significance of the moment, Graham Greene whispered to me as we descended the plane's ramp, 'My God, the things that happen to the United States!' Carter himself had to laugh, flashing his television-ad teeth, when General Torrijos told him what he'd done.

Graham described the scene in a letter to me:

> Washington was amusing. I was pleased to find that I got under Stroessner's skin as I got under Duvalier's. At the huge reception at the Organization of American States a girl introduced me to one of his [Stroessner's] ministers who directly he heard my name froze, said 'You once passed through Paraguay,' and turned on his heel without a handshake. At that moment too I was in spitting distance of Stroessner. The General's [Torrijos's] speech at the signing was much better than Carter's and Carter was practically inaudible although I was only in the fifth row of the audience.

Graham later delighted in telling me how he had squeezed close to Paraguay's General-President Stroessner, prepared to say something nasty but that the South American dictator was hidden by a circle of flunkies. (Alfredo Stroessner, known as a ruthless army officer, came to power in Paraguay in 1954 and lasted a remarkable thirty-five years in power, until 1989. El Excelentísimo, as he preferred to be called, was noted for his statement that strongman rule was 'the price of peace'. He was overthrown in 1989 and died in exile in Brazil in 2006 at the age of ninety-three. He also renamed a town 'Puerto Stroessner'. His Colorado Party was required membership, and he was known to torture his victims. El Excelentísimo had welcomed Anastasio Somoza Debayle following his overthrow in Nicaragua in 1979. Shortly after getting settled in Somoza was ambushed and killed in Asunción. Among others, Stroessner gave haven to was the infamous Josef Mengele, the Nazi doctor known as the Angel of Death.)

As for Chilean strongman General Augusto Pinochet, Graham likened him to a Boris Karloff who 'didn't even need to grunt'. I asked Graham why did he not go with García Márquez when the latter joined a group demonstrating against Pinochet before the White House. 'I didn't think the Americans could make any distinction between the generals,' he replied. I thought it a rather lame excuse for someone who touted his own personal Chilean-wine boycott against the Chilean strongman. Graham did add, when I teased him for turning down the chance to demonstrate before the White House, that he didn't wish to embarrass Omar as he was an official member of the Panamanian delegation. García Márquez had felt no such constraints. Prior to their departure for Washington Graham said he had been consulted by Torrijos on the Panamanian leader's speech; he added modestly that his help was not really needed, but it did testify to Graham's commitment to Panama's cause.

In another letter following Graham's visit to the US capital and dated 20 September he expressed additional concern regarding the landmark Canal Treaty endeavour:

> My fear in Panama is slightly different to yours. I am rather afraid of what may happen if the Senate do ratify the treaty. 300 square miles and more of real estate plus a lot of money will be a big temptation to the [Panamanian] bourgeoisie. They won't like the idea of the General spending it on school meals, free milk and pleasure grounds for children. I think the General's life might well be in danger if the Senate ratify.

16 | FAIR WIND FOR THE ISTHMUS

'I wonder what will happen next [in Panama]. I shall trust you to tell me,' Graham wrote in early 1978, adding, 'I am sorry to hear that Chuchu has mended his little plane. I am terrified at the thought of one day having to fly in it.' He wasn't really terrified of flying or fearful of Chuchu's little plane. In fact Graham enjoyed it. His correspondence could be misleading to anyone who didn't know his little private jokes. He loved teasing Chuchu about his secondhand Cessna.

Graham's Panama fever had become perennial. 'So far, apart from two weeks in Spain, my summer remains open to any wind that blows,' he said in a letter dated 15 May 1978. 'I would be quite happy if one blew me back to Panama, so do keep me informed of the situation there.' Then on 3 July he wrote, 'With a certain unwillingness I am drifting with the tide and going back to Panama in mid-August. I can't give you the exact date yet but it will be somewhere around August 12 I imagine. I would feel very much happier about a third return if you were going to be there for at least some of my stay. I fear I may be rather bored this time.' Eight days later Graham announced that he was booked on a KLM flight 'arriving in Panama at 9.00 or so on the morning of August 15. What a pleasure it would be to find you there to have you join me. What about an interview with ex-President Arias for *Time*? And all the other leaders of the opposition? Something I would find difficult to do because of my relationship to Torrijos.' The wind was favourable, and it blew us both back to Panama in August 1978.

A plebiscite giving the Canal Treaty overwhelming popular approval had been held in Panama in October 1977. The hard sell was in Washington where, under the US Constitution, any foreign treaty must be ratified by the US Senate. Some senators were discussing the possibility of amending the treaty before ratification, in effect gutting it. Such an action would in all probability force Torrijos to reject the agreement. Like snowbirds migrating south to flee the winter, US Senators flocked to Panama. Their squawking drove Omar close to the edge. He had become the treaty's chief salesman for visiting US congressional delegations. It was not an easy task.

Omar said he had grown tired of constantly being lectured by *yanqui* congressmen on how to run Panama. To limit what he called their 'cajoling' he took the wind out of their sails by trotting them through rural Panama. They 'perspired buckets' in the hot, humid jungle and acquired, Torrijos said, 'a good taste for our village dust'. He introduced them to his poorest constituents. It was a far cry from the well-groomed antiseptic Canal Zone and Panama City restaurants. However, most of the congressional visits ended amicably with Omar handing out cigars bearing his personal cigar band. The Cohibas, he said, were supplied personally by Fidel Castro. They were also illegal in the United States.

Omar pledged to aid the congressmen, if they supported ratification, by allowing political parties to function again in Panama and permitting exiles to return. Freedom of speech would be guaranteed. But he warned one group of US senators he was escorting, hopping around the country in his twin-engine Otto plane, 'You are our friends. We know you are our friends. Please do not carry out justice with a shotgun.'

In Washington during the spring of 1978 it was touch and go. Anti-treaty senators took delight in insulting Torrijos and exaggerating labour disturbances in Panama. Kansas' Republican Robert Dole, perennially cast by much of the media as a 'hatchet man', led an attack on the treaty and tried unsuccessfully to sabotage ratification by dragging drugs into the debate, which, as *Time* pointed out, 'was a bust'. US narcotics agents found no evidence to support Dole's assertion that Torrijos was soft on drugs.

Torrijos, for his part, was losing his patience. Opposition by the anti-treaty bloc in the US Congress was having its effect. US intelligence sources reported that Torrijos was seriously considering sabotaging the Canal if ratification were lost and that he had imported a team of Israeli demolition experts to do the job. He later hinted to both Graham and me that it was no idle threat. Finally on 18 April, with sixty-eight for ratification and thirty-two against, one of the most emotional and controversial treaties to go before the US Senate managed to squeak through with all the help it could get from the Carter White House. To the treaty's foes Jimmy Carter went down in history as the man who 'gave away the Canal'.

Exhausted and smarting from all the insults from Washington, Omar retired to Coclesito. On 16 June he returned to Panama City to join President Carter in officially signing the treaty in the crowded colosseum. The public ceremony during which Carter and Torrijos spoke drew a record crowd of more than two hundred thousand to Plaza Cinco de Mayo and adjacent streets. Carter spoke in Spanish, telling the jubilant Panamanians, 'This day marks the beginning of a new partnership between Panama and the United States.' It was still not over. Implementing legislation had to be voted into law, and the political battle in Washington was to continue until 27 September 1979.

*

Across the Caribbean, in the Dominican Republic, the generals had halted the vote count in the presidential election on 16 May 1978 when it appeared that their candidate, Joaquín Balaguer, was losing. The count resumed only after Venezuela threatened to cut off petroleum shipments and President Carter threatened to cut off US aid. The durable old Balaguer's monopoly on the presidency had been broken (temporarily, as later history turned out). Opposition candidate Antonio Guzmán's victory was recognized. In case the generals hadn't got the message, Carter sent an impressive 27-member delegation to President Guzmán's inauguration. The delegation was headed by Secretary of State Cyrus Vance and included UN Ambassador Andrew Young and Lieutenant-General Dennis McAuliffe, commander of the US Southern Command based in the Panama Canal Zone. Also prominent among the invited guests: Panama's Omar Torrijos. He was there as a show of support for his friends in the Socialist International, the victorious Dominican Revolutionary Party (PRD).

Carter's policy was a radical departure from that of his predecessor, President Lyndon Johnson, who thirteen years earlier had sent in US Marines and the 82nd Airborne Division to halt a popular uprising demanding the restoration of the PRD's ousted President Juan Bosch as the country's constitutionally elected leader. Johnson feared 'another Cuba'. Carter supported the PRD's triumph at the polls, fearing the loss of democracy. The United States was not the only one to have changed. Panama's Torrijos was on his best behaviour *vis-à-vis* Uncle Sam and in good humour. The irony of the situation was not lost on him since he himself had ousted a constitutionally elected civilian president from power a decade earlier. I had been covering the Dominican election and transfer of power, and Omar invited me to accompany him back to Panama. We would arrive before Graham.

Omar's bodyguards had been engrossed in reading the Spanish translation of my book on the 1961 assassination of Dominican dictator Rafael Trujillo. 'Either they are reading it to learn how to protect me or to kill me,' Omar joked. I asked him whether he felt safer now that the US Congress had placed a ban on CIA-sponsored assassinations. The ban followed Senator Frank Church's investigation into the agency's involvement in past 'eliminations with extreme prejudice'. Omar chuckled and said that an article in *Newsweek* on 11 June 1973 had reported that according to President Nixon's White House counsel, John Dean III, the infamous Watergate 'plumbers' had been given a contract to assassinate him in 1971. Dean said Torrijos had an uncooperative attitude towards the Panama Canal Treaty negotiations. The plan was said to have been aborted before the assassination team reached Panama.

Graham arrived in Panama on a KLM flight on 19 August, the day after the General and I returned from Santo Domingo. Graham was happy to be back, even though, like the General, he had a cough. There had been a goodly supply of Bols gin during the fifteen-hour flight from Amsterdam, Graham said, but he was in need of one of good-looking and friendly barmaid Flor's rum punches. Chuchu drove him from the airport to the Señorial Bar on a quiet tree-shaded downtown street in Panama City, where I met them. Holding high his first planter's punch and saluting Flor, Graham pronounced it a 'marvellous laxative after such a long flight'.

At the bar Flor looked on sympathetically as Graham regaled us with his adventures in trying to reach Panama. The origin of his cough, he explained, was the London Ritz Hotel. Pausing to savour the punch and to receive our undivided attention, Graham declared that things had a habit of going wrong at the Ritz, and for that reason he liked to stay there. During the night he had awakened coughing to find his hotel room filled with a most unpleasant acrid smoke. After a struggle, he said, he had managed to open the window, noting, 'Of course it is the wrong thing to do in a fire.' A plastic tarpaulin covering a neighbouring building under construction had caught on fire. It was, he continued, 'an awful morning'. 'Sautéed by the fumes and particles of the burning plastic, I boarded the wrong plane at Heathrow Airport, and ended up in Rotterdam instead of Amsterdam.' He finally made his airline connection by taking a taxi to Amsterdam. Having not a guilder in his pocket, he convinced the Dutch cab driver to settle for his fare in American dollars. Then on arrival in Panama he had had to wait endlessly for Chuchu.

'But, Graham,' Chuchu protested, 'your goddamn Dutch plane arrived an hour early! The crazy Dutch have the only airline in the world that can arrive so far ahead of schedule.'

'I want to live until Christmas,' Graham further declared enigmatically in the dimly lit Señorial. It seemed a simple enough request, and he had our full attention as we sipped our second rum punch. 'I have a play, a new play. It's a bit of a farce, but I like it. I don't know whether it will go over . . .' he went on seriously. Graham was now looking directly at Chuchu, waving his arms about like the wings of a plane.

Chuchu got the message and was profusely reassuring. 'Don't worry, Graham. My plane is OK. I am the best pilot. Yes, Graham, yes, you'll live until Christmas – and for many more Christmases, I guarantee you.'

Graham went on to confess that he wished he had begun writing plays earlier in life. They seemed to be his new passion.

Chuchu talked of his success with his play *La Guerra del Banano*. Then he abruptly asked Graham about the title of his 1957 play *The Potting Shed*. 'What the hell is a potting shed, Graham? Is it a toilet?'

When the laughter died down Graham explained: 'It is a little shed in which the gardener keeps his implements, bulbs and that sort of thing . . . They don't have them in America. They are a very old English tradition, and when we were children they were a place of mystery and romance.' He added archly, 'The play got rather good reviews in New York.'

When Graham registered at the El Panama Hotel he drew our attention to his departure date, which he had written down as 3 September. 'This is the official end of the summer holidays in Europe, and the tourists go home,' he explained with glee. He added that during the off-season his friend Yvonne could reach his place in Antibes in just five minutes from her home in Juan-les-Pins, but in the summer the crush of traffic was such that it took twenty minutes or more.

'Do you drive?' Chuchu asked.

'No, no, I don't own a car. Yvonne has a car and is a very good driver.'

That evening we dined under the stars at the seaside Panamar restaurant. There was hardly a ripple in the Pacific Ocean, which occasionally came alive with dancing phosphorescence that rolled in with the wake of returning fishing boats. Relaxed and happy, Graham extolled the beauty of a balmy Panama night.

Chuchu, however, was not his usual bouncy, expansive self. He admitted he was preoccupied. In fact, he was deeply concerned about the General's ideological compass, which Chuchu claimed had literally gone out of whack. Torrijos, he feared, was opting for social democracy.

Graham fussed with the waiter, making sure the bottle of white Chilean wine he had ordered was not post-Allende. Each time he ordered wine he took pleasure in announcing his boycott. 'I don't give any money to General Pinochet!'

Returning to our conversation, he suggested jokingly that Chuchu had fallen down on his job of proselytizing. 'You've lost the General to the opposition,' Graham chided.

Chuchu, ever the loyal Marxist, took it as a serious reprimand and launched into a tirade against what he claimed were the many wicked weaknesses of the social democrats. Graham, enjoying baiting Chuchu, said he thought the General had made a wise choice and that he himself was beginning to believe social democracy was the best political choice.

Stunned, Chuchu kept repeating, 'But, Graham, Graham, you've got to *know* those corrupt goddamned social democrats!'

It was a long, agitated evening for Chuchu, but it ended on a happy note as he announced that the General had instructed him to fly us up to Torrijos's beach house at Farallon the next day. The General was recuperating from a cold he caught in Santo Domingo. Graham looked at me and shook his head, once again pretending that we had more confidence in Chuchu's poetry than his piloting.

Chuchu protested, 'Graham, I promised to keep you alive till Christmas.' Then he asked, 'What is the name of your new play?'

'*For Whom the Bell Chimes*,' Graham replied.

Chuchu laughed. Then he learned it was no joke but the real name of Graham's play.

At breakfast the following day Graham announced with a certain dignity the good news that Flor's punch had been grandly successful. Only Englishmen, it appears, find the subject of bowel movements agreeable news to share over breakfast.

At the little Paitilla airport Chuchu showed off his little Cessna with pride. It was painted Panama's national colours of red, blue and white with the country's flag embossed on its tail. 'I've done thirteen hours in it since it was fixed up. I gave it a good overhaul,' he said proudly, patting the wings. I insisted on taking some colour photographs of Graham and Chuchu with the little plane, noting that the pictures could be for our families, just in case.

Graham shrugged. 'You can only die once.'

We flew the seventy drowsy miles along the Pacific coast to Farallon, Chuchu at the controls, Graham sitting next to him while I sat behind them. The baking sun streamed in through the side window, making it difficult to stay awake even in the noisy cockpit. Years later Graham would marvel at the fact that Chuchu had managed to transport weapons and ammunition in this small plane to his Sandinista and Salvadorean rebel friends.

With Graham's arrival Omar's cold seemed to improve. Torrijos turned his back abruptly on members of his government team, including the vice-president, with whom he was meeting on the terrace, and ushered us into the interior of his house. It was as if he really wished to turn his back on politics. We watched through a window as the government officials gathered up their papers and quietly departed. Once the terrace was vacated Omar suggested the sea air was better for his cold. He relaxed in his hammock on the terrace and appeared happy to see Graham again. With the birth of the new Canal Treaty, after such a long pregnancy, Torrijos said, he was 'suffering the blues'.

Chuchu identified his illness as 'postpartum psychosis'. We all laughed.

Omar confessed to a feeling of emptiness.

'It's not a fatal illness,' Graham assured him. 'It is the same after completing a book.'

We had lunch on the terrace, and the conversation turned to Panamanian politics. Omar allowed me to record it on my tape-recorder. I later furnished Graham with a translated transcript, and he faithfully recounted extracts of the conversation in *Getting to Know the General*. 'I'm going to give the politicians a big surprise,' Omar said. 'I'm designing a system – a political party – in order to get out. They think I am designing a system to stay in. The politicians are aiming their guns in the wrong direction. They will waste their ammunition and then they will say, "but the son of a bitch is unpredictable".' Then he looked at Graham, as if for approval, and added, 'All I want is a house, rum and a girl.' Chuchu couldn't have agreed more.

Graham saw the down side to such a withdrawal into self. 'You would soon get fed up with such a boring existence, as well as the girl,' he predicted. Graham didn't believe in the archetypal dream of getting away from it all. To him boredom was a cause of depression. The way Graham explained it, he needed stimulus, at least his creativity did, and travel helped. Graham had to recharge his batteries and rejuvenate his senses in order to write.

Chuchu said he recharged his batteries by going out with women.

As Graham talked, I realized that the General seemed to be growing old before our very eyes. He was much more contemplative and nostalgic than in the past. 'I haven't even decided whether I have done good or bad,' he muttered. 'It's like going to the petrol station. You pay and the pump returns to zero. Every time I wake up I'm back to zero.'

Graham and I could not understand the General's pessimism. In addition to negotiating the Panama Canal Treaty, Torrijos could take credit for some impressive infrastructure projects – a hydroelectric dam, schools, health clinics. He had lifted his people up more than any other Panamanian leader and was prepared now to give them participatory democracy.

Chuchu, sensing that the discussion was leading towards a philosophy with which he completely disagreed, stood up and transformed himself back into Sergeant Martínez. 'General,' he said, 'permission to check the aircraft.'

Torrijos nodded and gave him a military salute. Then he smiled as Chuchu disappeared in the direction of Hato Rey airfield. 'To fill the political void,' he said – referring to a void he had helped create with his 1968 coup, and the outlawing of what he termed the corrupt, parasitic political parties – 'we are forming a new kind of political party.'

After a pause he climbed back into his colourful blue, white and red hammock. He could have been Colonel Aureliano Buendía in Gabriel García Márquez's *One Hundred Years of Solitude* returning to Macondo from his wars. Omar made no secret of his distaste for what he described as the 'ridiculous ritualistic rules' and 'pompous and pedantic protocol' that went with governing a country. He preferred the isolation of his rustic ranch house at Coclesito, his Macondo. Farallon, he told us, was far too ostentatious.

There were indeed similarities between Coclesito and García Márquez's mythical village in *One Hundred Years of Solitude*. The General had found Coclesito by accident, dropping down from the sky one day in his helicopter and being shocked by the poverty of the area's subsistence farmers, who were isolated by mountains and ignored and neglected by their government. Coclesito's river flooded regularly. To help the forgotten community the

General built his rustic home and a small airstrip and had helped launch a cooperative to import water buffaloes that could thrive in the region's wet climate. The idea of a pineapple plantation was understandable to Graham and me, but a water buffalo cooperative was a puzzle. Neither of us got a satisfactory explanation about the water buffaloes. For the General, Coclesito was the closest place to heaven. He often dragooned his visitors there and led them on rugged hikes into the hills.

As his soul-searching continued, Omar's words came slowly with each gentle sway of the hammock. Panama was now a much more mature nation, he asserted. An anomaly among nations, it had been born as little more than a simple crossing path from one ocean to another. Now the possibilities for Panama were enormous, he declared. After a long pause he stirred again. 'We must organize a political party for elections . . .' The party would be officially founded in October, the tenth anniversary of the coup that brought the General to power.

'I'm too old to talk about the future,' he said. 'The future belongs to the youth, to our young technocrats. A political party, democracy, is necessary.' He said the country had been in great need of change, and he believed that he had brought about that change and pre-empted the ultra-left, and 'stolen the ammunition they needed for a revolution. We are too small to have a bloody revolution – and for what? Panamanians need to own their land, have pride in their country, their own national identity, and not be simply a fresh water and vegetable market for foreign vessels transiting the Canal, or servants of the *gringos* and the *rabiblancos* (upper-class Establishment) of the Union Club.'

As for himself, it was evident that Omar was experiencing political exhaustion. 'When people find a leader,' he said, 'they work him to death like a peasant works a good ox to death. The peasants speak to me frankly, and the peasant knows when you have to limp even when you may be curled up in a hammock.'

Omar knew that Chuchu would be taking us to meet his Nicaraguan-exile friends, and he asked us not to mention that we had met him. Father Ernesto Cardenal, the Nicaraguan poet-priest, Torrijos explained, had been asking to meet with him. None the less, as we left Omar said in an aside to me, 'They [the Sandinista rebels] will get up steam.'

I had asked him what he thought might happen in Nicaragua, since a new offensive proclaimed by the Sandinistas against President Anastasio Somoza appeared to be stalled.

'The guerrilla offensive is like a locomotive,' he said. 'To get up speed you must first build up steam.'

Graham, Chuchu and I flew back to Panama City in Chuchu's Cessna through a harrowing electrical storm. Upon arriving safely Graham noted dryly that he had never considered meeting death by electrocution. *Time* reduced my story on Graham's meeting with Omar to an item in the People section in the issue of 4 September 1978. It was illustrated with a colour photograph, snapped by me, of the General lolling in his hammock conversing with Graham.

The night of 21 August was hot and humid. Graham and I were led by Chuchu into the small Panama City apartment of Dr Ramiro (Camilo) Contreras, brother of dead Nicaraguan rebel Eduardo Contreras Escobar. As we arrived Chuchu told us that we had been invited to help celebrate the thirty-seventh birthday of another famous anti-Somoza Nicaraguan guerrilla, El Danto. Chuchu hugged and kissed the female guerrillas who were present, obviously thriving on close-quarters combat. Graham, on the other hand, detested such parties. I could see it on his face. He told me he was feeling awkward and pronounced himself allergic to organized social gatherings and the singing of Happy Birthday, or *Las Mañanitas*, no matter where they took place.

Graham implemented various defensive tactics to keep Father Ernesto Cardenal at bay. The priest, Graham felt, was 'just a little ridiculous; a caricature with his flowing white beard and hair under a black beret'. Once he got to know him Graham would change his opinion about the revolutionary cleric-poet, considering him sincere and committed. (Many of Graham's early critical appraisals of the Nicaraguan guerrillas' leaders were later modified as he became better acquainted with them. For example, at first he didn't like Daniel Ortega, who was to become president of Nicaragua, or Tomás Borge, the powerful interior minister, but once Graham got to know them his views of these men changed. It was unusual because Graham's snap judgements of people often proved to be quite accurate.)

Father Cardenal succeeded in cornering Graham between toasts and the ceremonial slicing of the birthday cake. The rebel priest was persistent. He kept telling Graham that he should visit Nicaragua and witness the war. It was an invitation that Chuchu and I did not encourage, as the logistics of joining the guerrillas in the mountains of Nicaragua would be difficult and risky. The rebels at the party emphasized that they were revolutionaries who were simply recharging their energies with some rest and relaxation, and were in no way refugees or exiles. Some of the women guerrillas were in Panama to see their gynaecologists.

We found El Danto, whose real name was Germán Pomares Ordoñez, seated with his back to a wall wearing a black beret. Guerrillas can be deceptive-looking, but there was nothing deceptive about the swarthy physically powerful Pomares whose birthday we were celebrating. He had been one of the founders of the Sandinista National Liberation Front (FSLN) in 1962. He was a weapons expert and considered the FSLN's top combat commander. As a child he had toiled in cotton fields, and he had moved up the leftist ranks through youth and union organizations. Only recently he had been taken prisoner in Honduras by the Honduran army, but when the Honduran authorities threatened to return him to Nicaragua sympathetic Honduran students took to the streets of Tegucigalpa in protest. The Honduran military finally handed Pomares over to Panama, where he had been granted political asylum.

At our guerrilla party, Pomares, never once removing his black beret, talked quietly of their coming battles. It was difficult to hear him above the din of the dance music and impossible for me to translate his words for Graham. Nevertheless, by cocking an ear closely I could absorb Pomares's message. El Danto described his great fear of a coup d'état that would rob the Sandinistas of their ultimate victory, leaving 'Somocismo sin Somoza' (Somozaism without Somoza) intact in Nicaragua. 'The whole rotten, corrupt system must be eradicated, not just the removal of one man,' Pomares declared. Radical change, he was convinced, could come only with a people's war.

I told him we had nearly met once before. He had been the FSLN military commander of a notorious guerrilla operation in 1974 and I was one of the newsmen covering that story. He smiled and said it had been a successful operation. Shortly before 11 p.m. on 27 December 1974 Sandinista commandos with guns blazing crashed a fashionable post-Christmas party in Managua. The party host, Managua businessman José María Castillo Quant, was shot to death when he tried to resist. The Sandinistas held hostage a number of relatives of Somoza and other influential friends of the regime. They were eventually exchanged for fourteen imprisoned Sandinistas. Among the latter, freed after seven years in prison, was Daniel Ortega. He flew off to Havana on 30 December with thirteen ex-prisoner companions and the thirteen commandos.

During our conversation at the Panama party Pomares conceded that the Sandinistas had suffered serious setbacks since then. Eduardo Contreras Escobar, the handsome Comandante Zero (Sandinistas always code-named the leader of an operation 'Cero' or 'Zero' and the second-in-command as 'Number One'), who had led the Christmas party raid in Managua, had been killed on 7 November 1976 in a shoot-out with one of Somoza's special anti-terrorist patrols. Two days later the Sandinistas lost their leader, Carlos Fonseca Amador, who was killed in action in the Nicaraguan mountains.

However, much else of what El Danto said was lost to the music as his comrades and several compañeras in the last stages of pregnancy danced determinedly to a Panamanian tamborito. He declined to predict how long their struggle would take.

Irritated at not being able to talk with Pomares and deafened by the loud music, Graham said he'd had enough.

'Let's get out of here. Let's leave Chuchu. He is enjoying himself.' Graham grabbed his throat dramatically to indicate he was suffocating. We walked until a taxi came along, and we returned to the hotel.

That night over a quiet drink Graham talked about the curious fact that the late Comandante Zero's pretty Panamanian wife, María Isabel, who had been our hostess at the birthday party, now lived with Dr Ramiro Contreras, brother of the slain commander. What Graham had found especially strange was that María Isabel had shown him a large portrait of her dead guerrilla husband peering down from a wall in her and Dr Contreras's bedroom. 'How could it be? It is strange. Maybe guerrillas look at life and death differently,' Graham mused. 'How can they make love with her dead husband looking down on them all the time?'

Graham pretended to be a timid soul. He abhorred wars and revolutions, he said. Yet the night we met Pomares Graham told me, 'I would go to Nicaragua if I could go with him. I trust him.'

We never saw El Danto again. He was soon back in Nicaragua battling Somoza. A year later, covering the war in Nicaragua, I was promised an interview in the field with Pomares. The interview was postponed. Then I was told it was off. No reason was given. Then I learned why. On Sunday 30 May 1979 a final offensive was to be launched against Somoza's forces. It was a final battle for Comandante Pomares. He was killed leading his men in an attempt to take the town of Jinotega.

17 | OPERATION SIR FRANCIS DRAKE

'What is this thing with El Draque [Drake]? Is he a relative of Graham?'
General Torrijos asked, mystified, as he ordered his helicopter for our early-morning flight to the Caribbean coast for 'Operation El Draque', as we had nicknamed Graham's project.

'No, General,' I said. 'Sir Francis Drake is related to his boyhood.' Both Chuchu and I did our best to explain how British schools, even in the colonies, taught students about the sterling exploits of the great English sea captain and navigator and how he had wrested control of the high seas from Spain for England.

Omar shook his head, muttering something about how the English were a strange race. Maybe it's good, he conceded, for a man of Graham's age to seek to satisfy a boyhood yearning. Torrijos relished the humour in the cultural dichotomy. 'We learned at school,' he said, 'that El Draque was a red-bearded *hijo de puta* [son of a whore], a *pinche pirata* [plundering pirate] like that other son-of-a-bitch Englishman, Henry Morgan, who sacked Panama.'

'Morgan,' Graham corrected the General, 'was a Welshman.'

At a very young age, Graham said, he had seen a pageant play in London in which Drake attacked a Spanish mule train laden with gold and silver crossing the isthmus of Panama to Nombre de Dios, the Spanish King's Caribbean treasure house. Loot from the Spanish colonies in America was stored there to await the annual convoy to Cadíz. The play had made a lasting impression on Graham. 'With the aid of roundshot,' he explained, 'Drake hijacked gold stolen by the Spaniards from the Incas for his Queen.' The exchange between Graham and Omar soared to the level of macro-economic theory. The kindest thing the General could say about El Draque was that he had really been working for the state (the Crown) and that his piratical activities were an early form of capitalist enterprise. Surprisingly, Graham agreed with the General. In fact, Graham had implied a similar conclusion in his book *Travels with My Aunt*. I mentioned this to Omar, and we all laughed, even though Graham never liked to quote from his own books. In that book wonderful old Aunt Augusta says, 'A little honest thieving hurts no one, especially when it is a question of gold. Gold needs free circulation. The Spanish Empire would have decayed far more quickly if Sir Francis Drake had not kept a portion of the Spanish gold in circulation.'

With a mischievous glint in his eyes, and clearly relishing the topic, Graham added that he had learned from reading history at Oxford that Drake was indeed a gentleman who had wined and dined the defeated Spanish galleon captains. This gave pause to Omar, who said Drake seemed like his kind of guy – as Omar had wined and dined *his* own enemies, even the *gringo* Canal negotiators. Graham continued building his case for Sir Francis, declaring that Drake whenever possible had put captured Spanish crews ashore. (Only recently I had told Graham about a contemporary Nicaraguan poem that cited Drake as behaving in the best tradition of a gentleman. The poet had obtained his research from actual files in the colonial archives in Madrid. The poem recounts that Drake had dined with the Spanish governor of what is today Nicaragua on silver plates, and Drake had apologized for taking some of the governor's silver for the Queen of England.)

Omar appreciated Graham's English history lesson but remained unconvinced of the lofty humanity of El Draque. However, the General was duly impressed by the legend that Drake, a really cool character, had delayed the battle with the Spanish Armada until he completed his game of bowls.

In 1596 Drake had died of a fever and was buried at sea in a lead coffin off Panama, which was one reason for our helicopter expedition to the coast. Despite the differences in historical interpretation, we took off for Panama's Caribbean shore in high spirits. Soon the city of Colón on the Atlantic side of the Canal hove into view. Graham, who was the unofficial commander of the expedition, began signalling that he was thirsty and we should drop down for a drink at the George Washington Hotel. Chuchu agreed and instructed the pilot to land. The pilot followed his orders to the letter and descended in the hotel's garden, forcing the palm trees to bend in salute to our rotor. We immediately went in search of a barman and had him open the bar even though it was still long before noon.

Graham was in rare form. He pronounced the George Washington Hotel's planter's punch pure nectar, and we toasted Sir Francis and George Washington. Rejuvenated, we choppered off into the sun in search of Nombre de Dios, alighting near an Indian village. However, we came up empty. With a look of disbelief, Graham lamented that we couldn't find a single trace of the fabled embarkation port – the end of the Camino Real (Royal Road) over which mules laden with Spanish plunder plodded across the rugged isthmus.

'What a reassuring sight the colonial town must have been to the tough muleteers,' Graham reflected, adjusting his floppy gardener's hat that kept obscuring his view. He wanted to see what they saw, but nature defied us. 'There must be *some* old fortifications left, surely!' Graham protested.

But we found none, not even a stone from the ballast that the Spanish ships carried *en route* to the Indies. 'It [Nombre de Dios] was built on blood and plunder and man's greed,' Graham said as he surveyed the trees and heavy undergrowth. Nevertheless, like García Márquez's mythical Macondo, Nombre de Dios had evidently surrendered to the jungle after more than two hundred years of solitude.

The Indians and blacks that lived side by side in separate villages near by were not particularly interested in sharing Graham's historic fervour. The sun was overhead, and they were sensibly indoors and seemed to know all about the saying 'Only mad dogs and Englishmen go out in the midday sun', which Graham recited for Chuchu's benefit.

Graham was ecstatic with his search and moved through the jungle at a good pace. He said the jungle reminded him of Indochina but that the Malay jungle was the densest he had ever penetrated. We stopped to rest in the shade on the stoop of a thatched house, where he began chatting to the Indians in English. They seemed amused by the rosy-faced man wearing a comical hat. An indigenous inhabitant with an enormous head replied to his questions in English and joined us in plodding along the beach where our shoes sank into the sand.

Suddenly Graham stopped. Poised like a bird dog, he looked seawards. 'I feel vibes. Drake is near,' he announced dramatically.

Chuchu, who always seemed prepared to believe anything, was the first to respond. 'Where, Graham, where?'

Graham stood anchored in the fine sand, which reached up to his ankles. We all waited in silence for more precise directional data from Graham's vibes, but the spell was broken when our two helicopter pilots in their orange flight suits trudged up to show Chuchu a point on their map.

'They want to apologize,' Chuchu explained. 'They dropped us in the wrong place. It's up there.' And he gestured towards an area further up the beach. So much for Graham's vibes!

We trudged along to another strip of sand. Undeterred, Graham was still animated by the adventure. When we rested again, he suggested that Drake had probably drifted a considerable distance in his lead coffin during his three hundred years in the water. He continued to act like a hunting hound, sniffing the air occasionally and surveying the sea. The George Washington Hotel's planter's punches and the sun were a powerful combination that made communication with the dead – even the long dead – possible. Unfortunately, Graham, who despite the heat was enjoying himself immensely, received no more vibes from his 'spiritual sonar system', as Chuchu called it.

Chuchu suggested that we had covered enough of the Panamanian coastline for one day. Graham was sunburned, lobster-red, despite his wide-brimmed floppy hat. We trudged back to our waiting chopper and flew on to the ancient town of Puertobello to examine its colonial fortifications, which Drake had managed to pierce before he died at sea.

'The casket is still there somewhere,' Graham avowed, adding that a psychic had once said he would have been a good medium.

After we landed in Panama City one of our pilots, when thanked for the trip, wanted to know what kind of treasure 'the old man' was looking for. 'He's just a history buff,' Chuchu replied.

When Omar heard of our expeditionary failure he joined in the game and offered Graham a dredge to continue the search in a more practical manner.

My file to *Time* was brief:

> British author Graham Greene can recite what he calls the 'good bad' poem of Henry Newbolt verse after verse about the death at sea off the coast of Panama of Sir Francis Drake, that gallant British navigator. He made a sentimental journey back to what is left of Nombre de Dios bay where the British poet suggests Drake's remains were buried at sea, in a lead chest and weighed down with roundshot. Just in case he also visited Puertobello, the famous Spanish ruins further along the coast near the Atlantic mouth of the Panama Canal where . . . an expedition searched as recently as three years ago for Sir Francis in a lead box, without success.

After a lobster lunch at the Panamar restaurant and careful wine selection, we returned to the hotel for an afternoon siesta. It was a rare luxury, but it proved to be my last siesta for a long time. The persistent ringing of the telephone awoke me.

'Hello, hello,' said a far-off voice.

'Yes,' I answered.

'Why aren't you in Nicaragua?' the voice said disapprovingly.

I was about to say, 'Because I'm in Panama,' but as my head began to clear I asked, 'Why?'

'The story is in Managua,' the voice said excitedly. 'Rebels have seized the palace there.' It was the foreign editor of the *Washington Star,* which *Time* had recently acquired. He wanted me to file a story on the takeover of the palace for that evening's edition. I told the editor it might not be that big a story because Nicaraguan President Somoza didn't use the palace, one of the few buildings to survive the 1972 Managua earthquake. Somoza preferred to work from his so-called 'bunker' or at his nearby home. 'It's not Somoza we are concerned with,' the editor said. 'The rebels are reportedly holding four thousand people hostage in the palace, including the Nicaraguan congress, which was in session at the time.'

'OK, OK,' I replied and got out of bed. 'I'm on my way.'

I decided against waking Graham from his siesta and instead slipped a note under his door advising him of my departure. I then raced to the airport to catch the afternoon Pan American Airways flight to Managua. Anxiously I had checked the condition of my Olivetti portable typewriter and camera in anticipation of a good story, but as the plane neared Managua the captain announced that because of the unsettled political situation we would not be landing there.

I pleaded with the stewardess to tell the captain to let me off. I assured her the airport was safe. 'It's a long way from the trouble in the city,' I said.

But it was no use. We flew on to Guatemala City.

The following day, Wednesday 23 August, with a whole gang of foreign correspondents from Mexico and Miami, I was able to fly into Managua. It was indeed a major story. Sandinista commandos, numbering only twenty-two, had captured not only thousands of ordinary citizens paying their taxes in the government offices but Somoza's entire rubber-stamp congress which had been in session at the time. Several of the hostages were relatives of Somoza. It was a guerrilla record, the largest hostage-taking in Central America.

Ultimately Somoza called off an initial attack to retake the palace, which had not been successful, and agreed to negotiate. Negotiations were under way when we arrived. The Sandinistas were demanding the release of fifty-nine of their comrades being held as political prisoners, $10 million in cash, the repeated broadcast over government radio stations of a two-hour-long Sandinista communiqué and their choice of air transport out of the country. They asked for Mexican, Venezuelan or Panamanian aircraft. Somoza bowed to their demands, although he cut a bargain with the Sandinistas to reduce the ransom money to half a million dollars. (The Sandinistas' communiqué was read three times a day for the next two days over the radio and on television and also published in the press.) The next day, Thursday, government police and soldiers were ordered to allow the guerrillas and their freed political prisoners open passage to the airport. It was a carnival scene. The police had disappeared. And when the people of Managua heard that the police had been ordered off the streets everyone seemed to converge on the airport highway and terminal to catch a glimpse of the Sandinistas, whom they treated as heroes. Driving a rental car with two photographers, I tailgated the caravan of buses from the palace, on to the tarmac and up to the waiting aircraft, a Venezuelan Air Force C-130 and a COPA Panamanian airliner. The leader of the twenty-two Sandinista commandos, Edén Pastora, stopped before entering the aircraft and posed for photographers, his rifle held high in a gesture of triumph. The picture became a popular Sandinista poster and Edén Pastora an instant hero of the revolution.

It was only the beginning of the Nicaraguan story. In the wake of the palace seizure a general strike was called by the Broad Opposition Front (FAO), made up mostly of business groups demanding the resignation of President

Somoza, the third family member to rule Nicaragua over more than thirty years. Youthful rebels, calling themselves Los Muchachos (the Boys), rose up and seized much of the picturesque town of Matagalpa. Suddenly it was shades of the Spanish Civil War and Guernica as Somoza ordered his air force to bomb his own people. As the guerrilla war spread Matagalpa, Estelí, Jinotega and Masaya as well as Managua became my datelines in the months that followed. For the next eleven months Nicaragua became my second home.

Back in Panama, Chuchu was so jubilant at the Sandinistas' hostage-taking coup that he got drunk and deprived Graham of his front-row seat in the Nicaragua drama. 'Chuchu and I were supposed to go on the plane fetching the hostages and commandos,' Graham wrote on his return to Antibes, 'but unfortunately Chuchu misunderstood the General's instructions [Chuchu later confirmed that he was too drunk to fully comprehend the General's orders] to spend the night at the airport and the plane left at four in the morning and we only arrived to get it at five! Chuchu received a reprimand from the General. But it wasn't serious.'

Chuchu did take Graham to see the newly freed prisoners and members of the audacious commando team who had freed them. They were being held temporarily at a Panamanian army base. Graham, like the General, was impressed with Edén Pastora, who was as handsome as a film star and a symbol of Sandinista defiance.

Graham wrote from Antibes:

> How good it was to see you for those few days in Panama. I very much liked your piece in *Time* [which now gave correspondents bylines] about the fighting in Matagalpa and I am glad that you came out alive to write it. I think unless something dramatic happens this is my last visit to Panama. I found the journey rather exhausting. Torrijos sent me and Chuchu up to Belize to see [Prime Minister George] Price and I enjoyed that trip except that there was nothing to eat except shrimps and we were stuck for long periods both ways in Salvador. At first I didn't care for Price but afterwards I came to the conclusion that he had been shy and we got along very well. An interesting and curious man. Another disappointment, I missed my caviar lunch on the way back to Amsterdam because we over-flew Lisbon and all we had in place of a luxurious meal was a selection of Dutch cheese.

Gabriel García Márquez, he added, had come to Panama City, and they had introduced him to Flor's rum punches at the Señorial.

On their return to Panama from Belize, Graham related, Chuchu had said he needed to stop over in San José, Costa Rica, to talk with an important Sandinista. While Chuchu met with his Sandinista contact, Graham had the pleasure of chatting with the 'lovely' Nicaraguan poet Rosario Murillo who had once been an occupant of Chuchu's guerrilla safe house in Panama City. Much later Graham learned that Chuchu's contact, who was with Rosario in San José that night, was Daniel Ortega, the man who was destined to become head of the Sandinista Junta and later President of Nicaragua.

He wrote on 9 October 1978:

> A hasty line, I'm afraid, to thank you for your most interesting and detailed letter of September 26 as I am just off to Anacapri for about two weeks. You must have had a terrifying time in Nicaragua and you were much in the thoughts of Chuchu and me. It's a terrible thing that Somoza has been allowed to run riot in this way. To think that he excused paying up for the hostages in the National Palace in order, as he said, to save human life! I should be sorry to see him going into a comfortable retirement and I do trust the Sandinistas will end by bumping him off.
>
> Alas, I seem to have been wrong about Drake's burial. It was off an island in Portobelo Bay according to the only book I have here. I think I did write to you when I got back but my memory is very hazy so you will know that Chuchu and I had a very interesting two days in Belize – it was the General's idea. George Price is well worth a visit. So is the Vice-Premier who looks like a black Edward VII. An interesting point emerged from him that the British contingent of troops is apt to make manoeuvres on the Guatemala side of the frontier without informing the Government. [Guatemala had long asserted claims on Belizean territory, challenging Britain's influence in its former colony.] There might be a story there. We angered the opposition by giving a radio interview stressing the friendship between Price and Torrijos. The leading opposition paper in an editorial referred to us as 'the so-called author Green [*sic*] and agent Martinez of Panama'.

In a letter dated 8 November Graham wrote:

> I have only just got your letter of September 29 partly because of the French post strikes and partly because I have been away for about two weeks in London and Switzerland. No news yet on *When the Bell Chimes* [*sic*].
>
> Don't bother to send me any further background on the Sandinistas. I doubt whether I shall see any of them again and your articles in *Time*

have really covered the ground admirably. I must say I rather like the idea of the Wild Pigs (a Panamanian anti-guerrilla unit) going to fight beside the Sandinistas, though I suppose it would be a disaster for the continent.

At the end of 1978 my editors at *Time* agreed with my suggestion that we ask Graham to write an article about the Caribbean, including Belize. They also assented to my further proposal that Graham and I wind up a trip in Cuba with an interview with Fidel Castro. Excited, I telephoned Graham in Antibes to discuss the project and was shocked to discover that he was scheduled to undergo an operation in London to remove part of his intestines. Apart from such a dire medical prospect, he was not enthusiastic about the project in any case. In a letter he wrote on 9 January 1979, he said:

> It was very nice hearing your voice on the telephone. I feel more and more doubtful about the *Time* magazine project. 4,000 words anyway scares me. I don't like to be committed to such a large article by accepting payment as if it were in advance for my expenses. [I could hear him again telling the story of his assignment for *Life* magazine, which involved his going into Malaya at the end of 1950 to report on the Communist guerrilla war, and then moving on to Vietnam. 'They were very generous,' he had said, 'and paid me $5,000 for one article they didn't even publish and which I later published in *Paris Match*. It was a lot of money in those days.'] As far as talking to Fidel is concerned you would do it far better than I as a practised interviewer. Let's leave our plans for the moment as something vaguely in the Caribbean. Do you know Belize? It's really a very charming place and worth a visit. My love to you and Ginette.

In a letter dated 19 March 1979 from Antibes, thanking me for a 'long and interesting letter' and then leaving the important things to last, Graham wrote, 'You must forgive a very brief reply as I have been having a rather nasty operation in a hospital in London for two weeks and still feel a bit feeble. I hope I shall be feeling all right when summer comes and we can make plans, but I have been told that I must do no travelling for the next two months.'

He also commented on a meeting that I had reported on between Pope John Paul II and the bishops of the western hemisphere in Puebla, Mexico.

> I had a different impression reading about the Pope's speech in Puebla. I took it as an encouragement for the progressives and simply a discouragement for priests actually to take up arms. That should be left to the laymen. This point of view seems to me reasonable. Rogelio,

the Panamanian Sandinista, visited me a month or two back and I sent a little money to their bank account in Panama – only enough I am afraid to buy a silver bullet to shoot Somoza with.

It proved a very difficult year for Graham. Not only did he have his intestinal tract to worry about; he was highly distressed about an interview he had given to the *New Yorker* magazine – or, more precisely, its rendition of the interview. A month later, on 19 April, he wrote:

> I have just seen a copy of the *New Yorker* which you may have seen with a so-called Profile by Mrs Gilliatt. I little thought the *New Yorker* were capable of publishing such inaccuracies or Mrs Gilliatt of writing them. I have written the enclosed letters to the *New Yorker* but of course they don't publish letters but it may warn the editor and cause some discomfort to Mrs Gilliatt . . . I wish there was some way of getting at her through *Time* magazine!

One of Graham's letters to the editor of the *New Yorker,* dated 18 April and which was enclosed, stated:

> Dear Sir, I was shocked to read in a paper like the *New Yorker* the Profile made by Mrs Gilliatt on my poor self. If your magazine printed correspondence I would ask you to print the enclosed. Surely there must be some way of drawing attention to her mistakes and misstatements . . . having counted more than fifty misstatements, misquotations and inaccuracies in Mrs Gilliatt's Profile, I gave up the job. I advise your readers not to take any sentence on trust as reporting what I thought or said or have done. To take a few large and small inaccuracies: I was never invited to an internment camp in Argentina, if any exists, there are no vultures in Antibes, I never saw Miss Tutin act in Russia, no Communist from the Czech Federal Ministry of Foreign Affairs has ever called me on the BBC 'a liar', etc. These epithets were published by Dr Duvalier of Haiti. The Czech official, like all but a few lines of Mrs Gilliatt's article, is the product of her very odd imagination and her very imperfect memory. I advise her in the future to use a tape-recorder and make sure that there is no vulture under her bed.

Graham could become extremely cross with what he called, 'the silly things people write about me'. He complained that they were constantly searching for some deeper meaning but became intellectually lost in the process.

*

I would like to think the Nicaraguan revolution ended on 18 July 1979, my fifty-third birthday, but the Sandinistas declared the 19th as the official end of hostilities and the day they took over the country. On returning to my base in Mexico City after spending the preceding three months covering the war, I found a letter dated 1 June from Graham in which he wrote:

> I am sorry I simply can't remember the name of Contreras's wife. I ought to as I have seen a great deal of her but I'm very bad at remembering names.
>
> I fear we will have to leave our Caribbean journey until next year. My operation in March and difficulties in Yvonne's family has meant that I haven't yet got to my little house in Anacapri and I think we will have to go there in late August. That only leaves me a few possible weeks in early August to arrange anything and I'm not sure yet that I feel fit enough. I have to go to London at the end of June for an examination and of course a good deal depends on that.
>
> I believe the General and Chuchu are going to be over in Europe this summer. I had a visitor from Panama a week or two back – the political counsellor who was there when we went to have lunch with Torrijos last time – and he was very pessimistic about the situation. Apparently Panama has lost the support of Colombia since the elections, Venezuela are very feeble supporters and they find themselves again alone. They believe that the emendations to the [Panama Canal] Treaty which will be made by the [US] Congress will make it impossible to accept it, and then there is going to be trouble in October. I imagine that's one of the points of the General's visit to Europe and also one of the reasons why he has gone back to the army. Anyway let's keep in touch.
>
> By the way I gained a very optimistic impression of the Sandinistas from the political adviser. He said the Western press had gone far astray and that the fight in Estelí was a real victory. The Sandinistas only lost a very few men and finally left town with more than a thousand recruits unstopped by the National Guard. He gave Somoza only a few more months to survive. Let's hope he wasn't being over-optimistic like the General was last year. It's a very good idea you should write a book on him [Somoza].

The political adviser had been correct regarding Estelí, as I and my press colleagues all were. In fact, none of us covering the war had underestimated the results of the climactic battle in Estelí, and we all knew that Somoza's days were indeed numbered.

On 7 August Graham wrote:

> I have received an invitation from the President, Royo . . . for [Panama's] celebration at the end of September of the symbolic entry into the Canal Zone. I imagine you'll be there, but I am not absolutely sure that I'll go this time as I feel lazy after my February operation and I may be in Capri. Anyway do let me know if you will be there as it would help to sway my decision.

Graham missed a day of great emotion, at least for Panamanians. US President Jimmy Carter, armed with the necessary implementing legislation voted by Congress, had signed the Panama Canal Act three days earlier, and Vice-President Walter Mondale headed a large delegation from Washington. It was a truly festive time. At dawn on 1 October Panama's new civilian President, Aristides Royo, led a march by members of his government and thousands of Panamanian citizens up Ancon Hill in what was now the former Canal Zone and unfurled a gigantic Panamanian flag. As the flag of Panama reached the top of the flagstaff, Royo declared, 'A state within a state no longer exists.'

Meanwhile leftist guerrillas were on the move in El Salvador. Eleven business-men had already been kidnapped that year for ransom money that would go to the guerrillas' war chest. Washington, fearful of another Nicaragua, was pressing the government of General Carlos Humberto Romero to institute political reforms, but El Salvador's powerful oligarchy warned against any concessions to the left. At the same time the United States was secretly talking to progressive elements in the military that Washington hoped might forestall another bloody revolution in Central America. Yet while the big story in the region in the autumn of 1979 was El Salvador, there was yet another story back in Panama: the Shah of Iran.

A popular uprising had forced Shah Mohammad Reza Pahlavi and his wife Farah to flee Iran in January 1979. While bouncing from one refuge to another they descended virtually in my backyard, in the lovely eternal-spring resort of Cuernavaca, just over the mountains from Mexico City. Then shortly before Christmas the royal couple landed on the beach of Contadora Island off Panama. President Carter's press secretary, Hamilton Jordan, who was on good terms with Omar Torrijos, had arrived to consult with the General. Without hesitation, between puffs of his Cohiba cigar, Omar agreed to take in the Shah as a favour to Panama's friend President Carter, who was by now in deep political trouble over the seizing of American hostages in Tehran. Carter had allowed the Shah to fly to New York for medical reasons, and

Islamic fundamentalist rebels in Iran had reacted by seizing the US embassy and holding its staff of fifty as hostages. The rebels demanded the Shah's return to stand trial in exchange for the hostages' freedom. For the United States the hostage crisis became the drama of 1980 and was to cost Carter his bid for re-election.

Mexico, already angered at the Shah for showing a preference for New York's medical facilities over their own, refused to allow the Shah back into the country, and the Carter administration felt duty-bound to find another haven for the exiled Iranian ruler.

By the time I arrived on Contadora Island to report on the Shah's move there, the pretty young aide whom Omar had designated to act as liaison with the Shah and his party was fed up. She pleaded with me to tell Omar she couldn't stand playing nursemaid to rude royalty. Ideologically, she would have preferred to have been on Via España in Panama City with the scores of students who were demonstrating against the Shah's presence in Panama. (Torrijos's National Guardsmen viciously repressed the anti-Shah demonstrators, several of whom required hospitalization.)

The bungalow belonging to the former Panamanian ambassador to the United States, Gabriel Lewis Galindo, where the Shah and his family were staying. It was hardly big enough for even a petite Peacock Throne, but the Shah and his wife managed. Almost daily they went out to play tennis with some of the chic guests at the new Contadora Hotel, a short drive down the hill from the bungalow. The Shah finally decamped from Panama for Egypt in March 1980.

Graham wrote in a letter dated 17 June 1980:

> A tardy good wishes for the anniversary you must have been celebrat-
> ing last Saturday. How time flies! You must have been very newly
> married when I first met you and Ginette. I very much look forward to
> reading your book on the Somozas. A young reporter who came to
> interview me this year – I think he was Dutch – apparently at one time
> knew the Somozas and was a friend of Tacho. He told me that Tacho
> used to read my books! Well, one isn't responsible for one's readers.
>
> About Managua in August. I can't for the moment decide as it all
> depends on the situation here. Yvonne and [her daughter] Martine are
> having a good deal of trouble with the ex-husband of Martine who
> belongs to the Mafia and I don't like leaving them for too long at a time.
> I have to leave them on July 6 to go to Spain at the invitation of the
> Mayor of Madrid and afterwards to do my annual trip with my friend
> Father Duran, and I hope the trip will revive my interest in a comic novel
> [*Monsignor Quixote*] I began. But let's keep in touch about Managua.

18 | WAITING FOR THE GUERRILLA

In a letter dated 30 July 1980 Graham wrote, 'Chuchu has been on the phone and I have told him that I'd go out to Panama some time between 16 and 20 August. Apparently the General wants me to have a look at Nicaragua. It would be great fun if you came too.'

He now stood at the corner window in Suite 921 in the Hotel El Continental and looked out at the vacant lot across the street where a circus was setting up. He was fascinated by the effort of two elephants, tethered to stakes in the ground, swinging their trunks back and forth in desperation, trying to reach what little straw was left in the mud just out of their reach.

'The poor devils are starved,' he said.

I joined him at the window. Via España, Panama City's main thoroughfare, was filled with traffic. I drew his attention to the buses with their bright, exotic artwork, reminiscent of Haiti.

We had just returned from a gluttonous meal of *bacalao* (dried codfish), preceded by our customary rum punch ordered by Graham as 'not too sweet and with an extra dash of Meyers's [rum], please'.

Not only did he show sympathy for the hapless elephants, but he saw their predicament as a metaphor for our own. We were virtually shackled to the room, waiting. Graham hated waiting. The past three days had been just that: waiting. But in this case a man's life was at stake, and we had no alternative but to wait. The conversation over lunch had been about family, which was rare for him; he rarely discussed his family.

'Last year I put my money in a trust for my two children. I might live to ninety, and there is no reason why they shouldn't enjoy it before they get old,' he said.

I had picked up the bill for the rum punches at the Holiday Inn, and because they were made to his instructions the cost for the two drinks came to an incredible $37 – tip not included. Graham offered to pay with the credit card to which he charged all his expenses, but I insisted and put the bill on my *Time* expense account.

'How generous they are,' Graham said of *Time* and *Life* and told me again of his reporting for *Life* in South-East Asia. It was also the year that *Time* had honoured Graham with a cover story introducing his works to millions of the magazine's readers. (The fact that Graham had written articles for *Life* in no way influenced the editors of *Time* in their choice of Graham as a cover subject.) *Time* pegged their story to the publication of Graham's latest book, *The End of the Affair*, and pronounced him the writer of the day.

Graham was happy with the article in *Time*, which ended its long and provocative cover piece as follows:

> How much fuss will posterity make about Graham Greene? Will it rate him as high as Hemingway or Faulkner? Will he outlast Evelyn Waugh? Will he be mentioned in the same breath as Dostoevsky? Only posterity can answer. But with these three contemporaries, at any rate, Greene can hold up his head. He is as accomplished a craftsman as they, and without the mannerisms with which the two Americans have begun to burlesque their own styles. He has neither the snigger nor the snobbery that are Waugh's trademarks. But when Greene is compared with Dostoevsky, the great shocker of the 19th century, all his books together would not match one *Brothers Karamazov*. That the comparison should even come to mind, however, suggests its inevitability. Graham Greene, like Dostoevsky, is primarily and passionately concerned with Good and Evil. There are not many competitors in that field.

In Panama City on 22 August 1980 the weather was as hot and humid as it always is in the midst of the rainy season. Graham had arrived three days earlier on a KLM flight from Amsterdam. It was his fourth trip to Panama, and this time he was on a mission. He could have been playing the part of a character in one of his books. The year before he had had an operation, and he had become obsessed with the complex marital misfortunes of Yvonne's daughter. It was not Martine's divorce that bothered him but the unjust and corrupt system that, he said, confined her to an area of the Riviera that was literally under the nose of the 'scoundrel ex-husband' whom he said was terrorizing the family.

Still, he had found time to write another book, *Doctor Fischer of Geneva or The Bomb Party*. He dedicated the book to his daughter, Caroline Bourget, 'at whose Christmas table at Jongny [Switzerland] this story first came to me'. The idea for the book, he said, came from the gaily wrapped Christmas crackers that produce a small bang and a few goodies when tugged apart.

One night in April 1979, an hour or so after midnight, Graham was awakened from sleep in his Antibes home by the persistent ringing of the telephone. It was Chuchu, wanting to know when Graham was coming to Panama. 'Graham,' he said, 'the General is sending someone to meet you.'

A few nights later the envoy from the General arrived in Antibes and telephoned Graham. When they met the young messenger explained that General Torrijos was concerned about the fate of two English bankers kidnapped by the Salvadorean guerrillas. The rebels holding the two bankers had lost contact with the bankers' home office. Torrijos's messenger brought a mysterious Mexico City telephone number with him to be passed on to the bankers' home office to enable them to re-establish contact with the guerrillas and complete the negotiations for their release. The messenger explained that all they wanted Graham to do was find the home office of the bankers. Graham had never heard of the Bank of London, but his sister Elisabeth managed to track down their head office.

The guerrillas wanted the bank to know that they had modified their demands. Only the ransom remained to be paid.

Graham said that when they finally located the bank, 'I told the bank people who were suspicious and surprised by my call that I had spent time in Central America and had good contacts there. It was a simple enough task,' he said, brushing off his involvement and ultimately saving the lives of two fellow Britons.

Whenever he told this story Graham said he had half-expected to receive a case of Scotch from the bank for his role in gaining the two bankers' freedom. No such expression of thanks ever arrived. 'But then again,' Graham added, 'they probably thought I got my cut from the $5 million ransom money they paid out.'

In January 1980 Graham received another cloak-and-dagger telephone call. He believed the caller was from the South African intelligence service. He introduced himself as Mr Shearer, Pretoria's *chargé d'affaires* in the French capital and explained that South Africa's ambassador to El Salvador, Archibald Gardner Dunn, had been kidnapped by the guerrillas there. No one had been able to establish contact with his captors. Shearer asked Graham for help.

In recounting the incident in *Getting to Know the General*, he wrote, 'It almost seemed at that moment as though Antibes had become a small island anchored off the coast of Central America and involved in all the problems there.'

As he later told me, he remembered how the Mexico City telephone number had worked for the two kidnapped bankers. But he said he had destroyed it, 'washed it down the loo'. He suggested Shearer contact an investigator at Lloyd's International who might still have the number. Indeed, the Lloyd's man had the number. He gave it to Shearer, who in turn gave it to Graham, asking him to see what he could do. After talking with his government in Pretoria, Shearer told Graham that no one in the Dunn family was up to the job of negotiating with the guerrillas. The ambassador's wife was dying of cancer in California, and his son, who ran a nightclub in

El Salvador, was not considered a good enough communicator. Dunn's daughter was too young. Graham said he had suggested that someone pretend to be a member of the family and initiate the negotiations.

It took a many attempts with the telephone before Graham got through to Mexico City. The mysterious telephone number was that of Habeas, a centre set up by Gabriel García Márquez. The 52-year-old Colombian writer lived part of the time in Mexico City and had created Habeas (short for habeas corpus) several years earlier to promote human rights and to help save lives whenever possible.

Gabo liked to keep a low profile. He felt the less publicity Habeas got the more effective it could be. From France Graham telephoned García Márquez and asked him for help. Gabo was opposed to political kidnapping, and he did what he could to help the victims in an anonymous way, but he was aghast at Graham's request because the hostage represented the white supremacist pariah state of South Africa.

I visited Gabo at his house in San Ángel in Mexico City, and he reiterated his position. When I told Graham of this he told me to ask Gabo if he had read *The Human Factor*. 'If he has,' Graham said, 'he will know how I feel about the South African government.'

There were five different Salvadorean guerrilla groups in the field, and establishing contact with the faction holding the ambassador was no small feat. Yet, despite his philosophical distaste for the kidnap victim, Gabo called Graham back a few days later and told him the guerrilla group holding Gardner was the largest rebel faction, the FPL. The guerrillas deemed South Africa to be the devil incarnate; therefore contact with them should be made by the family and not a representative of the South African government. To everyone's surprise, and possibly thanks to a little prodding from General Torrijos, the guerrillas indicated that they would consider a plea from Graham Greene and agreed to meet him to discuss Ambassador Dunn, who at this point had become known as the 'forgotten hostage'.

Thus six months later Graham went to Panama again and invited me to join him there. He also wrote to Shearer to inform him of his trip and the fact that the guerrillas appeared ready to meet him to discuss the case. Shearer thanked Graham but said that contact had been established and it was best to leave it to 'people in Washington'. The South African government, Shearer added, had a very clear policy in such cases: no dealing with kidnappers. When Graham later briefed me in Panama I asked whether he thought *The Human Factor* had affected his contact with Shearer and his superiors.

'Perhaps,' Graham replied.

After ten months in the hands of the FPL guerrillas, the life of South African ambassador Gardner Dunn seemed lost. It was, Graham noted, eerily similar to the human tragedy he had written about in *The Honorary Consul* – almost like life imitating art. Kidnapping had become a thriving industry for the Salvadorean guerrillas. Ransom money from the rich was needed to make war on them. Unknown to us at the time, a fund had been set up by friends of the hapless Dunn in both South Africa and El Salvador to try to meet the ransom conditions. The guerrillas were demanding an incredible $20 million and the publication in sixty-five languages in 110 countries of their manifesto.

They were also demanding that El Salvador's ruling *junta* sever diplomatic ties with South Africa, Israel and Chile. Ironically, on 28 November 1979, the day ten young guerrillas had seized Dunn as he left the South African embassy in San Salvador, the *junta*, which had been in power only six weeks, was actually in the process of severing diplomatic relations with Pretoria and Dunn was about to retire from a long diplomatic career.

For three days we had been waiting in Panama City for the rendezvous. We assumed it would happen in a safe house, perhaps outside the city. Graham thought it wouldn't entail blindfolds and that sort of rubbish, because he could be trusted. However, extreme precautions would still have to be taken in meeting with the most wanted and active guerrilla leader in all of Latin America, a man who had been seldom seen and we suspected had a large price on his head – dead or alive – by the Salvadorean and perhaps American intelligence agencies.

'It's so boring waiting,' Graham repeated over and over. We also had a date at some point in Managua, so we decided to go ahead and plan that trip. Besides seeing revolutionary Nicaragua, Graham wanted to visit Belize again and discuss with Premier George Price the status of its independence from Great Britain. Graham had recently written a letter to *The Times* stating his distrust of the Guatemalan military, which he feared might gobble up their little neighbour once Britain pulled out. Nor did he have much confidence in British Prime Minister Margaret Thatcher who, Graham believed, just wanted to dump Belize, even if it was into the lap of the Guatemalan military.

On Friday morning, as we waited for Chuchu to arrive, Graham read aloud his horoscope in the *Miami Herald*. He'd had breakfast alone in his room, reading the proofs of *The Letters of Evelyn Waugh*, a 664-page book edited by Mark Amory, a well-known author and journalist. I tapped on his door and handed him the *Herald*. He chuckled as he read out loud. 'Breakthrough occurs – green light flashes for new project, adventure.' Graham was a Libra, born on 2 October 1904. He marvelled at the forecast and read on. 'Take cold plunge into future; let go of imagined security blanket!' 'Well,' he sniffed, 'superstitious I am, but I've never had need of a security blanket. It's the opposite with me.' The *Herald's* horoscope had been prepared by Sydney

Omarr, a syndicated columnist. Laughing at the name, Graham mused, 'I wonder if our Omar didn't have something to do with this.'

Our Omar could indeed make things happen. My horoscope was even more intriguing. 'Time is on your side. Know it and play waiting game. See places, people in realistic light. Scenario abounds with clandestine arrangements, mystery, temporary seclusion and romance . . .' My editors at *Time* would have been impressed, since I was in Panama on the off-chance Graham's presence would produce a story.

We spent the morning with Chuchu rummaging about the waterfront market expecting to make contact at any moment. Knowing Omar's enjoyment of pranks, we half expected him to arrange the 'contact' as they do in the movies, complete with secret passwords.

Several *curanderas* (healers) pointed out the merits of their herbs, and one began to tease Graham, proclaiming that a certain plant possessed just the right rejuvenating qualities for him. Chuchu, our womanizing Marxist, insisted that the *curandera* was right and that her concoction was known for its aphrodisiac power, which ensured that a man of a hundred could enjoy sex. Graham, his hands folded behind his back as if not trusting them with the medicinal plants, laughed and tactfully changed the subject. Pointing to black vultures perched on nearby wharf pilings, 'I can't stand those horrible creatures,' he said. Chuchu suggested that instead of aphrodisiacs we seek an antidote for his fear of vultures.

The evening before we were supposed to depart to Managua we went to meet Omar at Rory Gonzalez's house at Calle Cincuenta for a small party. One of the visitors that evening was the General's oldest daughter, Carmen Alicia, who was studying to be a dentist. Looking very prim and proper in a school-style blazer, she came in and kissed her father, who was obviously very proud of her. She shook hands with each of us and left. Another guest was Omar's pretty former secretary who arrived with their baby daughter, only a few months old. 'When I can communicate with her [the baby],' Omar joked to the distress of his mother, 'I won't need you.' She spoke excellent English and engaged Graham in conversation. 'What will happen to our child if something happens to the General?' she asked.

'Nothing to worry about,' Graham said.

Graham, who was seemingly immune to the effects of alcohol, had been handed a special edition of Black Label scotch dubbed 'Swing' by the General. Graham looked at the bottle and suggested 'swig' was a more appropriate name. The General and I were drinking champagne, a gift, someone mentioned, from Tony Noriega. The General was wearing sandals and a sports shirt. He had come out of his rustic retreat at Coclesito just to see Graham.

The mood was convivial, and there was plenty of laughter. At this point we were all getting a little drunk. Close to midnight we sat down to a Chinese take-away, and after dinner the General switched to cognac.

Omar asked Graham about the characters in his book, *Doctor Fischer of Geneva or The Bomb Party*, but the plot was just a little too foreign for him. We settled it by saying it was just like our party but set in Switzerland. The conversation moved on to poetry, prose, philosophy and politics. There was an especially emotional discussion on what would happen to the region if Ronald Reagan won the US presidency. 'Carter listened and understood us. Reagan will not try and understand us if he is elected,' Torrijos said. 'Without trying to be an election prophet, these elections will be won by Carter by a close margin, but I would prefer Reagan emotionally as it would allow me to put my spurs on again and see if he is as *macho* as he claims to be.'

Concerning the principal purpose of Graham's visit to Panama, the General advised us to put off our trip to Managua for a day as he was sure the Salvadorean guerrillas, despite the delays we had encountered, wanted to talk with Graham. He added that representatives of the five guerrilla groups were at that very moment holding a unity meeting in Panama City. By now we were alone with the General; it was already early morning. He was stretched out on the sofa, his eyes closing.

'Buenas noches, mi General,' we each said and he offered his hand, unable to rise. He was sound asleep before we left the house.

The lobby of the Continental Hotel was empty, and only a few dedicated gamblers remained in the casino. 'Let's have a nightcap,' Graham suggested. He appeared astoundingly fresh, displaying no sign of weariness. He wanted to discuss our remarkable evening with the General. It was his habit. No matter how late or liquid an evening had been he liked to go over the day's activities in case he had missed something. It was a sort of end-of-the-night debriefing. When he returned to his room, he told me, he usually wrote up a few notes.

Later that afternoon as we watched the elephants there was a sharp knock on the door of Graham's hotel suite. We looked at each other. It couldn't be Chuchu; he normally called from the lobby before he came up. There was a second sharp knock, full of authority. I went to the door. I glanced at my watch. It was 5.45 p.m. I opened the door. A small nondescript man and a young woman stood in the hallway waiting. The man, his face the texture of old leather, peered at me through rimless spectacles. Only recently I had seen a photograph of the man, but even without seeing his picture I sensed that I would have known him. He was the legendary Salvadorean revolutionary, Salvador Cayetano Carpio, code-named Marcial. Cayetano was a tough ideologue of the left who believed in the theory of prolonged popular war. He was widely regarded as El Salvador's Ho Chi Minh. The unsmiling young woman, obviously a guerrilla herself, turned and left without a word.

I welcomed him, introduced myself and Señor Graham Greene, the celebrated English author. Cayetano sat on the sofa, his small feet dangling. He had been a baker as a young man and entered politics through El Salvador's bakers' union. He was one of the most successful guerrilla leaders in Central America, an almost mythical figure, but one would hardly have guessed it from seeing him in Graham's hotel room. Maybe it was the spectacles, but Cayetano looked more like a kindly grandfather with an air of wanting to please. He appeared much older than his reported age of sixty-one. Sitting in a chair opposite him, Graham had become suddenly brittle, all business. He leaned forward just a little menacingly, like a wound-up clock or an over-alert MI6 officer.

I told Cayetano that Graham had covered guerrilla wars elsewhere, and I mentioned Indochina, the Malay Emergency and Kenya during the Mau-Mau uprising.

Graham became irritated by the direction the introduction was taking. 'I'm not a reporter,' he snapped.

His annoyance was obvious, but Marcial's expression didn't change. There was not even a twitch in his sagging cheeks.

'I am a reporter,' I said and explained that Mr Greene was not. Then I went on to tell Marcial that I would not be taking part in any formal talks or negotiations but that Mr Greene would. I was interested in a story and wished to interview him at some later date.

'Yes,' Cayetano said, adding that he very much wanted to talk to me. I was excited by the prospect of an interview. I had a lot of questions about El Salvador's guerrilla war.

As we sat there I wondered whether Graham was actually angry at the man. The day before, Graham had read a bullying 'interview' with Ambassador Dunn, which had ostensibly been conducted in a 'people's prison' somewhere in El Salvador. The interview was published in the 14 February 1980 English-language edition of the Cuban Communist Party daily, *Granma*. The pain of it had deeply affected Graham. He had let the paper drop to the floor, declaring angrily, 'Abominable, abominable.' His face twisted in disgust. 'I'll never read that newspaper again. This is filthy treatment of anyone who is obviously sick.'

The *Granma* article was accompanied by a photograph of Ambassador Dunn lying in bed with a tape-recorder thrust next to his face. The caption read: 'Dunn is a veteran officer of the Pretoria intelligence service in Central America.' The interviewer was the Mexican newsman Mario Menéndez. He was a descendant from an old Mérida newspaper family, a leftist who in the 1960s had provided me with photographs of Latin American guerrilla leaders for *Time* and *Life en Español*. Menéndez had interviewed most of those guerrilla chieftains in the mountains of Central America and Venezuela. He had since moved to Havana and was reporting for *Granma*. He had written a whole series on El Salvador. Despite his other attributes he was not a sensitive interviewer, nor was he a doctor. Menéndez's opinion, expressed in the Dunn interview article, was that ' He [Dunn] thought that by playing sick he might be able to exert psychological pressure on his captors through the press. So he refused to get out of bed. The content of his statements, the tone of his voice and his cynical laugh before the tape-recorder revealed him to be the individual described by South Africa's Freedom Fighters.'

Menéndez grudgingly reported that Dunn had withstood the verbal attacks of his inquisitor, who had blamed him for his government's sins. 'Why don't you speak, Mr Dunn?' the interviewer asked. 'Once again, the cynical laugh. Then Dunn said, "The problem is that people don't understand my country's government"' Despite the obvious bullying by the interviewer, Dunn struck a note not unlike a Greene character in one of his human tragedies. 'Look, let's get something straight,' Dunn was quoted as saying with a touch of finality and defiance. 'I have consciously served the government of South Africa; I identify with its apartheid policy; and I don't care what they do to me.'

Suddenly, there was another knock at the hotel room door. I stood and quickly moved to the door. '*Quien es?*' ('Who is it?') I asked.

The voice was muffled by the closed door. All I could understand was that the visitor was on a special assignment for General Torrijos. There was a deep urgency to the voice. I opened the door slowly. A young overweight lieutenant of Panama's National Guard, sweating profusely, burst into the room and stopped short before Marcial. 'My God,' he exclaimed. 'I found you!' The old man's face brightened in a fleeting smile of triumph. He had managed to elude the young intelligence officer. Four other Salvadorean guerrilla commandants were waiting downstairs. It was time to talk.

The meeting moved into Graham's bedroom where Cayetano sat at the bedside, separated from the Graham by proofs of *Evelyn Waugh's Collected Letters*. The young Panamanian officer was excluded from the session. Marcial asked whether the other guerrilla representatives downstairs could join the meeting with Graham as the guerrillas were discussing a unified command of the five guerrilla factions. This now concerned all of them, and at least one of them spoke English and could act as interpreter. (Out of their historic unity meeting in Panama came the formation of the guerrillas' umbrella group, the Frente Farabundo Martí para la Liberación National, or FMLN). Graham acceded to the request. I closed the door behind the guerrillas and with the young lieutenant waited in the living-room hoping that we would have no unexpected visitors.

After two hours Graham, politely indicating that the meeting had concluded, ushered Marcial and the other guerrilla commanders out of the bedroom. He showed no sign of being elated. By now he had learned too much about the reality of life in these volatile latitudes to expect charity or kindness for the kidnapped diplomat. These were true revolutionaries who were in a life-and-death struggle. Human life in El Salvador had, it seemed, lost all value.

Once the guerrillas had left the room Graham gave me an account of their meeting. He said he had realized he had few cards to play, but he told the guerrillas he would do what he could to correct any wrong impression in the European media of their struggle – by that he meant with accurate information, not propaganda. He also said the guerrilla commander who spoke English forced him to listen to a long harangue on their efforts to free their small country from feudalism and a repressive military that had been at the service of the landed oligarchy and claimed that armed struggle was the only path to freedom.

There had been problems with unity, but unity had been achieved. Marcial had agreed there was still work to be done to perfect this new consortium, but only with unity and the support of the people could they go forward to victory. They had no doubts that they would win in the end. (Seven months earlier Marcial had removed his own customary hood, which he and his guerrilla commanders had adopted to conceal their identity not only from the government's security forces but from each other. They were ultra-clandestine and believed that their movement's survival depended on absolute secrecy. They had good reason to be paranoid. The end of wearing hoods came only when the guerrillas felt strong enough. The time had come for their leadership to go public.)

When the subject of Dunn came up – Graham said he had to finally broach the subject – South Africa was roundly denounced for its apartheid policy and its racist repression of blacks. Yet Cayetano appeared to understand that mercy in this case might help the guerrillas more than a dead Dunn. However, guerrilla unity also meant that Marcial could not act unilaterally, even if he was favourably disposed to heed Graham's plea for Dunn's life. The other four groups (after August 1980 it became five) had to be consulted and had to agree to allow the agent of the 'despicable racist country that oppressed the blacks', as the guerrilla who was interpreting put it, to go free.

The old man talked to me before they left. I secured an agreement for an interview for *Time* at some future date. At that point Marcial had not given any interviews to the Western press. 'I have read your book, *Kidnapping and Hoods*,' I told Cayetano, adding that I was aware of his own experiences as a kidnap victim of government agents. They had tortured and held him in a secret prison for a year, during which time they kept him hooded at all times. What bothered me about these guerrillas, however – and I posed the question to Cayetano – was how they could summarily execute suspected enemy spies in villages and expect to win the support of the people in those villages. The military and the right-wing death squads had committed countless crimes and massacres, but was the guerrilla policy of *ajusticiamiento* (execution) necessary?

Cayetano's response was that those who had been executed were members of the rural militia, Orden, a paramilitary group organized by the government. He spoke in a calm, almost gentle voice, saying that such action had been necessary. 'But we recently changed that policy,' he added.

'Did you notice his eyes?' Graham asked me later.

Indeed, I had noted Cayetano's heavy-lidded eyes behind his glasses, but still I thought the man looked like anything but a fanatical guerrilla.

'His eyes are hard,' Graham mused thoughtfully. 'I wouldn't like to be his prisoner.'

That evening over dinner – the next day we were going to Nicaragua – Graham now seemed buoyant about Dunn's release. 'Maybe they would free the ambassador,' Graham said, 'if they believed they had a need to enhance their image in the world. However, it's not done until it's done.' Once again he was right, only this time tragically so.

I wrote a report for *Time* on the meeting between Graham and the guerrilla leader, but the story was embargoed by all involved, including the editors, until the kidnap victim was released. My editors in New York felt that it was only a story if Graham's intervention helped save the ambassador's life. However, an editor took Graham's description of Marcial's hard eyes out of that story and inserted it in a story I reported the following year on the Salvadorean guerrillas. Graham was livid. He wrote to *Time* and to me. He objected to the quote, and noting that it was taken out of context said it made him sound like a supporter of the Salvadorean governing *junta*. 'The opposite is true,' he protested. 'I was not criticizing Señor Cayetano, but describing what I believe to be the result of the imprisonment and cruel torture he has suffered.' Indeed my original file to *Time* had observed: 'A man who has lived most of his life in hiding, hounded by security agents, informers, and spent a year in a secret government jail hooded and tortured would not be expected to have smiling eyes. There is absolutely nothing to smile about in El Salvador. Hard eyes come naturally to the guerrilla fighters. Cayetano's survival, all these years, is an incredible feat and story. His eyes mirror that Calvary.'

The next morning we were waiting again, this time for the General's jet. There was nothing left to do but continue that scheduled August trip to Managua. The Salvadorean guerrilla leaders went back to fighting their bloody war. Marcial, the gentle-appearing old man, was to become, five months later, commander-in-chief of the combined guerrilla forces, the FMLN. We awaited news of his kidnap victim.

19 | OUR MAN IN PANAMA

Before our guerrilla rendezvous Graham and I were sitting alone on the hotel terrace in Panama. I had invited Reece Smith, my Panama stringer, to join us for lunch at the Balboa American Legion Club in the Panama Canal Zone.

'Your man Smith,' Graham paused and looked in the direction of the driveway, 'works for us.'

The white-haired Smith, with his rhubarb complexion and Santa Claus belly, was normally a jolly fellow with a ready sense of humour, but around Graham he was uncharacteristically quiet. I sensed that he felt intimidated, as some people were around Graham.

Smith didn't own a car and was habitually late for meetings, preferring to walk and save the taxi fare. As we waited for him I suddenly realized that by 'us' Graham didn't mean British newspapers but, instead, Her Majesty's Government. For a journalist to be accused of working for a government was a serious charge.

'No, definitely not!' The alarm in my voice caused Graham to frown. I noticed a certain reproach in his look, but I found his allegation preposterous. I wondered whether Graham wasn't a bit of a spy-confectioner, having been a British agent himself during the Second World War.

In Panama Chuchu, perhaps because of his Marxist leanings, was quick to label any American as a CIA agent. He had told Graham that a certain American author and teacher living in Panama was a CIA operative. I had warned Graham not to take Chuchu's accusations seriously. That particular American, I advised Graham, had written a respectable novel set in Panama that he would enjoy reading. He was also stringing for my competition.

Graham laughed when I suggested that Flor, the barmaid at the Señorial bar, was probably working for Panama's G2, the country's intelligence arm, then under the control of Colonel Manuel Noriega. Still, if Graham's remark about Reece Smith was correct, I would have to fire him. During the Cold War days foreign correspondents for US publications were permitted informal contacts with CIA station chiefs in order to glean information, but such contacts were severely curbed after a US Senate Select Committee, led by Senator Frank Church, revealed in 1976 that fifty American newsmen had at different times been on the CIA's payroll. Others had been 'unwitting sources'.

That year I had forwarded a directive from the chief of correspondents of the Time-Life News Service in New York to all my part-time correspondents in Central America and the Caribbean, reminding them that they could not work for *Time* if they had any kind of inappropriate relationship with any intelligence agency. As we waited, Graham opened a wide-ranging discussion on espionage, a subject that he thoroughly enjoyed and which led to his discussing his former MI6 boss, Harold Adrian Russell 'Kim' Philby (who had worked as a reporter as well as for the Soviet Union), who, as Graham put it, 'had taken great risks for what he believed in'. Graham described how he himself had left MI6 near the end of the war, before the Normandy landings. He admitted he was not cut out for the job, and on arrival at his post in Africa during the war he had accidentally locked his codebook as well as the key in the safe. It was on the whole, he said, a 'bloody boring business'.

'Why did you quit?' I asked.

Graham explained he felt he was wasting his time shuffling paper in London, so when Kim let him know that he wanted to promote him he became angry and felt he was being used as there was another agent far better suited that he was. Graham conceded that today's world was a good deal different from the old days and told me how he had contrived to have a little fun, even during his wartime post in Africa, by devising funny lines in his coded messages. His superiors were not amused. His project, he said, to use a pro-Gaullist madame to organize a brothel in Portuguese Bissau to glean information from Vichy French visitors was foolishly rejected by London. It wasn't an original idea, he added, because the combination of the oldest profession being used by the second oldest was as venerable as espionage itself. He had likewise got into hot water by poking fun at MI6 in *Our Man in Havana*. The book revealed how he felt about the service.

I ventured the observation that Panama City was of little interest to the British. Graham listened patiently as I argued that London could not possibly have any interest in maintaining a presence or wasting money on what was strictly US intelligence turf. Besides the Central Intelligence Agency, in Panama the US Defense Intelligence Agency (DIA) and National Security Agency (NSA) were operating, along with the US Army Southern Command's intelligence unit. (The highly sensitive NSA operation in Panama was later given unwelcome publicity by General Alexander Haig who revealed during the Falklands War that Washington was providing its ally, Great Britain, with secret satellite information – information that reportedly led to the sinking of the Argentine battleship *General Belgrano* in 1982.)

As in Mexico, in Panama the CIA was known to spend most of its time, energies and money targeting the pro-Castro Cubans who were present in both countries. Cuba's spy chief, Comandante (Major) Manuel Piñeiro Losada, nicknamed Barba Roja for his red beard, was the CIA's main headache in Panama. 'Red Beard' was coordinator of Cuban activities in the western hemisphere, and agents of his 'Americas Department' were said to use Panama as their springboard to Central and South America. Everyone visiting the Cuban Embassy in Mexico City was secretly photographed by the CIA from a building across the street, and it was assumed that the same held true in Panama. To enliven the CIA's photo archives we newsmen would make faces, scowl or pose on entering or leaving the Cuban Embassy's consular section in Mexico City when applying for a visa to Havana.

When I first met Piñeiro on 3 January 1959 in Santiago de Cuba, where he had taken command two days after Castro's revolutionary victory, his beard was long and flaming red. Just ten years later it was grey. When, still later, Graham eventually met him in Havana his beard was white. Such presumably were the pressures of revolutionary spying! He had ended decades of intelligence gathering and retired to his home in Havana. Graham was to marvel that such a high-ranking spy did not know the difference between MI5 (Britain's internal security organization, overseeing counter-espionage on British territory) and MI6, its international spying service.

There were, however, other agents representing other interests. They included the Israelis, who were in the arms business and who also kept a close eye on the Libyans and the Palestine Liberation Organization, both of whom had offices in Panama. Mike Harari, a former officer in Israel's spy agency Mossad, had built up a special relationship with the Panamanians, but the few times we spotted him we were not introduced. In those years Noriega was equally stand-offish. On the rare occasions when Graham and I sighted him Omar would simply say, 'You know Tony? Everyone knows Tony', and would not bother to introduce us. The Soviet Union's KGB, according to Torrijos, had only one agent responsible for local operations, and he was a non-resident living in Mexico City, a Russian journalist. A high-ranking Russian official had presented Omar with a fine samovar, saying it was a present from then Soviet President Leonid Brezhnev. Omar had no use for tea.

The only British agents that my news colleagues and I believed were present in the area were one covering Central America (notably Guatemala) out of Mexico City and a young man attached to the political section of the British High Commission's office in Kingston, Jamaica, whom we used to encounter around the Caribbean. We assumed he was the lone MI6 or MI5 agent covering the British Caribbean and former territories. His main reporting chore appeared to be Belize, formerly British Honduras, where British troops were still stationed to ward off any invasion from Guatemala, which had long had claims on Belizean territory.

London's Embassy in Panama City was located in an elegant ancient residence near the American Embassy on Avenida Bolívar. Time seemed to have passed it by. At one time, in the distant past, the British Embassy had had to provide consular services for the thousands of British West Indian subjects, mostly Jamaican, who worked on the Panama Canal. But as Jamaica and other British Caribbean territories became independent their citizens in Panama were no longer the Embassy's responsibility. Beginning in the late 1950s, Britain's most illustrious resident subject, who provided the Embassy with the most excitement, was Dame Margot Fonteyn, one of the world's great ballerinas and a one-time acquaintance of Graham. In 1955 she had married Roberto E. Arias, a Panamanian politician, lawyer, editor (of *El Panamá América*) and diplomat, while he was Ambassador to the Court of St James in London. Arias, who was nicknamed Tito, was the son of Harmodio Arias, a businessman of humble birth who was President of Panama from 1932 to 1936. Tito had first seen Dame Margot dance in 1937 when he was an eighteen-year-old student at St John's College, Cambridge.

Two decades later, during the heady days of the Cuban revolution in 1959, Margot and her husband gave the British Embassy in Panama an unseemly headache with their putative participation in what the media dubbed the 'Aquatic Ballet'. Arias and Fonteyn were accused of providing arms for a failed comic-opera invasion of Panama from Cuba. The invaders' goal had been to unseat Panamanian President Ernesto de la Guardia. Fidel Castro was temporarily absent from Cuba at the time and was described as furious when he heard the news that Panama had been invaded from Cuba. The adventure did not, he protested, have his backing or blessing. Tito's yacht was allegedly involved. Margot was detained and then unceremoniously deported to Great Britain, while Arias took refuge in the Brazilian Embassy.

Even more tragic for Tito Arias was the night five years later in 1964 when, having just won election to Panama's legislative assembly, he was shot at close range by a friend and political party associate. The attempted assassination left him paralysed and confined to a wheelchair for the rest of his life. Dame Margot cared for him until his death in 1989, often taking him along on tour with her. The British Embassy in Panama closed its book on Dame Margot Fonteyn in February 1991 when, at the age of seventy-one, having been permitted back into Panama with her husband many years earlier, she died in Panama City's Paitilla Hospital. It was only much later that I learned of Graham's friendship with Dame Margot, and it was ironic that they had both been so close to Panama. Strangely, he hadn't mentioned her, perhaps because he was so caught up in our daily activity and preoccupied by thoughts of Yvonne.

For one terrible moment I wondered whether Graham was going to write another book poking fun at the British Secret Service and had spotted Reece

Smith as a protagonist. Admittedly, Reece could have made a great model for 'Our Man in Panama'. However, the difference between Smith and Wormold of *Our Man in Havana*, I hazarded to suggest to Graham, was Smith's extraordinary capacity for beer, far above even his New Zealand countrymen's considerable average intake. 'Surely MI6 wouldn't employ such a heavy drinker,' I suggested.

Graham chuckled, then he realized my *faux pas*. MI6, I remembered from my own reading, had a record for harbouring some of the thirstiest barstool elbow-benders in the spy business. Graham's one-time superior Kim Philby, the world's most famous spy after Mata Hari, was a notorious alcoholic. The late David Holden of *The Times* had confirmed to me the reports of Philby's drinking, as had a number of other colleagues who had known him in Beirut and Turkey.

None the less, Reece Smith did have some habits which, viewed from a cloak-and-dagger perspective, might have been deemed suspicious. He never seemed to take day-to-day things around him seriously. Among friends he had a witty, irreverent sense of humour, but he didn't always display it in front of strangers. He ordered milk delivered daily in the morning to his Panama City flat, as he had done when he lived for a time in Bogotá, Colombia. Then in ritual fashion he would pour the milk down the drain and drink beer for the rest of the day, even in his parked aeroplane (he was an accomplished pilot). His Latino neighbours believed the red-nosed gentleman wearing floral shirts was a good, decent man because he drank milk. He would send mail with the most outlandish postmarks – giving letters to friends travelling abroad to mail – and he had often asked me to post letters for him from faraway places. Like an Australian Aborigine he sometimes went walkabout, disappearing for days; none of his acquaintances knew where he was.

Reece was British-born, had grown up in New Zealand and served as a bombardier in the Burma theatre during the Second World War. He returned to New Zealand to become a top reporter for the Wellington *Evening Post* but left abruptly and appeared in Panama in 1950, lured there by a job offer from a fellow New Zealander, Edward (Ted) Scott, editor of *El Panamá América*. When I finally told Smith about Graham's suspicions, he spluttered into his beer, his belly shaking, 'What a bloody honour!' Graham's suspicions about him were erroneous, he said. 'If I worked for them,' he said when he eventually controlled his laughter, 'it was without my knowledge. Who knows where our reporting ends up.'

Graham seemed to enjoy talking about Philby. At first I thought, as a writer, he wanted to get inside his one-time spy boss's head. Graham was happy to have re-established contact with Philby, who by then had retired in Moscow, and seemed to relish their correspondence. It had begun a year earlier, with a postcard from Philby in Havana. It evidently represented a curious challenge of sorts for Graham. He wanted to know more about how his former boss had fared, and he seemed to treat their communication as a game of chess. Was his old chief feeding him misinformation on world trouble spots? Graham wondered. 'There was nothing really secret about it,' Graham said. 'They know about it.'

Gradually I learned that Graham had a genuine fondness for his old boss. They had spent many hours together at a pub near their office in St James's during the war. His feelings for Kim were real. Kim was a charmer and born to be a spy. Even though he was an ordinary-looking individual, he had charisma and was cultured. They had plenty to talk about besides the service, and they shared the same sense of humour. With his 1968 introduction to Philby's book *My Silent War*, in which Philby explains his work as a Soviet 'Master Agent', Graham admitted he won no friends at home in England. (My American edition of Philby's book didn't contain his introduction, and he promised to send me the English edition.)

Graham and Philby had worked together in 1943–4 in MI6's V section, which was counter-espionage on the Iberian peninsula. Graham said he knew Philby had been a leftist, but at the time they worked together he didn't know he was a spy for Moscow. If he had had proof that Philby was a Soviet agent he stressed that he would have given him twenty-four hours, a sporting chance to run, then reported him. In what appeared to many as somewhat strained logic Graham said he still respected Philby because he had worked for the Soviets not for money but because of genuine belief in his leftist ideology.

'Did I send you a copy of *The Virtue of Disloyalty*?' Graham asked me and then quoted from the privately printed speech of that title which he had delivered in 1969 on being awarded the Shakespeare prize in Hamburg: '"for if there is a virtue in disloyalty it can only be that the disloyalty is committed in the service of what a man believes to be a greater loyalty". It's a game after a while, and the spy plays with both sides,' Graham reflected. I believed he would have welcomed me writing a story on him making contact with Philby. But my story was on Graham and the Salvadorean guerrillas.

Graham also described his own visit to the USSR in 1961, how it was winter and he had caught a 'terrible flu' and 'thoroughly hated having to address a group there'. His flu had turned to pneumonia, he said, and on his return doctors even suspected he might have cancer.

He spoke of his son Francis, explaining that he had been posted to the USSR in the British diplomatic service. Graham had frozen his own relations with the Soviet Union over the imprisonment of two Soviet writers. His boycott was to last until 1986; he explained that he had refused to go there again until the two dissident writers, Daniel and Sinyavsky, had been released from detention. He said he had asked his Russian publisher to give royalties from his books sold there to the wives of the two writers. The publisher declined, not wishing to get involved. Daniel and Sinyavsky were eventually released and went to live in the West. Sinyavsky later died in France.

There have been allegations since Graham's death that during all those post-war years he continued to work for MI6. In my opinion this is a ridiculous charge. Graham would have found it amusing. There was, for example, little of interest to MI6 in the areas we travelled together. If Graham at times appeared to be playing the part of a latter-day Wormold, it was just an act, spurred by his intrinsic fascination with the world of espionage. He did say, however, that he had occasionally, over the years, had a drink with an old friend whose name I have forgotten who had risen in the ranks of MI6. And Graham was very much looking forward to one day having another drink with Philby. As it turned out that reunion was just around the corner.

The day we were lunching at the American Legion in Balboa in the Panama Canal Zone, an American friend of Reece Smith, a Greene fan whom we met casually, came over to our table and praised not only the prophetic quality of *The Quiet American* but also *Our Man in Havana*. He actually thought Graham had predicted that the Russians would establish offensive missiles in Cuba. Graham gave the man a generous smile as he returned to his table. It was not the first time people had said this to him, he said. They overlooked the fact that the book was published in 1958, even before Fidel Castro came to power and four years before President John F. Kennedy and Nikita Khrushchev locked horns in October 1962 in a crisis that shook the world. The crisis over the installation of offensive Russian ballistic missiles in Cuba, ninety miles from the US mainland, exposed weaknesses in both the US and Soviet intelligence services that brought the world close to nuclear cataclysm. Neither side knew what the other was up to.

20 | MANAGUA NIGHTS

It was a long wait for Omar's Falcon jet to be made ready for our trip to Managua. Chuchu had gone off to see what had happened to the plane. Now, facing a new adventure in visiting war-torn Nicaragua, if the plane ever arrived, Graham overcame his characteristic distress at having to wait by talking about writing and the importance of privacy to a writer. 'A writer must be alone to be able to work,' he explained. 'And one has to appreciate that, and I do find it very easy to be alone. It's one of the reasons I travel a great deal.' He went on to say how it was a great way to get away from family and friends, albeit those he loved. 'Loneliness,' he added, 'has never been a problem for me.' A novelist makes a rotten husband, he said.

Yet there was something more to his need to escape. He was continually searching. A writer, he said, must continue to search and observe life. He went on to recommend that I read Henry James and discussed James's influence on him. He had written essays on James, he noted in *The Lost Childhood*. (Years later, in reading one of those essays, 'Henry James: The Private Universe', I recognized the similarity in Graham's musing that day while waiting for the General's jet. In the essay Graham had written: 'There was no victory for human beings, that was his [James's] conclusion; you were punished in your own way, whether you were of God's or the devil's party. James believed in the supernatural, but he saw evil as an equal force with good. Humanity was cannon fodder in a war too balanced ever to be concluded.')

The Falcon jet finally arrived, and we boarded. Chuchu spent most of the trip to Managua in the cockpit learning to fly the hot little private jet. Sighting his first Nicaraguan volcano, Graham, acting like a headmaster giving an oral examination, asked question after question. He was intrigued by the similarities among autocratic Latin American regimes, especially Nicaragua's 42-year-long Somoza dynasty that was born out of the US Marine occupation and the thirty-year reign of Rafael Trujillo Molina in the Dominican Republic, likewise an offspring of the Marines.

Graham already knew much of Nicaragua's sad history. This was a country that appeared rich only in poets. Graham thought the quote attributed to US President Franklin Delano Roosevelt describing Anastasio Somoza García (Tacho I), the founder of the dynasty, as 'a son-of-a-bitch but our son-of-a-bitch' was probably applied by US foreign policy-makers to characterize Trujillo and other dictators as well. They had all had obviously survived with Washington's support.

Of course their rule was facilitated by their images as bulwarks against Communism. More concerned about their own virility and that of their horses and bulls than their own people (Somoza the elder used to invite visiting VIPs to his ranch to witness his prize bull servicing cows), they gave their countries back virtually nothing. The Somoza dictatorship in Nicaragua had been prototypical. Despite its considerable natural resources, the country remained among the world's poorest and least developed. Malnutrition and disease saw to it that it maintained a relatively small population of 3 million. The Somozas invested most of their resources abroad while leaving Nicaragua with over $1 billion in foreign debt, an empty treasury and a country wrecked by war.

The war had now been over for more than a year. The euphoria that had greeted the end of the tyranny had dissipated as the Sandinistas struggled to get their act together. After two decades as guerrilla fighters, the Sandinistas had entered Managua to find Somoza's forces had evaporated with the morning mist. That day they moved from running a guerrilla war to running a government, and they soon found out that being guerrilla fighters was not the same as being skilled bureaucrats.

When we arrived in Managua we were greeted by María Isabel, the attractive Panamanian who had been our hostess at the Panama City guerrilla party. She had been appointed special assistant to Minister Tomás Borge and looked chic in her Interior Ministry uniform. We were whisked away to a VIP villa outside Managua. A skinny youth sat before the door cradling a Thompson submachine-gun. After we had been shown our respective rooms and María Isabel had departed, Graham looked at me. 'Have we been kidnapped?'

Perhaps, I thought.

Being left alone in isolation, even with a well-stocked bar, was not Graham's idea of seeing Nicaragua.

Chuchu had left us at the airport. He had gone off to see Borge and his own son, who was a member of Borge's personal security detail and who had recently recovered from shooting himself in the leg accidentally. At one point Graham had commented that this was a sign that the young man was in the wrong profession.

Those first hours in Nicaragua were distressing. Graham hated being marooned. Slightly querulous, he took umbrage over the way the Sandinista revolution was going. It was obviously too bourgeois.

I explained that the country's new leaders were inexperienced and undecided even about what brand of socialism they wanted.

Graham doubted that Washington would allow the Sandinistas to succeed. Even though some Sandinista *comandantes* were from the ranks of Nicaragua's upper class, he didn't believe that would matter to US policy-makers. Again he was right.

When a maid arrived and announced that lunch was ready Graham took a step to set the Sandinista revolution on a more egalitarian course. 'If this is a revolution,' he declared, 'let us all eat together. At least we'll have some company.'

I translated his invitation, but inviting the servants to join us at the table was not easy. They were mystified and uneasy. 'What about the cook?' Graham asked after counting noses. I went back to the kitchen and fetched the cook. Flustered and embarrassed, she couldn't understand why she was being invited to sit with us and required a good deal of persuasion.

A pretty maid was equally nervous and wanted to know what would happen if the *comandante* arrived and found them all at the table.

'It is an order from the honoured guest,' I assured her. 'You have nothing to fear.'

Graham enjoyed the lunch and the proletarian table immensely. But the servants did not. They eyed each other in confusion, as if intimating, 'These crazy *gringos*.'

The table conversation was strained and contrived, to say the least. And it was only later that Graham realized he had forgotten to invite the young guard on the stoop with the tommy-gun.

Fearful of what might happen next, with Graham fretting about being stuck away from the action, I telephoned the InterContinental Hotel and had no trouble finding rooms for us the following day. Graham was pacified. I warned him that there was no such thing as a city centre in Managua, only the ruins from the devastating 1972 earthquake. Nevertheless he wanted to see things and hated being cooped up in an outlying villa.

Waiting for us to be picked up for a Sandinista rally dedicated to the completion of the literacy campaign, Graham talked of his latest book, *Ways of Escape*. 'It's autobiographical,' he explained, 'about escaping boredom.' It had been published in England on his seventy-sixth birthday and he was particularly happy about having given the Canadian rights to his niece, Louise Dennys (daughter of Graham's sister Elisabeth), whom he said had her own publishing house, Lester and Orpen Dennys, in Toronto. In an uncharacteristic display of familial feeling, Graham said he relished the thought of his niece receiving the book. He was also proud of her sister Amanda who had taken the photograph for the jacket of the new book. He also told me he had more than one unfinished manuscript that he was still carrying around. One was entitled 'How Father Quixote Became a Monsignor'. 'I don't expect I'll finish it,' he said. A California company called Sylvester and Orphanos, which specialized in publishing attractive limited editions, had produced seventeen pages of the unfinished book. He didn't care to autograph books, but he had signed all 330 copies of this special edition. *On the Way Back* was another novel he was working on. It was set in Panama and had been going nowhere until now.

We were interrupted by the arrival of María Isabel, who drove us to the new Nineteenth of July Plaza the Sandinistas had built outside the city. (The name commemorated the date of their takeover in 1979.) They had simply paved a huge field and set up reviewing stands. As invited guests, we were shown to wooden bleachers on a roofless stand where we were to sit for the next five hours. Thousands – the official figure was three hundred thousand – had gathered in the new plaza to celebrate the end of the literacy campaign. Nearly half were *brigadistas* (members of special cadres), some as young as thirteen years old, who during the campaign had been granted special leave from their schools to help teach over seven hundred thousand people, a quarter of Nicaragua's population, to read and write.

In spite of the hard wooden bench and the blazing sun, Graham was in good spirits. He spent a lot of time shading his eyes from the sun while scanning the crowd. He sighted a little Roman Catholic nun weaving her way through the multitude. Her presence symbolized the liberal clergy's support for the Sandinistas, although a higher-ranking prelate who was on hand – Bishop Sergio Méndez Arceo of Cuernavaca, Mexico, whom some Mexican conservatives called the 'Red Bishop' – kept his words brief. The guest of honour was the president of Costa Rica, Rodrigo Carazo. The Sandinistas owed this wartime ally a debt of gratitude, but his plea for elections during his speech did not sit well with the assembled *comandantes* or with the crowd. Defence Minister Humberto Ortega's answer in his discourse, punctuated by revolutionary hyperbole, was that there would be no elections before 1985. (Elections were actually held in November 1984 and his brother Daniel was elected president.) When the applause died down Humberto Ortega droned on for more than an hour and eventually lost the attention of even this fervent crowd.

To display his displeasure with Ortega's long-winded rhetoric, Graham heartily applauded the shortest speech from the podium, delivered by Interior Minister Tomás Borge, whom Graham gave top marks for a rousing brief five-minute discourse.

The heavy politics of the moment failed to spark Graham's interest. The Sandinistas had promised pluralism; that was enough, he said. Even if some hard-liners wanted a single-party Marxist-Leninist state, the revolution would work itself out – they always do. Graham preferred watching the reaction of the crowd to listening to a translation of what the speakers were saying. Tired of shading himself from the sun, he began talking of the first translation of the Bible from Latin to English. He mused on, recalling that the first book he had learned to read was entitled *Reading Without Tears*. Then he pretended to be reading it once again, reciting, 'A dog ate a frog . . .' However, I had gathered earlier that Graham had been traumatized by his school days at Berkhamsted, where his father had been headmaster. 'The fears and pain of childhood,' he reflected, looking out at the young Nicaraguan faces, 'stay with us.'

He said there had been an awful article in the *Daily Telegraph* by Robert Moss, whom he described as a right-wing Australian who thinks of himself as an expert on espionage. Moss had attacked the Nicaraguan literacy crusade, saying it had been used for political indoctrination and that the teaching students involved had been forced to go to the hills to participate. 'It is a shame Moss is not here to see this . . . They do look so happy and proud,' he said as we watched the youths parading before us.

Whatever its political objectives, the literacy crusade had not been a picnic. It had been tough, arduous and dangerous. At least fifty-six youths lost their lives in various ways. Several had died in accidents, eight had died from illnesses compounded by primitive living conditions – some youths had contracted diseases such as mountain leprosy and malaria, and seven had been assassinated by counter-revolutionaries, the forerunners of the US-backed Contra army.

'The Catholic Church once considered the Bible too dangerous to put in the hands of the people,' Graham observed as he looked over a copy of the 126-page Sandinista textbook, *Dawn of the People*, used in the literacy crusade. The textbook material was developed by Paulo Freire, a Brazilian educator. It was known as 'conscientization' or 'liberating education'.

Since I was doing a story on the crusade for *Time* Graham was helpful in offering all kinds of suggestions. 'We bring up our children on fairy stories, but it doesn't mean that they are going to believe in fairies all their lives,' he said, contending that concern over the political content of the textbooks was misplaced. He found no reference to Karl Marx or Communist Cuba in the book. It did stress the history of the 'New Nicaragua', depicting Augusto César Sandino as the father of the nation. Sandino was the Nicaraguan guerrilla leader who fought the US Marine occupation forces in the 1920s and 1930s, only to be assassinated in 1934, reportedly on orders of Anastasio Somoza García, Tacho I, founder of the family dynasty. (He was assassinated himself by a young poet in 1956.)

'Surely,' Graham said, 'it is better for them to read Marx than to have it expounded to them. If one is taught to read by reading Marx, that person is able to criticize Marx.'

A woman from the mountains who had learned to read and write during the crusade recited a poem she had written, proving once again that Nicaragua is indeed the land of poets. As the parade finally ended and the sun dipped below the horizon we were escorted to the neighbouring grandstand to meet the Sandinista *comandantes*. We found Chuchu near the stand with his son, who was still hobbling from his self-inflicted leg wound. With them was Chuchu's pretty young daughter with whom he was angry, adamant that she had to first complete her college studies before enlisting in the Sandinista army. The *comandantes* were too euphoric for anything more than a quick salutation to Graham and me.

Dangerously dehydrated by sun and weary of rhetoric, we were happy to accept an invitation to dinner at the home of Xavier Chamorro, a close friend of Borge who had only recently launched his own pro-Sandinista newspaper, *El Nuevo Diario*. As we left the rally Graham said, 'I like [Edén] Pastora's face, not Borge.'

'So does Omar,' I replied. It was interesting how Graham managed to sort out the various actors in any situation and categorize them.

We were intrigued as to why Torrijos had sent Graham to Managua, since Omar's own relationship with the Sandinistas had soured considerably. He had decided against attending their 19 July celebration a month earlier. Perhaps dispatching Graham in his personal jet was his way of sending a message to the Sandinistas that relations were not that bad. Torrijos was always careful to lard his public statements on Nicaragua and the Sandinistas with so much ambiguity that few could understand what his message really was. In private, though, he could be devastatingly blunt. Prior to the trip with Graham, when I had asked him about his relations with the Sandinistas, Omar grimaced and moved his head as if the subject had given him an instant headache. They were, he said, screwing up fast. They were too young and reckless to govern. They were playing with fire, 'pulling the monkey's [United States'] tail too hard' by bringing the Soviets, Bulgarians and Cubans into the United States' sphere of influence. 'They only listen to themselves. They don't even listen to Castro,' he said.

Chuchu was working furiously to keep relations between Panama and Nicaragua on an even keel, and Graham and I began to wonder whether it hadn't been Chuchu's idea for Graham to visit Managua under Omar's auspices.

At the end of 1979 when a delegation of Sandinistas had visited Panama everything seemed cordial enough on the surface, but there was an undeniable rift in relations over policy towards the Communist bloc. The Sandinistas, for example, said that only Cuba had a reservoir of doctors, teachers and technicians to loan to a sister country. Most other Central American countries were in dire straits themselves and could ill afford to help a neighbour on any significant scale. There was never any mention of an early US offer to help Nicaragua which was rejected by the Sandinista Directorate on the grounds that the United States would use its humanitarian volunteers to infiltrate CIA agents into the country.

Torrijos had made it seem to the Sandinistas that he had no qualms over the presence of thousands of Cubans in Nicaragua, but the Sandinistas had to realize, he cautioned, that they were making the military in neighbouring El Salvador, Honduras and Guatemala nervous. As far as he was concerned, he had told Panamanian television viewers at the end of 1979, it didn't matter if there were one thousand or five thousand Cuban teachers in Nicaragua helping in the literacy campaign because the 'alphabet has never overthrown anyone, nor has it destabilized anyone in the civilized world'. Along with other volunteers dispatched from Cuba, two thousand Cuban teachers participated in the crusade along with eight hundred Cuban medics. The Nicaraguans reported that, although their goal had been to reduce illiteracy from over 50 per cent to zero, they had managed to bring it down to an astounding 12 per cent.

The Sandinistas had drawn support during the war from several international political sectors and countries, but both Cuba and Panama were recognized as the main sources of the military hardware that allowed the Nicaraguan rebels to out-gun Tacho II Somoza in the end. (In Washington the Carter administration had also helped by cutting off Somoza's arms supplies.) Torrijos had even sent a Panamanian brigade to fight on the Southern Front with Edén Pastora, and they tied down some of Somoza's best troops during the conflict. And when, shortly after the Sandinistas' victory, a Nicaraguan delegation attended a 26 July celebration in Cuba, its members presented Fidel Castro with an Israeli-made Galil automatic rifle, the preferred weapon of Somoza's élite National Guard troops, and damned Israel as the dictator's chief arms supplier. When Omar had been invited to Managua a month after the rebel victory, the Sandinistas had also presented him with a Galil, but mindful of his close relations with Israel and the fact that his wife's father was Jewish they said nothing about Israel's role as arms merchant to the Somoza regime.

Moreover, the last shot had hardly been fired in the Nicaragua civil war, and Somoza had barely fled, before Omar dispatched a training team under Colonel Rubén Darío Paredes, known in the Panamanian National Guard as a lumbering right-of-centre officer. Paredes's task was to help organize the new Sandinista police force. The Cubans had arrived even earlier, speeding across the border from Costa Rica. Then, following the graduation of the first class of the new Sandinista police, Torrijos ordered the Panamanian instructors, as well as the remaining members of his expeditionary brigade, to pack up and return home to Panama. Some Sandinistas complained privately that the Panamanian police instructors were teaching the neophyte rebel police how to extract a *mordida* (bite) or bribe.

Xavier Chamorro and his wife Sonia were gracious hosts. A bottle of whisky was placed before us, and we quickly quenched our thirst. I had known Xavier since the late 1960s. He had worked at the newspaper *La Prensa* with his brother Pedro Joaquín Chamorro, whose assassination in January 1978 was the catalyst for the revolt against Somoza. Graham could not get over the lovely bourgeois setting of their home. Whenever we were left alone he signalled with his hands and eyes his impressions. Tomás Borge finally arrived with his cadre of bodyguards. He sat opposite us, across a low, round wooden coffee table, and ordered milk. Graham looked shocked; in disgust he refreshed his glass of scotch.

Short and Mayan-looking, with a head that appeared too large for his body, especially in his smartly tailored olive-green uniform, Borge wore the star of *comandante* of the revolution on his lapel. As the only surviving founder of the Frente Sandinista de Liberacion Nacional he had already, at forty-nine, entered Nicaraguan folklore. He could be eloquent, verbose and often poetic. In fact he was a good poet. He had also been a Marxist, at least initially. Upon his release from a Somoza prison in August 1978 he had declared at a Panamanian press conference: 'Yes, I am a Marxist-Leninist.' Three months later in Mexico City, where I interviewed him, he was no longer so sure. 'Somoza painted us Marxist. We have some Marxists with us, but the FSLN is much wider,' he answered. The concept of the 'prolonged people's war' (advocated by his faction), he maintained, was 'not Marxist, but a military concept which will lead to taking advantage of the favourable moment'.

During the early days after the Sandinista victory Borge was the most public of all nine rebel *comandantes*. He had personally forgiven the man who had tortured him during his long years of imprisonment. In his office on the top floor of what had been the electric company building in Managua there were fourteen crucifixes on the wall, by my count, and in the reception room were four more sculptured crucifixes of Jesus Christ. Furthermore, he had praised the Catholic Church and asserted that the Church's virtues and Sandinista ideals were one and the same. It was an interesting reflection of the philosophical parallels between a dogmatic religion and a doctrinaire political ideology.

A Borge show was often the best show in town, if for no other reason than for being refreshingly frank. However, whether it was the milk or the audience, that night was not a typical Borge show. He droned on about the divisions within the FSLN and discussed each of the Sandinista factions in exhaustive detail. Most of what he described was public knowledge. In *Time* we had treated the subject thoroughly, and I had included an analysis of the rebels' divisions in my book on Nicaragua, which E.P. Dutton in New York was about to publish.

Listening without comments to Borge's remarks, translated by Xavier, Graham's demeanour was that of a patient visitor, exhibiting outward calm. His face reflected too much sun, and even his eyes had turned red. Flor de Caña rum and Scotch whisky were flowing freely on our side of the round coffee table – in fact, far too freely. I decided that just in case the *comandante* said something new I should tape the conversation in order later to provide Graham with a clearer picture of the evening. I went out to the car and retrieved my little bag with my tape-recorder. I placed it on the coffee table before Borge. As he was totally absorbed in his monologue I thought it would be rude to interrupt and request permission to tape him. In fact I had taped him on numerous occasions before. However, paranoia was alive and well in the Sandinista ranks. Hardly had I set it down than one of Borge's bodyguards bent down and whispered in my ear, 'You are not recording the *comandante*, are you?' I reached over and shut off the recorder.

Later that night when we returned to our VIP villa and discussed the day's activities Graham said he hadn't noticed the glares I had received from Borge's vigilant bodyguards. It was then that I opened my tape-recorder to find the tape that I had placed in it was gone. A sleight of hand by one of Borge's bodyguards had evidently confiscated the cassette. I was angry but also embarrassed and humiliated. I half expected Graham to say with his characteristic acerbity, 'Bad show.' Instead his only reaction was to declare it a bloody boring evening. He really wasn't interested in the divisions within the ranks of the Sandinistas, he said. Noting that Borge, as Interior Minister, was in charge not only of the police but also of prisons, Graham observed that there was probably still room for me in one of his crowded penitentiaries. When Chuchu came to fetch us the next day and I told him about Borge's bodyguard's having seized my tape, he was not happy. Nor was he happy to hear from Graham that we were moving out of the 'secure' villa to Managua's Hotel InterContinental.

After we checked into the hotel that morning, Borge showed up with his entourage of bodyguards. We met at the hotel reception desk, and I immediately brought up the subject of the missing tape. He was not in his usual buoyant mood. In fact, he was angry. He told me I should not have taped him without permission. I explained that I didn't want to interrupt his talk by asking for permission. I had taped him, I explained, in order to give Graham a good briefing on his talk later that evening and requested the return of my cassette. He ignored my request and joined Graham, who had been explaining to Chuchu why we had moved to the hotel. Borge, I realized, was clearly upset that we had moved to the InterContinental and out of his VIP villa, insulting his hospitality; he probably suspected it was all my doing.

I often wondered what the Sandinistas thought of the recording on my tape of Graham's expounding his theory on why high-rise apartment buildings for the poor breed crime, which I had recorded during a drive in Panama City. We had spied several high-rise buildings that had replaced the old tin-and-wood dwellings of the poor and recorded his views on the topic. I also wondered whether Borge thought we were spying for Omar. It was no secret that Torrijos had his own intelligence-gathering methods in Central America and that he was known to prefer that his agents used tape-recorders in place of long-winded typed reports, the authenticity of which were not always verifiable. Borge left us, and we set out on a sightseeing tour of war-torn Nicaragua. During the testy morning only Graham was happy. His room had a clear view of the Momotombo volcano across Lake Managua.

I drove Graham around and pointed out areas of combat in the countryside during the rebellion against Somoza. Graham was interested, but Chuchu, who accompanied us, was obviously still fretting over letting Tomás Borge down. We motored on to Masaya and then to Monimbó, where in October 1977 the flames of revolution and popular insurrection against the Somozas had been further ignited by Indians living in the poor neglected *barrio*. Those places all brought back memories of mangled corpses and shallow graves. The damage inflicted by the war was still evident.

I reflected on how miraculous it was that more journalists were not killed during the war. ABC News television correspondent Bill Stewart was one of the unlucky ones. He had been forced to lie down and had been executed in the middle of a public street in Managua by a Somoza National Guardsman. His gutsy crew had managed to film the cold-blooded killing, which was broadcast across the United States and brought home to the American people the ruthlessness of Somoza's troops. President Carter called the killing of the newsman 'an act of barbarism that all civilized people condemn'. Those few minutes of videotape helped seal Somoza's fate.

In the beautiful town of Granada, the one-time capital of Nicaragua and the site of American mercenary William Walker's brief presidency (1856–7), Chuchu completely lost his cool. Unlike many Nicaraguan cities Granada had witnessed hardly any fighting during the Sandinista revolution. Chuchu picked an argument with the local correspondent of *La Prensa*. The newspaper was anti-Sandinista, and Chuchu cursed the reporter for his politics and working for such a 'load of shit as *La Prensa*'.

It was easy to lose your good humour, Chuchu later complained, because 'assassin and rapist counter-revolutionaries were becoming more and more bold'. Only a week earlier, he noted, the counter-revolutionaries had crossed the Honduras border to strike at a Sandinista army post in Nicaragua's north. He worried that thousands of Somoza National Guardsmen who had fled into exile in Honduras would become counter-revolutionaries.

Graham was sympathetic, saying it was frightful to think of more fighting. Chuchu said the Sandinista leadership had no illusions that if then Governor Ronald Reagan, the Republican candidate for the presidency, won the November election that year they would be in deep trouble. The Sandinistas had read the Republican platform, which described them as Marxist and deplored their takeover of Nicaragua, accusing them of attempting to destabilize El Salvador, Guatemala and Honduras.

'The old Indochina domino theory,' Graham observed.

Storm clouds were gathering, Chuchu went on, quoting Fidel Castro as charging that the Republican Party platform 'threatens again to apply the big stick to Latin America'.

The following day Graham and I were left alone. We paid a visit to our priest friend, Ernesto Cardenal, the new Minister of Culture who was full of plans. Culture, he said, had been neglected under the dictatorship. His government ministry was located in Tacho II Somoza's Spanish-style former home, El Retiro. We visited the city of León and the tomb, in the ancient Catholic cathedral, of Rubén Darío, the modernist Nicaraguan poet who brought recognition to his country at the beginning of the century by promoting Latin Americanism and wresting the Spanish language from its academic subservience to Spain. Dario had also warned against the 'terrible rifleman' Teddy Roosevelt who then symbolized to Latin Americans the dangers threatened by the 'Colossus of the North'. On a more contemporary note, the local Sandinistas in León showed off their ingenious arms caches that had been used during the war – false walls, floors and underground rooms.

Following our return to Managua Graham and I had accompanied María Isabel home so she could freshen up. She was no longer living with Ramiro. Left in the living-room with a Mickey Mouse cartoon blaring on the television, I moved across the room to lower the volume. There slumped in an easy chair, half hidden and hypnotized by the antics of capitalist America's most famous rodent, was a Sandinista officer. He offered Graham and me only a grunt of recognition and remained glued to the Spanish-speaking Mickey.

'One must get terribly bored in the mountains year after year,' Graham shouted to me. We broke into a fit of laughter. Mickey Mouse even robbed the beautiful María Isabel of a goodbye wave from her new beau.

That night, at Los Ranchos restaurant, Graham concluded we were surrounded by counter-revolutionaries, and he did not enjoy his meal featuring typical Nicaraguan dishes. I told Graham the bourgeois types in the restaurant could have well been anti-Somoza and even pro-Sandinista, such were the complexities of this revolution. Many Nicaraguans in the business sector had contributed to the overthrow of Somoza. Graham still felt they were too well dressed for our restaurant setting and that they eyed us suspiciously. He pronounced it enemy territory and was happy only when we left.

Whether it was the stress of her new job in the Interior Ministry or the distraction of the Mickey Mouse fan, María Isabel, as helpful as she tried to be, made a logistical mess of Graham's and Chuchu's departure. She booked a reservation for them on a non-existent flight. I flew back to Mexico while Graham and Chuchu suffered more delays. Graham told me as we parted that it was time for him to go home; he was missing Yvonne and was anxious about his own 'war' with her daughter's former husband.

Graham later recounted that when Omar asked him his opinion of Borge, Graham said he had been sceptical of the man at first but gradually came to appreciate him. Omar had agreed. 'For the first few minutes you dislike him.' For all his personality faults Borge was a fine poet. Daniel Ortega, dour and distant, also a poet, likewise grew on Graham. On the other hand, Ortega's companion, the poet Rosario Murillo, was an instant hit. This handsome, vivacious woman, a grand-niece of Sandino, had once worked for *La Prensa* publisher Pedro Joaquín Chamorro and spoke excellent English. She had attended secondary school in England and finishing school in Switzerland and was an immediate favourite of Graham's when they first met in Costa Rica. In the new government she was Vice-Minister of Culture.

The following month, in Asunción, Paraguay – where he was living in exile with his mistress – Tacho II was killed when his white Mercedes was blown apart by a rocket-propelled grenade in an ambush by an Argentine guerrilla group. Argentine army specialists skilled in the art of clandestine operations were already moving into Honduras to shape the ragged bands of anti-Somoza border raiders into a fighting force. The Argentines eventually worked with the CIA in launching the not-so-secret war to overthrow the Sandinistas. With Ronald Reagan now occupying the White House, Ortega and the Sandinistas were indeed in deep trouble, as Chuchu had predicted. Tacho II Somoza was buried in Miami, Florida.

When I returned to Managua several weeks later I learned from the Foreign Minister, Father Miguel D'Escoto (a Roman Catholic priest), that he had been expecting Graham and me for dinner and had assembled the rest of the governing *junta*. No one had advised us, not even our friend Borge. We had unintentionally stood up the Reverend Father of the Maryknoll Order and the *junta*. So much for communications within the Sandinista leadership.

Around that time I received encouraging news from Gabriel García Márquez in Mexico City. I passed the news on to Graham in Antibes: the guerrillas were ready to release Ambassador Dunn. Unbeknownst to us at the time, the

Ambassador's friends in South Africa, the United States, Chile (where he had also served) and El Salvador had quietly been collecting ransom money. They were equally ignorant of Graham's efforts to save Dunn. By mid-September they had collected more than $1 million and the money was transferred to the US Embassy in San Salvador for safekeeping. By early October the guerrillas were demanding that the money be handed over. The negotiators first wanted proof that Dunn was alive.

But less than two months after Graham's meeting in Panama with Marcial the FMLN announced to the media on Thursday 9 October 1980 that a final deadline had expired and that they had executed Ambassador Dunn for non-compliance with their demands. 'The Salvadorean government, the racist government of South Africa and the Dunn family are responsible for the justifiable execution of the criminal ambassador Dunn,' the guerrillas declared. They presented no proof that Dunn had in fact been executed. However, it was later confirmed that Dunn had cheated his captors. The FMLN had actually been prepared to accede to Graham's plea and to collect the ransom money, but the Ambassador had deprived them of the deal by dying and leaving them to dig his grave.

'I have got nothing further to write you about poor Mr Dunn. I wish you could write a piece about the forgotten hostage, quoting from that abominable article in *Granma*,' Graham wrote in a letter dated 5 January 1981. 'You'll be amused to hear that the Red Brigade [West Germany's terrorist group] were on the telephone to me the other day but I refused to play. [Graham did not elaborate.] Don't mention this in *Time*!' The late Ambassador Dunn would not turn out to be a character in Graham's unwritten novel. The Dunns of the world, caught up in human tragedy, already peopled his books.

My dateline had shifted back and forth between Nicaragua and El Salvador. The year 1980 had been a particularly bloody one for the Catholic Church in Central America. It had begun with the assassination in San Salvador of Monsignor Óscar Arnulfo Romero y Galdámez, a saintly man whom I had interviewed a number of times. He had been shot dead as he said Mass on 24 March, during the consecration of the Eucharist. More were to die at the archbishop's funeral service when a noise bomb exploded and the crowd panicked. The year was to end with the torture, rape and killing of three American nuns and a female lay worker in El Salavador by members of the government security forces.

The following year, in the summer of 1981, *Time* decided to reopen its Miami/ Caribbean bureau. I was transferred with my family from Mexico City to Miami, from where I continued to cover Central America.

The move shocked Graham. 'Your letter was a complete surprise! I never expected to find you living in Miami but of course I understand very well the reasons,' he wrote in a letter dated 9 June 1981. In early April Graham had gone to Jerusalem, where he received the $2,000 'Jerusalem Prize' award from Mayor Teddy Kollek.

'I have just finished reading the proofs of your *Somoza*,' Graham added and went on to critique my new book on Nicaragua. His critical response was another rare reflection of his personal literary standards and acumen.

I know you want me to be frank and I shall be frank. I think it is an excellent book of research which will be invaluable to future historians. I found that you went into too great detail and there were too many quotations from speeches etc., which were repeated over and over again. You wanted to cover every moment on the ground. I felt you should have got up in a mountainside and looked down and seen the main points before writing. My fear is that only people like myself who have a particular interest in Central America will appreciate the work you have done. The last chapters were excellent because you were dealing with actions and not words. If I was your editor I would advise you to cut out the notes. Notes in a book of this kind are only useful if they really cover all references, which you don't, or add something to what has been written in the text. Over and over again I looked for the source of a story and found it was not there, although many more trivial points were attributed to some newspaperman or other. I would be bold and eliminate the notes. A little point on p. 223. You say that Somoza threw an evening cocktail party for 40 foreign correspondents and make a point that he served a 34-dollar bottle of Russian vodka. The bottle wouldn't have gone very far among 40 people! Somewhere else I think you emphasized the point that Somoza tossed down his vodka neat but that is the usual way of drinking it. Oh yes, that's on p. 235. I would have been horrified if he had mixed it with orange juice or some awful concoction.

Please don't be discouraged by my criticisms. The book is of value, but I'm afraid it will be very heavy reading for the ordinary public. You have been too anxious I think to put in all the information which you have gathered without thinking of it as a book which must have a shape and appeal to a reader who is not necessarily deeply interested in the subject.

P.S. I don't know what my summer plans are yet. My Spanish priest [friend] is having an operation on his throat and we may not be able to go off on our usual tour before August. I have only heard one word in recent months from Chuchu and I don't really expect to be invited for the fifth time to Panama! If I am I will try and fit it in. Otherwise I must find some other escape route. P.P.S. If your publisher want a quote which is an honest quote I suggest: 'Bernard Diederich with his books on Somoza proves himself an indispensable historian for Central America.'

Graham's editorial suggestions were of immeasurable value. He was correct. Published in the United States by E.P. Dutton, my book was the first of many to appear on Nicaragua after the fall of the Somoza dynasty. It did well, even in the United Kingdom.

21 | THE GENERAL IS DEAD!

A macho gambles with destiny, ready to win or lose. He gambles with
death, he gambles with God. A burning love affair is a victory over
Destiny; a revolution, a victory over death; sin a victory over God.
When the three come together, man has accomplished his fulfilment.

Julius Rivera, *Latin America: A Sociocultural Interpretation*

A cable from Graham arrived on Saturday 1 August 1981 at our new home in
Miami. He hoped I would be joining him for yet another trip to Panama. 'I
don't think I'll go this time,' I told my wife Ginette. Call it a premonition,
but I had strange, unsettling feeling that something disastrous was about to
happen. My thoughts were that Chuchu's little plane might not make it
through the rainy season, and I didn't want to be in it when it went crashing
down into the Panamanian jungle. I was about to call Chuchu in Panama and
advise him of my decision not to travel to Panama to join Graham, who was
due to arrive in Panama City on 6 August, when the phone rang. It was one
of my colleagues at the *Miami Herald* asking whether I had any information
about what was happening in Panama. According to a brief news agency
bulletin out of Panama City General Torrijos was missing.

There were no details. I called Chuchu. 'Chuchu is not here.' His Italian
wife sounded as if she was crying. 'He believes something terrible has happened
to the General . . . He thinks there has been an attempted coup.'

It was the same with all my other sources in Panama. All that was known
was that the General was missing. There was nothing to do but wait. My
thoughts went back to our 1972 helicopter ride, when were lost in a rainstorm
and Omar had told me, his eyes merry with laughter, that he could get us
out of the jungle if we went down because he had graduated from the US
Army's jungle survival course.

Panama's terrain is no joke. Its formidable rainforests, steep mountains, tidal
mud flats, mangrove swamps and rolling savannah blanketed with towering
elephant grass are quite capable of hiding secrets. The General was famous
for changing his flight plan in mid-flight. This might have been good for his
personal security, but it also made it difficult for his headquarters to keep

track of his whereabouts. No one ever seemed to know where he was at any given time. Travelling with Omar, one never knew one's real destination.

It was a Saturday filled with anxiety. News out of Panama was a long time in coming. Even its National Guard seemed unsure of where the General was headed or what had happened. Colonel Roberto Díaz Herrera, the secretary-general of the National Guard, later claimed that he had been informed by intelligence chief Noriega at 7 a.m. on Saturday morning, more than eighteen hours after the General was first reported missing.

'My father had trouble with a crown on one of his teeth,' Carmen Alicia, Torrijos's eldest daughter, recalled. She was the last member of the family to have seen Omar alive. 'He had insisted on driving over from Farallon to our dental clinic that Friday [31 July], even though we were little better than a rural clinic. This was his third trip to our clinic in Penonomé in seven days. He was challenging us to fix his tooth, even though I told him he should go to the dentist in Panama City who had made the crown in the first place.'

Carmen Alicia was doing her odontology studies social service work at the time in Penonomé in the province of Coclé, a 25-minute drive from Farallon and some sixty miles from Panama City.

Following his dental work that Friday morning Omar invited his daughter to accompany him. A plane was waiting at a nearby airstrip. 'I told him, "No, Papi, I have my work to do,"' Carmen Alicia told me. She said she had earlier admonished her father, saying he shouldn't go around disrupting the country's health services. Not long before, the General had taken the entire medical staff from a Chiriquí clinic with him to see at first hand the conditions in a rural area. 'I told him such things were disruptive to our work. He understood, but that was how he was, he often made decisions on the spur of the moment. When he left for his plane he told me, "I'll see you in Farallon in the afternoon when you have finished your work." Those were, for me, his last words. The weather was fine at Penonome when he left,' she recounted. 'When we had finished working we went to Farallon and waited and waited. When my father didn't show up we thought he had stood us up. He had a habit of changing his destination even when we flew with him. "Didn't you see we changed course and crossed the canal? You must always keep your wits about you," he instructed us.'

Chuchu had stayed at home to translate key passages of French President François Mitterand's book into Spanish, since Torrijos was planning a visit to France. Then an officer telephoned, reporting that the General was missing. Chuchu immediately suspected a plot.

The next day, Saturday afternoon, a farmer appeared at a National Guard post near Coclesito and reported that he had heard an explosion on a nearby mountain. He led a rescue party to the site, which turned out to be where Torrijos's plane had crashed. By then US Air Force planes had joined the

Panamanians in their search for the General. Major Domingo Ocalagan, the National Guard public relations chief, finally confirmed that Omar's plane had crashed and announced, 'There are no survivors.'

Normally it was a fifteen-minute flight to Coclesito from Penonomé. At the controls of the De Havilland Twin Otter 205 carrying Torrijos were a veteran pilot and co-pilot. The mountains had suddenly become cloaked in a storm. It was the rainy season, but storms didn't ground the General, and his pilots were far too macho to admit being defeated by the weather. The General's awful flying habits were legendary. He could unnerve visiting US senators by changing their destinations in mid-air. One night the US Ambassador, Ambler Moss, was visiting Omar at Coclesito. The General, relaxing in his hammock on the veranda, suddenly remembered he had to go somewhere. It was 9 p.m. Ambassador Moss asked him, 'How?' The airstrip had no lights. Simple, Torrijos explained. 'We place a truck with its lights on at one end of the runway as a guide, and if we don't hit the truck we are airborne.' And off he flew without hitting the truck.

That fateful Friday morning poor visibility had forced Omar's pilots to abort a second try at landing on Coclesito's dirt airstrip. The plane was gaining altitude as the pilots intended to circle again to make a third try. As the Canadian-built aircraft ascended, the right wing clipped a tall tree, sending the Otto crashing into Cerro Marta only a few feet below its summit. The National Guard blamed the crash on bad weather. Along with Omar, six others aboard the aircraft perished. It was not until the next afternoon, 1 August, that rescue workers finally reached the crash site and removed the remains of the General, two other passengers, the crew and two guardsmen.

It was as if Omar had chosen the place and manner of his death: the rural Panama he loved, high above Coclesito. His friend, Gabriel García Márquez, in his tribute to Torrijos, whom he had visited only two weeks before the fatal crash, noted they had flown together in mid-July in the same plane. Omar, knowing García Márquez's fear of flying, made sure that the Colombian novelist flew with a glass of whisky in his hand. In the 'ultimate instance', García Márquez later wrote:

> Torrijos trusted his good, mysterious and true intuition! It was his only orientation in the darkness of fate! . . . He didn't realize that servitude to his supernatural intuition, which perhaps saved his life many times, ended in the long run being his most vulnerable side since at the end he gave as many opportunities to fate as to his enemies. [Torrijos] had reserved for himself the privilege of choosing his time and method of death. He had reserved it for his last and decisive card of his historic fate. It was the vocation of martyr which was perhaps the most negative

aspect of his personality but also the most splendid and moving. The disaster, accidental or provoked, frustrated this design, but the sad mourners who attended his funeral were without a doubt moved by the secret wisdom the impertinent death without grandeur, one of the most dignified forms of martyrdom.

In Washington the White House announced that President Ronald Reagan, who had once called Torrijos a 'tinhorn dictator', had sent 'most sincere condolences' to Omar's family and the people of Panama: 'General Torrijos is one of the outstanding figures in Panama's history,' a White House statement said.

Former President Jimmy Carter issued a statement from his home in Plains, Georgia, declaring, 'The untimely death of General Omar Torrijos is a tragic loss for the people of Panama and for all who admired him as a wise and effective leader. I knew him personally as a dedicated and unselfish man committed to a better life for those who looked to him for leadership.'

The news hit me hard. It was like a death in the family. I had lost a good friend. That fateful Saturday I telephoned Graham to break the news. There was no answer at his Antibes flat. I finally reached him on Sunday. By then he had heard the reports of Torrijos's tragic end. We talked a long time about Omar. I could hear, in Graham's voice and the way he spoke, that Omar's death had affected him, too.

Three years later, on the eve of Graham's eightieth birthday, he told the author Martin Amis about it. Amis recounted it in a magazine article entitled 'Encounter in Paris'. 'One is shocked when a bit of one's life disappears. I felt that with Omar Torrijos. I think that's why, in the case of Torrijos, I embarked on what I hoped would be a memoir but what turned into a rather unsatisfactory blend of things. I felt that a whole segment of my life had been cut out.'

I was not able to attend the funeral. But afterwards I talked by telephone with Chuchu. 'Why didn't Graham come to the General's funeral?' he asked with a hint of reproach in his voice.

I explained as best I could that the General's death had affected us all but that we each mourn in different ways and funerals were only part of the mourning process. One didn't have to fly to Panama to attend the very public mourning in order to pay one's respects. I also reminded Chuchu that Omar himself would have hated his own state funeral, so filled with the pomp and protocol he detested. Likewise absent, along with Graham, was García Márquez, who said simply, 'I never had the heart to bury friends.' But thousands of other mourners were there. The public outpouring of grief throughout Panama when word came of Omar's death was something the country had never witnessed.

'I imagine when we were trying to telephone Chuchu he was off identifying the bodies,' Graham wrote in a letter dated 26 August. 'I very much feel the loss of Omar. It seems to have brought an end to my Central American life, though I received a telegram of invitation from George Price to the independence celebration in Belize. However things here are difficult and I won't be able to get away there. I suspect that the celebrations may be a bit riotous . . . ?'

'It was a bomb,' Chuchu said with finality when I talked to him again on the phone. Farmers in the region, he said, had heard the General's plane and then an explosion. No one would dissuade him: in his adamant judgement, it had to be the work of the CIA. Who else would want to kill the General? Chuchu would not entertain any other suspects although *bolas* (rumours) in Panama encompassed a long list of potential perpetrators, including Chuchu's own friends within the ranks of the Sandinistas. There was concern in Managua that Omar was about to lend support to Edén Pastora, who earlier that month had quit his post in Managua and driven across the border to Costa Rica and then all the way to Panama. It was known that Pastora and his wartime fighting friend, Panama's Dr Hugo Spadafora, were spending a great deal of time at Farallon and Coclesito with the General, happily discussing a grand plan to bring social democracy to Central America. There was speculation that Pastora was supposed to have been on the plane along with Omar but had been late for his rendezvous. (Indeed, Pastora himself narrowly escape a bomb on 30 May 1984 when he had mounted his own offensive against the Sandinistas from the border with Costa Rica. Seven people killed and twenty-eight wounded along with Pastora.) In fact Pastora was with Spadafora, in his Panama City apartment, when they heard the first news of Omar's disappearance. Fearing it might be a night of the long knives, they sped to Farallon believing it was the safest place to be until the situation cleared. Spadafora later claimed that spy chief Noriega had kept them for days as 'virtual prisoners' at the Farallon compound. Others suspected that the placing of a bomb on Omar's aircraft could only have been Noriega's handiwork. Thus there was no shortage of suspects or motives. But there was not a shred of evidence to support any of the plethora of stories.

Rory Gonzalez said he didn't believe the bomb theory at first, but after what happened in the years following he had to wonder. There had already been infighting in the Panamanian National Guard, and Torrijos had sent Gonzalez to tell Noriega and Rubén Darío Paredes to stop their power plays. The two were positioning themselves to be Omar's successor even before the fateful day.

Few among Panama's political establishment listened when an expert for the Canadian manufacturer of the General's plane examined the wreckage and concluded that a combination of bad weather and pilot error was responsible for the crash. There was, the expert declared, no evidence of a bomb explosion. Still, Chuchu stubbornly held to his theory that it was the work of the CIA, even though such a view flew in the face of the evidence. Not only had a 1977 Act of the US Congress placed a ban on the CIA's participation in the assassination of foreign leaders; there was seemingly little reason for the CIA to target Torrijos at this juncture. The Panama Canal treaties were a *fait accompli* and the General was doing his best to bring peace to Central America. He had moved to the political centre himself, and it should have been obvious to even the greenest Washington spook that Omar's death would touch off a dangerous power struggle within the Panamanian National Guard – which in fact occurred.

In *Getting to Know the General* Graham wrote that he had been struck by Torrijos's aura of near despair. 'You and I have something in common,' the General told Graham. 'We are both self-destructive.'

Graham once asked Omar what he dreamed about most, and the reply was almost predictable: *'La muerte.'* An awareness of death ran through many of the General's conversations with Graham, so when death finally came, Graham wrote in *Getting to Know the General*, 'it was not so much a shock that I felt as a long-expected sadness for what has seemed to me over the years an inevitable end'.

Particularly ironic to me was the fact that one of the first and last groups of exiles Omar sought to help were Haitians. Shortly before he died, the General had given his blessing to a 'Continental Solidarity Conference with Haiti', an effort to unite the fragmented Haitian opposition to the regime of Jean-Claude Duvalier. Among the members of the conference's International Committee were Graham Greene, Gabriel García Márquez, the widow of Chilean President Salvador Allende and former Venezuelan President Carlos Andrés Pérez.

Now there would be no more such humanitarian gestures from the General. The charismatic populist who had dreamed and talked so often of death had finally met death at fifty-two. In his thirteenth year as Panama's strongman, the young officer from Santiago de Veraguas had changed the face of his country. To be sure, he himself was a dictator whose regime suffered from some of the trappings of a Latin American dictatorship. His failings are perhaps best described by author John Dinges in his book *The Underside of the Torrijos Legacy*. Dinges wrote of

> a National Guard that was unchecked and unmonitored, that was run for the personal benefit of those who comprised its upper échelons. In sweeping away the old-style cronyism of the Union Club, Torrijos had left

the country in political adolescence. By repression and exile, he had emasculated the political parties, rendering them incapable of governing or even mounting an effective campaign for honest government. It may not have occurred to Torrijos to challenge Panama's ingrained tradition of influence peddling and payoffs – the idea that the time of rule is a time of enrichment. Common parlance in Panama lacked even the terminology to express such concepts as conflict of interest and ethics in government.

Instead, Torrijos attempted to channel the fruits of corruption to promote his revolution, to serve both his selfish and his enlightened purposes. The system was disarmingly simple: Torrijos bought or gained control of businesses and arranged for them to have a monopoly or to receive other kinds of preferential treatment. The companies provided second salaries for National Guard officers and their profits were available for special projects not covered in the national budget.

Nevertheless, Torrijos, above all, wanted his people to take pride in their small but strategic country – to see it no longer as just an international cross-roads serving the world's shipping but as a nation with its own culture and interests. He had broken the upper-class *rabiblancos'* monopoly on power and by so doing pre-empted the Marxists.

As Dinges also writes:

As if by accident, without the oratorical or ideological flourishes of a Fidel Castro, his military revolution had wrought enormous social, racial, even psychological changes in the lives of the vast majority of Panamanians. More than the reforms in land distribution, health care, education, the essence of 'Torrijismo' was the inchoate national pride he instilled in a people who had been more servants than slaves, more bought-out than downtrodden. By peaceful settling of Panama's historic score with the United States, he gave concrete reality to Panama as a country; by imposing a government that flaunted its middle-class, multiracial character, he had halted social polarization and short-circuited the appeal of Marxist radicalism.

With such achievements the General became a hero not only in his own country but also to others. In Nicaragua a group of poor people in the city of Estelí rechristened their *barrio* 'Omar Torrijos'.

After our last meeting with the General, Graham had mused about his failed Panama novel *On the Way Back*. He said it featured the failure of a revolution, which would be the book's main *raison d'être*. But while he had a villain he couldn't handle Chuchu. The problem, as I saw it – and it was the only time I offered my opinion on the subject – was that there was no room for the exuberant Chuchu in Graham's subconscious because Chuchu already so resembled a fictional character. I had observed Graham crafting characters from real life into *The Comedians,* but Chuchu seemed far too much for Graham's creative imagination to handle in a novel. Moreover, at times it seemed as if Chuchu was trying to micro-manage Graham's novel. I knew all about the futility of this because I had tried the same tactic with Graham and *The Comedians.* In writing, as in many other areas, Graham marched to his own drum.

Chuchu had other irritating qualities. He had a propensity for uttering fatuous phrases, some hyperbolic, others simply nonsensical. 'I believe in the Devil, I don't believe in God,' he used to say, as if such a sacrilegious declaration would shock the world about him. He was unabashedly excited about the prospect of being a fictional character in 'Greeneland', a name-place that Graham had grown to detest thoroughly. On their first trip together into the Panamanian hinterland Graham had made the mistake of revealing that he was thinking of a new novel. For Chuchu this was like an open door, and he stepped right in. When Graham asked him whether he would mind being killed off in the book Chuchu accepted the offer of literary martyrdom with pleasure but then warned, 'I am never going to die.'

In a letter to me after returning to Antibes from that first visit to Panama Graham wrote on 30 December 1976, 'I even got an idea for a novel when I was in the country with Chuchu and, if it does seem to take root, I shall go back to Panama in July.' Three weeks later he wrote, 'I really believe a novel is emerging into my self-conscious as the result of Panama with Chuchu as the main character.'

The book he had been carrying around for all those years was ultimately published in 1978 as *The Human Factor.* It was to bring Graham's career as a novelist full circle. Despite his own misgivings *The Human Factor* was one of his best novels and the last of the best ones, a masterful work. Graham had revealed to me earlier in Panama that the novel dealt with a British double agent, Maurice Castle, who married a black South African (Sarah). Graham had feared that critics might believe he was writing about Kim Philby because Castle, like Philby, ends up marooned in Moscow – a sorry finale – but does not receive the numerous perquisites provided by his Soviet handlers that Philby enjoyed. (Philby actually objected to Graham's portrayal of Moscow's bleakness – at least as experienced by the fictitious Castle.) His double agent Castle, Graham assured me, was in no manner or form based on Philby.

He had let the novel languish, without even a working title, for all those years. When he finally published *The Human Factor* he sent a copy to Philby. I read the book with anticipation and was not disappointed. I later told Graham that I agreed that no one familiar with Kim could possibly confuse Graham's character Maurice Castle with Philby, that Castle was the antithesis of Philby.

The title, *The Human Factor,* is well chosen. Again Graham treats the phenomena of betrayal, espionage, conspiracy and clandestine behaviour. There are also love, pain and anguish as well as a marked tenderness and compassion. The protagonist, Castle, who is the loneliest of spies and double agents, has a moral debt to pay to those who helped him spirit his black wife Sarah out of apartheid South Africa, which ultimately places him alone in the stark isolation of Moscow pining for the ones he loved.

(In *Ways of Escape* Graham had written: 'Perhaps the hypocrisy of our relations with South Africa nagged me on to work too. It was obvious that, however much opposed the governments of the West Alliance might pretend to be to apartheid, however much our leaders talked of its immorality, they simply could not let South Africa succumb to Black Power and Communism. If Operation Uncle Remus [a top-secret contingency plan for the defence of South Africa by the Western alliance that Castle learns about] did not exist, it would certainly come into existence before long. It was less an invitation than a prediction.')

As a book *The Human Factor* was a success, but, Graham reported, unfortunately Otto Preminger's film was not. Preminger, Graham added, had had problems financing the production and he was forced to do it 'on the cheap'.

Through 1977 Graham continued to struggle with his Panamanian novel. It often seemed that the key to unlocking his writer's block was to remind him of Bocas del Toro, the ancient dilapidated Panamanian banana port of which Graham had read in *The South American Handbook*, 'No tourist ever goes there.' Precisely for that reason he wanted to go there, literally to follow Columbus's footsteps to the 'Mouths of the Bull'. After several false starts, on his 1980 trip Graham finally got to fly – through a tropical thunderstorm – to Bocas del Toro. He found it a dismal place, with the cats in his decrepit hotel too busy having sex to bother chasing the free-roving rats. He wrote that he had awakened in Bocas del Toro after a long night's discussion with an independent political candidate, an impressive black Panamanian, with a new book in mind. No longer would Omar or Chuchu be characters in the novel, and instead of Panama it would all happen in an imaginary Central American country. A year later not only was the General dead but so was this latest inspiration for a novel.

The first chapter of the initial version that Graham had written in Anacapri did, however, appear as a short story the year following Omar's death, in a publication called *Firebird* and entitled 'On the Way Back'.

Then, as a tribute to his friendship with the General, Graham decided to write a non-fiction book about that friendship. The book proved also to be a tribute to Chuchu. In *Getting to Know the General* Graham noted, 'As we drove I told Chuchu of the novel which I was planning, and perhaps that is the reason why it never came to be written beyond the first chapter. To tell a story is much the same as to write it – it is a substitute for the writing.'

Even while in Central America, where war was very real, Graham was seriously preoccupied, even obsessed, by his own war at home. Many an evening would end with his talking of his anxiety and fears about what 'the scoundrel from Nice with Mafia connections' would do next. He worried aloud about Yvonne and her daughter Martine, and his thoughts were often with them on the faraway Côte d'Azur.

Graham would become uncharacteristically emotional and angry in telling the story of his war. Stoking the fires of controversy and provoking polemics in the exogenous realm were not new to Graham, but this was different. The matter was so serious that he had gone public and was forced, he said, to use his own literary guerrilla tactics.

Graham recounted that Martine had become fed up with the horrible man to whom she was married. She had obtained a divorce as well as custody of their child. (She was pregnant at the time of the divorce with their second child.) 'But the conditions of the divorce,' Graham explained, 'restricted Martine to live with her children within a five-mile radius of her angry ex-husband. The injustice of it all was outrageous.'

Graham had called Guy Daniel, the ex-husband, to his small apartment to discuss Martine's rights. Daniel was adamant. She and the two children must remain within the restricted area. Graham claimed that the ex-husband was making all their lives impossible, in fact terrorizing the family. The French police, he said, did nothing. It was then, he said, that he began his own inquiry and learned the depth and pervasiveness of corruption and organized crime in Nice where Martine's ex-husband lived. The family skirmish had turned into a political war that engulfed Nice. One evening in Panama City Graham talked at length about the then-mayor of Nice, Jacques Médicin, and his alleged ties to the 'Mafia mob', as well as Daniel's purported connection. He was extremely worked up about the lack of recourse and what he termed 'justice'.

Indeed when Graham read our *Time* cover story (23 November 1981) on South Florida entitled 'Paradise Lost – Trouble in Paradise' and headlining the fact that Miami had been hit by a hurricane of crime, drugs and refugees, Graham saw a parallel to the underside of the picture-postcard French Riviera city of Nice. In a letter dated 29 November 1981 he wrote:

Congratulations on your story in *Time* about Florida. It reminded me only too uncomfortably of the position here with Nice. As I think you know I have been engaged with my friends in a war which has lasted nearly three years with the criminal *milieu* there. It has involved an Inspecteur Général coming down to Nice from the Ministry of Justice and a Controlleur Général from the Ministry of the Interior. A few days ago I was in Paris and we saw the Inspecteur Général of the Police at the Ministry.

He went on to describe the situation in Nice as

a wall formed by corrupt police officers, corrupt magistrates and corrupt *avocats* which it is very difficult to pierce. You mustn't quote this. All the same if your man in Paris wants one day to do a story of Florida in France we can give him lots of material but I must have due warning and have confidence that nothing will be printed which I feel undesirable . . . I am thinking indeed of writing a book which Max Reinhardt would publish in French and English called like Zola's *J'accuse*.'

I did as Graham suggested and passed on word to my editors in New York to advise our Paris bureau that Graham was prepared to talk to them about his personal war. Then on 18 February 1982 Graham wrote:

Many thanks for your letter of February 3. As you will have seen *Time* did a small and rather ineffective story I thought but a nice a Dutchman called Van der Veen came to see me. However as a result of his visit I did have one that was rather more important from Madame Le Roux whom perhaps you know lost a daughter who has disappeared probably forever during the war of the Casinos here. She is a valuable ally and a very formidable woman. The counter-attack is taking form now . . . I shall have to go to Paris in a few days to see my allies.

In May Graham published *J'accuse: The Dark Side of Nice*. The book actually made it to the bookstores on the Riviera, but every copy was purchased and burned. The French courts then banned the book, and Martine's ex-husband won a libel suit of 52,000 francs against Graham and his publisher.

An Englishman attacking the French judicial system was not popular in France. Graham was attacked in some French newspapers. In a page out of the small-world encyclopaedia, Richard Eder, the *New York Times* correspondent whom Graham had met in Port-au-Prince during the Haiti crisis in 1963, had by now become the *New York Times*'s bureau chief in Paris. Eder flew to Antibes, interviewed Graham and filed a story on the troubles Graham termed the 'criminal *milieu*' of Nice. Both Graham and Eder were sued, but the case was eventually dropped.

The war had ballooned into a war of principle, and Graham had unleashed his talent and every other resource at his disposal to fight what he branded as an evil. When Eder asked the 77-year-old author, who had just finished *Monsignor Quixote*, whether he didn't think what he was doing was a parallel to the book's protagonist, a parish priest in Spain, and duelling with windmills, Graham smiled and replied, 'I wrote a sonnet when I was 20. It was about the peace of old age. Now I find it not so peaceful at all!' (*New York Times*, 3 February 1982).

A month earlier Graham decided to send a copy of *Monsignor Quixote*, his book about faith and doubt, to the Mayor of Nice, the notorious Jacques Médecin. In return he received a copy of an expensively printed book entitled *Cuisine niçoise* by Médecin himself. The author thanked Graham for his book and in his dedication stated, 'To Graham Greene, to whom the title *Cuisine niçoise* keeps a lot of secrets'. '*Cuisine niçoise*' can have a double meaning and imply more than cooking.

In his letter of 18 February 1982 Graham had also written:

> Chuchu rang me up about a week ago from Panama. He says that he knows that Omar was killed by a bomb in the plane but that he couldn't give me the details over the telephone. He is very anxious that I should come back in the summer, but I doubt whether I will be able to. I am not keen on doing so now that Omar has gone and I'm not anxious to lose my life in El Salvador.
>
> P.S. I also wonder whether the war with the *milieu* will allow me to leave Antibes. I can't leave Yvonne on her own to deal with things. My letter to *The Times* [about the situation in Nice] caused a bigger explosion than I had expected and I am rather exhausted with journalists, telephone calls and parlaphone calls. For the moment I wouldn't ask *Time* to do any more about the Antibes story.

By the following month, on 29 March, Graham had changed his mind about the *Time* stringer-correspondent and was in a combative mood, describing him as 'an awful little man' who had published after a 'poor piece in *Time* a really nasty piece in *People*, packed with inaccuracies and venom. I long to see him down here because then I will give him a couple of blows on the ears. But I think you might warn your office that he is a thoroughly unreliable reporter who shouldn't be left at large.'

'Yes, the battle still continues,' he wrote on 30 August,

> and it's impossible to make many plans for the summer. I have escaped
> to England for about ten days and have now started a book on Torrijos
> called *Getting to Know the General* – a very personal one which I hope
> will come off. I shall get you to read it in proof if it gets so far. I had
> read your story about Cuba in the European edition of *Time*, but I
> enjoyed reading it again. I do think the Reagan administration is badly
> mishandling Fidel. I get telephone calls occasionally from Chuchu
> who urges me to return to Panama, but I feel it would be like going
> to see Hamlet played by an understudy. The other day he told me that
> there were two Salvadorean guerrillas in Paris who were coming down
> to see me in Antibes, but I had to tell him I was away that weekend
> and they never showed up. He also sent Gaetano's [Cayetano's] regards!
> He's convinced that Omar was killed by a bomb. If that was the case
> I suppose it was the *junta* in Salvador who were responsible. I'm asking
> my sister to send you a copy of *J'accuse*, but she is away on holiday at
> the moment and it will be some time before it arrives. I do wish *Time*
> magazine wouldn't keep on sending me the appalling Dutchman
> whom they have in Marseilles. I won't speak to him.

'Many thanks for the cuttings about Panama,' he wrote on 4 October. 'I
have started a book called *Getting to Know the General* in which the General
and Chuchu will be the main characters. If it is ever finished (I have done
15,000 words so far) of course I'll let you see the typescript as you play a part
in the story. I hope you won't lose your life in Haiti.' Graham was concerned
about the danger of being 'bumped off' by Interior Minister Dr Roger
Lafontant, who opposed my return in 1980 to interview President-for-Life
Jean-Claude (Baby Doc) Duvalier. Reporting from Haiti in subsequent years
I took particular care to keep out of the way of Lafontant and other Macoutes.

Then on 7 October Graham reported, 'I have done more than a quarter
of the book about Omar and I will certainly call on your help and criticism
if I ever get it finished. I had a telephone call from Nicaragua and old Father
Cardenal a few nights back inviting me on behalf of the *junta* to go there. I
hedged because I am very busy here and said it might be possible in November
but I doubt if it will.'

Still later he announced in a letter dated 22 December that he was
returning to Panama on 3 January 1983 and would 'then go on with Chuchu
to Nicaragua. The *junta* are inviting me there. It would be good if there was
a chance of your visiting at the same time, but I realize that it is no longer
your field of action.'

Chuchu had finally succeeded in persuading Graham to pick up a ticket from the KLM office in Amsterdam that Omar had ordered for him and been held there since his death. Chuchu would not take no for an answer. In January 1983 Graham flew to Panama, and when the pilot announced that they were about to land at the newly renamed Omar Torrijos Herrera International Airport, Graham recalled, he had a somewhat comforted feeling. The fact that the airport, which Omar had rebuilt, now bore his name filled a little of the void. However, when he found he was booked not in the old Continental Hotel but in the plush new Marriot's presidential suite, and had been assigned a member of the Panamanian National Guard's G2 as bodyguard, he wondered what had happened to Omar's proletarian Panama.

Graham was soon to learn that the struggle to fill Torrijos's boots had begun even before his demise. At his death Omar left his youthful former education minister, Aristides Royo, in the presidency and Colonel Florencio Florez as chief of staff of the National Guard. In March 1982 Colonel Florez, a gum-chewing career officer with a reputation for honesty, had been easily shoved aside by a trio that included Deputy Chief of Staff Colonel Rubén Darío Paredes, Intelligence Chief Manuel Noriega and the Guard's secretary-general Colonel Roberto Díaz Herrera. On 30 July 1982, the eve of the first anniversary of Omar's death, Paredes made his move. He replaced President Royo. In resigning the presidency Royo explained to a national television audience that he was suffering from a sore throat. It became a historic removal of a president in Panama in what instantly became known as the '*gargantazo*'– 'sore-throat coup'. With Paredes's nod, Vice-President Ricardo de la Espriella, a former chief executive of Panama's national bank, moved up to the presidency. Behind the scenes Noriega was consolidating his power and combining both the police and National Guard into what became known as the Panama Defense Forces (PDF). The Guardia was in effect turning its back on Omar's promised transition to democracy and popular rule.

Graham liked Ricardo de la Espriella but didn't particularly take to Paredes, who was known as a heavy-footed right-winger and who later proved no match for the more nimble Manuel Noriega (whom Graham didn't like either). Chuchu did not feel it was necessary to fill Graham in on the Byzantine intricacies of the Guardia power play that was now part of the Panamanian landscape. The new leadership, Chuchu said, wanted Graham to go on to Nicaragua and then to Havana to sprinkle a little stardust of friendship. Panama's new strongmen were in need of friends. None of the ambitious Guardia officers, Graham later told me, could hold a candle to Omar. Paredes had moved into Rory's house on Calle Cincuenta and was acting like the new leader.

Almost as embarrassing was Paredes's present to Graham of an expensive

Rolex watch with the inscription 'To an English brother of General Omar Torrijos from General Paredes.' On his return to Antibes Graham wrote, on 15 April 1983, 'General Paredes embarrassed me by presenting me at lunch with an inscribed gold Rolex watch which I noticed in the Faubourg in Paris was sold at 66,000 frs! I couldn't very well refuse it but I am having it demolished for its gold bracelet . . . so that it becomes possible to wear!'

Encouraging Graham to go to Nicaragua was the fact that he now felt only sympathy for the plight of the Sandinista revolution, partly because all of his prophecies had come to pass. Reagan was determined to oust the Sandinistas and was secretly funding and training their foes, who had become known as the Contras. He had written from France:

> I am doing what I can here but it is very little. The Nicaraguan ambassador rang me up and asked me to sign a letter proposed by [Sergio] Ramirez of the [Sandinista] *junta* – quite a ferocious letter which García Márquez and author Carlos Fuentes are also signing. I have also signed a telegram to the Nicaraguan Press Agency here, which they are sending out to all chiefs of state. The Mickey Mouse bomb [a reference to a booby trap Contra bomb placed in a child's lunch box] has also been useful and I have publicized it to the best of my ability. Just off to London now for my surgical check-up.

Much later Graham revealed to me that his earlier operation on his 'gut' had been identified as cancer. During his check-up he had received the heartening news that his cancer had not reappeared.

Before he had left Panama for Nicaragua, President de la Espriella, in a ceremony at Panama City's Palace of Herons, and in the presence of Omar's two strapping sons, the National Guard high command and a beaming Chuchu, presented Graham with the country's Grand Cross of the Order of Vasco Nuñez de Balboa. While Graham said he was embarrassed by the award, he was none the less moved. 'I had done nothing to justify such a decoration,' he protested to Espriella. He was later to write in *Getting to Know the General*, 'My sense of embarrassment increased when I became tangled up in the ribbon and the stars. I felt like a Christmas tree in the process of being hung with presents.' (He was not the only Brit to be honoured. His friend, the ballerina Dame Margot Fonteyn, had also received the decoration.) Another moving moment occurred when he flew over Cerro Marta, the crash site of Omar's plane, in a bucking helicopter along with Torrijos's eldest daughter Carmen Alicia and Chuchu. It was the first time that Chuchu, for all his certainty about a bomb, had gone near the crash site.

In January 1983 I met up with Graham and Chuchu in Managua while reporting an article headlined 'Rising Tides of War in Central America' for *Time*. The story appeared in the 14 February 1983 issue of the magazine in which the cover story was 'The KGB Today: Andropov's Eyes on the World'. Interestingly Graham had expounded a pet theory to Omar that the KGB could well be the vehicle for change in the Soviet Union. Graham really believed that the USSR's Communist Party chief Yuri Andropov – a former head of the KGB – was a dove. In Nicaragua, meanwhile, the clashes between the US-backed counter-revolutionaries and Sandinista military forces were becoming more frequent.

Graham was impressed by the Church people, both Catholic and Protestant. Most were outspoken critics of Reagan's policy of aiding the Contras. Graham met with nuns in Ciudad Sandino and was taken on a tour of the war zone near Nicaragua's border with Honduras. On his return he asked me whether he had been shown a quiet sector of the Contra war. I assured him that there was no peaceful area near that border.

On Graham's last night in Nicaragua, at dinner at an outdoor Mexican restaurant, Los Antojitos, across the street from Managua's InterContinental Hotel, he appeared tired and somewhat bewildered. He was staying in what he described as 'a posh, well-guarded residence of a wealthy Sandinista'. However, his overall mood was good for having survived the war zone trip. 'An ambush would have made it a little more exciting,' he chuckled.

The Sandinista Land-Rover jeeps were, he commented, the closest he had been to a coffin. In an ambush he felt there would be no way of getting out the back of the vehicle. (Three months after Graham's trip *Time's* chief of correspondents Richard Duncan, along with two editors from the magazine and veteran foreign correspondent Karen DeYoung of the *Washington Post*, were ambushed although unharmed by Contra rebels while travelling in a Sandinista military convoy. They were moving down the road from the little town of Jalapa, near the Honduran border, to an airfield to return to Managua when the mortar attack occurred. Five government soldiers guarding the journalists were killed and six wounded.)

Sandinista Interior Minister Tomás Borge had introduced Graham to Lenin Cerna, the head of state security. Graham received the tour Lenin customarily gave the foreign media, some of whom were sceptical of Cerna's display of lethal boobytrapped toys he accused the rebels of manufacturing for use against the civilian population. Graham accepted them as evidence of the purported barbarity of the Contras. The *pièce de résistance* was the child's Mickey Mouse school lunch-box bomb. What Graham saw, and was shown, during his visit heightened his anger against President Reagan and what was becoming known as Reagan's secret war.

Graham confessed at Los Antojitos, when Chuchu went to use the telephone, that 'it has been a strange trip. I don't mind being used when it is for a good cause but I am a little mystified about our and Chuchu's next stop, Havana. I am still not certain whether I am invited by Fidel or Casa de Las Americas [the Cuban cultural centre]. Frankly I am a little tired and it is time to go home.'

When I thought how arduous and tense travelling around rural Nicaragua with the Sandinistas could be, stopping and starting and visually sweeping the road ahead for an ambush, I felt sympathy for Graham, who was about to turn eighty. It was the last time the three of us would be together in Central America.

23 | A NIGHT IN HAVANA

Gabriel García Márquez happened to be in Havana when Graham arrived. The two writers were now old friends, and it was Gabo who helped break the ice when Fidel Castro dropped in to visit Graham Greene. García Márquez's original report of the meeting was reprinted in the Cuban newspaper *Granma* on 14 April 1991 after Graham's death.

Graham Greene stopped over in Havana for 20 hours, and the local correspondents of the foreign press read all kinds of things into it. Naturally. He arrived on an executive plane belonging to the government of Nicaragua and was accompanied by José de Jesús Martínez [Chuchu], a Panamanian poet and professor of mathematics who was one of the men closest to General Omar Torrijos. Moreover, they were met at the airport by protocol officials, and the meeting was wrapped in so much discretion that no journalist found out about the visit until it was over. They were taken to a house for visiting dignitaries that is usually reserved for heads of state of friendly countries, a black Mercedes Benz was placed at their disposal – the kind that was used only during the 6th Summit Meeting of Non-Aligned Countries, nine years ago. Actually, they didn't need it, because they didn't leave the house. Old Cuban friends of theirs came to see them – friends who knew they were there because the writer himself told them. Painter René Portocarrero who became Greene's friend when the writer came to Havana to study the setting for *Our Man in Havana*, got the message too late, and, when he got there, the writer had already gone back. Greene ate only once during the 20 hours, nibbling at a lot of things like a wet bird, but he had a bottle of good Spanish red wine, and the two of them and their guests polished off six bottles of whisky.

When Greene departed, he left the impression that not even he knew why he had come – a thing that could happen only to one of his characters in his novels, fomented by doubts about God.

I went to his house two hours after he arrived because he phoned as soon as he heard I was in the city. This made me very happy, not only because I've admired him for a long time as a writer and as a human being but also because many years had gone by since we'd seen each other last.

After so many years, I found a rejuvenated Graham Greene whose clear thinking continues to be his most surprising and unalterable virtue. As always, we talked about everything under the sun. What most caught my attention was the sense of humor with which he referred to the four trials in which he had to appear in various French courts, as a result of the accusatory pamphlet he published against the Mafia in Nice. For many familiar with the Côte d'Azur's underworld, Greene's revelations were nothing new. But we, his friends, feared for his life. He held to his course, however, and went ahead with his denunciation. 'I'd rather die of a bullet in the head than a cancer of the prostate,' he said. And I said then – I don't remember where – that Graham Greene was playing literary Russian roulette, as he had done in his youth with a .32 Smith and Wesson, as reported in his memoirs. He remembered my statement during the visit and took it as a starting point for telling us the details of his four trials.

At around 1.00 a.m. Fidel Castro dropped by to visit. He and Greene had first met shortly after the triumph of the Revolution, when Greene attended the filming of *Our Man in Havana*. They saw each other several times since then, during Greene's periodic visits, but it seemed that they hadn't gotten together the last two times, because, when they shook hands, Graham Greene, said, 'We haven't seen each other for 16 years.' It seemed to me that they were both a little daunted, and it wasn't easy for them to start talking. Therefore I asked Graham Greene how much truth there was in the episode of Russian roulette that he'd told about in his memoirs. His blue eyes, the clearest I've ever seen, lit up with the memory. 'That was when I was 19,' he said, 'when I fell in love with my sister's teacher.' He said that, in fact, he had played a solitary game of Russian roulette with an old revolver belonging to an older brother and that he'd done so on four different occasions.

'There was a week between the first and the second time, but the last two were just a few minutes apart.' Fidel Castro, who couldn't let a fact such as that go by without exploring it in depth, asked him how many bullets could fit in the cylinder of the revolver. 'Six,' Graham Greene replied. Then Fidel Castro closed his eyes and began to murmur multiplication figures. Finally, he looked at the writer in astonishment and said, 'According to the calculation of probabilities, you should be dead.' Graham Greene smiled with the serenity of all writers when they feel they are living an episode from one of their own books and said, 'It's a good thing I was always terrible at maths.' Perhaps because they had been speaking about death, Fidel Castro quickly noted the writer's youthful appearance and good health and asked him what exercises he did. It was a question that was bound to come up, because Fidel Castro considers physical culture to be one of the keys of life. He does several hours of exercise every day, in the same enormous proportions in which he does everything, and he urges his friends to do the same. His physical condition is exceptional for a man of his age, and he attributes his good mental health to this. Therefore he was taken back when Graham Greene replied that he'd never done any exercises at all, yet he felt very alert and had no health problems at 79. Moreover, he said that he didn't have any special diet. That he slept between seven and eight hours a night – which was also surprising in an old man with sedentary habits – and that, at times, he drank up to a bottle of whisky a day and a liter of wine with each meal, yet he'd never become a slave to alcohol.

For a moment, Fidel Castro seemed to doubt the efficacy of his regimen of health, but he quickly realized that Graham Greene was an admirable exception –admirable, but an exception. By the time we said goodbye, I was sure that, sooner or later, that meeting would be described in a book of memoirs by one of the three of us – or perhaps by all.

When Graham returned to Antibes he wrote in a letter to me dated 2 February 1983, 'It was an amusing meeting with Fidel in my twenty-four hours in Cuba. He looked to me much younger than he had done in 1966 and much more relaxed.' An article reported by a colleague of mine had appeared in *Time* that had enraged Graham. He was so upset by this article and the treatment of the Sandinistas that he went on French television to excoriate it. He said he had promised to send a copy to Chuchu.

In a letter two weeks later he said:

I wrote to you after I returned but I was very tired and I don't know what I told you! Did I tell you that we had had a visit from Marcial who was very friendly? I was very shocked by that piece in *Time* magazine so that I broke all my resolutions and went on television on the Third Regional to contradict the story of which I said I did not believe a word as I had spoken to many priests and American nuns in Nicaragua who would certainly have had some knowledge of such things going on. [The *Time* story, 'A Defector's Firsthand Account of Massacres and Torture', was full of allegations which the Sandinistas denied.] I have also written a long letter to *The Tablet* [the British edition of the Catholic newspaper] on the unreliability of Archbishop Obando y Bravo. I will send you a cutting when it appears. A crazy young documentary Australian film director Bradbury has sent me a student's ticket to Managua and back because he wants me to help him in a film he is doing with Bianca Jagger. He is a good documentary man and on the right side and I expect he will be trying to look you up. Did I tell you that Fidel prophesied a guerrilla victory in San Salvador in a year's time?

Pope John Paul II descended on Sandinista-ruled Nicaragua less than two months after Graham departed. The Pope's visit began with his humiliating Father Ernesto Cardenal, the Minister of Culture. As Father Cardenal knelt to kiss his papal ring the Pope withdrew his hand and wagged his papal finger in the priest's face. The Pope was admonishing him and other Catholic clerics for taking an active role in the revolutionary government. Then the papal Mass turned into a free-for-all. Youthful Sandinistas in the huge throng baited nuns sitting before them in the stands who were trying to keep the youths quiet. Badgered by hecklers in the crowd, the Pope grew impatient and asked them to be silent. The agitators loved it. The Pope had suddenly lost his infallibility and descended to their level.

John Paul II had angered many Sandinistas not only by his public scolding of Father Cardenal but by reaffirming his support for Nicaraguan Archbishop Miguel Obando y Bravo, a harsh critic of the Sandinistas. The *comandantes* sat through the Mass, making no effort to intervene to restore order.

Following the Pope from Nicaragua to Port-au-Prince on his tour, I found it interesting that he faced a different kind of political drama in Haiti. Led by Bishop Willy Romulus of Jeremie, the liberal wing of the Haitian Catholic Church took heart when the Pope declared, 'Things must change here.' This papal declaration was pounced on by young oppositionists who used it as their battle cry against the Duvalier regime. The ensuing popular uprising succeeded, and Jean-Claude Duvalier ceased to be President-for-Life on the morning of 7 February 1986.

Graham, who was already deeply concerned by the Polish Pope's actions, wrote in a letter to me on 28 March 1983, 'I haven't a very high opinion of [Daniel] Ortega and I thought he behaved rather stupidly – but then so did the Pope. I am glad the rum punches are still good at the Oloffson. I have no summer plans for the time being, but I'll let you know if I travel west.'

In Nicaragua, three months after Salvadorean guerrilla leader Marcial had visited Graham in Managua, the commander of the strongest arm of the Salvadorean guerrilla force was dead. His end came days after his second-in-command, Mélida Anaya Montes, known by her *nom de guerre* Ana María, was brutally murdered in a safe house in a prestigious suburb of Managua. Her throat was slashed, and according to the Nicaraguan Interior Ministry her body revealed eighty stab wounds. Marcial was in Libya at the time and returned to Managua for the funeral. Reporters who saw him described Marcial as looking much older than his sixty-four years and wearing a sweater under a coat despite the intense summer heat. Six days later, on 12 April, Salvador Cayetano Carpio, 'Marcial', was found dead, reportedly by his own hand, of a bullet in the heart. His role in the killing of Anaya Montes had been established.

In a letter dated 22 May Graham wrote:

> I haven't yet any settled plans for the summer except that I hope to find time to get on a bit with the book I am writing about Omar. I was shocked by Marcial's death. When I saw him in Nicaragua he was full of optimism for the future. The death of his woman deputy seems to have been a peculiarly brutal one. I am glad the men responsible have been arrested. Chuchu keeps on ringing up and the story of Cayetano's death becomes more and more mysterious. Now they are blaming the murder of this woman on him.

24 | MASTER OF CONTRADICTION

'I have finished my book on Torrijos,' Graham announced, 'but I am not sure yet whether I will publish it. After four revisions I am not happy about it. Maybe I will let Chuchu make the final decision.' But publish he did. *Getting to Know the General* hit the bookstores in January 1984. At the end of May 1983 Chuchu had descended on Antibes. Graham was happy to see him and wrote:

> Chuchu arrived safely and corrected many misspellings of mine. I would have liked you to have seen the book before publication but we are anxious to get it out before the American elections – Chuchu is especially anxious. He likes it better than I do. His character really overshadows Omar in the book and I feel it an uneasy falling between two stools of memoirs and autobiography. However I will follow Chuchu's advice and publish.

Graham later agreed that the tome was too dispersed, not clearly enough a memoir, an autobiography or a travel book. (*Time's* reviewer, J.D. Reed, had asked, 'How much of this strange biography – travel book, escapist yarn, memoir – is documentary? It is certain that in his 45th book Greene remains a master of contradiction.')

Following the publication of *Getting to Know the General*, Graham concluded a letter to me with a comment on the US elections.

> I have hope that [US Senator Gary] Hart will beat both Mondale and Reagan. I don't feel it likely somehow that Reagan will go whole-hog on an invasion of Nicaragua. After all the Pentagon decided that it would need a hundred thousand troops to guard the Canal so I should imagine it would need close to half a million to do anything in Nicaragua.
>
> I begin to feel old and tired so though Chuchu brought me letters from Colonel Díaz, Noriega and [Panamanian President] Espriella who sent me a picture also I doubt whether I shall take off again for Central America. I shall probably go no further than Spain this year.

When I received my copy of *Getting to Know the General* I realized that Graham was not simply being modest in saying that he was not satisfied with even the fourth version he had written. I thought he had given a faithful and truthful account of his peregrinations in Panama, but much was missing that could have been covered only in a novel. The book could have worked so much better as fiction. General Omar Torrijos was a complicated human being to whom Graham could have done justice only in fictional form. At the end of the book it also became apparent that Chuchu did more than correct spelling mistakes, that Graham had allowed him to exert editorial influence to make his (Chuchu's) easy view of the Sandinistas appear to be shared by General Torrijos, when it was not. Omar had said more than once that the Sandinistas were 'neither a model nor a menace'. He confessed that he did not like what he considered the Sandinistas' dangerous growing dependency on the East when they were in the West.

Getting to Know the General offered a revealing portrait of Graham's inner thoughts. While being driven by Chuchu into the Panamanian mountains one day, Graham recounts, 'to me it was like a return back to life after a long sickness – the malignant sickness of a writer's block. My writing days, I thought, were not over after all.' With the General's death

> the idea came to me to write a short personal memoir, based on the diaries which I had kept over the last five years, as a tribute to a man whom during that time I had grown to love. But as soon as I had written the first sentence after the title, *Getting to Know the General*, I realized that it was not only about the General whom I had got to know over those five years . . . it was also about Chuchu, one of the few men in the National Guard whom the General trusted completely, and it was this bizarre and beautiful little country, split in two by the Canal and the American Zone, a country which had become, thanks to the General, of great practical importance in the struggle for liberation taking place in Nicaragua and El Salvador.

Two outstanding foreign correspondents, the previously mentioned Karen DeYoung of the *Washington Post* (who had escaped injury during the mortar ambush in Nicaragua) and Alan Riding of the *New York Times*, were covering Panama and Central America at the time, and both reviewed *Getting to Know the General*.

DeYoung thought the book should have been a novel rather than the non-fiction account that Graham had written. She noted that Graham had developed a close relationship with Torrijos and had kept a journal that he hoped to turn into a tale tentatively titled *On the Way Back*, but that all had changed with Torrijos's death. She wrote:

Some of Greene's critics, and even fans, say his books are not political enough. For better or for worse, his novels often are considered too entertaining to be profound. But for this reader and fan, the moment when *On the Way Back* became *Getting to Know the General* was an unfortunate one. What could have been both good politics and good entertainment as fiction turns out to be a disappointment as real life . . . Omar Torrijos was a compelling, unique man who combined the Latin American *caudillo* tradition of military dictatorship with a curious kind of humanism and humanity, a 'dictator with heart,' as he used to call himself . . . By Latin standards, his rule was benign and relatively progressive. He dedicated himself to negotiating the return of US control of the Panama Canal and Canal Zone, and wrestled the long-languishing treaty negotiations to a political victory through will power and clever diplomacy . . . One longs for the larger-than-life complicated character that Greene could have made of a fictionalized Torrijos; for the sense of place and time, and even political meaning, that the Greene treatment could have evoked of Panama and Central America at a time when national pride and revolution were awakening.

The best passages in the book are those about the process of creating characters and writing fiction, about *On the Way Back* before it was discarded in favor of a pale paean to the General. Only one small bit of it is preserved here, but it is worth comparing to real life. In *Getting to Know the General*, Greene describes his arrival for his first meeting with Torrijos. 'It was a small insignificant suburban house, only made to look out of the ordinary by the number of men in camouflage uniform clustered around the entrance and by a small cement pad at the rear in place of a garden, smaller than a tennis court, on which a helicopter could land.'

Much later in the book, as Greene recounts his efforts back at home in France to begin the subsequently aborted novel, *On the Way Back*, the scene is transformed. The fictional protagonist, a journalist named Marie-Claire, arrives at the same suburban house to interview the as yet unknown General. 'She found herself surrounded in the small courtyard of a white suburban villa with half-Indian faces. The men all carried revolvers on their belts and one had a walkie-talkie which he kept pressed closely to his ear as though he were waiting with the intensity of a priest for one of his Indian gods to proclaim something. The men are as strange to me, she thought, as the Indians must have seemed to Columbus five centuries ago. The camouflage of their uniforms was like painted designs on naked skin.'

DeYoung's fellow foreign correspondent Alan Riding concluded his review in the 4 November 1984 *New York Times*:

> On Greene's last trip to Panama, in 1983, some of Torrijos's followers were eager to use him as a symbol that the general's political ideas were still alive. Greene didn't mind. 'I have never hesitated to be "used" in a cause I believe in,' he noted. And he headed off in a Panamanian Government plane, first to Nicaragua, where he met top Sandinista leaders, and then to Cuba for the same reason, where he greeted Fidel Castro with the words, 'I am not a messenger. I am the message.'
>
> Greene omits the detailed analysis required to support his case, but it remains valid – the death of Torrijos removed a vital force for moderation from the Central American scene. At his death, he was somewhat disillusioned with both the Sandinistas and Fidel Castro, but he kept his lines open to the left, just as he did to the United States. And his death, Greene concludes, 'was not only the end of his dream of moderate socialism but perhaps the end of any hope of a reasonable peace in Central America.' Coming out shortly after Graham Greene's 80th birthday, *Getting to Know the General* reassures us that the writer's dreams and hopes have not died. From a literary point of view, this book is perhaps not among his most memorable – he has conceded he found it difficult to write. But from a human point of view, it is compellingly compassionate.

'I am glad you found something you liked in *The General*,' Graham wrote to me on 2 January 1984. He was responding to my favourable comment.

> I was disappointed in the book myself. It seemed to fall between too many stools, but it was the best I could do. Of course I haven't seen much of the American press, but I was surprised by the number of good reviews that I did see – including the *New York Times*, *Time* itself, and *Newsweek*, and there were others . . . I do hope we meet again in not so long a time in Central America or elsewhere.

Graham ended a long letter with 'Forgive a hasty line, but this bloody 80th birthday is filling all my time and my post box.'

For all his eight decades of life, Graham's correspondence – and mind – seemed as sharp as ever. He wrote on 29 September 1984:

> I am sorry you are out of Central America for the moment, but I suspect after the election you will be well in again. I don't see any chance

of joining you in the Caribbean for our war [a reference to Yvonne's domestic tribulations] is still continuing and I don't feel able to get away for any length of time. I have been invited to Bulgaria and to Russia – Bulgaria in October and Russia in the spring – but I am very doubtful of getting to either of them . . . I went back to Spain for a little more than a week in August but I plan no real travels . . . Let me know if you come to Paris.

Back in New Zealand my eldest sister, a Catholic nun and a great admirer of Graham Greene, had been diagnosed with cancer and had been given only a few weeks to live. I had made an urgent journey to visit her. On my return to Miami I received a letter from Graham, dated 27 June 1985, saying he was sorry to hear the news.

As one grows older there seem to be many more deaths than births to record. I don't know exactly what I shall be doing this summer except I hope that I escape from the Côte a bit. The affair [Yvonne's problems] is still a bit of a bother but not so much as it used to be. Chuchu rings up from time to time and it's just possible that I might go to Panama and Nicaragua in late July, but I find it difficult to make up my mind. I shall certainly let you know if I do go. Reagan is a real nightmare. Russia and the USA seem to be the same face looking at each other in the same glass and there are times when I certainly prefer the Russian face to the American face similar though they both are. I miss Omar more and more and I haven't the same confidence in Noriega . . . Anyway let's keep in touch.

In his postscript he reported, 'I was invited to the 6th anniversary of the Sandinista revolution on I think July 19 but it's a date very difficult for me and I was glad to have an excuse to refuse. If I go to Nicaragua I would much rather go on my own and not with a bunch to make propaganda.'

25 | WE'LL MEET AGAIN

One day in September 1985 I watched as Graham walked swiftly across the little Antibes railway station to greet me. I had finally found time to take up his invitation and visit him. Apprehensive, in his heavily accented French, Graham questioned the female receptionist at the old Hotel Terminus et Suisse across from the station: 'You have held your good corner room? I specifically asked for it weeks ago, chamber 12,' he insisted.

She nodded. '*Oui, monsieur.*'

'*Merci, mademoiselle.*'

Graham personally made reservations for his visitors weeks in advance and troubled about their comfort. But he was always relieved when they left and the reunion was over. He never made any secret of how much he treasured his privacy or his aversion to any form of domesticity. 'One needs to be free of all the taxing chores of domestic life, family feuds and that sort of thing,' he said, adding that that didn't mean he didn't love his family. In fact, he emphasized, he loved his family very much and tried to help and provide for them as much as possible.

We went to his small apartment overlooking Antibes and the French Riviera and sipped a noontime vodka (not really a martini) which he had poured himself. He had managed to simplify his lifestyle, he said, with few commitments, and Yvonne was most understanding, She arrived on the scene most days at noon after he had completed his day's work.

Graham had just emerged from his war with the Mafia. Much of the publicity that had accompanied it, he confessed, was his doing. In addition, all the fuss over his eightieth birthday had robbed him of much of the privacy he held so dear. He had allowed himself to be interviewed and decorated. He had received the Companion of Literature award from the Royal Society of Literature in England and the Ordre des Arts et des Lettres in France. During the outset of his war he was so disgusted with the French judicial system that he had returned his Légion d'honneur to Paris, but the government had returned it saying that it remained his until 'death or dishonour'.

He sat in his rattan armchair, mocking himself as a fool for having succumbed to the publicity. He wondered out loud whether it wasn't all part of the rites of becoming an octogenarian. The fall-out from all the publicity was almost a daily routine, and he had to be on his guard. Relishing his vodka, he pondered whether it had not cast too much illumination on his private life. For decades he had preferred to live quietly and unseen; now he complained he was being badgered by perfect strangers. 'When I returned from Capri there were over sixty letters. I couldn't possibly reply to them. I'd be writing all day,' he said.

At the little *tabac* across from Chez Félix au Port they had finally learned the identity of the tall Englishman who for years had purchased English and French newspapers and magazines there. In 1984 those newspapers carried big photographs and stories on him to mark his eightieth birthday. He now dreaded his front-door buzzer and intercom.

Graham's living-room was his workroom. The bright Mediterranean sun slanted through the glass doors on to the wooden dining table that doubled as his writing desk. He rose, went over and sat down behind the table, his back to the wall, and explained how he worked. He lifted his right hand, his long slender finger bent from rheumatism. The disease was Dupuytren's contracture. 'My ideas flow from the right side of my head down to this hand,' he explained, demonstrating the right hand with which he composed in longhand, using a fountain pen, not a pencil. In the morning, he said, his favourite working time, he was now lucky to produce two hundred words. When the first draft of a manuscript was complete, he added, he would read it page by page into a Dictaphone and then send the tapes to England where his sister, Elisabeth, would do the typing. When the typescript came back he would do his own trimming and other editing.

Work came first, and he built his life around it; like a turtle, he joked, he had his shell. He did his writing in the morning. By noon he was ready to relax. Yvonne joined him for lunch. He now believed in an afternoon siesta. The evenings were free, although, he said, 'Yvonne and I drive [she did the driving] into the hills sometimes to a restaurant for an early dinner.' (Often when he telephoned for a reservation Graham found his name written as Gram Grim.)

He devoted a great deal of time to reading, and often reread books that he particularly liked. He talked enthusiastically about R.K. Narayan, the Indian writer, whom Graham had helped find a publisher earlier in life and with whom he continued to correspond.

We reminisced about the General. Graham wondered whether many of the crazy things Torrijos had threatened to do had only been clever tactics designed to force Washington's hand. There was, for instance, the team of Israeli experts Omar said he had brought to Panama to sabotage the Canal by blowing up its locks if the US Senate refused to ratify the Panama Canal Treaty. It was commonly accepted that Omar's agents had set off the harmless bombs in the Canal Zone on the eve of Graham's first visit to Panama in 1976.

Graham wanted to know whether there was any truth to the rumour that Reagan would invade Nicaragua. He believed that the US president might have adopted Omar's threatening tactics.

'How can Reagan get away with it?' he asked, referring to Washington's belligerent policy towards the Sandinistas.

Many Americans shared Graham's concern. It was the first time since the Vietnam War that a US President was being accused of waging an undeclared war without the consent of Congress. The Reagan administration had argued that it was in compliance with the law because the purpose was merely to harass the Sandinista government, not to overthrow it.

Smiling, Graham said, 'The General would have found that ingenious . . .'

Later, Yvonne arrived. She entered with a flurry and a *'Bonjour, Gram.'*

Speculation over Torrijos's reaction to Reagan's policy in Central America ended in mid-sentence. Graham's mood brightened. He towered over the trim, petite figure as he rose to greet her. After introductions she excused herself and set about straightening up the small kitchen. He had spoken so often about Yvonne in Central America that I felt I already knew her.

Then the phone rang. 'Where are my glasses?' Graham fretted. Yvonne found them and handed them to him.

After he hung up Yvonne said that Graham and I had a lot to talk about and that she would not join us for lunch.

It was a straight walk from his apartment building down the hill to Chez Félix au Port, the old Le Men family restaurant at the entrance to the port, now a fashionable marina. Albert Le Men greeted Graham as an old friend. Chagrined, our host realized that someone was seated at Graham's favourite table. Graham was visibly annoyed. As soon as he set his reading spectacles down on our allocated table he hurried across the street to the small *tabac* and bought *The Times*. 'The *Guardian* has really become unreadable,' he said, 'but the British *Tablet* is quite good. I read it regularly.'

He placed the financial section of the newspaper on the windowsill behind him, and Albert retrieved them. Albert was interested in financial matters; Graham was not. We looked out at the old town gateway in the wall that dated from the seventeenth century and led to the marina. During the summer, he said, the little street would be jammed with pedestrians and vehicle traffic. Chez Félix could no longer be his hideaway, nor could his other favourite local restaurant, Auberge Provençale. The newspaper and magazine stories on his eightieth birthday describing his life in Antibes and naming his two favourite restaurants had ruined all that. Albert agreed. He was often pestered by 'Greeneophiles' requesting introductions.

We drank two bottles of wine during lunch and continued our talk about Central America. 'I was very interested in the World Court case [Nicaragua's

Sandinistas versus the USA over its backing of the Contra rebels],' Graham said. 'I was going to write a letter to Reagan in reply to his famous terrorist speech, accusing the US of being the chief terrorist, but next day I read that Fidel had done just that.'

There was nothing extreme about Graham, except for his political conversation. While he talked about opium, he was not a dope addict, and while he enjoyed his vodka, rum punches, wine, whisky and good British beer, he was not an alcoholic. Torrijos admired Graham's capacity for liquor and once asked me, 'Graham is a heavy drinker, yes?'

I told Graham and he told the General, 'No, I am not a heavy drinker. I am a steady drinker.'

There was a lesson in the manner in which he lived. He configured his living arrangements to be as free as possible from stressful domestic distractions. It was as if his books were his family. His surroundings were almost Spartan, not at all bourgeois. He had everything he needed, but there were no frills and few trinkets from his foreign trips, no unnecessary extras, just a tidy one-bedroom apartment with no room for guests. Yet it was a place where even Salvadorean guerrillas could feel at home, although Graham had been a little tart with the Haitian guerrilla Fred Baptiste and his suspicious army friend when they visited him during the filming of sequences of *The Comedians,* which were being shot in the hills above St Raphael further down the Riviera.

'Fred said that their train left at 9.50 p.m. and when we got to the station we found its departure time was 8.50. He had a long wait for the next train. How can they run a revolution if they can't get such a simple thing as their train schedule right?' Graham complained.

Panama's Chuchu had been somewhat taken aback by Graham's simple lifestyle on the French Riviera. It was in stark contrast to the way other rich and famous people lived in big villas on Cap Antibes, hidden behind high walls and scraggly Mediterranean pines or further along the coast in such sprawling white villas as that of the late author Somerset Maugham, visible in the distance on Cap Ferrat. Graham's apartment, on the other hand – apart from his library containing two thousand-odd well-worn books, many of which he often reread, and some of which were stacked under a wooden liquor cabinet which also served as a bar – was a very ordinary middle-class bachelor pad.

Publishers and authors, Graham explained, sent him a great number of unsolicited books. 'I have no room for them. Some I read, some I don't, and the man who collects those I cast off is very lucky – he gets a lot of books,' he said; he avoided calling the collector the dustman.

He did complain that his flat was no longer as comfortable as it had once been because of the noise. 'Confounded cars and motorbikes, changing gears and roaring up the street,' he said, and he slid open the glass doors and stood on the balcony enveloped in the deafening roar of traffic. Graham said he had once poured a pot of water on one particularly noisy motorcyclist who had spent a long time revving his motor below. The water, Graham added, was dissipated into drops by the time it hit the cyclist. 'I do believe he thought I had peed on him. He was quite angry.'

Yvonne remained at her home in Juan-les-Pins that evening. Wheeling out a small black-and-white television set Graham said, 'Let's hear the evening news.' He never liked television the way he loved the cinema, he explained, but the evening news had a rather nice anchor lady. The news was tragic. There were pictures of Mexico City, my former *Time* base, devastated by an earthquake. Firefighters and rescue teams from nearby Marseilles, the woman anchor reported, were leaving to help in the faraway rescue work. Graham and I looked at each other in shock. There was nothing we could do. I worried about friends in Mexico City and later that evening called home for news of them, but there was none.

The Greenpeace ship *Rainbow Warrior* was also in the news. Graham bet me that the head of the French Secret Service (General Directorate of External Security, DGSE), Admiral Pierre Lacoste, would roll because of the scandal involving the environmentalist vessel. 'He will either quit or be fired,' Graham predicted. The *Rainbow Warrior*, berthed in Auckland, New Zealand, had been sunk on 10 July by two mines attached to its hull, and a photographer aboard had been killed. The ship had been due to sail on a protest voyage against French nuclear testing on the Mururoa atoll in Polynesia, and the DGSE agents responsible for sabotaging the *Rainbow Warrior* had been caught by the New Zealand police. Graham ridiculed the French Secret Service as 'terribly stupid, and one must agree they are a beastly lot of amateurs'. He won his bet. Admiral Lacoste later quit.

The uproar over the French Secret Service blunder in New Zealand brought him back to the old subject of Kim Philby. Graham said he drew great pleasure from their correspondence as a game between two old friends. It took them back to the days when they lunched together in London. He did say, however, that Philby's views (contained in his letters) on Soviet trouble spots such as their war in Afghanistan were quite 'doveish'.

After dinner we strolled around town, and Graham told me in two words how he had been drawn to Antibes: 'Love, Yvonne.' It was as if the darkened street were his confessional, and, like the confessor to the priest, only his profile was visible in the night. 'I settled here to be near her,' he said. 'She lives next door in Juan-les-Pins. We met in Africa, in Douala in the Cameroons in March

1959.' He had just spent six weeks at a leprosarium in the Belgian Congo and Yvonne called him as burnt out as his character Querry in *A Burnt-Out Case*. That same year Yvonne moved back from Africa to her home in Juan-les-Pins with her two children. (Martine was eight and Brigitte was nearly five.) Her husband Jacques, a Swiss working for the UAC, the Anglo-Dutch United African Company, whom she had met in Dakar and married in 1948, remained most of the year in Africa. Yvonne told me later that by 1959 she and Jacques were no longer a couple but that they had decided to stay together because of the children. She had gone to Africa with her mother at the end of the Second World War to join her father, who had made a career in Africa building the Benin-to-Niger railway.

Graham and Yvonne met again in August 1959 at the hotel La Voile d'Or in Saint-Jean-Cap-Ferrat. 'I first lived here in Antibes at the Royal Hotel,' Graham said. He enjoyed walking and had his own route along the quieter streets of Antibes after a stroll along the ramparts of the port. 'Then I got a small one-room flat on the sixth floor of the Floride. My next and last move was to this flat', and he pointed in the direction of Avenue Pasteur and his apartment, La Residence des Fleurs. 'Finally in June 1966 I bought it.'

I was glad it was dark. Graham rarely discussed such private matters, and I felt rather uncomfortable. He said Yvonne was no bother, no hindrance; in fact she was a great help to him. As a married man and a Catholic I wondered about Yvonne's husband.

Obviously the sin of adultery didn't bother Graham. He must have guessed what I was thinking and said, 'We [he, Yvonne and Jacques] have an understanding, an agreement. She is on the left, you know.' He was obviously very proud of her ideological leanings and intellect. It was only during this conversation that I learned Yvonne's last name, Cloetta. For years, during our travels, Graham had referred to her only as Yvonne and said how she had come along at the right moment in his life.

We went back to his flat for a nightcap and gazed down at the ancient Fort Carré and the lights of the beautiful yachts berthed in the marina below his flat. Graham shook his head. 'It is the most lavish exhibition of wealth, these multimillion-dollar yachts of the rich and famous. The yacht belonging to Fuad II, the last Egyptian king.' He pointed in the direction of the pier. 'It had its own helicopter.' Graham said he had first visited Antibes when he was invited to go sailing by his friend the famous movie-maker Sir Alexander Korda on Korda's yacht. Graham described how the Antibes harbour had been reclaimed and rebuilt and its ancient ramparts that served as a seawall were moved out further to allow even more yachts to anchor in the marina.

Graham said he was preparing to visit the Jesuit-run Georgetown University in Washington, DC. 'We are going to Washington next month, on October

5th, then to Charleston, West Virginia, and to New York. I don't care for New York. It's a dirty city, but Yvonne wants to see it, and this gives her a chance to see it. I'm writing to young Korda [Michael, Sir Alexander's nephew]. He'll help find a hotel there. I hope the students bring up politics. I will not, as it's supposed to be a literary meeting. But the rector sends students to pick coffee in Nicaragua.'

He also confessed he was back in the good graces of the Russians and that they were going to publish *Getting to Know the General*. Once more he found it necessary to comment, 'It is not a good book. There was too much Chuchu, but it was the best I could do.'

I told him he had paid off a debt to his friend Omar.

During our conversations I was reminded that Graham's shyness in personal encounters did not extend to letter writing. With the pen he could be outspoken and furious. With the pen he was in full control. He had an old-fashioned attachment to the post office and the tradition of letter writing and complained, 'The post in Antibes is terrible. There is only one person selling stamps.' Whenever he found something in a newspaper or magazine with which he disagreed he was apt to fire off a letter to the editor. He was always shockingly frank in his opinions.

As we reminisced about Haiti and Central America he said he had contributed half of the Spanish and Latin American royalties from *Monsignor Quixote* to the Salvadorean guerrillas. He was prompted in part, he said, by the viciousness of the Salvadorean military and the country's right-wing death squads. The rape and killing of the two American nuns in El Salvador in December 1980 and the assassination of Archbishop Romero had upset Graham a great deal. The other half of the Spanish royalties, Graham said, had gone to a Trappist monastery in Osera, Spain. He had visited the Trappists with his priest friend and had been happy to see them.

On my return to Florida I received a letter from Graham dated 4 October 1985. 'Can you put me in the picture about this Panama President scandal and the murder of Dr Hugo Spadafora plus the deposition of President Barletta. Noriega seems to be involved. I can't expect Chuchu to put me straight about this over the telephone.'

Then on the 24th he thanked me for updating him.

The position in Panama seems to be pretty complex and nasty. Chuchu should be ringing me up in the last week of October, but I wonder whether he may not have retired from the scene as Colonel Díaz Herrera seems to be in trouble. Yvonne and I had a good time in

Washington . . . but a pretty tiring one. I saw far more of the city than I had done on my previous two visits and I thought the Madison was one of the best hotels I have ever stayed in. Unlike the Hilton at Charlottesville where we spent one night before flying home.

On the 30th he wrote:

I am sure I wrote to you to thank you for the newspaper clips which were of great interest to me. I find too very interesting the quotation from your brief file. I look forward to getting the book you mention [the book in question is no longer on record]. I certainly won't throw it away. I begin to be nervous for poor old Chuchu, the friend of Díaz. I liked Díaz much better than I liked Noriega and I really believe him an honest man. It's all very puzzling and I don't feel inclined to return to Panama!

Nevertheless, a three-line note arrived from Graham's sister and secretary, Elisabeth Dennys, dated 22 November 1985, informing me that Graham has asked her to send me 'a hasty note to say that he is arriving in Panama on 30th November'.

While Panama's political machinations hadn't yet attracted international attention, the media was beginning to focus on Haiti. My photographer son, Jean-Bernard, and I had flown to Haiti, which was on the brink of a popular explosion against the Duvalier dynasty after the killing of three students in the town of Gonaïves at the end of November. During an Independence Day Mass at the Port-au-Prince Cathedral on 2 January 1986 we were arrested by Uzi-armed plain-clothes government agents. We knew the curtain was coming down on President-for-Life Jean-Claude Duvalier, and on 7 February Baby Doc and his wife and children flew into exile in France courtesy of the US Air Force.

Mail from Graham brought me up to date on Panama and Nicaragua. On 17 December 1985 he wrote:

We missed you this time in Panama. I have sent your two cuttings to Chuchu as they may interest him. I had a more interesting time in Nicaragua than before. Tomás Borge very cordial and close. Met Marcial's successor as Commander of the Salvadorean guerrillas. Daniel Ortega much improved and very friendly and open. I definitely don't like Noriega and Colonel Díaz seems to me to be getting rather feeble. The Cubans wanted me to go over but I felt tired and made for home. I said I might go for a real visit next year.

In Nicaragua Graham had granted an interview to a Reuters correspondent, and the story, datelined Managua, had been distributed on 12 December:

> In the lush, volcanic terrain of Nicaragua Graham Greene samples tropical revolution and searches for an idea that will put paid to more than 10 years' work. The idea has to be a good one, one which will allow him to ditch his present novel, a non-political work with the projected title of *The Captain and the Enemy*. He has given it up twice already. 'I have no confidence in it,' he said. 'I'm doing it very, very slowly and hoping that a real idea will come and I'll be able to abandon it for the third time.'

No idea came along, and he was still struck with *The Captain and the Enemy*. It was Nicaragua that now preoccupied Graham.

> When I was in Managua the other day I met Marcial's successor as military leader of the FMLN and he gave me a number of very amusing photographs of the happy daughter of [El Salvador's President Napoleón] Duarte in her so-called captivity [having been kidnapped by the leftist guerrillas]. Obviously not in any way faked. Would they be of interest to *Time* magazine? Some of them I got published the other day in *Le Matin*. P.S. If the answer is yes I am afraid there will be a little delay as I am off on the 9th to the Caribbean for a fortnight.

Then on the 27th he wrote again, thanking me for a copy of an article I had reported from Cuba about Castro's thoughts on religion. It ran in *Time* as 'Fidel and the Friar'.

> I suppose they [*Time*] slanted it a little more than you would have done against Fidel. The Cuban Ambassador came to see me in Managua and asked me to go over even if it was for only one day and night to Cuba, but I was feeling desperately tired and refused to alter my arrangements. However I said I wanted to go next time for a week or so in order to ride about the country a bit. He gave me Fidel's book on Liberation theology but it was in Spanish and I shall wait to read it until the English translation appears. I was not very contented with Panama this time. Colonel Díaz whom I like very much of course was still there, but I felt that he was a rather weak man. Noriega greeted me with all his staff very warmly, but I didn't feel any great trust in him. I was glad to get away and spend quite a lot of time with Tomás Borge

[in Nicaragua] whom I like more and more. What I plan to do next time is perhaps to take Aeroflot from London which goes direct to Havana and afterwards to Managua leaving out Panama except for perhaps a fleeting visit. Chuchu rather agrees with the idea.

I wrote to Graham suggesting he make a trip to Haiti. It had been unusually quiet, and general elections had been scheduled for the end of the year. There was still hope for the country. But he wrote back telling me of his plans and was almost apologetic:

> I have just got back from Italy and am off to Russia at the beginning of September. Chuchu was on the telephone yesterday and I have half promised to go to Nicaragua and Cuba with him in October. I wish I could join you in the Caribbean, but I am afraid it is impossible. Yvonne and I had a very interesting and amusing two weeks in the USSR and they wanted me to go back in this February but I don't intend to go. Yes, like three-quarters of the world I imagine, I am enjoying the Reagan affair [Irangate]. I don't think I want to go back to Haiti and the past.

Politics in Panama had been seemingly infected by sorcery and insanity. Graham wrote on 28 July 1987 that he had 'managed to get in touch with Chuchu about two weeks ago and he thought himself quite safe. I said I would go out to him if he were in danger. Díaz has gone completely off his head and he put Chuchu in handcuffs and he was a prisoner in Díaz's house for some hours. Díaz also accused Chuchu of having a homosexual relationship with me!' (In his book *Divorcing the Dictator: America's Bungled Affair with Noriega* Frederick Kempe writes, 'Yet the crazier Díaz Herrera acted, the less Noriega worried about him. Noriega knew his plot was working when he heard that Chuchu, long a friend of Díaz Herrera, alleged that he had been chained like a dog in Díaz Herrera's basement and made to bark.')
'I met Díaz twice in April,' Graham continued,

> when I was in Panama going to and coming from Nicaragua. On the first occasion I thought he had gone off his head as he talked for hours some meaningless metaphysical language which he had learnt from a medium in Panama City. On the second occasion I saw him at the National Guard and he seemed more sensible and told us how he had forged the elections and how necessary it was. Without forging them Arias would have returned and all Omar's work would have been wiped out. He didn't mention Noriega . . . I don't like Noriega

but at least he is against the United States. I wonder now whether I shall ever return.

(That same year a grand jury in Miami had handed down eleven counts of drug trafficking against Noriega.)

In April 1987 Graham did return to Nicaragua with Chuchu. At this time the Sandinistas were in dire need of friends, and Chuchu didn't shrink from aiding them, nor did Graham. The Sandinistas were at war. The *Guardian*, on 24 April, published a dispatch from its correspondent, Maurice Walsh, in Managua:

Nicaraguans are the first defenders in a war between civilization and barbarism, Graham Greene yesterday told poets, writers and statesmen gathered here to present him their premier cultural award in recognition of his contribution to world literature and support for the Third World. In a ceremony of some pomp but even more good humour, the author had the Order of Rubén Darío pinned to his shirt by President Daniel Ortega, himself a poet, while those watching included the novelist and vice-president, Mr Sergio Ramírez, the Interior Minister Tomás Borge, also a poet in his time, and President Ortega's wife Rosario Murillo, another poet.

Before the formal presentation, Mr Greene was treated to a discursive biography of his work by another poet, Carlos Martínez Rivas, who turned to the author at various points to ask: 'Am I right?' The citation said the award was in recognition of Mr Greene's 'fundamental contribution to contemporary literature which is recognized by all of humanity and also for his struggle against imperialist domination'.

In a short but emotional speech delivered through his interpreter, Mr Greene said he was touched by the award but also felt a certain feeling of shame that it was being presented to an Englishman. 'I am well aware that England, like France, has done very little for Nicaragua in her difficulties, therefore I don't feel as an Englishman that I deserve this decoration. I had known a bit about Central America before I came for the first time in 1980 but my real knowledge of your situation came in a mysterious telegram in 1976 signed by General Omar Torrijos inviting me to Panama. Then in the next years, until his death, I came each year to Panama and he was my tutor, my teacher about Central American affairs. But I see Nicaragua not only as a small country fighting a bully in the north. I see you even more as being in the front line of the trenches in a worldwide conflict . . . I am proud to be here, and I thank you with all my heart and I pray for your victory.'

Meanwhile in Haiti, in spite of a night of terror designed to keep voters away from the polls, determined citizens turned out in droves on the morning of 29 November 1987 to cast their ballots; it was the first time they had exercised that right. So ruthless were the Haitian army and its Macoute thugs in attempting to abort the voting that men and women at one polling station were gunned down and hacked to death as they waited patiently to cast their ballots. My son, Jean-Bernard, who was working as a photographer for *Time*, was wounded in the hand while escaping the site of the massacre. A Dominican cameraman was shot dead beside him. For a harrowing time Jean-Bernard had been reported killed. He appeared a while later and was airlifted out of Haiti with a wounded ABC News camera crew.

In March 1988 Jean-Bernard went to cover events in Panama. I put him in contact with Chuchu, who greeted him warmly and drove him in his dinky Russian-made Lada Gigoli to the modest Vera Cruz Hotel in downtown Panama City. Jean-Bernard said he noted a sadness about Chuchu, as if time had passed him by. He was still the extrovert, playing his part as a living Greene character whom the media sought out for interviews, but politically he was non-committal. He did not appear to have any influence or *entrée* with Noriega or his newly designed Panama Defence Force (PDF) high command.

While Jean-Bernard travelled around Panama photographing Noriega as he faced off against the Bush administration, Chuchu kept his distance. At the end of March, when the DINA – Noriega's secret police – chased the opposition Civilistas into Panama City's Marriott Hotel and began beating up journalists, Jean-Bernard ran to the aid of a sound man being battered by DINA agents. He was arrested, stripped of his cameras and packed off to a soccer stadium where the detained were placed in makeshift cells, fingerprinted and photographed before they were finally released. The members of the media who had been arrested were told their equipment would be returned to the hotel. It never was. Even Noriega couldn't return it. His secret agents had already reaped a tidy profit from selling the expensive equipment. Jean-Bernard called Chuchu to tell him what had happened, but Chuchu just hung up the phone. His political involvement, Jean-Bernard concluded, was over.

Graham had stated in a letter in April:

> Chuchu has still been ringing up at intervals and claims that he is in no danger. Noriega has now become a patriot in his eyes and I must admit that if I have to choose between a drug dealer and United States imperialism I prefer the drug dealer. I never much cared for him but Omar at least would have appreciated the way he is hanging on . . . I don't feel much like returning to Panama at the moment. It would be so easy for the CIA to bump me off and blame it on Noriega, and vice

versa, though I doubt if Noriega would do it. I seem to spend a lot of my time now going to and fro to Russia. I have been there four times in the last two years and we are probably going again towards the end of May. Yvonne and I had a very agreeable trip to Siberia. Tomsk, which for some reason is closed to foreigners, proved unclosed to us, and it's a most beautiful city. I never liked to ask why it was closed to foreigners. Of course I would always be delighted to see your son. If possible let him give me not too long a notice because I find it very difficult to plan very far ahead.

Graham had given a quote to the author of a book on Haiti, but the book turned out to contain regrettable inaccuracies. 'I am not up-to-date in the affairs of Haiti,' he wrote to me, 'but I hadn't realized how inaccurate the account was.' He rang up the American publisher to ask him to withdraw the quote, to no avail. 'It seems I have been made a fool of, but it was impossible for me to judge that moment. *Tant pis.* I shall now put it [the book] in the wastepaper basket.'

Elisabeth Dennys, Graham's sister who had arranged his wartime job with SIS and who for many years had typed his manuscripts and correspondence, had suffered a stroke. Her daughter Amanda took over the task of typing his mail. (He was working on the ending of another manuscript that had been around for almost a decade.) Elisabeth's illness affected Graham a great deal.

'Thank you so much and so does Yvonne for your good wishes. I admire your courage in staying on in Haiti,' he wrote to me on 10 December 1988 from Antibes.

I am afraid I wouldn't have the courage to return, all the more so because the picture you sent me must have enraged the Tonton. [It was a story I had reported on post-Duvalier Haiti.] It is a pity that you will have missed Gorbachev after all in Cuba. I have an enormous admiration for him and also considerable fear for his fate. I have now been three times to Russia – no, five times – in the last three years including Georgia, the Ukraine and Siberia. After 25 years' absence the changes were even more startling for me. I am afraid Noriega has been disappointed at my failure to turn up! I don't like the man and I have been resisting all the more as I have been travelling too much during the last year or two. I celebrated my 84th birthday at a party in Moscow when I had to blow out 84 candles! All the same I suspect I shall make the effort and go to Panama and Nicaragua sometime in the coming year. I hope it may coincide with your visit. When you see Daniel Ortega do give him my very warm regards. It would be delightful if you did come here with your son the photographer. You would be most welcome.

Then, on 16 May 1989 he wrote:

> I would love to see you again after all this time and I don't feel inclined at the moment to go to Panama. I have just been seeing Daniel Ortega in London – a very cordial meeting. I am afraid the end of May and beginning of June is not good for me. I am hoping to get away at that period to work in Capri and won't be back until late June. July would be a safer month as far as I am concerned.

In fact, although he did not mention it until we met again later that year in Antibes, Graham had taken a nasty fall in his favourite London hotel. He got tangled in a rug at the Ritz, fell and broke several ribs. Despite the pain, he had gone forth and introduced Daniel Ortega at a meeting in London.

It was also around this time that a Haitian publisher decided to publish *The Comedians* and asked for my help in obtaining the French-language rights for Haiti. 'It would be amusing to be published in Haiti,' Graham wrote back in his characteristically understated style.

Jean-Bernard and I joined Graham and Yvonne in Antibes to celebrate the bicentennial of the French Republic. The following day – Bastille Day – we joined what seemed like the entire French Riviera at a celebration in Juan-les-Pins. Graham appeared spry – he had recovered well from his fall – and was in high spirits when we arrived. His flat in Antibes looked the same as when I had visited four years earlier, except for a picturesque addition to the bathroom. Hanging on the wall and facing the toilet bowl was a large framed poster depicting Jean-Claude Duvalier in drag. He was resplendent in a red-lace dress with high-heel shoes, pointing a pistol to his head in the act of suicide.

'You sent it to me after Duvalier's overthrow,' Graham said.

'No,' I said. 'It was the Haitian artist.'

The apartment had been burgled twice, but the intruders had taken little of importance. In fact, aside from his books there *was* little of importance. Obviously the burglars were not artistically inclined as a small sculpture of *The Warrior* by Henry Moore was still on the glass-top coffee table. But even more surprising was the fact that the thieves had left a gold nugget that Graham kept in a drawer.

Graham relaxed in his rattan armchair facing the glass doors. He discussed Professor Norman Sherry's first volume of his biography, which had only recently been published. I confessed I hadn't yet read it.

'It's far too long,' Graham said bluntly. He said he was displeased and embarrassed by the biographer's examination of his personal life from 1904 to 1939. (My mind went back to our train ride across Panama when Graham had divulged that he was considering Sherry to be his biographer.) Almost in mid-sentence, Graham glanced at his watch; it was noon. 'Let's have a drink. What will you have?' he said. Then the phone rang. 'Blasted telephone. Where are my glasses?' Why he required glasses to answer the telephone was never clear to me. He found them and answered. It was Yvonne. She could join us for lunch. A few minutes later, vodka bottle in hand, he prepared the habitual midday martini and resumed his critique. 'Sherry has only reached the Second World War. Is there really any need to publish letters to one's wife in their entirety?' (Returning from Graham's funeral in Switzerland, Sherry defended the biography: 'My God, but there were more than 2,000 of those letters,' he told me.)

'I must say I much prefer the Victorian biography,' Graham went on. He got up, went to his book-lined shelves, took out a slim dark-covered volume and demonstrated its lightness in his hands. It was, he said, little more than a hundred pages. He then replaced it on the shelf without bothering to tell us what the book was or who wrote it.

I actually empathized with his biographer. How could Graham Greene's life be squeezed into a hundred pages? He had lived too many adventures. Moreover, precisely because he had guarded his privacy so jealously he had opened his life to much speculation.

To change the subject I congratulated him on finally publishing the manuscript he had carried around with him for fifteen years, *The Captain and the Enemy*.

'Yes,' he said, 'I am rather glad to get rid of it. A dream helped me in the end . . . It's probably my last.'

'I seriously doubt it,' I said.

He laughed and explained that the old manuscript had originally been entitled *Getting to Know the General*, and then after Omar's death he had given that title to the memoir instead.

The first part of *The Captain and the Enemy* is vintage Greene fiction built around his unhappy days at school in Berkhamsted where his father was headmaster and a brother head prefect. There were bullies, ferocious games and lots of prunes. Through the years he had often referred to this period of his life as an unhappy time. In the book, the narrator, a boy called Victor, is kidnapped by a peculiar Captain who says he won him in a game of backgammon. The last part of the book is contemporary Greene and contemporary Central America. I was fascinated, I told him, by the book's ending in which the Captain, with a plane full of explosives, attempts to crash and blow up Somoza, a kamikaze-type suicide run during which he manages to hurt no one but only kill himself.

The story reminded me how at precisely 1.00 a.m. on Thursday 21 June 1979 a low-flying aircraft flew so low over the safe house I was sharing with Alan Riding of the *New York Times* and Karen DeYoung of the *Washington Post* in Managua that we thought it might crash into our backyard. The plane came from the direction of Somoza's bunker and dropped nine concussion grenades miles off target, wounding a woman. The bombing had a psychological effect as the Sandinistas had warned that they intended to bomb Somoza's bunker and the InterContinental Hotel because it was filled with Somoza's rubber-stamp parliamentarians and assorted hangers-on. (Torrijos had also sent the US Intelligence Service in Panama into a panic one night when he ordered Venezuelan bombers to bomb Somoza's bunker. The Venezuelan aircraft had been flown to Panama and stationed there as part of an effort to pressure Somoza to quit. The bombers, it was later discovered, had no bombs.)

At the end of *The Captain and the Enemy* the narrator says, 'With the Captain dead what is the point of continuing it [writing]? I realize more than ever that I am no writer. A real writer's ambition doesn't die with his main character . . .' The last lines of the book, which was to be, as Graham predicted, his final novel, are intriguing: '"I'm on my own now," Victor says, before throwing what he has written into the wastepaper basket. "The line means Fini. I'm on my own now and I am following my own mules to find my own future."'

Graham had dedicated the book to Yvonne: 'For *Y* with all the memories we share of nearly thirty years.'

We talked of his thin manuscript about dreams, which lay on his work table. When I mentioned a nightmare I'd had in which Graham and I fell into a deep precipice in my Volkswagen during our trip along the Dominican–Haitian border more than twenty years ago, he said, 'I had quite forgotten that incident.'

It wasn't one of his own nightmares, but since he had made a habit of compiling his nightmares over the years, putting them down on paper, he could enthusiastically commiserate about other people's. He quickly warmed to the subject, went to his table and opened a folder with a thin sheaf of pages. It was the beginning of the manuscript. 'I've already decided on a title: *A World of My Own*. Oh yes, I have included my Papa Doc nightmare,' he said and conceded that Duvalier had inflicted on him what the author termed his longest-running personal nightmare – a transatlantic one, like a successful play.

Yvonne eventually published *A World of My Own* a year after Graham's death. The book is a strange, fascinating kaleidoscope, yet it opens a window into Graham's subconscious. The dreams he related also amount to a revealing postscript to his adventurous career in what, in his book, he terms the real-life 'Common World', laying bare many of the fears – and pleasures – which he experienced but which, reticent as he tended to be about himself, he rarely discussed.

With his pixie sense of humour, he begins *A World of My Own* with an introduction in which he points out that this is one book for which he can be neither sued nor prosecuted, since his dreams are a world 'shared with no one else. There are no witnesses . . . The characters I meet there have no memory of meeting me . . .'

It is well that such is the case because many of his dreams, were they to be presented as fact, would appear potentially actionable. For example, in one sequence Graham takes a country walk with the writer Ford Madox Ford. They are in a field with a large bull and a young bull. Graham retreats to the road but, looking back, notes that the young bull has mounted on Ford's shoulders. Ford doesn't seem disturbed.

Of special interest to me, of course, were Graham's dreams about Haiti. Predictably, many were nightmares in which Papa Doc figured prominently. Thus, in one surrealistic episode, 'Out in the yard [of the Grand Hotel Oloffson in Port-au-Prince] there were a number of cars. An old lady stood by a car . . . I had seen her before in the streets of Port-au-Prince. "I believe that's Papa Doc's wife," I said, and, sure enough, the President himself joined her and they rode away. I tried to hide my face with my hands, and I was very afraid.'

Graham was in good humour. The spirit in which he laughingly described his nightmare gave no sense of the terror that François Duvalier could inflict on a person when he was still alive.

I had my own Papa Doc nightmares, which plagued me for many years after I was freed from the National Penitentiary in Port-au-Prince. Graham and I compared nightmares. In Graham's dream, Duvalier is about to strike him. Like me, Graham is back in Port-au-Prince and trying to escape from Papa Doc. 'I am in Haiti and I feel something is going to happen to me at any moment,' he recounted to Jean-Bernard and me. 'I get into a car and go to the British Embassy or I try to get there, and when I get there I find the Embassy is no longer there . . .' The deafening roar of Antibes' ubiquitous motorbikes below his fifth-storey apartment window drowned out the rest of his story.

I noted to Graham that at least in one version of his bad dream he had had the advantage of a car. In my nightmare, which was realistic enough to wreck my sleep for years after my imprisonment, I find myself outside the penitentiary, naked and on foot. My main preoccupation, besides trying to get away while hiding my nakedness, is to disguise myself since most of Duvalier's top Tontons Macoutes know me. An old lady tending her open-air kitchen is frying *griot* (seasoned pork) while other *marchands* (market women) are walking down the street balancing baskets of produce on their heads. They are zombie-like and don't notice me. I usually woke up when the Macoutes arrived.

It was ironic that we were talking about Papa Doc when his son lived only twelve minutes away by car. Jean-Claude Duvalier and his wife Michele and their two children were living in a house loaned to them by a son of the international arms dealer Adnan Khashoggi. The house was situated in a hollow near the main highway to Nice and opposite a lettuce farm. When Jean-Bernard and I drove by the place, a farmer on a tractor ploughing his field in preparation for planting sent clouds of dust on to the former dictator's front lawn.

Graham confessed that when he and Yvonne drove into the hills for dinner they gave wide berth to restaurants Baby Doc was known to frequent.

'And our friend, the exiled Haitian priest,' Graham asked, 'whatever happened to him?' Bajeux's own faith had slowly died. There had been no dramatic rupture with the Church. Instead, he felt abandoned by it. He quit the priesthood in the wake of the reformist Second Vatican Council, at the time when thousands of other priests were choosing to free themselves from ecclesiastical discipline and return to secular life. Materially speaking, Bajeux was better off than many clerical colleagues who had abandoned the cloth. He taught at the University of Puerto Rico and later at Princeton University. He was a poet and literary critic, and he wrote a book on three outstanding Caribbean poets: Jamaican-born Claude McKay, Puerto Rican Luis Palés Matos and Aimé Césaire of Martinique. But he never stopped working to free his country from dictatorship.

After the fall of the Duvalier dictatorship in 1986 Bajeux didn't wait to be issued a Haitian passport and a re-entry visa to Haiti. Waving a blue-and-red Haitian flag, the original colours that Duvalier had changed to red and black, in front of startled immigration officials and saying, 'This is my visa,' he was eventually allowed into the country. He went on to open what he christened the Ecumenical Centre for Human Rights in February 1987 and helped lead-fund Haiti's largest post-Duvalier democratic political organization, Konakom (the Creole acronym for National Congress of Democratic Movements). Konakom brought together in its congress some 315 peasant and grassroots organizations from throughout Haiti and later become a political party.

In 1990 Bajeux threw his support behind Jean-Bertrand Aristide, who won a historic victory. However, by October 1993, after Haiti's military had once again seized control, Bajeux was back in exile in Puerto Rico after escaping assassination by neo-Duvalierists who sacked the house where he was living in Port-au-Prince. The beasts born of dictatorship are not easily tamed. The intercom system buzzed. 'Confounded thing,' Graham said as he got up to answer it.

All we heard was a long 'Yes.'

'Sorry,' he said when he returned, and he lifted both hands in exasperation. 'It was a Dutchman who wanted me to autograph a book. I asked him whether I knew him. I only autograph books for my friends.'

The talk of autographs reminded him of an event during his latest birthday celebration that he felt was perhaps the most fun. The Greene King Brewery, founded by his great-grandfather in England in 1799, had issued one hundred thousand bottles of an especially strong Graham Greene birthday ale from St Edmunds, with Graham's signature on the label. He lamented that he didn't have a bottle for us but gave us the address of a London pub that might still have a bottle or two.

With surprising receptiveness he acceded to Jean-Bernard's request for a photo session. He stood and walked to the little balcony. 'They usually like a photo here.' The backdrop was the marina and white-capped sea beyond.

'I would rather, if you don't mind, just do your thing. Don't take notice of me,' Jean-Bernard said.

'Oh,' Graham laughed, 'it is going to be painless, is it?'

Later he sat at his table and read out snippets of the unfinished dream manuscript while Jean-Bernard photographed his hands.

Yvonne drove us to Chez Félix au Port for lunch, and while Graham left us at the table to cross the street to purchase *The Times* Jean-Bernard snapped several more photographs of him. 'Please,' Graham said, 'don't take any more photos outside. It attracts unwanted attention.'

In Florida a colleague of mine who had covered the Vietnam War had asked me whether I might ask Graham if the character Pyle in *The Quiet American* was in fact Colonel Edward G. Landsdale of the USAF, an American army officer who had won fame as a guerrilla expert, helping Philippine President Ramon Magsaysay beat the Hukbalahap guerrillas and who later become Chief of the CIA's Military Mission in Saigon.

Graham laughed. 'I should get angry,' he said. 'I've been asked that question so many times, and no one seems to take any notice when I say no.' He leaned forward and shouted, 'No!' Then he added that Landsdale had not yet arrived in Vietnam when he was there. (Colonel Lansdale had been assigned to South Vietnam in June 1954. Graham had left four months earlier.) Besides, he didn't even know the man. Pyle, he added, was a very different character from the gung-ho Colonel Lansdale.

'They confuse *The Ugly American* with *The Quiet American*,' he said and pleaded jokingly that we should not spoil such a pleasant day discussing *The Quiet American*. Graham had not forgiven Joseph Mankiewicz for his film version of the book, which Graham declared was a travesty.

Graham decided against staying up for the bicentennial celebrations and retired early. In the morning he told us he had slept well but had briefly awoken. 'I heard a big bang!' he said.

We assured him it must have been fireworks.

He spoke of his trips to Russia and how he was happy to have seen Kim Philby before he died. Graham spoke of Philby as one would speak of a dear friend. Philby died in his sleep on 11 May 1988 and was buried in Moscow's Kuntsevo Cemetery. (Much later, Philby's Russian widow, who said she lived on the rouble equivalent of $53 a month, which the Russian government paid her, put some of Philby's possessions up for sale at Sotheby's. Included in the collection, which sold for nearly $50,000, were eleven letters from Graham.)

As was typically the case, there was nothing sad about bidding goodbye to Graham. It was always assumed that we would meet again, and we made plans to do so. Travel had a rejuvenating effect on him. He appeared as indestructible as ever. With Yvonne's help he had succeeded in reducing life's tedious trivial chores to a minimum.

We embraced as he saw us off. It was the last time I saw him.

On our return to Miami I sent him a copy of a *Newsweek* magazine article about dreams. He replied on 26 August saying thanks but that he was 'astonished that they didn't quote the ideas of J.W. Dunne in an experiment with time where he claims that dreams take their images from the future as well as from the past. It's a very convincing book and in my own experience a true one.' He concluded his letter with 'Yvonne and I both enjoyed your visit very much and I am glad that in spite of the awful hot weather J-B liked Antibes.'

Five months later, in November 1989, Graham returned unwell from a trip to Ireland where he had presided over a literary prize committee. He thought it was his heart, but his doctor in Antibes found nothing wrong. A month later, visiting his daughter Caroline at her home in Switzerland, he fainted. Blood tests revealed a lack of red blood cells, and his doctor ordered blood transfusions. His peregrinations were now limited to his dreams. Yet he made no mention of the seriousness of his illness in his letters.

Meanwhile our old haunt, Panama, had exploded and was making the world news. The US Joint Chiefs of Staff in Washington, DC, had been given President George Bush's approval for Operation Blue Spoon, and the world witnessed one of the United States' most bizarre geopolitical interventions. It was also the largest such action since the Vietnam War.

The principal announced goal of the Bush administration's invasion of Panama was to get their man – General Manuel Noriega, who had been indicted by a federal grand jury in Miami on charges of violating US drug laws. It was an enormously costly operation to catch Noriega, the one-time CIA asset who later was to claim he collected more than $10 million from the agency, even though government records show payments of only about $800,000. The action also called for neutralizing Noriega's Panama Defence Force (PDF) which by early 1988 had been listed by the US military as 'unfriendly'.

Shortly after midnight on 20 December 1989 Operation Blue Spoon shattered the Panama night, and once it was under way Washington changed its name to the more palatable Operation Just Cause. The Torrijos–Carter treaties had placed a ban on the United States intervening legally in Panama's internal affairs, hence the invasion.

No clear picture of the scope of the fighting was to emerge because of the tight control that American officials placed on news coverage. Yet in spite of the latest state-of-the art high-technology weaponry, such as laser-guided missiles, it is known that the US troops were surprised by the tough resistance put up by elements of the PDF, especially at its Comandancia (headquarters) and at Panama City's small Paitilla airport. The bearded black-shirted Machos del Monte battalion with their skull-and-crossbones emblem and tapir mascot had been moved from their Río Hato military base to the Comandancia weeks earlier. PDF troops at Río Hato were quickly overwhelmed by superior US airborne forces. American troops blew off the front door of Omar's Farallon beach house near by, only to find the aged maid huddling in fright in the kitchen and an old watchman hiding in the carport. Like circling black buzzards, US Delta Force helicopters searched in vain for the wanted man. Some say the midnight invasion caught Noriega literally with his pants down, that they couldn't find him because he was wandering around disrobed in an alcoholic stupor. The Navy Seals detailed to capture the Paitilla airport and decommission Noriega's Learjet encountered stiff resistance and took casualties. Four Seals lost their lives. But Noriega no longer had his private jet available, and Chuchu no longer had his Cessna.

The ramshackle, weathered two-storey tenements of El Chorrillo across from the Comandancia went up in flames. The hall in which Graham and I had watched Omar listen to 'the people' was obliterated. The sixteen-storey high-rise apartment building that Graham had so disliked was utilized as an effective sniper position by the PDF. There was some fighting at Fort Amador in the Canal Zone, which had reverted to Panama after the signing of the Torrijos–Carter treaties in 1978. Noriega had an office there. However, the American officer commanding troops manning 105-millimetre howitzer artillery and 50-cal machine-guns instructed his men to avoid hitting Omar Torrijos's granite mausoleum located near Fort Amador barracks where some members of the PDF were still holding out. (Some Panamanians believed Arnulfistas had stolen Omar's body after the invasion. In fact Omar's body had been so badly torn apart in the crash that his family had decided on cremation. The urn with the ashes was stolen after the invasion from its resting-place in a church and was eventually returned to the family.)

Across the Atlantic, Graham seethed. He told Reuters: 'Whatever he [Noriega] may have done cannot be half as bad as what the United States did in El Salvador, giving arms to those people who killed six Jesuit priests.'

I tried calling Chuchu repeatedly but got no answer. Philip Bennett, a correspondent of the *Boston Globe*, found him and reported that he had 'sneaked around the bars and back streets of post-invasion Panama, steps ahead of US troops and with an idea for a children's book forming inside his head'.

'It's a book for the Panamanian children of the next century,' Chuchu told Bennett, sitting with his back to the wall of an obscure Chinese restaurant. 'What's happening today, nobody's going to want to believe in the future.'

Bennett described Chuchu as

> perhaps the saddest man in the country generally happy to have been invaded. A 61-year-old lieutenant in the dissolved Panamanian Defense Force, he is famous as the muse of Gen. Omar Torrijos, the military leader whose attempt to build nationalism in Panama through populism, force and charm was cut short by a plane crash in 1981. For Chuchu, the US invasion of December 20 was the catastrophic finale of a tragedy sealed by Gen. Manuel Antonio Noriega, whose cruel and corrupted rule did as much as the Americans to destroy Torrijos's legacy. At the end, poor Panamanians waved American flags in gratitude from the rubble of their bombed homes.
>
> 'We haven't lost very much because we didn't have anything,' he said. 'Nothing remains of Torrijos. There is nothing to defend. I'm more pessimistic than ever.' Despite his enmity towards Noriega, Martínez is one of the few remaining officers in the Defense Force who has not surrendered himself to US Forces. Instead, his wife, who is Italian, and two children have left the country under diplomatic protection, leaving him semi-clandestine, writing articles and giving interviews in homes of friends.

Chuchu admitted to the reporter that he didn't fire a shot during the US invasion.

At home when the fighting started, he attempted to drive to his assigned barracks but was turned back by roadblocks. He spent two days at a state office before returning home to find his 9-year-old daughter cowering from gunfire in the neighborhood. He bitterly condemned the US bombing of the slum near Noriega headquarters, which killed a number of Panamanians and left more than 10,000 homeless. He said a seismograph at the National University registered 417 explosions during the first hours of the invasion. 'I could never hate the Yankees, but now we all see how cruel imperialism is.'

A denunciation of the invasion by Chuchu appeared in Cuba's Communist daily, *Granma*. It was vintage Chuchu. 'Panama,' he wrote, 'is only a trench. The war is against all of Latin America, whether or not Latin America wants it, whether or not they dare to realize it or admit it and assume their responsibilities.' He omitted any mention of Noriega and set out demands for indemnities for all the material damage the United States had caused in the country.

In a letter dated 3 April 1990, Graham complained:

> The posts are terrible at the moment. Forgive a very hurried note and thank you too for the *Boston Globe* piece about Chuchu, but I have been very unwell since Christmas – twice in hospital and bearing up with blood transfusions, vitamin injections and four different lots of pills! Yvonne thank goodness is well. Chuchu has been on the telephone to me several times and always sounds cheerful. I was very touched too to get a letter from [Vaclav] Hável asking after my health! Incidentally that's very bad and travel is impossible.

Then on 14 May he wrote:

> My sickness is not a painful one only boring because one sees no end to it. I do hope you will get back to Haiti for the Pope's visit. I was astonished to read that Fidel had sent him an invitation! Yvonne and I send our love to you and Ginette and Jean-Bernard and I look forward to his photographs.

On 6 June he wrote:

> It's good to have news of you. I'm glad too to have the message from George Price [of Belize] whom I like very much. I would have loved to have seen Bosch back as President [of the Dominican Republic] if only as a smack in the eye for the United States who drove him out the first

time. I am glad you are writing again on Haiti and look forward to reading it.

In a letter to Jean-Bernard dated 23 May Graham thanked him for

two very pretty photographs, which I will share with Yvonne. I'm getting on all right but all these transfusions and injections are a bit of a bore. I think your father was paying a visit to Haiti when I last heard from him. I hope this silence in the newspapers means their woman president is doing better than the man.

On 5 October I received a letter that made me realize this was not a passing illness.

It was good hearing from you but I wish we were seeing you closer. I was amused to read the other day that a priest had been kept for twenty-four hours at Haiti airport because his name happened to be Greene. I much look forward to your new Haiti book. Alas I'm not in very good health and I am unable to travel, but I do hope that one day you can come down here.

The last letter I received from Graham was dated 20 November 1990, not from Antibes but from his new residence in Corseaux, Switzerland. He thanked me for my most recent letter and said:

The *Daily Express*, as you could assume, have got things entirely wrong. Yvonne and I have taken this flat to escape from the noise and dirt that has developed in Antibes. I haven't given up Antibes and I am not living with my daughter. I expect to spend most of the year here except perhaps a month or two in the winter when we will go back to Antibes. I sold my house in Capri to pay for the flat which is a very nice one with a beautiful view. [He had said earlier that he had purchased the Anacapri house with proceeds from *The Third Man* and that it was the only house he ever owned. He had also forgotten he had a Haitian publisher for *The Comedians*.] I never knew that I had a Haitian publisher! Do send me a copy of the book if it comes out. I had no idea that Father Aristide was putting himself up for the Presidency. It would be wonderful if he got in, though I doubt whether he would survive long.

He sounded much better in this letter, if not a little forgetful. For some reason I believed he was indestructible and would recover. Perhaps that was because of his irrepressible zest for life. I promised I would visit him soon. However, I was busy covering Haiti. Father Jean-Bertrand Aristide had indeed made history by winning a landslide election victory on 16 December 1990. Aristide's platform was a simple one: he promised change, and above all justice and transparency. The vast majority of the people saw in Father Aristide a messiah, a non-politician, although for a priest he had a strange Caligula-like enthusiasm for street justice. Graham was among the foreign dignitaries invited to President-elect Aristide's inauguration on 7 February 1991. Yvonne herself sent a cable from Switzerland explaining that because of ill health he would not be able to accept the invitation.

On 29 January 1991, a year after the US invasion, Chuchu, aged sixty-one, died of a heart attack after his usual morning jog in Panama City. '*Chuchu Martínez murio de dolor y de rabia*,' declared the headline in *Seminario Universidad*, and it was quite possible that he had indeed died of pain and anger. Even international fame, which had come to him as a living Graham Greene character, was no longer gratifying. It did ensure, however, an obituary in England as well as in the *New York Times*. In the *Independent* David Adams reported, 'Despite the current political climate of Panama, where all references to militarism have been eradicated, it is a tribute to Martínez that his political enemies joined his friends this week in lamenting the loss of one of the country's most talented and colourful figures in recent history.' The *Independent* quoted Graham as commenting, 'Chuchu remained faithful to Marxism, but his first fidelity was always to Torrijos in spite of the general's belief in social democracy which to Chuchu must have seemed like a cup of very lukewarm tea.'

Chuchu's world and dreams had come crashing down around him. The Cold War was over. Noriega, after a ten-day stand-off at the Papal Nunciature, surrendered to US forces and was dragged off to Miami to face US justice as Federal Prisoner 41586.

Chuchu didn't live to witness Noriega's long and expensive trial, at the end of which he was sentenced to forty years in a US prison.

In Nicaragua Chuchu's friends, the Sandinistas, had been voted out of office on 25 February 1990, and Violeta de Chamorro, the widow of the slain publisher Pedro Joaquín Chamorro, had won the presidency. In El Salvador the UN had helped negotiate a peace accord after the loss of seventy-five thousand lives, and Marcial's vaunted guerrillas had reorganized themselves into a political party.

Graham had outlived both the General and Chuchu. There would be no more telephone calls in the middle of the night from Panama.

*

On 3 April 1991 Graham died in his flat in Corseaux. His long search for the definition of good and evil finally ended. The grand adventure was over, or, as he liked to say, another was just beginning. He had always said his preferred manner of death was a bullet, not a lingering infirmity. It was not to be.

Yvonne, who had been his constant companion during the last years of his life, described how he worried about his correspondence up until the very end. As reserved as he was about his private life, friendship meant a lot to him and the mail was an important part of his life. He made a habit of answering every letter, especially if it came from a friend. Ultimately, tired and feeble from his blood transfusions, he found it impossible to cope with his letter writing.

'Two weeks before he died,' Yvonne told me, 'he was in despair. One morning Caroline was in the flat. Suddenly he asked us to send a message to Amanda, who was then his secretary. It said, "Could you give a call to one of the English papers saying that Mr Greene is too tired and ill to reply to any letters. Would all his friends excuse him for not getting any answers." Useless to say how puzzled we were by the idea, but we didn't say anything. Caroline left a message on Amanda's answering machine. In the evening she called from her home in England. She was upset. "But, Yvonne," she said, "this will be a disaster for Graham. All the journalists and what not will be after him if they read that. Try to persuade him that this is the last thing to do." It didn't take me a long time to convince him that this was not the right thing to do, and he abandoned the project to our great relief.'

For those who knew this warm self-deprecating man, whose boyish exuberance followed him into old age, there was no doubting the sincerity of his concern about the human condition. His politics were driven by simple sympathy for the underdog. He was often more welcome in the Third World than the First. And, while he liked to use the cover of boredom for his travels, as the Indian author Maria Couto writes, many of his biographers 'fail to comprehend Greene's need for experience outside of himself to illuminate the tragic sense of his art'.

In a letter dated 9 May 1991 Amanda Saunders introduced herself to me.

> I am Graham Greene's secretary and also his niece. As an old and close friend of Graham's I felt sure you would like to have the enclosed information about the memorial service, which is being held for him. I would also like to ask for your help in advising me if there are any friends of Graham in Haiti or Central America who would like to be contacted about the memorial service. I was in Switzerland with Yvonne when Graham died and even though he had been ill for some time it still came as a shock – we somehow expected him to go on forever. We will miss him terribly.

EPILOGUE

One afternoon in 1991 I drove out to see the Voodoo Mambo Lolotte in the Cul de Sac plain a few miles outside of Port-au-Prince. Lolette and the other women of her family were sorting freshly harvested yams in her *peristyle* (the central part of the temple). I told her I wanted to leave a bottle at a Voodoo temple in the Voodoo manner for the departed. 'It is for a good friend, a *bon blan* [good white man], who died recently,' I explained. She interrupted her labours and unlocked the door to a small thatched hut, the *callie mystères*, home of the *lwas* – the spirits. It seemed like the natural thing to do. I told her the bottle was for the spirit of a writer who did what he could to help Haiti.

The priestess's muscular arms and legs were caked with mud from harvesting yams. She was a strong and handsome woman who did not live off her Voodoo but instead worked the land and never failed to pay dues to her gods, in the form of a rich ceremony to them. She traditionally celebrated the *manger-yam* Voodoo ceremony in her sanctuary, and it appeared to pay off. Most years she had a bumper crop. I think Graham would have liked her.

As she opened the door of the hut enough sunlight seeped in to guide me to the altar dedicated to the *lwas*. I chose a little space between the dust-laden bottles of liqueurs, wines and spirits, discernible only by their shapes, in which to place Graham's bottle of Stolichnaya. It would, I was confident, remain there and gather its own coat of dust from the neighbouring fields.

There was no need for a bottle of vermouth. Graham used just a drop when mixing a martini. Lolotte did not ask any questions. She murmured a prayer and called upon '*Bon Dieu*' to look after Graham's spirit.

'He wrote a book about Haiti,' I said, 'called *The Comedians*.' I went on to explain what Graham meant by comedians.

Mambo Lolotte understood. She exhibited surprising sophistication. As she left to prepare her yams for market she stood for a moment in the doorway of the little hut and looked at me. 'We are *les Komedyens*,' she said, using the Creole word. 'We Haitians are all actors. We must be to survive.'

Unlike Catholicism, Voodoo has no heaven or hell. Graham's soul would be free to wander. Perhaps he would even return to Haiti.

After Lolotte left I remained for a long time reflecting inside the cool

Voodoo sanctuary. Just as had happened at Graham's memorial Mass in Westminster Cathedral, memories of the man flooded back to me. Paradoxical as he often was, I believed Graham would have been more at home with this simple Voodoo tribute in Lolotte's *hounfor* than at high Mass at Westminster. The Voodoo priestess's prayer would have been less embarrassing for him. He was easily embarrassed.

I left the offering of Stolichnaya to repose in Lolotte's *bagui* and then wondered if I should have bought a larger bottle. The Voodoo gods liked to be abundantly pleased. When I walked out the light was fading. I said goodbye to Mambo Lolotte and noticed the irony that her *peristyle* was a neighbour to Pont Beudet, Haiti's ancient but still functioning insane asylum.

Not far down the road was what remained of Jean-Claude Duvalier's ranch. As I passed it on my return to Port-au-Prince I noticed the entrance gate to the property was broken and hanging on its hinges. The unmanned rusty guard turrets and high concrete wall were all that was left standing of the once-elaborate country retreat. Vegetation rotted in the swimming pool and cows and goats grazed in the garden. Peasants in the area said that the army had looted the ranch and then set it alight, blaming the local people. Even the mounds of lead from spent bullets on Jean-Claude's private shooting range had been collected for scrap.

Four years later, on Friday 26 May 1995, there was a rare official homage to Graham Greene in Port-au-Prince. The tribute was being offered by grateful Haitians who believed that with *The Comedians* Graham had managed to lift the shroud and expose Duvalier's tyranny to the world. The white walls of the newly established non-governmental Info-Service lecture hall, located in an old, renovated Port-au-Prince gingerbread mansion, were covered with posters (provided by the British Council) illustrating Graham's long and productive life. While carrying out his book research at the height of Papa Doc's terror in August 1963, Graham, travelling by taxi, often passed this house on Avenue Charles Sumner in Turgeau, a residential section of the capital, as he returned from the Hotel Sans Souci to the venerable Grand Hotel Oloffson. Now, thirty-two years later, Graham's niece Louise Dennys was present as a guest to represent the Greene family.

The republic's new Minister of Culture, Jean-Claude Bajeux – the former exiled priest who had accompanied Graham and me on our 1965 border trip – lectured on 'La Métaphysique du Mal Chez Graham Greene' ('The Metaphysics of Evil as Seen by Graham Greene'). The young university students in the audience craned forward in their seats. They shared an eagerness for knowledge of the lost decades in which the dictatorship had turned their country into an intellectual wasteland. They were all too familiar with the metaphysics of evil, their country having only just emerged from three bloody years of post-Duvalierist military repression during which many of these same students were forced to flee for their lives in boats or seek refuge in rural Haiti, becoming exiles in their own country. Many of their fellow students had been killed.

In his ninety-minute lecture Bajeux outlined Graham's literary form, emphasizing the author's belief in human value and purpose. He defined at length Graham's treatment of good and evil and stressed that through his anti-heroes such as the whisky priest in *The Power and the Glory* and Pinkie the murderer in *Brighton Rock* he showed that good and evil coexist within all of us. 'It is a lesson to all of us,' Bajeux said, 'to be reminded that good and evil coexist in our own souls, and that is where we have to look, not outside ourselves.'

Bajeux explained that when Graham stated that he had found evil (hell) in Duvalier's Haiti, what the author meant was that he had found some evil characters in Haiti – whom he later portrayed in *The Comedians*. The lecture ended with a discussion among professors attending the *hommage* on the origins of violence in Haiti, without reaching any conclusion. Nevertheless Bajeux made reference to the suggestion that a Macoute lies in all of us.

Haiti was no longer Graham's nightmare republic. Haitians were enjoying – at least for the moment – hope of a better future. A force of twenty-two thousand American troops had made a soft landing in Haiti in September 1994 and restored democratically elected President Father Jean-Bertrand Aristide to power after he had spent three years in exile. On 31 March 1995 President Bill Clinton, from a reviewing stand in front of the National Palace, watched the change of command from US to UN peacekeepers. It was a historic sight: an American President seated on a reviewing stand on the steps of what was once a palace of terror. As the bagpipes of a battalion of peacekeepers from Bangladesh wailed, the regimental colours and country flags of the various foreign troops and nations involved in the peacekeeping mission fluttered like colourful Voodoo flags (beaded Voodoo flags carry images of their gods in many colours) on the palace lawn.

Of Haiti and *The Comedians* Graham had written:

> I would have liked to return yet a fourth time before completing my novel, but I had written in the English press a description of Doctor Duvalier's dictatorship, and the best I could do in January 1965 was to make a trip down the Dominican and Haitian border – the scene of my last chapter [of *The Comedians*] – in the company of two exiles from Haiti. At least, without Doctor Duvalier's leave, we were able to pass along the edge of the country we loved and to exchange hopes of a happier future.

On the Monday following the lecture, Louise Dennys, her husband Ric, our friend Father Alberto Huerta, a Jesuit professor of literature from the University of San Francisco who had corresponded with Graham over his religious beliefs, and I were escorted to the Palace by Bajeux. I couldn't help thinking how pleased Graham would have been – a Greene in Papa Doc's palace! Graham's request for an interview with Dr Duvalier in 1963 had been refused. The closest he had come to the Palace was the Casernes Dr François Duvalier.

There were no military sentries at the Palace gate that Monday. In fact, Haiti no longer had an army. President Aristide had dissolved the armed forces upon his return from exile. The Palace itself had undergone several transformations since the hurried departure of Jean-Claude Duvalier nearly a decade earlier. One short-lived military-backed president had even called in a Voodoo priest to exorcise the place of Duvalier evil.

At our meeting with Aristide he talked amicably and enthusiastically to Ms Dennys about his hopes for a literacy campaign. A self-described voracious reader, Aristide said he had read *The Comedians* while studying at a seminary in La Vega, in the neighbouring Dominican Republic. (When I presented him with a first-edition copy of *The Comedians* while he was in exile in Washington, DC, he promised to read it.)

When Aristide, himself an author, learned that Ms Dennys once had her own publishing business and currently represented a prominent American publishing firm in Canada, the president invited us into his adjoining workroom to show off his books and to present her with a beautiful painted box – a modest but simple tribute to Graham. 'There is nothing inside the decorative box,' Aristide said, 'just the air of Haitian freedom.'

Later, as we sat relaxing on the balcony of the Grand Hotel Oloffson, I mentioned how I had left Graham's favourite midday aperitif, a bottle of Stolichnaya vodka, at Mambo Lolotte's *hounfor*. Louise loved the idea and asked if I could take them to meet Lolotte, so the following day we drove out from Port-au-Prince to the Cul de Sac plain. When we arrived the priestess was officiating with a group of faithful at prayers. We were given chairs, and we waited until the prayers ended. Mambo Lolotte greeted us and graciously agreed to open her *bagui* with its offerings. To my pleasant surprise, Graham's bottle of Stolichnaya had been elevated to repose on a red cushion on a miniature rocking-chair. Father Huerta asked the priestess whether he could say a prayer, to which she readily acceded. The four of us stood before the small altar with the Mambo, and Father Huerta led us in a silent prayer. It was the ultimate ecumenical act.

Graham would have understood.

AFTERWORD

On 5 August 2011 Jean-Claude Bajeux's infinite weariness from his fight for a better Haiti ended with his death. He fought and had never surrendered. His Calvary had ended. His soul was finally at peace, and his wishes for no religious service were respected. His body was cremated, and a small informal service was held at a funeral home in Port-au-Prince. He had helped many, having devoted his life to human rights in the human sense. His struggle for justice, transparency and an end to impunity never faulted – no one gave so much to fight for a new Haiti as he sought to extirpate the vile beast of despotism and its moral corruption from the country. All I could think of on the morning of his service was that he, for those who were privileged to know him, would live on for ever. I loved a dear friend.

INDEX

SOME AUTHORS WE HAVE PUBLISHED

James Agee • Bella Akhmadulina • Tariq Ali • Kenneth Allsop

Alfred Andersch • Guillaume Apollinaire • Machado de Assis • Miguel Angel Asturias

Duke of Bedford • Oliver Bernard • Thomas Blackburn • Jane Bowles • Paul Bowles

Richard Bradford • Ilse, Countess von Bredow • Lenny Bruce • Finn Carling

Blaise Cendrars • Marc Chagall • Giorgio de Chirico •Uno Chiyo • Hugo Claus

Jean Cocteau • Albert Cohen • Colette • Ithell Colquhoun • Richard Corson

Benedetto Croce • Margaret Crosland • e.e. cummings • Stig Dalager • Salvador Dalí

Osamu Dazai • Anita Desai • Charles Dickens • Fabián Dobles • William Donaldson

Autran Dourado • Yuri Druzhnikov • Lawrence Durrell • Isabelle Eberhardt

Sergei Eisenstein • Shusaku Endo • Erté • Knut Faldbakken • Ida Fink

Wolfgang George Fischer • Nicholas Freeling • Philip Freund • Carlo Emilio Gadda

Rhea Galanaki • Salvador Garmendia • Michel Gauquelin • André Gide

Natalia Ginzburg • Jean Giono • Geoffrey Gorer • William Goyen • Julien Gracq

Sue Grafton • Robert Graves • Angela Green • Julien Green • George Grosz

Barbara Hardy • H.D. • Rayner Heppenstall • David Herbert • Gustaw Herling

Hermann Hesse • Shere Hite • Stewart Home • Abdullah Hussein

King Hussein of Jordan • Ruth Inglis • Grace Ingoldby • Yasushi Inoue

Hans Henny Jahnn • Karl Jaspers • Takeshi Kaiko • Jaan Kaplinski • Anna Kavan

Yasunuri Kawabata • Nikos Kazantzakis • Orhan Kemal • Christer Kihlman

James Kirkup • Paul Klee • James Laughlin • Patricia Laurent • Violette Leduc

Lee Seung-U • Vernon Lee • József Lengyel • Robert Liddell • Francisco García Lorca

Moura Lympany • Dacia Maraini • Marcel Marceau • André Maurois • Henri Michaux

Henry Miller • Miranda Miller • Marga Minco • Yukio Mishima • Quim Monzó

Margaret Morris • Angus Wolfe Murray • Atle Næss • Gérard de Nerval • Anaïs Nin

Yoko Ono • Uri Orlev • Wendy Owen • Arto Paasilinna • Marco Pallis • Oscar Parland

Boris Pasternak • Cesare Pavese • Milorad Pavic • Octavio Paz • Mervyn Peake

Carlos Pedretti • Dame Margery Perham • Graciliano Ramos • Jeremy Reed

Rodrigo Rey Rosa • Joseph Roth • Ken Russell • Marquis de Sade • Cora Sandel

George Santayana • May Sarton • Jean-Paul Sartre • Ferdinand de Saussure

Gerald Scarfe • Albert Schweitzer • George Bernard Shaw • Isaac Bashevis Singer

Patwant Singh • Edith Sitwell • Suzanne St Albans • Stevie Smith

C.P. Snow • Bengt Söderbergh • Vladimir Soloukhin • Natsume Soseki

Muriel Spark Gertrude Stein • Bram Stoker • August Strindberg

Rabindranath Tagore • Tambimuttu • Elisabeth Russell Taylor • Anne Tibble

Roland Topor • Miloš Urban • Anne Valery • Peter Vansittart • José J. Veiga

Tarjei Vesaas • Noel Virtue • Max Weber • Edith Wharton • William Carlos Williams

Phyllis Willmott • G. Peter Winnington • Monique Wittig • A.B. Yehoshua

Marguerite Young • Fakhar Zaman • Alexander Zinoviev • Emile Zola